M000247610

Managing Organizational Behavior

Managing Organizational Behavior

RONALD R. SIMS

QUORUM BOOKS
Westport, Connecticut • London

Library of Congress Cataloging-in-Publication Data

Sims, Ronald R.
Managing organizational behavior / Ronald R. Sims.
p. cm.
Includes bibliographical references and index.
ISBN 1-56720-495-3 (alk. paper)
1. Organizational behavior. 2. Management. I. Title.
HD58.7.S587 2002
658.3—dc21 2001057869

British Library Cataloguing in Publication Data is available.

Library of Congress Catalog Card Number: 2001057869
ISBN: 1-56720-495-3

First published in 2002

Quorum Books, 88 Post Road West, Westport, CT 06881
An imprint of Greenwood Publishing Group, Inc.
www.quorumbooks.com

Printed in the United States of America

The paper used in this book complies with the Permanent Paper Standard issued by the National Information Standards Organization (Z39.48–1984).

10 9 8 7 6 5 4 3 2 1

Contents

Acknowledgments

A very special thank you goes to Herrington Bryce, who continues to serve as a colleague, mentor, and valued friend. The administrative support of Larry Pulley, Dean of the School of Business Administration at the College of William & Mary, is also acknowledged. I am also indebted to Eric Valentine, Publisher at Quorum Books, and all the others who encourage me to share my ideas with others.

My thanks and appreciation as usual also goes out to my wife, Serbrenia, and to our children, Nandi, Dangaia, Sieya, and Kani, who continue to show patience and support during my periods of writing. A special "keep movin' forward" goes out to Ronald, Jr., Marchet, Vellice, Shelley, and Sharisse.

Chapter 1

Setting the Stage

INTRODUCTION

This book brings together much of the extensive knowledge about managing people's behavior in organizations. Such information will help you better understand the behavior of others as well as your own. The understanding you gain from this book will help you better meet the ultimate challenge: managing organizational behavior.

WHAT IS AN ORGANIZATION?

An organization is a system of two or more people, engaged in cooperative action, trying to reach an agreed-upon purpose. Organizations are bound-bed systems of structured social interactions featuring the use of incentives, communication systems, and authority relations. Examples of organizations include retail stores, universities, businesses, and hospitals.

Whether we want to be or not, we are all part of organizations. In your daily activities you move from one organization to another. You may deal with a government agency, go to work, or shop at a store. Understanding organizations and their management can give us significant insights into systems that have major effects on us all.

WHAT IS ORGANIZATIONAL BEHAVIOR?

We define organizational behavior as the actions and attitudes of people in organizations. The field of organizational behavior (OB) is the body of knowledge derived from the study of these actions and attitudes. Organizational behavior can help managers identify problems, determine how to correct them, and establish whether the changes would make a difference. Such knowledge can help people better understand situations they face in the workplace and change their behavior so that their performance and the organization's effectiveness increase.

As a field of study, organizational behavior includes a collection of separate theories and models, ways of thinking about particular people and events. It has its roots in the disciplines of psychology, sociology, anthropology, economics, and political science. Organizational behavior can help managers understand the complexity within organizations and that most organizational problems have several causes. Organizational behavior principles play an essential role in assessing and increasing organizational effectiveness, which is a central responsibility of and focus for all managers.

Three Levels of Analysis: Individuals, Groups, and Organizations

To appreciate behavior in organizations, researchers and specialists in OB cannot focus exclusively on individuals acting alone. After all, in organizational settings, people frequently work together in groups and increasingly in teams. Furthermore, people—whether alone or in groups—both influence and are influenced by their work environment. Therefore, OB focuses on three distinct levels of analysis: individuals, groups, and organizations.

The field of OB recognizes that all three levels of analysis must be used to comprehend fully the complex dynamics of behavior in organizations. Careful attention to all three levels is a central theme of modern OB and is fully reflected in this book. For example, at the individual level, we describe how OB and managers are concerned with individual perceptions, attitudes, and personality. At the group level, we describe how people communicate with each other and coordinate their activities in work groups and teams. Finally, at the organizational level, we describe organizations as a whole—the way they are structured and operate in their environments, and the effects of their operations on their employees.

STUDYING THE BEHAVIOR OF PEOPLE AT WORK

Why do employees behave as they do in organizations? Why is one group or individual more productive than another? Why do organizations continually seek ways to delegate authority and empower their employees? These and similar questions are important to successfully managing behavior in today's organizations. Understanding the behavior of people in organizations has become increasingly important as management concerns—such as individual and team productivity, job stress, and career progression—continue to make headlines.

At its core, OB is interesting because it is about people and human nature. OB does not have to be exotic to be interesting. Anyone who has negotiated with a recalcitrant bureaucrat or had a really excellent boss has probably wondered what made them behave the way they did. Organizational behavior provides the tools to find out why.

Organizational behavior is important to leaders, managers, employees, and consumers; and understanding it can make us more effective leaders, managers, employees, and consumers. Organizational leaders and managers in organizations are challenged by many changes occurring within and outside their organizations. Increased calls for change and a more diverse workforce points out that organizational leaders are being asked to perform effectively in a changing world. Organizations are also expected to efficiently use and manage the available information technology so that they can compete globally.

Employees were not always so valued as they are today. Today's sense of caring about individuals has evolved over the years. Many of history's great philosophers have contributed to our understanding of leading or managing behavior in organizations. Niccolò Machiavelli, a sixteenth-century Florentine statesman and political theorist, wrote *The Prince*, a cynical guide to ruling people. He assumed that all people were lazy and self-centered and that tricking them into working made good sense. Machiavelli believed that the end justified the means. Indeed, we have come to associate his name with the process of manipulation. Thus, an individual utilizing his principle is called "Machiavellian."

Throughout history, people were members of various classes. Some were rulers (kings, nobles, and trusted aristocrats) and many more were followers. If one assumed that people of lower social status should be subservient, management of them would likely rely on exerting power or force. Managers with such assumptions did not give much thought to the importance of human relations as a means of effectively managing people—after all, lower-class people were seen as barely human.

The eventual breakdown of the rigid class system with the advent of democratic thinking called for new and different ways to manage. The notion that people are "created equal and endowed with certain unalienable rights," as Thomas Jefferson asserted, was a radically different way of thinking about people and human relationships. Today's successful organizations and managers must be concerned with the "people element" instead of dictating to their employees as the ancient aristocrats did.

Managers today must continue to find ways to better manage the behavior of people in their organizations. Today, the field of OB is filled with a rich variety of approaches. It is interesting to examine the various ways of viewing employee behavior that have emerged over the years. Taking a historical perspective on attitudes toward employee behavior helps us both understand where the management of organizational behavior stands today and visualize the directions it may take in the future.

The interest in questions such as the nature of leadership, how to motivate people, how to solve interpersonal conflicts, and how to develop effective teams is timeless. We say "timeless" because of the fundamental issues in managing organizational behavior—the rapidly changing workplace notwithstanding—aren't new. In fact, the roots of trying to manage organizational behavior go back thousands of years.

For example, ancient Chinese emperors grappled with how to efficiently organize a vast workforce of civil servants. In the Roman Empire, experiments with tenure-based wage classifications (what are called tiered wage systems today) created problems. But we'll spare you the details of some 4,000 years of history—you can pursue that on your own. The importance is that concerns about OB have always been with us.

In the next section, we'll jump ahead with our time line to the late 1800s in the United States, to what is referred to as the Industrial Revolution and Scientific Management—the roots of OB.

Scientific Management

During the late 1800s some of the earliest attempts to study behavior in organizations came out of a desire to improve worker productivity. During that time period, several famous "experiments" in human behavior were conducted in organizations. Robert Owen, for example, was a textile manufacturer who experimented with "innovations" such as providing breaks and hot meals for his employees. Likewise, the Pullman factory was seen by many as innovative in its day. Today, of course, what was viewed as an attractive workplace in the 1800s comes across as laughable. For example, at the *Boston Herald* in the 1870s, a company rule stated that "men employees will be given an evening off each week for courting purposes, or two evenings a week if they go regularly to church" ("8 rules for office workers," 1997).

The Industrial Revolution of the nineteenth century brought about many radical changes in the management of employees as experts in industrial efficiency grappled with the question: What could be done to get people to do more work in less time? In contrast to the work of craftspeople of earlier times, work became centrally located in factories. It was not particularly surprising that attempts to answer this question were made at the dawn of the twentieth century. This was a period of rapid industrialization and technological change in the United States. As engineers attempted to make machines more efficient, extending their efforts to work on the human side of the equation—making people more productive—was only natural. Especially since jobs required less skill because machines controlled production processes. Given this history, it should not be surprising that the earliest people to receive credit for their contributions to OB were industrial engineers.

Though production increased dramatically, other results of these sweeping changes were not all positive. Some writers, most notably Adam Smith and Karl Marx, pointed out that simplification of work processes beyond a certain point could have diminishing returns and produce feelings of alienation in workers.

Although we recognize the significance of these criticisms of work simplification today, the industrialists of the early twentieth century were not yet ready to do so. They preferred an engineering approach to managing worker behavior called scientific management. Scientific management, developed by Frederick Taylor, called for the detailed analysis of tasks and time-and-motion studies in conjunction with piece-rate pay schemes in order to improve productivity. Believers in scientific management searched for the "one best way" to perform a task. They introduced standard parts and procedures. In the extreme, the scientific management approach subscribes to the belief that one single best solution exists for a given situation.

Beyond identifying ways in which manual labor could be performed more efficiently, Taylor's scientific management approach was unique in its focus on the role of employees as individuals. Taylor advocated two ideas that hardly seem special today but were quite new a century ago. First, he recommended that employees be carefully selected and trained to perform their jobs—helping them become, in his own words, "first-class" at some task. Second, he believed that increasing workers' wages would raise their motivation and, in turn, their productivity. Although this idea is unsophisticated by today's standards—and also is not completely accurate—Taylor may be credited with recognizing the important role of motivation in job performance. Contributions like these stimulated further study of behavior in organizations, and they created an intellectual climate that eventually paved the way for the modern field of OB.

Scientific management stimulated several other scientists to expand on Taylor's ideas. For example, the psychologist Hugo Munsterberg worked to "humanize" jobs by explaining how the concepts of learning and motivation related to the behavior of people at work (Munsterberg, 1913). Similarly, management writer Mary Parker Follett claimed that organizations could benefit by recognizing the needs of employees (Metcalf and Urwick, 1942). Among Taylor's most famous disciples were the husband-and-wife consulting team of Frank and Lillian Gilbreth. Devotees of time-and-motion studies, the Gilbreths developed a highly ordered family life that received notoriety in the book *Cheaper by the Dozen*. Following time-and-motion principles, Frank Gilbreth redesigned the manner in which bricklaying was performed so as to greatly improve productivity. The Gilbreths also developed an elaborate system for redesigning jobs based on the notion of an irreducible time-and-motion unit of work task, termed a *therblig* (Gilbreth roughly spelled backward). Along with Taylor, the Gilbreths founded an association to promote scientific management.

A legacy of the concepts of time-and-motion studies, external analysis of tasks, and standards for productivity is that many jobs are still designed with the goal of maximizing short-run efficiency. The negative implications of employees performing simplified, repetitive tasks did not concern the advocates of scientific management.

The Human Relations Movement

Despite its important contributions, scientific management did not go far enough in directing our attention to the many factors that might influence behavior in work settings. Efficient performance of jobs and monetary incentives are important, to be sure, but emphasizing these factors makes people feel like cogs in a machine. In fact, many theorists and employees rejected Taylorism, favoring instead the human relations approach that focused on the employees' own abilities and emphasized a respect for individuals.

During the same period in which scientific management was popular, the human relations school of thought emerged. The human relations approach, which partially grew out of the field of psychology, emphasized the importance of motivation and attitudes in explaining employee behavior. At the forefront of this new approach was Elton W. Mayo, an organizational scientist and consultant widely regarded as the founder of the human relations movement. Mayo and other proponents of this movement were concerned with task performance, but they also realized that it was greatly influenced by the social conditions in organizations—the way employees were treated by management and the relationships they had with each other.

The approach drew much of its strength and following from the results of a series of studies that began in 1927 at the Hawthorne Plant of the Western Electric Company, located in the western suburbs of Chicago. Inspired by scientific management, these researchers were interested in determining, among other things, the effect of illumination on work productivity. They found that by making the workplace slightly brighter, they could increase output. So they cranked up a carefully measured increase in candlepower and found that the output increased even more. But being good scientific researchers, they also decided to check the other direction by reducing illumination. Output again went up. They reduced it even further. Output continued to increase! What was happening? They found that by either increasing or decreasing illumination, sometimes even dimming the lights to the brightness of a moonlit night, they almost always got increases in productivity. Something that couldn't be accounted for in terms of their scientific measurement was taking place.

After considerable analysis, the researchers determined that the very fact that the workers were being observed by the research team seemed to affect their output. The workers enjoyed being the center of the research team's attention and responded by producing more. What resulted is now known as the Hawthorne effect, a situation created when managers or researchers pay special attention to workers that seems to result in improved worker output. But from a scientific management perspective, paying attention to people shouldn't have caused them to work better. After all, they weren't being paid any more money! Other forces must have been at work.

Mayo and his group hypothesized that the increased production resulted from changed social situations of the workers (they received more attention), modifications in worker motivation and satisfaction, and altered patterns of supervision. Social and psychological factors were seen as playing a major role in determining worker satisfaction and productivity.

The Hawthorne Studies were important because they demonstrated that in addition to the job itself, certain social factors can influence employees' behavior. Informal social groups, management–employee relations, and the interrelatedness among the many facts of work setting were found to be quite influential. The Hawthorne Studies represented a major step forward in the attempt to systematically study worker behavior.

Many scholars believe that the Hawthorne Studies show the importance of the social nature of employees. The Hawthorne Studies suggest that to understand behavior on the job, we must fully appreciate the employees' attitudes and how they communicate with each other. This way of thinking, which is so fundamental to the modern field of OB, may be traced back to Mayo's pioneering Hawthorne Studies. Considering the scientific management views prevailing at the time, this perspective was quite novel.

Clearly, the impact of the Hawthorne Studies on the field of OB are considerable. The contribution has nothing to do with what the research revealed indirectly about the importance of human needs, attitudes, motives, and relationships in the workplace. In this respect, the work established a close link between the newly emerged field of OB and the behavioral sciences of psychology and sociology—a connection that persists today.

Contingency Approach

While scientific management and the human relations approaches have an enduring legacy, neither is dominant today. Instead, the contingency approach holds sway over thinking about organizational behavior. The contingency approach acknowledged the difficulty of offering simple general principles to explain or predict behavior in organizational settings.

Nonetheless, the contingency approach did not abandon the search for principles, but instead sought to specify the conditions under which we can expect to find certain relationships. As such, it represented a search for the factors that would aid in predicting and explaining behavior.

The contingency approach argues that there's no single best way to manage behavior. What works in any given context depends on the complex interplay between a variety of personal and situational factors. For example, employees' needs and sense of motivations are clearly related to their behavior. But also influential are management's skills, abilities, perceptions, and history of behavior toward employees. Plus, most employees work with others in a team, a department, or a unit. So employees usually behave within a group context of some kind. As a result, group norms, expectations, and cohesiveness—issues we'll tackle later in this book—can impact behavior as well.

Situational factors are also important. Factors internal to the organization might include the organizational culture, the organization's procedures, and the organizational structure within which employees work. All can influence individual behavior. Finally, the external context matters, too. For example, when an organization does poorly in the marketplace, employee morale often suffers and anxiety rises. Many people will shift their attention away from their work and worry instead about being fired or updating their resumes. Likewise, when organizations have done well, it can boost employee confidence, if not create an annoying level of hubris.

Throughout this book we embrace the contingency approach while also recognizing the frustration managers have with it. To many, "it depends" means "you have no answers for me." And in a sense, that's correct. The key to successful behavior management is for managers to both understand and develop the skills needed to find their own answers.

THE NATURE OF MANAGERIAL WORK

Over the years many have described what managers do or prescribed what they should do. For our purposes, we will focus on the classical way of viewing management. The classical management writers were the first to describe managerial work. Writers of the classical school proposed that managerial work consists of distinct, yet interrelated, functions which taken together constitute the managerial process. The view that management should be defined, described, and analyzed in terms of what managers (functions and processes) do has prevailed to this day, but with considerable modification as management functions and processes change in response to changing times and circumstances.

Henry Mintzberg's influential study identified three primary and overlapping managerial roles: interpersonal role, decisional role, and informational role (Mintzberg, 1980). Each role has several related activities that distinguishes one role from the others. But interpersonal role activities clearly involve the manager with other people both inside and outside the organization. Decisional role activities involve the manager in making decisions about operational matters, resource allocation, and negotiations with the organization's consequences. The informational role involves the manager as a receiver and sender of information to a variety of individuals and institutions.

The concept of management developed here is based upon the assumption that the necessity for managing arises whenever work is specialized and undertaken by two or more persons. Under such circumstances, the specialized work must be coordinated, creating the necessary managerial work. The nature of managerial work is to coordinate the work of individuals, groups, and organizations by performing four management functions: *planning, organizing, leading*, and *controlling.*

The list of management functions can be increased to include other functions, but these four can be defined with sufficient precision to differentiate them and, at the same time, to include others that management writers have proposed. For example, some managers and organizations include functions such as decision making, staffing, coordinating, implementing, and executing. You should remember that management and OB aren't exact sciences with uniform language and definitions. The various definitions of management reflect the specific expectations of the people who practice management in specific organizations (Drucker, 1998).

While the list provided here may be arbitrary, managers at all levels of the organization generally perform these functions. The relative importance of one function vis-à-vis another function differs depending upon where the manager is in the organization and what problems and issues the manager faces. But the ability to discern the relative importance of planning, organizing, leading, and controlling may distinguish effective managers from ineffective managers (Kraut, Pedigo, McKenna, and Dunnette, 1989).

Planning

The planning function involves defining and setting goals, figuring out ways for achieving these goals, and developing a comprehensive hierarchy of plans to integrate and coordinate activities to reach the goals. Setting goals keeps the work to be done in its proper perspective and helps organizational members keep their attention on what is most important.

Plans establish boundaries for people making decisions and carrying out assigned activities. Planning helps managers anticipate future events, study problems, and analyze causes of those problems. In an increasingly dynamic world, planning helps managers decide what to do before an action is taken. At the same time, a quality plan will have contingencies for other situations that develop.

Planning is considered the central function of management, and it pervades everything a manager does. In planning, a manager looks to the future, saying, "Here is what we want to achieve, and here is how we are going to do it." Decision making is usually a component of planning, because choices have to be made in the process of finalizing plans. Managers by their own decisions can affect how they and their organizations will be evaluated. They determine what ends are legitimate and, therefore, what criteria are relevant. And once appropriate means are determined, the next managerial function—organizing—must be undertaken.

Organizing

Organizing is the process of making sure the necessary human and physical resources are available to carry out a plan and achieve organizational goals. Organizing includes all managerial activities that translate required planned activities into a structure of tasks and authority. In a practical sense, the organizing function involves (1) designing the responsibility and authority of each individual job and (2) determining which of these jobs will be grouped in specific departments. For example, managers of an engineering organization will be assigned to the engineering department. The organizing function's outcome is the organization structure.

The organization structure consists of many different individuals and groups performing different activities. These different activities must be integrated into a coordinated whole. It is management's responsibility to devise integrating methods and processes. If the differences among jobs and departments aren't too great, then the simple exercise of authority is sufficient to integrate the differences.

The interrelationships between planning and organizing are apparent. The planning function results in determining organization ends and means; that is, it defines the "whats" and "hows." The organizing function results in determining the "whos" (who'll do what with whom to achieve the desired end results). The structure of tasks and authority should facilitate the fulfillment of planned results if the next management function leading is performed properly. See Chapter 11 for a more detailed discussion of the organizing function and organizational structure.

Leading

The leading function involves the manager in close day-to-day contact with individuals and groups. Thus, the leading function is uniquely personal and interpersonal. Leading is influencing others to achieve organizational objectives (Chapter 9 discusses the concept of leadership). Leading involves dozens of interpersonal processes: motivating, communicating, coaching, and showing employees how they can reach their goals. When managers motivate employees, direct the activities of others, select the most effective communication channel, or resolve conflicts among members, they are engaging in leading.

Leadership is such an important part of management that managing is sometimes defined as accomplishing results through people. Leadership in executive positions represents the organization to its external constituencies. In this role, effective executive leaders use words and symbols to express the organization's abstract ideals and what the organization stands for. The organization's mission statement provides a starting point for performing this leadership role. But without the ability to use powerful language and metaphors, the executive leader will fail even if he has effective interpersonal skills.

Controlling

The final management function is controlling. The controlling function includes activities that managers undertake to ensure that actual outcomes are consistent with planned outcomes. Controlling is ensuring that performance conforms to plans. That is, after the goals are set, the plans formulated, the organizing arrangements determined, and the people hired, trained, and motivated, something may still go amiss. To make sure that things are going as they should, managers must monitor a particular unit of the organization's performance. Managers must compare actual performance to the previously set goals. If there is a significant difference between actual and desired performance, the manager must take corrective action.

A secondary aspect of controlling is determining whether the original plan needs revision, given the realities of the day. The controlling function sometimes causes a manager to return to the planning function temporarily to fine-tune the original plan.

The large-scale use of computerized information has contributed to the complexity of the controlling process. Compared to the noncomputerized past, there is now much more information available to measure deviations from performance. The process of monitoring, comparing, and correcting is what comprises the controlling function.

The functions of management require technical and administrative skills. They also require human relations skills—the ability to deal with and relate to people. OB literature stresses the importance of people. Many observers and practitioners of management believe that managing people effectively is the key to improving the effectiveness of groups and organizations.

Planning, organizing, leading, and controlling are important management functions. Today's managers who are concerned with being successful must develop an understanding of and skills in these four functions. They must also become proficient at identifying and responding to important trends or changes occurring in the world of work.

KEY TRENDS AND CHALLENGES AFFECTING TODAY'S ORGANIZATIONS AND MANAGERS

In recent years increasing attention has been paid to the importance of effectively managing an organization's human resources in determining an organization's competitive advantage. Some have even declared that human resources represent the only enduring source of competitive advantage available to many of today's organizations. A number of factors have contributed to the increased attention on the value of effectively managing human resources or the behavior of the organization's employees. For example, there are a number of changes in organizations themselves and broader trends causing these changes to occur. Perhaps most important, organizations today are under intense pressure to be better, faster, and more competitive—there are more and more efforts to squeeze productivity out of organizations while others are merging and downsizing.

Throughout the foreseeable future, managers will have to understand and deal with an increasing number of complex environmental factors and trends that influence them. To be effective in today's changing world of work, managers must be adaptable and maintain their perspective in the face of a rapidly changing environment. For instance, global competition, the knowledge and information explosion, and diversity represent not only some of the latest buzzwords, but also a harsh reality that will continue to face managers and their organizations.

Twenty years ago issues like workforce diversity and globalization were not that important. Today there are many solutions being offered on how to deal with these complex challenges. Yet the simplest but most profound solutions may be found in the words of Sam Walton, founder of Wal-Mart and the richest person in the world when he died. When asked for the answer to successful organizations and management, Walton quickly replied, "People are the key."

Information Availability and Technology Advances

An important environmental development is the second generation of the Information Age. The first generation was characterized by relatively straightforward automated data processing. This second generation has moved to automated decision making, more technology-based telecommunications, and the information superhighway. Now commonplace, decision support systems, expert systems and e-mail allow organizations to make real-time, online decisions backed by quantitative data and multiple input.

Many organizations have been completely revamped because of technological advances, computers, robotics, automation, changing markets, and other competitive influences that demand both internal and external adaptations. The great expansion of information technology—computers, e-mail, faxes, beepers, cellular phones, voice mail, and so on—has profoundly changed the workplace. These devices have made it much easier for people to access information and to communicate with each other on the job. In many cases, managers no longer have to be the keepers of all information.

The computerization of tools and machines and the greater use of robots in manufacturing reduce the number of people needed in various jobs and, thus, in turn, the number of managers needed to manage those people. In other words, technology has affected management greatly, either by automating work formerly done by employees directed by managers or by giving employees direct access to information and people without having to go through their immediate supervisor. This change has freed managers to devote more time to other tasks, such as better planning, more coordination of work among teams, management of suppliers or vendors, and assisting their work groups or teams to improve processes.

Increases in information availability and technological change will increasingly require managers to have increased technical skills. Furthermore, these changes require more skilled and trained employees. This then increases the importance of the manager's role in training and overcoming resistance to change as discussed in Chapter 12. Therefore, managers must keep up to date on the latest developments so that they can effectively train their people. Higher-level skills and training require new approaches to motivation and leadership. Thus, managers need more skills in the interpersonal area.

Globalization

Managers and other employees throughout an organization must perform at higher and higher levels because the world has been changing more rapidly than ever before. In the last 20 years, both domestic and global competition have increased dramatically. The rise of global organizations—organizations that operate and compete in more than one country—has and will continue to put severe pressure on many organizations to improve their performance and to identify better ways to use their resources.

Many U.S. companies are increasingly challenged to think globally, something that does not come easily to organizations long accustomed to doing business in a large and expanding domestic market with minimal foreign competition. The Internet is fueling globalization, and most large organizations are actively involved in manufacturing overseas, international joint ventures, or collaboration with foreign organizations on specific projects.

The implications of a global economy on organizations and their managers are many. From boosting the productivity of a global labor force to formulating compensation policies for expatriate employees, managing globalization and its effects on competitiveness will thus present major management challenges in the years to come. Global challenges will continue to impact the manager. Substantial investment has been made in U.S. firms by the British, Germans, Swiss, Canadians, Japanese, and others. Identifying the various cultural/value system and work ethic differences is beyond the scope of this book. However, today's manager must recognize that management practices differ culturally and structurally in these organizations compared to the U.S.-owned and -operated companies. Today's managers will need to learn to operate in a one-world market made up of differing cultures and leadership styles, especially at the middle manager level.

More than ever before, talented people will be needed to represent firms on a global basis. Clearly, there is increasing evidence that globalization will impact managers and their organizations. Today's managers who make no attempt to learn and adapt to changes in the global environment will find themselves reacting rather than innovating, and their organizations will often become uncompetitive and fail.

Diversity in the Workforce

Managers across the United States are confronted almost daily with the increasing diversity of the workforce. Workforce diversity refers to the wider variety of today's employees, who vary with respect to gender, age, culture, and ethnic background, and who may have physical and/or mental disabilities. Whereas, globalization focuses on differences between people from different countries, workforce diversity addresses differences among people within a given country.

The workforce is continuing to become more diverse as women, minority-group members, and older workers flood the workforce. More specifically, one need only note that in many large urban centers, such as Miami, New York, and Los Angeles, the workforce is already at least half composed of minorities. Women with children under age six have also been one of the fastest-growing segments of the workforce. Additionally, as the workforce gets older, employees will also likely remain there well past the age at which their parents retired, due to Social Security and Medicare funding shortfalls and the termination of traditional benefit plans by many employers.

Workforce diversity has important implications for management practice. An important management challenge will be valuing the uniqueness of each employee, while forming cohesive work groups and teams with people of different backgrounds and values. Managers and their organizations will need to shift their philosophy from treating everyone alike to recognizing differences and responding to those differences in ways that will ensure employee retention and greater productivity while, at the same time, not discriminating. This shift includes, for instance, providing diversity training and revamping benefit programs to make them more "family friendly." Some organizations are not only changing the range of benefit choices they offer, but also changing the basic structure of their benefits as they recognize that the "one size fits all approach" to employee benefits does not always work.

Increased diversity presents both a significant change and a real opportunity for managers. Diversity, if positively managed, can increase creativity and innovation in organizations as well as improve decision making by providing different perspectives on problems. When diversity is not managed properly, there is potential for higher turnover, more difficult communication, and more interpersonal conflicts.

The Quality Revolution

Today's organizations operate quite differently than in past decades. For them the watchword is not "getting by," but, "making things better," what has been referred to as the quality revolution. The best organizations are ones that strive to deliver better quality goods and services to customers at lower prices than ever before. Those that do so flourish, and those that do not tend to fade away.

There is increasing evidence that the delivery of quality products and services to customers has a direct impact on the success of organizations. The key, of course, is to realize that the people in the organization, not advertising slogans or statistical quality control, deliver quality goods and services. The challenge for managers and organizations across the world is to have their employees deliver quality products and—especially—services to each other (internal customers) and to customers and clients.

In the future, organizations will continue their efforts to improve quality and service through organizational practices like total quality management (TQM) (an organizational strategy of commitment to improving customer satisfaction by developing techniques to manage output quality carefully and achieving ISO 9000 certification) and reengineering (the fundamental rethinking and radical redesign of business processes to achieve dramatic improvements in performance). Because of the recent optimism toward these approaches it is unlikely that they will become tomorrow's outdated fads.

New Organizational Forms

As noted earlier, technology has made it possible for fewer people to do more work than ever before. Unlike the gradual process of automation in the past, today's technology is occurring so rapidly that the very nature of work is changing as fast as we can keep up. More will be said about the changing nature of work later in this section. With this, many jobs disappeared during the last two decades, leaving organizations (at least the most successful ones) smaller than before.

Downsizing. Indeed, during the 1980s and 1990s organizations rapidly reduced the number of employees needed to operate effectively—a process known as downsizing. Typically, this process involved more than just laying off people in a move to save money. The process is directed at adjusting the number of employees needed to work in newly designed organizations and is therefore also known as rightsizing. Whatever you call it, the bottom line is clear: Even during today's economic boom many organizations still believe they need fewer people to operate today than in the past—sometimes, far fewer.

Outsourcing. Another way organizations are restructuring and doing more with less is by completely eliminating those parts that focus on noncore sectors of the business (i.e., tasks that are peripheral to the organization) and hiring outside firms to perform these functions instead—a practice known as outsourcing. Contracting with outsiders to do work previously done within the corporation is not a new phenomenon, but it has been rapidly growing. In an effort to cut costs, many organizations are farming out many varieties of work previously done by regular employees, resulting in layoffs and internal reorganization. By outsourcing secondary activities, an organization can focus on what it does best, its key capability—what is known as its *core competency.* For example, by outsourcing its payroll processing, a company may grow smaller and focus its resources on what it does best. Outsourcing, of course, creates layoffs and the associated problems, including union-management frictions which all undoubtedly pose challenges for managers.

Mergers. Combining two or more companies into one organization continues to be an epidemic frequently resulting in large layoffs. Mergers tend to create issues in addition to those associated with layoffs. For example, who will be in charge and what managers and other employees will be retained or laid off? Who, where, and how will the work be completed? The remaining managers, of course, must address all of these and other issues relative to their own operations if they are to assist the total organization effectively with the merger.

Virtual organization. As more and more organizations are outsourcing various organizational functions and pairing down to their core competencies, they might not be able to perform all the tasks required to complete a project. However, they can perform their own highly specialized part of it very well. If you put together several organizations whose competencies complement each other and have them work together on a special project, you would have a very strong group of collaborators. This is the idea behind an organizational arrangement that is growing in popularity—the *virtual organization.* A virtual organization is a highly flexible, temporary organization formed by a group of companies that join forces to exploit a specific opportunity.

Although virtual organizations are not an everyday occurrence, experts expect them to grow in popularity in the years ahead. As one consultant has put it, "It's not just a good idea; it's inevitable." More will be said about virtual organizations and other structural designs in Chapter 11.

Changes in the Nature of Work

The trends and changes discussed so far are also changing the nature of jobs and work. For one thing, there has been a pronounced shift from manufacturing jobs to service jobs in North America and Western Europe. As the number of manufacturing jobs have decreased over the past two decades, the number of part-time and service industry jobs in fast food, retailing, legal work, teaching, and consulting have increased. These service jobs will in turn require what have recently been referred to as "knowledge" workers and new human resources management (HRM) methods to manage them and a new focus on human capital.

The knowledge, education, training, skills, and expertise of an organization's workers refer to an organization's human capital. And human capital is more important than it has ever been before. Service jobs put a bigger premium on worker education and knowledge than do traditional manufacturing jobs. Even entry-level factory jobs have become more demanding. For example, factory jobs in textiles, auto, rubber, and steel industries are being replaced by knowledge-intensive, high-tech manufacturing in such industries as telecommunications, pharmaceuticals, medical instruments, aerospace, computers, and home electronics, and even heavy manufacturing jobs are becoming more high tech. Human capital is quickly replacing machines as the basis for most organizations' success.

An important realization for managers and organizations is that these new "knowledge" workers can't be just ordered around and closely monitored like their parents. New management systems and skills will be required to select, train, and motivate such employees and to win their commitment. In order to attract and retain the most qualified employees, today's organizations must offer flexible work schedules, telecommuting, opportunities for temporary, part-time, or contract positions, and changes in job design.

Work schedules. Like work rules, work schedules are a major condition of employee's acceptance of jobs. Work schedules refer to matters such as starting and stopping times, the number and length of work breaks, how work beyond the regularly scheduled day or week is administered, whether the work is done on company premises or at home, and whether the employee is full-time or part-time. Like work rules, work schedules have gained an increasing influence on the satisfaction, and frequently the performance, of employees. The manner in which those work schedules are monitored, administered, and changed is important. From the standpoint of the manager, work schedules are necessary to coordinate and control work. Further, a certain amount of uniformity is required (and expected) to meet employee expectations of equitable treatment. Work schedules are becoming more flexible, however, than has been traditionally assumed in many organizations.

Experimentation with different kinds of work schedules, such as the compressed work week, flextime, permanent part-time work, peak-time work, job sharing, telecommuting, and temporary employment will increasingly be the rule, not the exception. The reasons for this experimentation will undoubtedly continue to change work attitudes and lifestyles, desire for more leisure time, attempts to minimize traffic problems, advances in computer technology, and attempts by management to increase both morale and productivity. Some, if not all, of the experimentation is also partly based on pragmatic attempts by managers to cut costs.

In any case, today's manager must be sensitive to the importance of changing work schedules in addressing employee needs and problems and the impact these changes may have on employee morale and performance. Managers should conduct case-by-case analyses of the advantages and disadvantages of work schedule practices to evaluate their cost-effectiveness for their specific work units and organizations.

Telecommuting. Question: What current organizational activity simultaneously helps alleviate child-care problems, reduces traffic jams, and cuts air pollution and fuel consumption, while also saving millions of dollars on office space? The answer is *telecommuting* or teleworking—the practice of using communications technology (i.e., computer, modem, the telephone, and/or fax machine) to enable work to be performed by employees from remote locations, such as the home or a nearby telecenter. Imagine the following example: An after-hour request from one of Marston Technologies' customers is made for some assistance on a computer problem. Everyone has gone home for the day. A call is made to the on-call computer technician who has a computer/modem at home for diagnosing and addressing customers' problem. The request is completed, the customer is happy, and no one had to make a trip back to the Marston office.

Telecommuting results in increased separation from the principal office, while, at the same time, it increases connection to the home. Telecommuting is perhaps one of the most profound examples of how technology impacts work, jobs, and managers.

Contingent workforce. Increasingly, organizations are employing more part-time employees. That is, instead of eliminating entire organizational functions and buying them back through outside service providers, organizations are eliminating individual jobs and hiring people to perform them on an as-needed basis. Such individuals comprise what has been referred to as a contingent workforce. This workforce is comprised of people hired temporarily, part-time, or as contract employees who work as needed for finite periods of time.

The temporary or contingent workforce has grown rapidly, paralleling the restructuring and layoff phenomena. The contingent workforce is of considerable size and includes specialists of all kinds, including nurses, accountants, lawyers, engineers, and computer and software experts. A growing number of middle managers and top executives are also part of this temporary workforce.

The "leasing" of employees by staffing service companies has become a rapidly growing industry because of the demand for temporary workers. Some analysts predict that in just a few years, half of all working Americans—some 60 million people—will be working on a part-time or freelance basis. Specifically, British consultant Charles Handy has described the organization of the future as being more like an apartment than a home for life, "an association of temporary residents gathered together for mutual convenience." Although others believe this prospect is far-fetched, it is clear that a growing number of people are seeking the freedom and variety of temporary employment rather than facing repeated layoffs from ever-downsizing corporations. They are opting for "permanent impermanence" in their jobs, so to speak.

How will the manager motivate employees who consider themselves, at best, transient—that is, just working at the present organization until something better comes along? Numerous studies have indicated that lower productivity and increased accidents occur when employees are not fully committed to their jobs. Motivating employees who are not fully committed will be another management challenge.

Changes in job design. Changes in job design (the process of determining and organizing the specific tasks and responsibilities to be carried out by each member of the organization and/or teams) has and continues to drastically change the nature of work itself in many instances.

The widespread and growing use of self-managed teams (see Chapter 7) is an example of changes in job design. Organizations have moved toward the use of such teams to increase the flexibility of their workforce. They are redesigning work and jobs to allow employees with unique skills and backgrounds to tackle projects or problems together and to perform a wide variety of tasks, including dividing up the work, monitoring quality, ordering parts, interviewing applicants, and so on. The use of self-managed teams also frequently involves many organizational changes, including changes in technology, workflow, selection, training, and compensation.

As organizations continue to redesign jobs, they will also reshape the relationship between managers and the people they are supposedly responsible for managing. You will find more and more managers being called coaches, advisors, sponsors, or facilitators. And there will be a continued blurring between the roles of managers and their employees. More and more decision making will be pushed down to the operating level, where workers will be given the freedom to make choices about schedules, procedures, and solving work-related problems. Organizations will also continue to put employees in charge of what they do. And in doing so, managers will have to learn how to give up control to employees who must learn how to take responsibility for their work and make appropriate decisions. Empowerment (putting employees in charge of what they do) will change leadership styles, power relationships, the way work is designed, and the way organizations are structured. More will be said about empowerment later in this chapter.

The job skills gap. The U.S. service sector has experienced much faster growth than the manufacturing sector over the past 40 years. Service, technical, and managerial positions that require college degrees will make up half of all manufacturing and service jobs in the coming years. Unfortunately, most available workers will be too unskilled to fill those jobs (i.e., job skills gap). Even now many companies complain that the supply of skilled labor is dwindling and that they must provide their employees with basic training to make up for the shortcomings of public education systems.

Although in the last decade the overall education level of Americans has increased in terms of schooling and even fundamental literacy, so also have the demands of the workplace. As a group, high school graduates are simply not keeping pace with the kinds of skills required in the new business world. The report card on college-educated workers is not particularly flattering either.

To deal with these problems, some businesses have developed agreements in which their companies join with public schools to form a compact that reserves jobs for high school graduates who meet academic and attendance requirements. A second strategy is in-house training for current or prospective employees through formal training and on-the-job training programs. Companies currently spend in excess of an estimated $60 billion a year on a wide variety of training programs. This is in addition to the more than $24 billion spent on training programs by the federal government each year. Nonetheless, the job skills gap or shortage is likely to remain a challenge for managers and their organizations in the United States.

Changing Attitudes toward Work

American workers are changing their attitudes toward work. Employees now demand better coordination between lifestyle needs, including family and leisure, and employment needs. Leisure pursuits have become more highly valued than work goals. Even previously loyal employees have become cynical of the corporate world. This cynicism has spawned a new interest in organized labor and collective bargaining, even among professionals.

American workers are more interested in jobs with meaningful work, which allow for self-fulfillment and work satisfaction. They want jobs that provide greater challenges and enable them to use more skills and knowledge. These changes in employee attitudes and values require that managers and their organizations use different organizational strategies than those used in the past.

Lifestyles and expectations about life circumstances are also changing. Where people are willing to live and work is becoming a serious issue for a significant number of workers. People are prone to have decided preferences about where they want to live, whether in the city, the suburbs, or a rural setting, and in what region and climate. In addition, more and more people express concern about the appropriate balance of work and family and leisure and other aspects of their lives. They may not want the job interfering with taking a child to a Little League game or to a Girl Scout meeting or going to church. Thus they may be less willing to accept overtime assignments or to work long hours or weekends. However, fear of layoffs undoubtedly produces considerable acquiescence to management's wishes, but with resulting job dissatisfaction for many people.

Deregulation

Being better, faster, and more competitive is also more important because for many industries the comfortable protection provided by government regulations continues to be stripped away. Industries from airlines to banks to utilities must now compete nationally and internationally without the protection of government-regulated prices and entry tariffs in the United States and in many other industrialized countries such as England, France, and Japan.

One big consequence of deregulation has been the sudden and dramatic opening of various markets. One need only look at the long-distance phone companies efforts to enter the previously protected monopoly of companies like AT&T and start-ups in the airline industry to compete head-to-head with industry giants like Delta and American Airlines. Just as significant has been the impact that deregulation—and the resulting new competition—has had on prices, requiring these organizations to get and stay "lean and mean." Prices for hundreds of services like long-distance calls have dropped in some instances which means organizations must get their costs down too.

Achieving Societal Goals through Organizations

Over the past three decades there has been an increasing trend toward viewing organizations as vehicles for achieving social and political objectives. Most organizations are deeply concerned with potential liability resulting from HRM decisions that may violate laws enacted by local governments, state legislatures, and the U.S. Congress. Legislation like the 1964 Civil Rights Act requires organizations to respond to larger social, political, and legal issues. Other legislation requires that organizations provide reasonable accommodations for the disabled and for employees with HIV.

How successfully an organization manages its human resources depends to a large extent on its ability to deal effectively with government regulations. Operating within the legal framework requires keeping track of the external legal and social environments and developing internal systems (for example, management training and grievance procedures) to ensure compliance and minimize complaints.

Organizational responses to legislative requirements today generally follow a realization that important issues need national attention. As entities within the larger society, organizations can't help but be influenced by the ideology and culture around them. As changes occur in the larger society, organizations must adapt and change. The results of legislative and social changes are added pressures on organizations. Management and more contemporary practices are not formed in a vacuum but must represent the societal ideology in which they are embedded.

Managerial Changes

New management approaches are adding to the challenges facing today's managers. As organizations face more complex problems, they can't rely mainly or only on their managers to solve them. At the same time, executives have given their employees more autonomy and control over their work as a way of increasing their job satisfaction. Increased employee autonomy has combined with an emphasis on teamwork and collaboration in organizations. As a result, employees have become empowered to make decisions.

Empowerment of employees and self-managed teams are two specific management approaches that are having a significant impact on today's managers. Empowerment is a form of decentralization that involves giving employees substantial authority to make decisions. Under empowerment, managers express confidence in the ability of employees to perform their work. Employees are also encouraged to accept responsibility for their work. In many organizations now using self-managed teams, groups of employees do not report to a single manager; rather, groups of peers are responsible for a particular area or task. The breadth of changes in areas like managerial and employee responsibilities continues to have a powerful impact on today's managers.

The empowerment of the workforce and the increased use of self-managing teams in the workplace continue to blur the distinctions between managers and employees. Now employees often assume such responsibilities as planning staffing and rewarding other employees that used to be typically entrusted solely to managers. Managers have become more adept at using technology, often assuming word processing, analysis, and communication roles formerly delegated to staff employees. Managers have moved from a directive to a facilitative role and now coach and counsel employees. They create teams of workers, who often differ from the manager in gender, race, language, values, and lifestyle. Managers must then manage this diverse workforce in an uncertain and changing environment.

Knowledge workers have become a mainstay of computer, health care, communications operations, and those organizations in the information sector of the economy. These well-educated employees perform nonroutine work and make decisions in their organizations. Both blue-collar and white-collar employees are becoming knowledge workers and thus innovators in their organizations. These employees can require different skills from their managers, particularly those focused on helping, coaching, empowering, and listening.

MEETING TODAY'S ORGANIZATIONAL AND MANAGEMENT CHALLENGES

It has often been said that the only thing that remains constant is change—and it's true! (See Chapter 13 for more discussion on change.) Today's manager will, more than ever before, need to be prepared for changing events that will have a significant effect on their lives. Some of the more recent changes and challenges have been highlighted throughout this chapter. This section takes a closer summarizing look at how some of these changes are and will continue affecting managers in organizations.

Globalization affects managers in many ways. A boundaryless world introduces new challenges for managers. These range from how managers view people from different countries to how they develop an understanding of these immigrating employees' cultures. A specific challenge for managers is recognizing differences that might exist and finding ways to make their interactions with all employees more effective.

Although downsizing, quality improvements, and changing forms of work are activities that are initiated at the top-management level of an organization, they do have an effect on managers. Managers may be heavily involved in implementing the changes. They must be prepared to deal with the organizational issues these changes bring about. For example, when an organization downsizes, an important challenge for managers is motivating a workforce that feels less secure in their jobs and less committed to their employers. Managers must also ensure that their skills and those of their employees are kept up to date. Employees whose skills become obsolete are more likely to be candidates for downsizing. Those employees who keep their jobs will more than likely be doing the work of two or three people. This situation can create frustration, anxiety, and less motivation. For today's manager, this, too, can dramatically affect work unit productivity.

An emphasis on quality focuses on the customer, seeks continual improvements, strives to improve the quality of work, seeks accurate measurement, and involves employees. Each manager must clearly define what quality means to the jobs in his or her unit. This needs to be communicated to every staff member. Each individual must then exert the needed effort to move toward "perfection." Managers and their employees must recognize that failing to do so could lead to unsatisfied customers taking their purchasing power to competitors. Should that happen, jobs in the unit might be in jeopardy.

Effective quality initiatives can generate a positive outcome for managers and employees. Everyone involved may now have input into how work is best done. A focus on quality provides opportunities for managers to build the participation of the people closest to the work. As such, quality can eliminate bottlenecks that have hampered work efforts in the past. Quality can help create more satisfying jobs—for both the manager and his or her employees.

Few jobs today are unaffected by advances in computer technology. How specifically is it changing the manager's job? One need only to look at how the typical office is set up to answer this question. Today's organizations have become integrated communications centers. By linking computers, telephones, fax machines, copiers, printers, and the like, managers can get more complete information more quickly than ever before. With that information, managers can better formulate plans, make faster decisions, more clearly define the jobs that workers need to perform, and monitor work activities on an "as-they-happen" basis. In essence, technology today has enhanced managers' ability to more effectively and efficiently perform their jobs.

Technology is also changing where a manager's work is performed since they have immediate access to information that helps them in making decisions. Technological advances assist managers who have employees in remote locations, reducing the need for face-to-face interaction with these individuals. On the other hand, effectively communicating with individuals in remote locations (for example, teleworkers), as well as ensuring that performance objectives are being met, has become a major challenge for managers.

The implications of workforce diversity for managers are widespread. However, the most significant implication for managers is the requirement of sensitivity to the differences in each individual. That means they must shift their philosophy from treating everyone alike to recognizing, valuing, and responding to these differences in ways that will ensure employee retention and greater productivity.

Today's successful managers will be those who have learned to effectively respond to and manage change. Managers will work in an environment in which change is taking place at an unprecedented rate. New competitors spring up overnight and old ones disappear through mergers, acquisitions, or failure to keep up with the changing marketplace and customer demands. Downsized organizations mean fewer workers to complete the necessary work. Constant innovations in computer and telecommunications technologies are making communications instantaneous. These factors, combined with the globalization of product and financial markets, have created an environment of never-ending change. As a result, many traditional management practices—created for a world that was far more stable and predictable—no longer apply.

New governmental and societal issues will continue to complicate the manager's job in the future. Numerous environmental concerns will remain as serious long-term problems for managers and their organizations. Energy availability and costs will continue to be of great concern internationally and domestically. These types of issues and societal pressures have become part of the managers' and organizations' planning and operations.

Federal legislation affects managers. In addition, state and local governments have laws and regulations that impact business. The effect of such legislation can be quite costly, and managers and their organizations may be required to change their methods of operations in order to comply.

All indications are that these pressures will remain intense. In some instances today's manager has to be more like a lawyer, police officer, teacher, accountant, political scientist, and psychologist than a manager. While this may be overstating the point, it reflects a realistic aspect of every manager's contemporary role. Managers must be more flexible in their styles, smarter in how they work, quicker in making decisions, more efficient in handling scarce resources, better at satisfying the customer, and more confident in enacting massive and revolutionary changes. As management writer Tom Peters captured in one of his best selling books: "Today's managers must be able to thrive on change and uncertainty."

In bringing this introductory chapter to a close it is important to recognize that the workplace of today and tomorrow is indeed undergoing immense and permanent changes. Organizations are being challenged to change or be "reengineered" for greater speed, efficiency, and flexibility. Teams are pushing aside the individual as the primary building block of organizations. Command-and-control management is giving way to participative management and empowerment. Authoritative leaders are being replaced by charismatic and transformational leaders. Employees increasingly are being viewed as internal customers. All this creates a mandate for a new kind of manager today.

Managers will need a broader set of skills to achieve and maintain both their own, the department's, and organization's success today. The areas in which they will need to develop expertise include strategic planning; budgeting; quality management, benchmarking and best practices; and telecommunications and technology. Aside from honing these skills, managers can better prepare themselves for today's challenges by gaining a better understanding of the needs of their internal customers, recognizing the need for effective information systems for employees, building relationships with the best service providers, and aligning the manager's unit and organization strategies and their processes.

Today's managers, regardless of their level in the organization, must be true strategic partners in the organization. Each manager must effectively respond to the constantly changing world of work and the role managers are expected to successfully play in that world. As the pace of change quickens, managers must become a tougher and more durable, albeit more flexible, interface between their organization and the lumpy road of a changing environment.

CONTEMPORARY MANAGERS AND ORGANIZATIONAL BEHAVIOR

As highlighted in this chapter, today's world of work is indeed undergoing tremendous and constant change. Organizations are being changed for greater speed, efficiency, and flexibility. Teams are increasingly supplanting the individual as the main building block of organizations. Command-and-control management is giving way to participative management and empowerment. Customer-centered leaders are replacing egocentered leaders. Employees are increasingly being viewed as internal customers. All of this creates a mandate for a new kind of manager in today's organizations. Table 1.1 contrasts the characteristics of past and future managers.

PLAN FOR THE BOOK

Change and challenge are watchwords in organizations during these changing times. Managers and employees alike are challenged to meet

Table 1.1
Evolution of the Contemporary Manager

	Past Managers	Contemporary Managers
Primary role	Order giver, privileged elite, manipulator, controller	Facilitator, team member, teacher, advocate, sponsor, coach
Learning and knowledge	Periodic learning, narrow specialist	Continuous lifelong learning, generalist with multiple specialties
Compensation criteria	Time, effort, rank	Skills, results
Cultural orientation	Monocultural, monolingual	Multicultural, multilingual
Primary source of influence	Formal authority	Knowledge (technical and interpersonal)
View of people	Potential problem	Primary resource
Primary communication pattern	Vertical	Multidirectional
Decision-making style	Limited input for individual decisions	Broad-based input for joint decisions
Ethical considerations	Afterthought	Forethought
Nature of interpersonal relationships	Competitive (win-lose)	Cooperative (win-win)
Handling of power and key information	Hoard and restrict access	Share and broaden access
Approach to change	Resist	Facilitate

change in the workplace, change in how work gets done, change in who is working in the organization, and change in the basis for organizations. The major trends and challenges shaping the changes occurring in organizations throughout the world were discussed earlier in this chapter. For example, the increasing globalization of business has led to intense competition in various industries, and the changing demographics of the workplace have led to increased diversity among working populations.

We begin by looking at the foundations of individual behavior—perception, attitudes, and personality in Chapter 2. Then we consider various motivation theories and tools for effectively motivating today's employees in Chapter 3. Chapter 4 addresses performance appraisals in organizations. Chapter 5 considers managing stress at work. In Chapter 6 we consider issues important to successful communication. Chapter 7 discusses groups and teams. Individual and group decision making is the focus of Chapter

8. We then investigate the important topic of leadership in Chapter 9 and conflict and negotiation in Chapter 10. Chapter 11 discusses designing effective organizations. In Chapter 12 we discuss how each organization has its own culture that acts to shape the behavior of its members (i.e., ethical or unethical behavior and response to workforce diversity). Chapter 13 considers various organizational change issues and techniques that managers can use to affect behavior for the organization's benefit. Chapter 14 concludes the book with a look at the changing roles and responsibilities for career development and management in today's organizations.

REFERENCES

Drucker, P.F. 1998. Management's new paradigm. *Forbes* (October 6): 152–177.

8 rules for office workers at the *Boston Herald*, 1872. 1997. *Boston Herald* (October 5): 1.

Kraut, A.I., Pedigo, P.R., McKenna, D.D., and Dunnette, M.D. 1989. The role of the manager: What's really important in different management jobs. *Academy of Management Executive* (November): 286–293.

Metcalf, H., and Urwick, L.F. (eds.). 1942. *Dynamic administration: The collected papers of Mary Parker Follett.* New York: Harper and Row.

Mintzberg, H. 1980. *The nature of managerial work.* Englewood Cliffs, NJ: Prentice-Hall.

Munsterberg, H. 1913. *Psychology and industrial efficiency.* New York: Houghton Mifflin.

Chapter 2

Perception, Attitudes, and Personality

INTRODUCTION

In this chapter, we explore three related aspects of individuals that affect behavior in organizations: perceptions, attitudes, and personality. First, we discuss perception. We then explore the attributions that people make to explain the behaviors of themselves and others and the attribution process. The chapter closes with a discussion of personality and personality types. Understanding these basic individual differences should help managers to better understand behavior in organizations.

WHAT IS PERCEPTION?

Perceptions are important because we act based on our interpretation of events. Likewise, at other times we fail to take action because of those same perceptions. So when faced with the same objective events, we may see different things. Perception—like beauty—is in the eye of the beholder. This doesn't mean that perception is so idiosyncratic that it is not worth studying. To the contrary, it's a critical building block for effective behavior management.

Individuals use five senses to experience the environment: sight, touch, hearing, taste, and smell. Organizing the information from the environment so that it makes sense is called perception. Perception is a cognitive process. Perception helps individuals select, organize, store, and interpret stimuli into a meaningful and coherent picture of the world. Because each person gives his own meaning to stimuli, different individuals "see" the same thing in different ways (Nicholson, 1998). The way an employee sees a situation often has much greater meaning for understanding behavior than does the situation.

The cognitive map of the individual is not, then, a photographic representation of the physical world; it is, rather, a partial, personal construction in which certain objects, selected by the individual for a major role, are perceived in an individual manner. Every perceiver is to some degree a nonrepresentational artist, as it were, painting a picture of the world that express his or her individual view of reality (Krech, Crutchfield, and Ballachey, 1962, p. 20).

Each person selects various cues that influence his perceptions of people, objects, and symbols. Because of these factors and their potential imbalance, people often misperceive another person, group, or object. To a considerable extent, people interpret the behavior of others in the context of the setting in which they find themselves.

The following organizational examples point out how perception influences behavior:

1. A manager believes that an employee is given opportunities to use his judgment about how to do the job, while the employee feels that he has absolutely no freedom to make judgments.
2. A direct report's response to a supervisor's request is based on what she thought she heard the supervisor say, not on what was actually requested.
3. The manager considers the product sold to be of high quality, but the customer making a complaint feels that it's poorly made.
4. An employee is viewed by one colleague as a hard worker who gives good effort and by another colleague as a poor worker who expends no effort.
5. The salesperson regards his pay increase as totally inequitable, while the sales manager considers it a fair raise.
6. One line operator views working conditions as miserable; a coworker right across the line regards working conditions as pleasant.

These are a few of numerous daily examples of how perception can differ. Managers must recognize that perceptual differences exist. Table 2.1 illustrates how perception works. Suppose the worker has been told that she has the freedom to make decisions about how the job is to be designed. Note that the manager and the employee perceive the job design freedom in different ways; they have different perceptions of the employee's amount of freedom.

Research has shown that managers and direct reports often have different perceptions of the same events as illustrated in Table 2.1. Managers and direct reports both act based on their perceptions, regardless of their accuracy. And that can create problems. Imagine what might happen over time if managers feel they've adequately recognized employee's accomplish-

Table 2.1
Perceptual Differences and Behavior

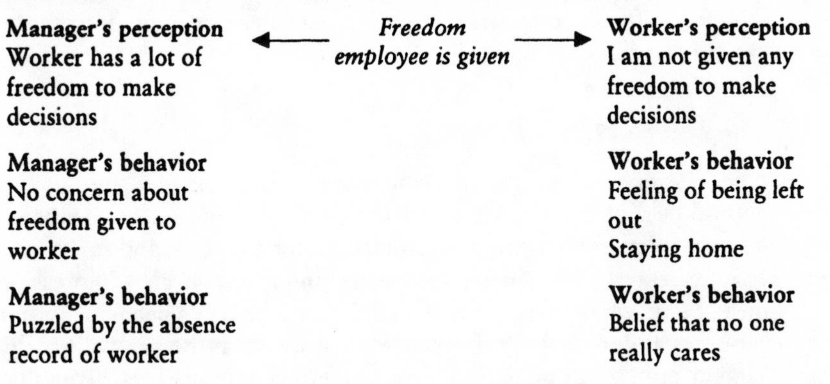

Manager's perception Worker has a lot of freedom to make decisions	← *Freedom employee is given* →	**Worker's perception** I am not given any freedom to make decisions
Manager's behavior No concern about freedom given to worker		**Worker's behavior** Feeling of being left out Staying home
Manager's behavior Puzzled by the absence record of worker		**Worker's behavior** Belief that no one really cares

ments, while employees feel underappreciated. Managers might feel little need to step up their rewards to employees, even as morale disintegrates. And without recognizing this basic truth about perception, managers are unequipped to handle growing employee dissatisfaction.

SOME OBSTACLES TO ACCURATE PERCEPTIONS

There are a number of obstacles, barriers (or biases) to the precise perception of others' behavior. Each obstacle is a possible source of misleading or distorted information.

Stereotyping

Stereotypes are judgments of others that are based on group membership. Such attributes as sex, race, ethnic group, and age are the basis of commonly held stereotypes. For example, the beliefs that older workers are not capable of being trained for new tasks and that younger workers cannot handle responsibility are commonly held stereotypes. Occupational groupings also frequently serve as the basis for stereotypes. For example, consider your own views of, say, politicians, union officials, top-level executives, and police officers. Even relatively superficial attributes can be the basis of stereotypes, as evidenced by such cliches as "redheads are short-tempered."

This is not to say that stereotypes are totally worthless and inaccurate. In some instances, stereotypes may, in fact, be based on group characteristics; this is the "kernel of truth" notion of stereotypes. The proposal argues that some stereotypical beliefs are based on an element of truth, in that the beliefs are derived from observations that hold for an entire group but that do not hold with much accuracy for given individuals in the group. While the popular stereotype of, say, police officers may have some accuracy, the variability of the traits of individual police officers is so great that it is extremely difficult to classify an individual officer accurately from the stereotypical information alone.

First Impression Error

First impressions are lasting impressions, so the saying goes. Individuals place a good deal of importance on first impressions, and for good reason. We tend to remember what we perceive first about a person, and sometimes we are quite reluctant to change our initial impressions. First-impression error means that we observe a very brief bit of a person's behavior in our first encounter and infer that this behavior reflects what the person is really like. Primacy effects can be particularly dangerous in interviews, given that we form first impressions quickly and that these impressions may be the basis for long-term employment relationships.

The Halo Effect

Another obstacle to accurate perceptions is labeled the halo effect: A person is good at one thing and so is assumed to be good at something else. The positive assumption, therefore, creates the halo. For example, assume that you are a supervisor in a machine shop. Ed, your employee, has been one of the best drill press operators in your section for over five years. A lathe operator is unexpectedly needed in another section. You recommend Ed, assuming that he will also do well at the lathe. Ed bombs! He may have excelled at one job, but he lacked the necessary skill or training to accomplish the other. Figuratively you had placed a halo over Ed's head.

Another instance of the halo effect could occur if two people have a violent fistfight on the job, and one is a personal friend with whom you regularly socialize off the job. Watch out for the tendency to place a halo over your friend's head by assuming that the other person must have been the cause of the conflict.

Projection

We have a tendency to ascribe our own feelings and attributes to others. This is known as projection. People who engage in projection tend to perceive others according to what they themselves are like rather than according to what the person being observed is really like. When observing others who actually are like them, these observers are quite accurate—not because they are perceptive but because they always judge people as being similar to themselves. So when they finally do find someone who is like them, they are naturally correct. When managers engage in projection, they compromise their ability to respond to individual differences. They tend to see people as more homogeneous than they really are.

Contrast Effects

There's an old adage among entertainers who perform in variety shows: Never follow an act that has kids or animals in it. Why? The common belief is that audiences love children and animals so much that you'll look bad in comparison. This example demonstrates how contrast effects can distort perceptions. We don't evaluate a person in isolation. Our reaction to one person is influenced by other people we have recently encountered.

An illustration of how contrast effects operate is an interview situation in which one sees a pool of job applicants. Distortions in any given candidate's evaluation can occur as a result of her or his place in the interview schedule. The candidate is likely to receive a more favorable evaluation if preceded by mediocre applicants and a less favorable evaluation if preceded by strong applicants.

Selective Perception

Yet another obstacle to accurate perceptions arises from the tendency to be influenced by our own interests. As it is not possible to take in all stimuli we receive, we tend to select out certain elements. As an illustration of this, consider the experience that follows the purchase of a car. Suddenly you begin to notice that type of car on the street much more frequently. Selective perception occurs in organizations when managers tend to interpret problem situations in light of their own background and interest. For example, given an ambiguous problematic situation, a sales manager will be inclined to see sales issues as the underlying cause while a production manager will be inclined to see manufacturing-related issues as the cause.

Implicit Personality Theories

Implicit personality theories can also lead to inaccurate perceptions. We tend to have our own mini-theories about how people look and behave. These theories help us organize our perceptions and take shortcuts instead of integrating new information all the time. We are cognitive misers. Because the world is complex and ambiguous and we have a limited mental capacity, we try to expend the least amount of effort possible in attempting to make sense of the world. We group traits and appearances into clusters that seem to go together. For example, you may believe that introverted people are also worriers and intellectuals, or that fashionable dressers are also up on current events and like modern music. These implicit personality theories are obstacles, because they limit our ability to take in new information when it is available.

IMPRESSION MANAGEMENT

Most people want to make favorable impressions on others. This is particularly true in organizations, where individuals compete for jobs, favorable performance evaluations, and salary increases. The process by which individuals try to control the impressions others have of them is called impression management. Individuals use several techniques to control others' impressions of them.

Some impression management techniques are self-enhancing. These techniques focus on enhancing others' impressions of the person using the technique. Name-dropping, which involves mentioning an association with important people in the hopes of improving one's image, is often used. Managing one's appearance is another technique for impression management. Individuals dress carefully for interviews because they want to "look the part" in order to get the job. Self-descriptions, or statements about one's characteristics, are used to influence impressions as well.

Another group of impression management techniques are other-enhancing. The aim of these techniques is to focus on the individual whose impression is to be managed. Flattery is a common other-enhancing technique whereby compliments are given to an individual in order to win her or his approval. Favors are also used to gain the approval of others. Agreement with someone's opinion is a technique often used to gain a positive impression.

Some employees may engage in impression management to intentionally look bad at work. Methods for creating a poor impression include decreasing performance, not working to one's potential, skipping work, displaying a bad attitude, or broadcasting one's limitations. Why would someone try to look bad to others? Sometimes employees want to avoid additional work or a particular task. They may try to look bad in hopes of being laid off, or they may create poor impressions in order to get attention.

Impression management seems to have an impact on others' impressions. As long as the impressions conveyed are accurate, this process can be a beneficial one in organizations. If the impressions are found to be false, however, a strongly negative overall impression may result. Further, excessive impression management can lead to the perception that the user is manipulative or insincere.

Lessons about Impression Management

So how can managers avoid being fooled by clever impression management? Alternatively, how can you capitalize on these impression tactics so as to present yourself in a favorable way to others (your direct reports, peers, superiors, etc.)? Let's start with some basic suggestions that can reduce unwanted impression management.

1. *Try to reduce ambiguity.* Impression management becomes more viable when performance criteria are unclear. When clear standards are lacking, resources are more likely to be doled out to those who are well-liked by superiors. Do a better job of making performance criteria specific and you'll reduce the incentive to manage impressions.
2. *Be aware of how circumstances and status impact your interactions.* As a manager, never forget that your status—and your ability to control rewards—can elicit ingratiation and "brown-nosing." And if you or your organization emphasizes status (special offices, elaborate titles, etc.), then don't be surprised when employees use such strategies. Beauty may be in the eye of the beholder, but money and rewards are in the hands of the employer. Reducing the emphasis on status can help curtail unbridled brown-nosing.
3. *Be aware of possible ulterior motives.* Often there's a fine line between impression management and reality. For example, a sports announcer for a local TV station seems very phony and overly dramatic in his delivery. And viewers have criticized him for it. A newspaper article, however, suggests that this style reflects the guy's real personality and that he has been hurt by the public's impression of him. Of course, people were skeptical of the announcer's delivery because they suspected an ulterior motive—that his style was designed to snare viewers in a competitive news market. Yet providing a bad impression isn't the worst thing here. The worse thing is to provide an inaccurate or phony presentation; that's unforgivable. So be aware of ulterior motives, but also know that there's a difference between pure self-promotion and true competence.

And what about the flip side? If impression management can make you more attractive as both a job candidate and an employee, then how can you capitalize on these tactics in presenting yourself?

1. *Looks are important.* Unfortunately, looks sometimes carry the day. But we don't just mean physical attractiveness, although that can be very important. We're also referring to the general impression that manipulating one's appearance can create.
2. *Avoid using some presentation methods.* Some presentation strategies are best left alone. Excuse-making and justifications—even if legitimate and accurate—are losing propositions. You're on the defensive to start with and it's tough to recover. Further, relying on these techniques leads people to suspect other things about you as well. Take a look at the best-selling business books. Most of them present very positive messages; pictures are painted of "servant" leaders, people who lead with their "hearts," and so on. How many people do you know whose careers have been filled with dispassionate, fair-minded, servant bosses. But the more positive (and less accurate) portrayal of business leaders is what sells. Perhaps this holds lessons for us all.

3. *Rely on more subtle techniques*. There's nothing wrong with a little well-timed and delivered self-promotion, but focus on relatively objective accomplishments. Likewise, indirect compliments about an organization can go a long way in interviews and on the job. A comment such as "I've noted that XYZ Corp. is listed as one of the best places to work in the United States" can have positive effects. Subtle agreement with interviewers and bosses (smiling, head nodding, and other nonverbal methods) also can be effective.

ATTRIBUTIONS: PERCEIVING THE CAUSES OF BEHAVIOR

The attribution process refers to the ways in which people come to understand the causes of their own and others' behaviors (Baron and Byrne, 1991; Myers, 1993). Attributions play an important role in the process of person perception. Attributions made about the reasons for someone's behavior may affect judgments about that individual's fundamental characteristics or traits (what he or she is really like).

The attributions that employees and managers make concerning the causes of behavior are important in understanding organizational behavior. For example, managers who attribute poor performance directly to their direct reports tend to behave more punitively than do managers who attribute poor performance to circumstances beyond their direct reports' control. A manager who believes that an employee failed to perform a task correctly because he lacked proper training might be understanding and give the employee better instructions or more training. The same manager might be quite angry if he believes that the direct report made mistakes simply because he didn't try very hard.

Behavioral reactions to the same outcome can be dramatically different, depending on perceptions of the situation and attributions made. For example, Table 2.2 lists some of the possible differences in managerial behavior when employees are perceived positively versus when they are perceived negatively.

The Attribution Process

People make attributions to understand the behavior of other people and to make better sense of their environments. Individuals don't consciously make attributions in all circumstances (although they may do so unconsciously much of the time) (Azar, 1996). However, under certain circumstances, people are likely to make causal attributions consciously. For example, causal attributions are common in the following situations.

- The perceiver has been asked an explicit question about another's behavior? (Why did Nandi do that?)

Table 2.2
Possible Results Stemming from Differences in Perceptions of Performance

Boss's Behavior Toward Perceived Strong Performers	Boss's Behavior Toward Perceived Weak Performers
Discusses project objectives. Gives direct reports the freedom to choose own approach to solving problems or reaching goals.	Gives specific directives when discussing tasks and goals.
Treats mistakes or incorrect judgments as learning opportunities.	Pays close attention to mistakes and incorrect judgments. Quick to emphasize what direct report is doing wrong.
Is open to direct report's suggestions. Solicits opinions from direct reports.	Pays little attention to direct report's suggestions. Rarely asks direct report for input.
Gives direct report interesting and challenging assignments.	Gives direct reports routine assignments.
May frequently defer to direct report's opinions in disagreements.	Usually imposes own views in disagreements.

- An unexpected event occurs. (I've never seen Stanley behave that way. I wonder what's going on.)
- The perceiver depends on another person for a desired outcome. (I wonder why my boss made that comment about my expense account.)
- The perceiver experiences feelings of failure or loss of control. (I can't believe I failed my midterm exam!)

In a basic model of the attribution process people infer "causes" to behaviors that they observe in others, and these interpretations often largely determine their reactions to those behaviors. The perceived causes of behavior reflect several antecedents: (1) the amount of information the perceiver has about the people and the situation and how that information is organized by the perceiver; (2) the perceiver's beliefs (implicit personality theories, what other people might do in a similar situation, and so on); and (3) the motivation of the perceiver (e.g., the importance to the perceiver of making an accurate assessment). Internal factors like learning, motivation, and personality influence the attribution process. The perceiver's information and beliefs depend on previous experiences and are influenced by the perceiver's personality.

Based on information, beliefs, and motives, the perceiver often distinguishes between internal and external causes of behavior; that is, whether people did something because of a real desire or because of the pressure of circumstances. The assigned cause of the behavior—whether internal or external—helps the perceiver attach meaning to the event and is important for understanding the subsequent consequences for the perceiver. Among the consequences of this attribution process are the subsequent behavior of the perceiver in response to the behavior of others, the impact on feelings or emotions (how the perceiver now feels about events, people, and circumstances), and the effects on the perceiver's expectations of future events or behavior.

A central question in the attribution process concerns how perceivers determine whether the behavior of another person stems from internal causes (personality traits, emotions, motives, or ability) or external causes (other people, the situation, or change). A widely accepted model proposed by Harold Kelley attempts to explain how people determine why others behave as they do (Kelley, 1973). This explanation states that in making attributions, people focus on three major factors:

- *Consistency*—the extent to which the person perceived behaviors in the same manner on other occasions when faced with the same situation.
- *Distinctiveness*—the extent to which the person perceived acts in the same manner in different situations.
- *Consensus*—the extent to which others, faced with the same situation, behave in a manner similar to the person perceived. (Kasof, 1999)

According to one researcher, under conditions of high consistency, high distinctiveness, and high consensus, the perceiver will tend to attribute the behavior of the person perceived to external causes (Myers, 1993). When distinctiveness and consensus are low, the perceiver will tend to attribute the behavior of the person to internal causes. Of course, other combinations of high and low consistency, distinctiveness, and consensus are possible. Some combination, however, may not provide the perceiver with a clear choice between internal and external causes.

One of the more interesting findings from attribution theory is that there are errors or biases that distort attributions. For instance, there is substantial evidence that when we make judgments about the behavior of other people, we have a tendency to underestimate the influence of external factors and overestimate the influence of internal or personal factors (Miller and Lawson, 1989). This is called the fundamental attribution error and can explain why a sales manager is prone to attribute poor performance of her sales agents to laziness rather than to the innovative product line introduced by a competitor. There is also a tendency for individuals to attribute their own successes to internal factors such as ability or effort while putting the blame for failure on external factors such as luck. This is called the self-serving bias and suggests that feedback provided to employees in performance reviews will be predictably distorted by recipients depending on whether it is positive or negative.

OVERCOMING OBSTACLES TO PERCEPTIONS OF OTHERS

In most instances, obstacles or people's biased perceptions of others do not result from any malicious intent to inflict harm. Instead, these obstacles or biases in perception tend to occur because we, as perceivers, are imperfect processors of information. We assume that people are internally responsible for their behavior; because we cannot be aware of all the possible situational factors that may be involved—hence, we make the fundamental attribution error. Furthermore, it is highly impractical to learn everything about someone that may guide our reactions—hence, we use stereotypes.

We can, however, minimize the impact of these other biases. Indeed, several steps can be taken to promote the accurate perception of others in the workplace. The following recommendations are useful in this regard:

- *Do not overlook external causes of others' behavior.* The fundamental attribution error leads us to discount the possibility that people's poor performance may result from conditions beyond their control. Therefore, we may ignore legitimate explanations for poor performance. You should ask yourself if anyone else may have performed just as poorly under the same conditions. If the answer is yes, then you should not automatically assume the poor performer is to blame. Good managers need to make such judgments accurately so that they can decide whether to focus their efforts on developing employees or on changing work conditions.
- *Identify and confront your stereotypes.* We all rely on stereotypes—especially when it comes to dealing with new people. Although this is natural, erroneous perceptions—quite possibly at the expense of someone else—are bound to result. Therefore, it is good to identify the stereotypes you hold. Doing so helps you become more aware of them, thus taking a giant step toward minimizing their impact on your behavior. After all, unless you are aware of your stereotypes, you may never be able to counter them.
- *Evaluate people based on objective factors.* The more objective the information you use to judge others, the less your judgments are subjected to perceptual distortion. People tend to bias subjective judgments in self-serving ways, such as positively evaluating the work of those we like and negatively evaluating the work of those we dislike. To the extent that evaluations are based on objective information, however, this is less likely to occur.
- *Avoid making rash judgments.* It is human nature to jump to conclusions about what people are like—even when we know very little about them. Get to know people better before convincing yourself you already know all you need to about them. What you learn may make a big difference in your opinion.

In reality, many of these tactics are far easier to say than to do. To the extent we conscientiously try to apply these suggestions to our everyday interactions with others in the workplace, however, we stand a good chance of perceiving people more accurately, and this is a fundamental ingredient in the recipe for successfully managing others in today's organizations.

ATTITUDES

Attitudes are determinants of behavior because they're linked with perception, personality, and motivation. An attitude is a positive or negative feeling or mental state of readiness, learned and organized through experience, that exerts specific influence on a person's response to people, objects, and situations. Each of us has attitudes on numerous topics—dieting, career goals, exercise, tax laws, and unions, for example. This definition of attitude has certain implications for managers. First, attitudes are learned. Second, attitudes define our predispositions toward given aspects of the world. Third, attitudes provide the emotional basis of our interpersonal relations and identification with others. And fourth, attitudes are organized and are close to the core of personality. Some attitudes are persistent and enduring; yet, attitudes are subject to change.

An attitude has three separate but related parts:

- *Cognitive.* Perceptions and beliefs about the object of the attitude; the person's perception of the distinguishing features of the object.
- *Affective.* Evaluation and feelings about the object of the attitude; a person's feeling of like or dislike for the object.
- *Behavioral intentions.* How the person wants to behave and what the person says about his behavior toward the object. It is not always the same as the behavior observed following the expression of the attitude. (Breckler, 1984)

Attitudes have many sources: family, peer groups, society, and previous job experiences. Early family experiences help shape individuals' attitudes. Young children's attitudes usually correspond to their parents'. As children reach their teens, they begin to be more strongly influenced by peers. Peer groups influence attitudes because individuals want to be accepted by others. Teenagers seek approval by sharing similar attitudes or by modifying attitudes to comply with those of a group.

Culture, mores, and language influence attitudes. Attitudes of Americans toward people in Russia, Cubans toward capitalism, and French Canadians toward France are learned in society. Within the United States are subcultures—ethnic communities, ghetto communities, and religious groups—that help shape people's attitudes.

Through job experiences, employees develop attitudes about pay equity, performance review, managerial capabilities, job design, and work group affiliation. Previous experiences account for some individual differences in attitudes toward performance, loyalty, and commitment.

Individuals strive to maintain consistency among the components of attitudes. But contradictions and inconsistencies often occur, resulting in a state of disequilibrium. The tension stemming from such a state is reduced only when some form of consistency is achieved.

The term cognitive dissonance describes a situation where there's a discrepancy between the cognitive and behavioral components of an attitude (Festinger, 1957). Any form of inconsistency is uncomfortable so individuals attempt to reduce dissonance. Dissonance, then, is viewed as a state within a person that, when aroused, elicits actions designed to return the person to a state of equilibrium (Elliott and Devine, 1994). For example, the chief executive officer (CEO) of a tobacco company may experience cognitive dissonance if she believes that she's honest and hardworking but that cigarettes contribute to lung cancer. She may think, "I'm a good human being, but I'm in charge of a firm producing a cancer-contributing product." These thoughts create inconsistency. Instead of quitting and giving up her successful career, she's more likely to modify her thoughts or cognitions. She could state, "Our firm has manufactured a cigarette that's now very safe and free of cancer-producing products." Or she may think that cigarette smoking actually improves smokers' well-being, that it helps them reduce or cope with stress. When inconsistency in attitudes arises, the person can attempt to work out the problem cognitively or behaviorally. Here the CEO used a cognitive process to reduce her dissonance.

Cognitive dissonance has important organizational implications. First, it helps explain the choices made by an individual with attitude inconsistency. Second, it can help predict a person's propensity to change attitudes. If individuals are required, for example, by the design of their jobs or occupations to say or do things that contradict their personal attitudes, they may change those attitudes to make them more compatible with what they've said or done.

Changing Attitudes

Managers often face the task of changing employees' attitudes because existing attitudes hinder job performance. Attitude change happens because (1) something persuades the person to shift his attitudes; (2) the norms of a social group important to the person affect her attitudes; or (3) the person becomes uncomfortable with some aspects of her beliefs about certain things.

Common sources of attitude change are the persuasive communications designed to affect our beliefs such as those found in radio, television, newspaper, and magazine advertising. Persuasive communication tries to change the cognitive part of an attitude and assumes the affective part will change in either a positive or negative direction.

Persuasive communication changes attitudes through four separate but related processes. First, the communication must win the target's attention. Television advertising, for example, often plays at a higher volume than the main program to get the attention of the viewer. Second, the target of the attitude change must comprehend the message. A persuasive communication must be presented in a language and format understandable by the target. The third process is acceptance. No matter how logical and persuasive a communication, if the target does not accept it, attitude change will not follow. The last process is retention. If the message is not memorable, attitude change will not last. The latter, of course, is central to the effectiveness of advertising. Our shopping behavior is little affected by advertising we easily forget.

The second major approach to attitude change views people as embedded in a social context and affected by the norms or standards held by the social groups a person experiences (Lewin, 1947). People who hold attitudes different from those of a group important to them will feel social pressures to conform to the norms of the group. Such pressures come from the tendency of social groups to reject people who do not conform to their norms. If the person with the differing attitude values membership in the group, he will likely bring the attitude into alignment with the group norms.

Hints for Shaping and Changing Employee Attitudes

It is difficult to change other people's attitudes. But it can be done. The following hints can help you as a manager to change employee attitudes.

1. *Give employees feedback.* Employees must be made aware of their negative attitudes if they are to change. The manager must talk to the employee about the negative attitude. The employee must understand that the attitude has negative consequences for the individual and the department. The manager should offer an alternative attitude.
2. *Accentuate positive conditions.* Employees tend to have positive attitudes toward the things they do well. Make working conditions as pleasant as possible; make sure employees have all the necessary resources and training to do a good job.
3. *Provide consequences.* Employees tend to repeat activities or events followed by positive consequences. On the other hand, they tend to avoid things followed by negative consequences. Encourage and reward employees with positive attitudes. Try to keep negative attitudes from developing and spreading.
4. *Be a positive role model.* If the manager has a positive attitude, employees may, too.

Attitudes and Values

Values are linked to attitudes in that a value serves as a way of organizing. Values are defined "as the constellation of likes, dislikes, viewpoints, shoulds, inner inclinations, rational and irrational judgments, prejudices, and association patterns that determine a person's view of the world" (Flowers, 1975; Spranger, 1928). Certainly, a person's work is an important aspect of her world. Moreover, the importance of a value constellation is that, once internalized, it becomes (consciously or subconsciously) a standard or criterion for guiding one's actions. The study of values, therefore, is fundamental to the study of managing. There's evidence that values are also extremely important for understanding effective managerial behavior (Flowers, 1975).

Values affect the perceptions not only of appropriate ends but also of appropriate means to those ends. From the design and development of organizational structures and processes to the utilization of particular leadership styles and the evaluation of the performance of direct reports, value systems are persuasive. An influential theory of leadership is based on the argument that managers can't be expected to adopt a leadership style that's contrary to their "need structures" or value orientations (Fiedler, 1967). Moreover, when managers evaluate direct reports' performance, the effects of the managers' values are noticeable. For example, one researcher reports that managers can be expected to evaluate direct reports with values similar to their own as more effective than direct reports with dissimilar values (Senger, 1971). The impact of values is more pronounced in decisions involving little objective information and, consequently, a greater degree of subjectivity.

Another aspect of the importance of values occurs when the interpersonal activities of managers bring them into a confrontation with different, and potentially contradictory, values. Assembly-line workers, scientists, and persons in various professional occupations are characterized by particular, if not unique, value orientations. Day-to-day activities create numerous situations in which managers must relate to others with different views of what's right or wrong. Conflicts between managers and workers, administrators and teachers, and line and staff personnel have been documented and discussed in the literature of management. The manner in which these conflicts are resolved is particularly crucial to the organization's effectiveness.

Attitudes and Job Satisfaction

Job satisfaction is an attitude that individuals have about their jobs. It results from their perceptions of their jobs, based on factors of the work environment, such as the supervisor's style, policies and procedures, work group affiliation, working conditions, and fringe benefits. While numerous dimensions have been associated with job satisfaction, five in particular have crucial characteristics (Smith, Kendall and Hulin, 1969).

1. *Pay.* The amount received and the perceived equity of pay.
2. *Job.* The extent to which job tasks are considered interesting and provide opportunities for learning and for accepting responsibility.
3. *Promotion opportunities.* The availability of opportunities for advancement.
4. *Supervisor.* The supervisor's abilities to demonstrate interest in and concern about employees.
5. *Coworkers.* The extent to which co-workers are friendly, competent, and supportive.

In some studies, these five job-satisfaction dimensions have been measured by the Job Descriptive Index (JDI). Employees are asked to respond "yes, no, or can't decide" as to whether a word or phrase describes their attitudes about their jobs. The JDI attempts to measure a person's satisfaction with specific facts of the job. Other measures of job satisfaction, such as the Brayfield-Rothe measures are more general.

A major reason for studying job satisfaction is to provide managers with ideas about how to improve employee attitudes. Many organizations use attitude surveys to determine levels of employee job satisfaction.

Changing Attitudes

The environment around us influences our attitudes. Usually we cannot control our environment, but we can control our attitudes. We can choose to be optimistic or pessimistic. We can look for the positive and be happier and get more out of life. The following hints can help you change your attitudes:

1. *Be aware of your attitudes.* People who are optimistic have higher levels of job satisfaction. Consciously try to have and maintain a positive attitude. If a situation gives you lemons—make lemonade. If you catch yourself complaining or being negative in any way, stop and change to a positive attitude. With time you can become more positive.
2. *Think for yourself.* Develop your own attitudes based on others' input; don't simply copy others' attitudes.
3. *Realize that there are few, if any, benefits to harboring negative attitudes.* Negative attitudes, like holding a grudge, can only hurt your human relations, and hurt yourself in the end, and it's stressful.
4. *Keep an open mind.* Listen to other people's input. Use it do develop your positive attitudes.

PERSONALITY

We have all probably heard phases such as "that person has a pleasant personality" or "that person has an outgoing personality." The word personality carries many meanings for psychologists and lay people. For example, personality is defined by some as a set of traits, characteristics, and predispositions held by a person. For others, personality is the unique and relatively stable pattern of behavior, thoughts, and emotions shown by individuals. In either definition, personality refers to the lasting ways in which any one person is different from all others. And as you can imagine, personality characteristics can be very important when it comes to organizational behavior.

Personality usually matures and stabilizes by age 30. The collection of factors that make up an individual's personality affects how the person adjusts to different environments.

Personality Theories

Since the early twentieth century, psychologists have developed three major classes of personality theories. Each theory makes different assumptions about human personality and offers a different perspective of how personality develops.

Cognitive theory describes people as developing their thinking patterns as their lives unfold (Kenrich, Montello, and MacFarlane, 1985). A person's patterns of thinking affect how the person interprets and internalizes life's events. People move through a series of cognitive development stages (Shafer, 1988). The stages begin shortly after birth with the reflexive behavior of the infant and proceed through increasingly more complex modes of perceptions and interpretation of events in the child's environment. This class of personality theory views a child as neither driven by instincts nor unwittingly shaped by environmental influences. Children are curious and actively explore their social world to understand it. They respond to their environments according to how they understand and interpret their environment's features. Two children in the same environment could interpret and react to it differently.

Learning theories of personality have appeared in several forms since the early 1990s. The earliest versions assumed a child was a blank sheet of paper, shaped almost entirely by the social environment. Instincts played no role in these theories. A need to satisfy a set of internal states, drives, motivated a person's behavior (Dollard and Miller, 1950; Watson, 1913, 1928).

A person learns behavior from social interaction with other people. The young child learns acceptable behaviors during early family socialization. Adults continuously interact in different social environments and with different people. As behavior stabilizes, it forms the basic qualities of an individual's personality. Some learning theories view personality development as a continuous process from birth to death. The uniqueness of each personality follows from the variability in each person's social experiences (Dollard and Miller, 1950).

Operant-Learning Theory offers another view of social learning (Skinner, 1953, 1971). People learn behavior because external stimuli reinforce the behavior. Reinforcement increase the likelihood of the behavior in the future. The proper application of reinforcers develops complete behavior patterns, which form an individual's personality.

The cognitive social-learning theory developed by Bandura accepts the role of reinforcement but sees behavior as largely learned by observation (Bandura, 1977). People learn by observing behavior and its consequences, not by directly responding to reinforcers. They learn by observation and try to imitate the behavior they see.

Biological theories of personality development have developed from two different sets of research. Ethological theory describes the ways in which the members of a given species, say, human beings, develop common characteristics as a result of evolution. Behavior genetics describe how an individual's unique gene structure affects personality development (Kenrich et al., 1985). The accumulated research evidence points to strong genetic effects on human personality (Bouchard, 1997).

Ethological theory has deep roots in an evolutionary perspective of human behavior (Cairns, 1979; Jones, 1972). Behavioral characteristics that have helped humans survive through successive generations become the inborn characteristics of all humans. The simplest example is the distress-like cry of an infant and the response of a person responsible for the infant's care. The infant cries because of hunger or other pain. The caregiver responds to the cry by caring for the infant. Ethologists view both behavioral responses as inborn characteristics common to all humans. Ethologists also believe humans learn from their social experiences. A child who cries, but does not consistently get a warm and nurturing response from a caregiver, may develop a personality characterized by distrust of others (Sroufe, Fox, and Pancake, 1983).

Behavior genetics describes personality development as a process of behaviorally expressing a person's genotype or set of inherited genes. Behavior geneticists do not view emerging behaviors, abilities, predispositions, and other characteristics of the personality as solely a function of genes. They see personality development as an involved series of interactions between a person's genetically-based predispositions and influences from the person's social environment.

Although some aspects of personality can come from inborn qualities, others are learned. Modern personality researchers largely agree that personality develops from an interaction of internal qualities and the external environment.

The Big Five Personality Dimensions

After almost a century of research, scientists largely agree that five basic dimensions can describe personality (Digman, 1990; Salgado, 1997). These dimensions have appeared in many studies, across many samples, and in studies done in several countries outside the United States. Although some psychologists feel the dimensions are not precisely specified, fewer than five dimensions exist, or a different set of five dimensions exist, these dimensions are now widely used in personality psychology (Waller and Ben-Porath, 1987). The "Big Five" factors are:

- *Extraversion.* This dimension captures one's comfort level with relationships. Extraverts tend to be gregarious, assertive, and sociable. Introverts tend to be reserved, timid, and quiet.
- *Agreeableness.* This dimension refers to an individual's propensity to defer to others. Highly agreeable people are cooperative, warm, and trusting. People who score low on agreeableness are cold, disagreeable, and antagonistic.
- *Conscientiousness.* This dimension is a measure of reliability. A highly conscientious person is responsible, organized, dependable, and persistent. Those who score low on this dimension are easily distracted, disorganized, and unreliable.
- *Emotional stability.* This dimension taps a person's ability to withstand stress. People with positive emotional stability tend to be calm, self-confident, and secure. Those with highly negative scores tend to be nervous, anxious, depressed, and insecure.
- *Openness to experience.* The final dimension addresses an individual's range of interests and fascination with novelty. Extremely open people are creative, curious, and artistically sensitive. Those at the other end of the openness category are conventional and find comfort in the familiar.

As you might imagine, the Big Five dimensions of personality play an important role in organizational behavior. For example, research has shown that employees who are highly conscientious tend to perform better than those who are not so conscientious. Organizational scientists also have found that people who are highly extraverted tend to succed on managerial and sales jobs—much as the stereotype suggests (Barrick and Mount, 1993). However, not all research findings are as easily explained. For example, neither agreeableness nor emotional stability have been linked to success in various kinds of jobs. This may well be because large numbers of disagreeable and unstable people leave their jobs early. As a result, those who are left behind, and whose performance is measured by researchers, tend to be relatively agreeable and stable. Clearly, as you can see, personality plays an important—but often unpredictable—role when it comes to understanding behavior in organizations.

Personality Types

Human personality characteristics and dispositions are also described as personality types. Many types are useful for understanding and managing behavior in organizations. The following paragraphs describe some personality types that can give you insight into their behavior.

Locus of control. People differ in whether they feel they control the consequences of their actions or they are controlled by external factors. External control personality types believe that luck, fate, or powerful external forces control their destiny. Internal control personality types believe they control what happens to them (Rotter, 1966).

Machiavellianism. A Machiavellian personality holds cynical views of other people's motives, places little value on honesty, and approaches the world with manipulative intent. Machiavellians maintain distance between themselves and others and are emotionally detached from other people in their lives. Their suspicious interpersonal orientation can contribute to high interpersonal conflict. Machiavellian personalities focus on personal goals, even if reaching them requires unethical behavior or manipulating other people. Their suspicious orientation also leads them to view their organizational world as a web of political processes (Wilson, Near, and Miller, 1996).

Type A and B personalities. During the 1960s and 1970s, much research focused on personality patterns associated with coronary heart disease. The Type A personality emerged as a significant risk factor for that disease. Type A personalities are "aggressively involved in a chronic, incessant struggle to achieve more in less and less time, and, if required to do so, against the opposing efforts of other things or other persons" (Friedman and Rosenman, 1974; Friedman and Ulmer, 1984). Type A personalities have strong desires to dominate other people and quickly explode in anger over what others consider trivial events. For example, lines at a bank or a stalled vehicle in an intersection can throw a Type A personality into a rage.

In contrast to the Type A personality is the Type B, who is exactly the opposite. Type B's have no sense of time urgency and often stop to review their achievements and think about where they are headed in the future. They have high self-esteem, a characteristic that distinguishes them from Type A personalities. Type B personalities are even tempered, are not bothered by common everyday events, and approach the world in a calmer way than Type A personalities.

Myers-Briggs Type Indicator (MBTI). The Myers-Briggs Type Indicator (MBTI) is a popular personality assessment device based on Jung's personality theory (Jung, 1971). This device assigns people to one of 16 personality types based on four bi-polar dimensions: extroverted (E)–introverted (I); sensing (S)–intuitive (I); thinking (T)–feeling (F); perceiving (P)–judging (J). Extroverts look outward; introverts turn inward. Sensers use data; intuitives use hunches. Thinkers are objective; feelers are subjective. Perceivers are flexible; judgers want closure. The letters in parentheses form type indicators. An ESTJ, for example, is an extroverted, sensing, thinking, and judging type.

There is no hard evidence that the MBTI is a valid measure of personality. But lack of evidence doesn't seem to deter its use in a wide range of organizations. Companies like AT&T, Exxon, and Honeywell have used the MBTI in their management development programs to help employees understand the different viewpoints of others in the organization. The MBTI can be used for team building. Hewlett-Packard and Armstrong World Industries have used the MBTI to help teams realize that diversity and differences lead to successful performance.

Type theory is valued by managers for its simplicity and accuracy in depicting personalities. It is a useful tool for helping managers develop interpersonal skills. Type theory is also used by managers to build teams that capitalize on individuals' strengths and to help individual team members appreciate differences.

It should be recognized that there is the potential for individuals to misuse the information from the MBTI in organizational settings. Some inappropriate uses include labeling one another, providing a convenient excuse that they simply can't work with someone else, and avoiding responsibility for their own personal development with respect to working with others and becoming more flexible. One's type is not an excuse for inappropriate behavior.

SUMMARY

Organizing the information from the environment so that it makes sense is called perception. Perception is a cognitive process. Perception helps individuals select, organize, store, and interpret stimuli into a meaningful and coherent picture of the world. There are a number of obstacles, barriers (or biases) to the precise perception of others' behavior. Stereotypes, first impressions, halo effect, projection, contrast effect, selective perception, and implicit personality theories are examples of some of the obstacles that managers must overcome in order to prevent imprecise perceptions of others' behavior.

Attribution deals with the perceived causes of behavior. People infer causes for the behavior of others, and their perceptions of why certain behaviors occur influence their own subsequent behavioral responses and feelings.

Attitudes are favorable or unfavorable dispositions about an object. The three related parts of an attitude are cognitive, affective, and behavioral intention. Attitudes can change because something persuades the person to shift his attitudes; the norms of a social group affect his attitudes; or the person becomes cognitively uncomfortable (cognitive dissonance) with some aspects of his beliefs compared to others.

Personality is defined by some as a set of traits, characteristics, and predispositions held by a person. Three views of personality development came from cognitive theory, learning theories, and biological explanations of personality development. Among the personality traits most likely to affect behavior in organizations are: The "Big Five" dimensions of personality, locus of control, the Type A and B behavior patterns, and Machiavellianism.

REFERENCES

Azar, B. 1996. Influences from the mind's inner layers. *The APA Monitor* (February): 1, 25.

Bandura, A. 1977. *Social learning theory*. Englewood Cliffs, NJ: Prentice-Hall.

Baron, R.A., and Byrne, D. 1991. *Social psychology: Understanding human interaction*. 6th ed. Boston: Allyn & Bacon.

Barrick, M.R., and Mount, M.K. 1993. Autonomy as a moderator of the relationships between the big five personality dimensions and job performance. *Journal of Applied Psychology* 78: 111–118.

Bouchard, T.J., Jr. 1997. Genetic influence on mental abilities, personality, vocational interests and work attitudes. In C.L. Cooper and I.T. Robertson (eds.), *International review of industrial and organizational psychology*, vol. 12. Chichester, England: John Wiley & Sons, pp. 373–396.

Breckler, S.J. 1984. Empirical validation of affect, behavior, and cognition as distinct components of attitude. *Journal of Personality and Social Psychology* 47: 1191–1205.

Cairns, R.B. 1979. *Social development: The origins of plasticity of interchanges*. New York: W.H. Freeman.

Digman, J.M. 1990. Personality structure: Emergence of the five-factor model. *Annual Review of Psychology* 41: 417–440.

Dollard, J., and Miller, N.E. 1950. *Personality and psychotherapy: An analysis in terms of learning, thinking, and culture*. New York: McGraw-Hill.

Elliott, A.J., and Devine, P.G. 1994. On the motivational nature of cognitive dissonance: Dissonance as psychological discomfort. *Journal of Personality and Social Psychology* (September): 382–394.

Festinger, L. 1957. *A theory of cognitive dissonance*. Evanston, IL: Row, Peterson.

Fiedler, F.E. 1967. *A theory of leadership effectiveness*. New York: McGraw-Hill.

Flowers, V.S. 1975. *Managerial values for working*. New York: American Management Association.

Friedman, M., and Rosenman, R. 1974. *Type A behavior and your heart*. New York: Alfred A. Knopf.

Friedman, M., and Ulmer, D. 1984. *Treating type A behavior—and your heart.* New York: Alfred A. Knopf.

Jones, N.B. 1972. Characteristics of ethological studies of human behavior studies of human behavior. In N.B. Jones (ed.), *Ethological studies of child behavior.* London: Cambridge University Press, pp. 3–33.

Jung, C.J. 1971. *The collected works of C.G. Jung, vol. 6: Psychological types.* Translated by H.G. Baynes; revised by R.F. Hull. Princeton, NJ: Princeton University Press. (Originally published 1921.)

Kasof, J. 1999. Attribution and creativity. In M.A. Runco and S.R. Pritsker (eds.), *Encylopedia of creativity*, vol. 1. San Diego: Academic Press, pp. 147–156.

Kelley, H.H. 1973. The process of causal attribution. *American Psychologist* 28: 107–128.

Kenrich, D.T., Montello, D.R., and MacFarlane, S. 1985. Personality: Social learning, social cognition, or sociobiology? In R. Hogan and W.H. Jones (eds.), *Perspectives in personality: A research annual*, vol. 1. Greenwich, CT: JAI Press, pp. 215–219.

Krech, D., Crutchfield, R.S., and Ballachey, E.L. 1962. *Individual and society*. New York: McGraw-Hill.

Lewin, K. 1947. Group decision and social change. In T. Newcomb and E. Hartley (eds.), *Readings in social psychology*. New York: Holt, pp. 330–344.

McGuire, W.J. 1985. Attitudes and attitude change. In G. Lindzey and E. Aronson (eds.), *Handbook of social psychology*, vol. 2. New York: Random House, pp. 233–346.

Miller, A.G., and Lawson, T. 1989. The effect of an informational option on the fundamental attribution error. *Personality and Social Psychology Bulletin* (June): 194–204.

Myers, D.G. 1993. *Social psychology*. 4th ed. New York: McGraw-Hill.

Nam, S. 1992. Cultural and managerial attributions for group performance. Unpublished doctoral dissertation, University of Oregon. Cited in Steers, R.M., Bischoff, S.J., and Higgins, L.H. (1992) Cross-cultural management research. *Journal of Management Inquiry* (December): 325–326.

Nicholson, N. 1998. How hardwired is human behavior? *Harvard Business Review* (July–August): 133–147.

Rotter, J.B. 1966. Generalized expectancies for internal and external control of reinforcement. *Psychological Monographs* 80: 1–28.

Salgado, J.F. 1997. The five factor model of personality and job performance in the European Community. *Journal of Applied Psychology* 82: 30–43.

Senger, J. 1971. Managers' perceptions of subordinates' competence as a function of personal value orientations. *Academy of Management Journal* (December): 415–424.

Shafer, D.R. 1988. *Social and personality development*. Pacific Grove, CA: Brooks/Cole.

Skinner, B.F. 1953. *Science and human behavior*. New York: Free Press.

Skinner, B.F. 1971. *Beyond freedom and dignity*. New York: Bantam.

Smith, P.C., Kendall, L.M., and Hulin, C.L. 1969. *The measurement of satisfaction in work and retirement*. Skokie, IL: Rand McNally.

Spranger, E. 1928. *Types of men*. Halle, Germany: Max Niemeyer Verlag.

Sroufe, L.A., Fox, N.E., and Pancake, V.R. 1983. Attachment and dependence in developmental perspective. *Child Development* 54: 1615–1627.

Waller, N.G., and Ben-Porath, Y.S. 1987. Is it time for clinical psychology to embrace the five-factor model of personality? *American Psychologist* 42: 887–889.

Watson, J.B. 1913. Psychology as the behaviorist views it. *Psychological Review* 20: 158–177.

Watson, J.B. 1928. *Psychological care of the infant and child.* New York: Norton.

Wilson, D.S., Near, D., and Miller, R.R. 1996. Machiavellianism: A synthesis of the evolutionary and psychological literatures. *Psychological Bulletin* 119: 285–299.

Chapter 3

Motivating Today's Workforce

INTRODUCTION

"Nobody wants to work like they did in the good old days." "Half the problems we have around here are due to a lack of personal motivation." "Workers just don't seem to care." Such sentiments are often expressed by many of today's managers. However, motivating employees is not a new problem. Much of the pioneering work in the field of management, which took place early in the twentieth century, was concerned with motivation. One can even find examples showing motivation problems existed back in biblical times.

One reason why leading is such an important management activity is that it entails ensuring that each member of a team is motivated to perform highly and help the organization achieve its goals. When managers are effective, the outcome of the leading process is a highly motivated workforce.

Managers frequently ask the following questions:

- What does it take to motivate my direct reports?
- How do I get people to do things?
- Why is motivation so complicated and difficult to understand?
- Can basic principles of motivation apply to today's individual employees and teams?
- Am I motivated?

No two managers will answer these questions in exactly the same manner. Motivation is an individual phenomenon affecting each person in a different way. Although motivation continues to be a popular word, it is extremely difficult to define. Yet its importance cannot be overemphasized. In reality, managers are not evaluated on what they do, but, instead, on what they cause their direct reports to do. The mark of a successful manager is to be able to motivate people, causing them to advance their best efforts to accomplish and possibly exceed organizational goals and objectives.

In this chapter we describe what motivation is and the importance to managers in promoting high levels of motivation in order for an organization to achieve its goals. We examine the major theories of motivation. Each of these theories provides managers with important insights about how to motivate organizational members. The theories are complementary in that each focuses on a somewhat different aspect of motivation. We then consider specific methods for motivating today's workforce.

WHAT IS MOTIVATION?

We see examples of motivation all the time. Rocky, the prizefighter down for the count, sees his wife through bleary eyes and rises slowly from the mat, summoning energy from within himself that allows him to attack the challenger and win. During halftime, the lackluster football team is transformed by the coach into screaming, aggressive, and highly motivated players who go on to win the game.

The study of motivation is concerned primarily with the question of why and how people behave as they do. Motivation is derived from the root of the Latin word meaning "to move." It is, basically, to impel someone to act. An overwhelming amount of time and energy has been devoted to finding the answers to this question.

In many work situations, some managers do not believe that motivation is part of their job. They think that once an employee is hired, it is the employee's responsibility to ensure that the job is done. They unfortunately envision their job as simply making corrections and adjustments when necessary, and they erroneously believe that motivation is the responsibility of the individual employee.

Today's organizations cannot be successful if they rely on this premise. Managers and various team leaders are the movers and shakers whose primary responsibility is to get things done through others. The first thing that those in leadership positions must accept is that motivation is a primary part of their job. In order to motivate effectively, they must understand the process and theory of motivation, as well as its components. What is more, they must readily recognize the negative consequences of unmotivated employees.

Managers must realize that people behave with a purpose or pattern. Patterns of behavior are influenced by motives that stem from psychological and physiological needs. Employees are individual by nature, making the total concept of motivation somewhat complicated.

Motivation is the process of satisfying internal needs through actions and behaviors. It is concerned with a composite of mental and physical drives, combined with the environment that makes people behave the way they do.

If today's organizations wish to be successful in getting employees to achieve organizational objectives, their supervisors and managers must understand the fundamentals of motivation. This is not an easy job. Motivation is psychological by nature. Although it cannot be seen, its presence or absence can be recognized by observing employee behavior. When a manager observes an employee, "doing" a task, the logical assumption is that the employee is motivated. If, on the other hand, an employee is frequently observed wasting time, it can be assumed that the employee is not motivated. The same application can be made to group behavior.

Harmful Myths about Motivation

Two harmful myths about motivation are widely held: (1) that it can be gained from "motivational" speakers and (2) that it can be triggered simply with economic rewards. Motivational speakers seldom, if ever, provide lasting motivation. A lot of advice is dispensed by motivational gurus about how to motivate employees and customers. Serious students of motivation recognize this as being like worthless "snake oil" sold in a bottle. The value of pep talks (along with sales meetings, convention speeches, and posters or calendars with motivational messages) has been oversold. They may be entertaining and fun, but they are not permanently motivational. Lasting motivation comes from within the person.

Likewise, the notion that economic rewards necessarily trigger motivation is a gross oversimplication. According to this approach, all you have to do to get the behavior you want is to provide the right amount of money or other rewards. Economists assume that people act rationally in their own self-interest. However, as we all know, the perfectly rational human being does not exist. Each of us has a point after which extra money does not motivate us.

Dispelling these myths leads to an important lesson about motivation: motivation is not enthusiasm, and motivating a person only with money is not a guarantee of productivity. Lasting, persistent motivation comes from within; it is initiated and maintained by the self.

The Importance of Needs and Motivation

All of us have needs. Although we might be able to survive without such gadgets as video telephones and digital compact disc players with random-access programming, we wouldn't survive for long without food, drink, sleep, air to breathe, and appropriate atmosphere conditions. A need, in effect, gives a person a feeling of deprivation, that something is missing from his or her life, at least at the moment. The missing things may be physiological (food and drink), security (medical insurance), social (friends), or psychological (self-esteem, status, and a feeling of achievement). When you are deprived of various things, something to drink for example, you feel a type of tension that moves (motivates) you to engage in activity intended to quench (satisfy) your thirst. Certain types of deprivation on the job can also influence your attitude—that is, morale—at the workplace.

The need satisfaction model is used to illustrate motivation from a simplified point of view. In this model, a need or motive serves as the basis for action. The person then takes an action, directly leading to satisfaction of the need. For example, thirst may lead an individual to go to the store and buy a soft drink. The need satisfaction model has obvious job implications: for example, the need for additional money may lead an individual to work overtime.

THE MOTIVATION PROCESS

In order to understand the motivation process, we need to consider various job-related factors. These include general factors, such as the organizational environment and the rewards or punishments provided for particular behaviors. It also includes factors that are unique to each employee: individual perceptions, the personal importance of different needs, personal traits, the ability to perform different types of work, and the amount of effort the employee is willing to expend.

The following provides a detailed explanation of the motivation process. The process begins with the identification of a need. Money, status, recognition, and promotion are typical job-related needs. For example, let's follow an employee who wants to be promoted. The same steps and rationale explored below would apply to many identified needs.

Once the employee wants a promotion, the satisfaction of that desire is subject to steps 2, 3, and 4. In step 2, the employee assesses the degree of importance attached to being promoted. Is the employee willing to make the necessary sacrifices? Is the promotion so important that the employee is willing to put aside other activities in favor of seeking it? For example, if promotion is based on superior performance, is the employee willing to commit the extra time and effort necessary to perform in a superior manner? If not, the process terminates at this stage. If the employee is willing to make the commitment, the process proceeds to the third step.

In step 3, pre-evaluation, the employee attempts to determine the availability of a promotion. The process is likely to terminate at this stage if no higher position is available. However, it is conceivable that the employee will continue with the evaluation even though the promotion is not available, with the intention of securing a promotion in another organization. Assuming a promotion is available, the employee must consider any environmental constraints to securing it. The employee might ask, "Have I been here long enough? What does the job require? Do I have the necessary education? Do I have the necessary training and skills? Am I capable? Am I likely to get it? Is the boss's son or daughter standing in my way?" Again, a negative answer to one or more of these questions is likely to terminate the process.

If the responses to the questions raised in step 3 are encouraging, step 4 is initiated. In this step, the employee puts forth the effort necessary to cause the desired outcome. The employee makes a self-assessment to determine if he or she is meeting the employer's standards. In step 5, the employee evaluates the outcome, asking: "Did I get my reward? Will I receive it in the near future? Why or why not?" Step 6 analyzes the outcomes of step 5. Were the employee's efforts justified? If not, the long-term implications (step 7) could be serious; but if so, the long-term implications can be positive, giving the employee the self-confidence to tackle the process of satisfying new needs.

Just like the employee in our example, today's managers must recognize that other employees may be motivated by a bonus or the opportunity for a pay increase and may be willing to work harder to get it. For today's organizations to be successful in motivating employees it pays for their leaders to understand the process of motivation.

Each of the theories of motivation discussed in this chapter focuses on a different set of issues that managers need to address to have a highly motivated workforce. Each theory in a distinct way adds to the motivation puzzle. Together, the theories provide a comprehensive set of guidelines that can be used to motivate today's employees. The next section discusses the major motivation theories.

MAJOR MOTIVATION THEORIES

A few theories of what motivates people have been so intuitively appealing to managers that they have become "classics." Their popularity largely stems from ease of understanding and general acceptance in the early years of the study of motivation rather than a firm foundation of research data. They have provided a foundation upon which many other theories have built their conclusions and they have substantially influenced thousands of managers who accept their principles.

Maslow's Hierarchy of Needs

Organizations that strive to meet the needs of their employees attract the best people and motivate them to do excellent work. Some insight into how this may come about is provided by psychologist Abraham Maslow's hierarchy of needs theory. Maslow's basic idea was simple: People will not be healthy and well-adjusted unless they have their needs met. This idea applies whether we're talking about becoming a functioning member of society, Maslow's original focus, or a productive employee of an organization, a later application of his work.

Specifically, Maslow (1954) proposed that all people seek to satisfy five basic kinds of needs: psychological needs, safety needs, belongingness needs, esteem needs, and self-actualization needs. Maslow suggested that these needs constitute a hierarchy of needs, with the most basic or compelling—physiological and safety needs—at the bottom. Maslow argued that these lowest-level needs must be met before a person will strive to satisfy needs higher up in the hierarchy, such as self-esteem needs. Once a need is satisfied, he proposed, it ceases to operate as a source of motivation. The lowest level of unmet needs in the hierarchy is the prime motivator of behavior; if and when this level is satisfied, needs at the next highest level in the hierarchy motivate behavior.

Maslow's impact on management. Maslow's theory is widely covered—yet heavily debated. Some theorists argue the precise order and sequence of the needs. Of greater importance is the fact that Maslow has identified those needs that are of paramount importance to the individual. Managers must constantly ensure the on-the-job ability to satisfy these needs for themselves and for their employees.

Some key conclusions that can be drawn from Maslow's hierarchy are: (1) there are several aspects of the workplace other than money (to provide for physiological needs); (2) since people can be at any of the levels of the hierarchy, what substantially motivates one person may provide only minimal motivation to another—thus managers must be aware of the needs of each individual; and (3) what motivates a person may change over time, thus the assessment of a person's needs must be continuous.

Individual growth is the key vehicle for organizational success. Managers must attempt to identify individual employee needs and foster satisfaction. If they do so, employees will progress toward self-actualization, permitting the organization to be all that it can be.

McClelland's Achievement Theory

Maslow described needs that people seem to be born with. In other words, all people seem to have such needs instinctually, and they fulfill them through various behaviors. David McClelland suggested refining some of Maslow's higher-order needs to make them relevant to life in organizations. McClelland called these refinements acquired needs, because people learn that fulfilling these needs is desirable if they want to excel. McClelland (1961) theorized that individuals have three basic motivational needs: affiliation, power, and achievement.

The affiliation motive can be explained as a strong desire for individual and group approval, and it reflects the desire for social acceptance and friendship. The power motive can be satisfied by being in control. It is expressed as a strong desire to change events and to exercise influence over others. The achievement motive is based on the need to achieve and win. It is characterized by seeking a challenge, establishing goals, working hard, and succeeding.

For managers, all three motives—affiliation, power, and achievement—are important when it comes to motivating employees. What is more, McClelland found that learning, education, and training can stimulate a greater need to achieve.

Managers can use their understanding of the three needs to match employees to tasks that help them fulfill these needs, resulting in high performance. For example, it is wasteful to place a person with a high need for achievement in a job with routine demands. This person would not feel challenged, would probably become bored, lose interest, and perhaps leave the job. People with a high need for affiliation are likely to perform better in jobs with a lot of interpersonal contact, as well as personal support and approval tied to their performance.

People high in their need for power are likely to excel in leadership positions and are the most likely candidates for promotion to management, where they can influence others. How can you tell which people have such needs? There is no test, but their actions on the job will give you a good idea. Those seeking power will take extra assignments that involve leadership, those seeking achievement will look for challenging work assignments, and those seeking affiliation will be good socializers.

Herzberg's Motivation–Hygiene Theory

"First, describe situations in which you felt exceptionally good about your job. Second, describe situations in which you felt exceptionally bad about your job." Adopting an approach different from Maslow's and McClelland's, Frederick Herzberg asked these two questions of a number of workers. He then tabulated and categorized their responses. What he found was that the replies people gave when they felt good about their jobs were significantly different from the replies given when they felt bad.

Herzberg (1996) took these results and formulated his motivation–hygiene theory which focuses on two factors: (1) outcomes that can lead to high levels of motivation and job satisfaction and (2) outcomes that can prevent people from being dissatisfied. According to Herzberg's theory, people have two sets of needs or requirements: motivator needs and hygiene needs. Motivator needs are related to the nature of the work itself and how challenging it is. Outcomes such as interesting work, autonomy, responsibility, being able to grow and develop on the job, and a sense of accomplishment and achievement help to satisfy motivator needs. In order to have a highly motivated and satisfied workforce, Herzberg suggested, managers should take steps to ensure that employees' motivator needs are being met.

Hygiene needs are related to the physical and psychological context in which the work is performed. Hygiene needs are satisfied by outcomes such as pleasant and comfortable working conditions, pay, job security, good relationships with coworkers, and effective supervision. According to Herzberg, when hygiene needs are not met, workers will be dissatisfied, and when hygiene needs are met, workers will be satisfied. Satisfying hygiene needs, however, will not result in high levels of motivation or even high levels of job satisfaction. For motivation and job satisfaction to be high, motivator needs must be met.

Some of the various motivators (work itself) identified by Herzberg include: recognition, advancement, work content, possibility of growth, achievement, and responsibility. Various hygiene factors (environment) include status, working conditions, company policy and administration, money, supervision, interpersonal relations, and security. Managers should apply the conclusions of Herzberg's research because they are relevant to understanding motivation. According to his findings, an organization may provide adequate salary, safe working conditions, and job security—yet still have low motivation. Physical conditions are not as important as psychological conditions when it comes to motivating people. In conclusion, Herzberg's theory stresses the importance of helping individuals satisfy all their needs, not just lower-level needs.

Comparison and Application of Maslow, McClelland, and Herzberg

Careful review of the three major theories presented thus far points out distinct similarities. In essence, Maslow provides a list of hierarchical needs explaining motivation. McClelland advances a three-factor approach, whereas Herzberg presents a two-factor model, but both parallel Maslow's theory. See Table 3.1 and note that the relationship between the higher-order needs as advanced by Maslow and the motivators and hygiene factors as presented by Herzberg is in total synchronization with McClelland's achievement motivators.

Each theorist approached motivation from a different perspective yet arrived at similar conclusions. In turn, through mutual reinforcement, they have provided clues to help in understanding motivation.

Table 3.1
A Comparison of the Motivation Theories of Maslow, McClelland, and Herzberg

McClelland	Maslow	Herzberg
		MOTIVATORS
Achievement motive	Self-actualization	Achievement
		Work content
		Growth
Power motive	Self-esteem	Recognition
		Status
		Advancement
		HYGIENE FACTORS
Affiliation	Social	Interpersonal relations
		Quality of supervision
	Safety	Company policies
		Job security
		Working conditions
	Physiological	Salary
		Wages

In conclusion, probably the greatest value of the above three theories lies in the practical implications they have for supervision. In particular, the theories are important insofar as they suggest specific things that managers can do to help their employees become self-actualized. Because self-actualized employees are likely to work at their maximum creative potential, it makes sense to help people attain this state by helping them meet their needs. With this in mind, it is worthwhile to consider what today's managers and organizations may do to help satisfy their employees' needs.

1. *Promote a healthy workforce*. Some companies are helping satisfy their employees' physiological needs by providing incentives to keep them healthy. For example, some organizations give insurance rebates to employees with healthy lifestyles, while charging extra premiums to those whose habits (e.g., smoking) put them at greater risk for health problems. To the extent that these incentives encourage employees to adapt healthier lifestyles, the likelihood of satisfying their physiological needs is increased.
2. *Provide financial security*. Financial security is an important type of safety need. In this regard, some organizations are going beyond the more traditional forms of payroll savings and profit-sharing plans. Financial security is a key aspect of job security, particularly in troubled economic times, when layoffs are inevitable.

To help soften the blow of layoffs, more and more organizations are providing outplacement services—assistance in securing new employment.

3. *Provide opportunities to socialize.* To help satisfy its employees' social needs, IBM each spring holds a "Family Day" picnic near its Armonk, New York headquarters.
4. *Recognize employees' accomplishments.* Recognizing employees' accomplishments is an important way to satisfy their esteem needs. In this connection, some companies give awards to employees who develop ways of improving customer satisfaction or business performance. Some other organizations recognize their employees' organizational contributions by touting them on the pages of their corporate newsletters.
5. *Recognize that today's employees are motivated by different things.* Try to understand each employee as a unique individual, one who is likely to differ from other employees, but particularly from the manager, in their level of need fulfillment.

Vroom's Expectancy Theory

Victor Vroom's expectancy theory examines motivation through the perception of what a person believes will happen (Mitchell, 1982; Vroom, 1964). According to the expectancy theory, human motivation is affected by anticipated rewards and costs. An employee will be motivated to work toward a particular goal if it is perceived that a personal need will be satisfied. The employee's desire for a goal (valence) multiplied by what the organization expects (expectancy) will equal satisfaction and motivation (see Figure 3.1).

To illustrate Vroom's expectancy theory, suppose that an employee desires a promotion, which results from superior performance with minimum absenteeism. Now the employee understands the organization's expectations in relation to promotion (see Table 3.2).

For promotion to occur, job performance must be superior. Other forms of behavior fall short, as demonstrated in the illustration. Hence, promotion is based on how important the promotion is (valence) or the ability to make 100 widgets with minimum absenteeism (expectation), and the ability of management to recognize and assess high performance through proper evaluation (instrumentation).

The important thing for managers to understand about expectancy theory is that it has proven to provide a powerful explanation of employee motivation. It helps explain why a lot of employees are not motivated on their jobs and merely do the minimum necessary to get by. Managers should strive to show employees that increased effort will lead to improved work performance which in turn will result in increased rewards.

Expectancy theory helps managers zero in on key leverage points for influencing motivation. The following implications are crucial:

Figure 3.1
Desire for a Goal

Valence (strength of individual's desire for goal)	x	Expectancy (ease of accomplishment and strength of others' expectations)	=	Motivation and job satisfaction

Table 3.2
Vroom's Expectancy Theory

Standards of Performance (Widgets per Day)	Absenteeism on Annual Basis (Days)	Instrumentation Result (Evaluations)
100 (superior)	0–3	Receives promotion
75 (above average)	4–7	Falls short
50 (average)	8–11	Falls short
40 (below average)	12–15	Falls short
Less than 40 (undesirable)	15+	Falls short

- Provide a work environment that facilitates good performance, and set realistically attainable goals.
- Provide training, support, and encouragement so that people are confident they can perform at the levels expected of them.
- Understand what people want to get out of work. Think about what their jobs provide them and what is not but could be provided.
- Make sure that good performance is followed by personal recognition and praise, favorable performance reviews, pay increases, and other positive results.
- Make sure that working hard and doing things well will have as few negative results as possible.
- Ensure that poor performance has fewer positive and more negative outcomes than good performance.

METHODS USED TO MOTIVATE EMPLOYEES: PUTTING THEORY INTO PRACTICE

Experts are saying that today's organizations must concentrate on the three R's, recruiting, retraining, and retaining high-quality people (Perry, 1991). Motivation is involved in all of them, as organizations try to appeal to employees' high-level needs. As industry trends continue to shift toward self-managing teams, employees cannot be expected to turn into motivated self-managers overnight. They need to be given the proper tools through development and training programs.

> The adaptive organization . . . provides openings for the creativity and initiative too often found [only] in small, entrepreneurial companies. It does this by aligning what the corporation wants—innovation and improvement—with what turns people on—namely, a chance to use their heads and expand their skills. (Anderson, 1991)

As the trend continues to shift toward self-managing teams, employees cannot be expected to turn into motivated self-managers overnight; they need to be given the proper tools through development and training programs.

When employees appear to be unmotivated, managers will need to size up the leadership situation, identify and understand what is happening, and formulate a response. Knowledge about the theories of motivation, discussed in the previous section, should help managers identify and understand the motivational problems they face. In this section, we describe methods that can be used to motivate employees.

One reason these motivation methods are widely used is the fact that they have strong foundations in motivation theory and research. For example, empowering employees is based in part on self-efficacy—namely, on the idea that people differ in their estimates of how they will perform on a task. Therefore, building their skills and self-confidence by empowering them should bolster their self-efficacy and thus their motivation.

PAY FOR PERFORMANCE

Pay for performance is probably the first thing that comes to mind when most people think about motivating employees. Pay for performance refers to any compensation method that ties pay to the quantity or quality of work the person produces. Piecework pay plans are probably the most familiar: Earnings are tied directly to what the worker produces in the form of a "piece rate" for each unit he or she turns out. Thus, if an employee gets 40 cents apiece for stamping out circuit boards, the individual would make $40.00 for stamping out 100 a day and $80.00 for stamping out 200. Sales commissions are another familiar example.

Piecework plans have a firm foundation in motivation theory. Vroom's expectancy approach describes motivation as depending on employees' seeing the link between performance and rewards, and pay for performance plans should emphasize precisely that. Similarly, behavior modification emphasizes that people will continue behavior that is rewarded, and pay for performance plans, of course, tie rewards directly to behavior.

New pay for performance plans are becoming more popular. Some of these are discussed below.

Variable Pay Plans and Gainsharing Plans

Variable pay plans put some portion of the employee's pay at risk, subject to the organization meeting its financial goals. In one such plan at the DuPont Company, employees could voluntarily place up to 6 percent of their base pay at risk (McNutt, 1990). If they then met the department's earnings projections, they would get that 6 percent back plus additional percentages, depending on how much the department exceeded its earnings projections.

Other organizations have gainsharing plans, incentive plans that engage many or all employees in a common effort to achieve a company's productivity goals. Implementing a gainsharing plan requires several steps. Specific performance measures, such as cost per unit produced, are chosen, as is a funding formula, such as "47 percent of savings go to employees." Management thus decides how to divide and distribute cost savings between the employees and the company, and among employees themselves. If employees are then able to achieve cost savings in line with their performance goals, they share in the resulting gains.

Implementing Successful Pay for Performance Plans

Not all pay for performance plans succeed. However, the following five suggestions make success more likely, given our discussion on motivation.

- *Ensure that effort and rewards are directly related.* The incentive plan should reward employees in direct proportion to their increased productivity. Employees must also believe that they can actually do the tasks required. Thus, the standard has to be attainable and the manager and organization have to provide the necessary tools, equipment, and training to meet it.
- *Make the plan understandable and easily calculable by the employees.* It should be easy for employees to calculate the rewards they will receive for various levels of effort.
- *Set effective standards that will benefit the organization.* The standards should be viewed as fair by employees. They should be high but reasonable; that is, there should be about a 50–50 chance of success. The goal should also be specific, such as, "decrease the work order by 10 percent." This is much more effective than telling someone to "do your best."
- *Guarantee your program.* The rewards offered for a particular level of work should be viewed as a contract between the organization and the employees. Once the plan is operational, great caution should be used before decreasing the size of the incentive in any way.

- *Guarantee a base rate.* It is often advisable to give employees a safety net by providing them with a base pay. They will know that no matter what happens, they can at least earn a guaranteed minimum amount.

Merit Pay

Most employees, when they do a good job, expect to be rewarded with at least a merit raise at the end of the year. A merit raise is a salary increase—usually permanent—that is based on the employee's individual performance. It is different from a bonus in that it represents a continuing increment, whereas the bonus represents a one-time payment. Gradually, however, traditional merit raises are being replaced by lump-sum merit raises, which are merit raises awarded in one lump sum that does not become part of the employee's continuing pay.

To the extent that it is actually tied to performance, the prospect for a merit raise may focus the employee's attention on the link between performance and rewards, which is in line with the expectancy approach to motivation. However, relying too heavily on merit raises for rewards is a bit dangerous. A year is a long time to wait for a reward, so the reinforcement benefits of merit pay are somewhat suspect. The motivational basis for the merit plan can also be undermined by inadequate employee evaluations. You may have personally experienced the questionable nature of some performance appraisal systems, including the fact that some managers take the easy way out and rate everyone's performance about the same, regardless of actual effort. This type of problem can eliminate any possible benefits of a merit pay plan unless merit plans are paid quarterly.

Spot Awards

As its name implies, a spot award is a financial award given to an employee literally "on the spot" as soon as the laudable performance is observed. Programs like this have actually been around for some time. For example, Thomas J. Watson, Sr., founder of IBM, reportedly wrote checks on the spot to employees doing an outstanding job.

These cash awards are used increasingly today. Federal Express's Bravo-Zulu voucher program is an example. This program was established to give managers the ability to provide immediate rewards to employees for outstanding performance above and beyond the normal requirements of the job. (Bravo-Zulu is a title borrowed from the U.S. Navy's semaphore signal for "well done.") Bravo-Zulu vouchers average about $50 and may be in the form of a check or some other form of reward, such as dinner vouchers or theater tickets. It is estimated that Federal Express managers present employees with these awards more than 150,000 times a year (Federal Express Corporation, 1998).

Other organizations use spot cash incentive awards as well. For example, Victor Kiam, president of Remington Products (who liked Remington shavers so much that "I bought the company"), maintains a $25,000 discretionary fund to give instant cash awards to workers spotted by their managers doing an exceptional job. Kiam invites these people to his office and awards them checks ranging from $200 to $500 (Nelson, 1994).

Spot rewards like these have a sound basis in what we know about motivation. For example, to the extent that the rewards are both contingent on good performance and awarded immediately, they are certainly consistent with the expectancy approach, and provide the recognition most people desire.

A manager has many kinds of rewards to draw from in creating an environment to motivate both individuals and groups. Many of these rewards are relatively inexpensive. See Table 3.3 for a number of such examples.

Skill-Based Pay

You are probably aware of the fact that in most organizations pay is determined by the level of the job's responsibilities. Thus, presidents generally make more than vice presidents, sales managers make more than assistant sales managers, and secretary IVs make more than secretary IIIs, because higher-level jobs are meant to have more responsibility.

Skill-based pay is different in that you are paid for the range, depth, and types of skills and knowledge you are capable of using, rather than for the job you currently hold (Ledford, 1991). The difference is important: It is conceivable that, in a company with a skill-based pay plan, secretary III could be paid more per hour than secretary IV, for instance, if it turns out that the person who happened to be secretary III had more skills than did the person in the secretary IV job.

A skill-based pay plan was implemented at a General Mills manufacturing facility (Ledford and Bergel, 1991). In this case, General Mills was trying to boost the flexibility of its factory workforce by implementing a pay plan that would encourage all employees to develop a wider range of skills which would make it easier for employees to take over whatever job needed to be done in the plant as needs changed.

In this plant, the employees were paid based on their attained skill levels. For each of the several types of jobs in the plant, workers could attain three levels of skill: limited ability (ability to perform simple tasks without direction), partial proficiency (ability to analyze and solve problems associated with that job), and full competence (ability to analyze and solve problems associated with that job). After starting a job, employees were tested periodically to see whether they had earned certification at the next higher level. If so, they received higher pay even though they had the same job. This system allowed higher-skilled workers on the same job to receive

Table 3.3
The Manager's List of Good Rewards

Money or Its Equivalent
• Raises and bonuses
• Cash
• Day off or time off
• A parking space
Social Functions and Outings
• A night on the town
• A nice meal with the manager
• Lunch as a group that the manager buys
• Dinner provided by the organization
• A pizza party
• Picnics for teams
• Golf or other sporting events involving managers and employees
Tangible Reward
• Tickets to spring events, concerts, and so on, that the employees can attend by themselves
• Certificates and plaques
• Shirts, phones, pins, hats, cups, and other tokens
Praise and Recognition
• Direct verbal praise
• Peer recognition
• Letters of recognition put in the file and perhaps placed where customers can see them
• Passing on customer compliments and commendations
• Written praise from upper management
• A personal call or visit from the senior executive
Improvements to the Job Itself
• Additional responsibilities
• Opportunities to excel
• Additional training
• Better tool
• Ability to bid on preferred projects

Source: Adapted from P. Meyer, "Can You Give Good, Inexpensive Rewards? Some Real-Life Answers," *Business Horizons* (November–December 1994): 85.

higher pay than others doing the same job. Employees could then switch to other jobs in the plant, again starting at skill level one and working their way up if they so desired. In this way, employees could earn more pay for more skills, particularly as they became proficient at a variety of jobs, and the company ended up with a more highly skilled and therefore more flexible workforce.

Skill-based pay makes sense in terms of what we know about motivation. People have a vision—a self-concept of who they can be, and they seek to fulfill their potential. The individual development emphasis of skill-based pay helps employees do exactly that. Skill-based pay also appeals to an employee's sense of self-efficacy in that the reward is a formal and concrete recognition that the person can do the more challenging job and do it well.

Recognition

Most people like to feel appreciated. In one study over two-thirds of employee respondents said they highly valued day-to-day recognition from their manager, peers, and team members (Nelson, 1994). If you have ever spent half a day cooking a meal for someone who gobbled it up without saying a word about how it tasted, or two weeks doing a report for a boss who did not even say "Thanks," let alone "Good job," you know how important having your work recognized and appreciated can be.

Being recognized for a job well done—and not necessarily just financially—makes a lot of sense in terms of motivation theory. Immediate recognition can be a powerful reinforcer, for instance, and can provide some immediate outcomes to counterbalance the employees' inputs or efforts. Recognition also underscores the performance-reward-expectancy link, and it helps appeal to and satisfy the need people have to achieve and be recognized for their achievement.

Consequently, many companies formalize the common-sense process of saying "Thank you for a job well done." For example, Xerox Corporation gives what it calls bell-ringer awards for good work: a bell is rung in the corridor while the person is formally recognized by his or her boss (Nelson, 1994). At Busch Gardens in Tampa, Florida, the company reportedly gives a "pat on the back" award to employees who do an outstanding job, embodied by a notice of the award in the employee's file. At Metro Motors in Montclair, California, the name of the employee of the month goes up on the electronic billboard over the dealership (Nelson, 1994). Bell Atlantic names cellular telephone sites after top employees.

Managers must identify which kinds of behaviors they reward. "The things that get rewarded get done" is what one author calls The Greatest Management Principle in the World. With this in mind, here are 11 types of behavior that should be recognized by organizations and individual managers to motivate high performance (LeBoeuf, 1991):

- solid solutions instead of quick fixes
- risk taking instead of risk avoiding
- applied creativity instead of mindless conformity
- decisive action instead of paralysis by analysis
- smart work instead of busywork
- simplification instead of needless complication
- quietly effective behavior instead of squeaky wheels
- quality work instead of fast work
- loyalty instead of turnover
- working together instead of working against
- lack of absenteeism and tardiness

Job Redesign

Managers have long been concerned about the monotonous and boring qualities of highly specialized, short-cycle, assembly-line jobs. In an effort to respond to these concerns, many employers set up programs aimed at redesigning their workers' job. Job design refers to the number and nature of activities in a job; the basic issue in job design is whether jobs should be more specialized or, at the other extreme, more "enriched" and non-routine.

Job enlargement and job rotation. Initial attempts at job redesign centered on job enlargement and job rotation. Job enlargement assigns workers additional same-level tasks to increase the number of tasks they have to perform. For example, if the work is assembling chairs, the worker who previously only bolted the seat to the legs might take on the additional tasks of assembling the legs and attaching the back. Job rotation systematically moves workers from job to job. Thus, on an auto assembly line, a worker might spend an hour fitting doors, the next hour installing head lamps, the next hour fitting bumpers, and so on.

Job enrichment contends that having several boring jobs to do instead of one is not what employees want. Maslow and others believe that what employees want from their jobs is a sense of achievement from completing a challenging task successfully and the recognition that comes from using their skills and potential.

Job enrichment means building motivators like opportunities for achievement into the job by making it more interesting and challenging. This is often accomplished by giving employees more autonomy and allowing them to do much of the planning and inspection normally done by the their managers.

Job enrichment can be accomplished in several ways:

- *Form natural work groups.* Change the job in such a way that each person is responsible for or "owns" an identifiable body of work. For example, instead of having the typist in a typing pool do work for all departments, make the work of one or two departments the continuing responsibility of each typist.
- *Combine tasks.* Let one person assemble a product from start to finish or complete a series of tasks, instead of having it go through several separate operations that are performed by different people. Combining tasks in this way is also often called job enlargement.
- *Establish client relationships.* Let the employees have contact as often as possible with the clients of their work. For example, let an assistant research and respond to customers' requests, instead of automatically referring all problems to his or her boss.
- *Vertically load the job.* Have the employees plan and control their jobs, rather than letting them be controlled by others. For example, let the employees set a schedule, do their own troubleshooting, and decide when to start and stop working.

Under what conditions would a manager want to consider implementing a job enrichment program? To find the answer, managers should carefully diagnose the leadership situation, specifically addressing the following questions:

- Is motivation central to the problem? Or is there some other problem (a poorly designed flow of work in the office, for instance)?
- Is the job low in motivating potential? Is the job the source of the motivation problem identified in step 1? Or, for instance, is it the fact that pay is unusually low, or that several members of the work group continually argue against working harder?
- What specific aspects of the job are causing the difficulty, if it is the job? Here, consider inadequacies in the following core job dimensions:
  - —Skill variety: to what degree does the job require the employee to perform activities that challenge his or her skills and abilities?
  - —Task identity: to what degree does the job require completion of a whole, an identifiable piece of work?
  - —Task significance: to what degree does the job have a substantial and perceptible effect on the lives of other people in the organization or the world at large?
  - —Autonomy: to what degree does the job give the employee freedom and independence?
  - —Knowledge of results: to what degree does the employee get information about the effectiveness of his or her job efforts?
- How ready are the employees for change? Not all employees will prefer enriched jobs, and in any case some may not be ready to assume more responsibility. It may be futile to proceed with the change if the employees themselves will vigorously resist it.

Empowering Employees

As briefly discussed in Chapter 1, empowering employees is a popular approach to work organizations. It means giving employees the authority, tools, and information they need to do their jobs with greater autonomy, as well as the self-confidence required to perform the new jobs effectively. Empowering is inherently a motivational approach. It boosts employees' feelings of self-efficacy and enables them to more fully use their potential, satisfying high-level needs for achievement, recognition, and self-actualization. Empowerment results in changes in employees' beliefs—from feeling powerless to believing strongly in their own personal effectiveness. The result is that people take more initiative and persevere in achieving their goals and their leader's vision even in the face of obstacles.

Today, organizations are increasingly empowering their work teams. At Saturn Corporation, empowered, self-managing work teams are responsible for a variety of duties. For each team, these duties include resolving its own conflicts; planning its own work and schedule; designing and determining its own job assignments; making selection decisions of new members into the work unit; working directly with suppliers, customers, and other partners; performing their own equipment maintenance; seeking improvements in quality, cost, and the work environment; performing within its own budget; providing for their own absentee replacements; and performing their own repairs.

Empowering does not just mean assigning broad responsibilities. Teams also need the training, skills, and tools to allow them to do their jobs, such as in consensus decision making. Firms like Saturn also make sure their managers actually let their people do their jobs as assigned.

Not all empowerment programs are as comprehensive as that at Saturn Corporation. At Scandinavian Air System (SAS) for instance, empowering the workforce meant letting employees make more decisions themselves. Ticket agents now have the authority to re-ticket a passenger or even move the passenger up a class, if they feel the situation warrants it. At one Marriott chain subsidiary, each and every hotel employee, from management to maintenance, is empowered to offer guests a free night's stay if, in the employee's opinion, the hotel has been lax in serving the guest. And at engine-maker Pratt & Whitney, salespeople can now authorize multimillion-dollar repairs on the spot, instead of having to wait for approvals from up the line. In virtually all such cases, employees find empowerment exciting, while employers find it helps workers to self-actualize and exhibit self-efficacy, and thereby boost motivation and employee commitment (Thomas and Velthouse, 1990). The guidelines below can make managers more successful in empowering their employees (Tracey, 1990):

- Make sure people understand their responsibilities.
- Give them authority equal to the responsibilities assigned to them.
- Set standards of excellence that will require employees to strive to do all work "right the first time."
- Provide them with training that will enable them to meet the standards.
- Give them information that they need to do their jobs well.
- Trust them.
- Give them permission to fail.
- Treat them with dignity and respect.
- Provide them with feedback on their performance.
- Recognize them for their achievements.

Goal-Setting

Have you ever set your sights on a goal—becoming a manager or earning enough money for a trip abroad, for instance? What effect did setting the goal have on you? Setting specific goals with employees can be one of the simplest yet most powerful ways of motivating them.

Managers and employees need to understand each other's goals. In addition, managers are responsible for helping employees in setting goals or objectives. With a clear understanding of explicit goals or objectives, managers and employees can work together to achieve specific outcomes. Several attributes of goals are especially important for improving performance: goal specificity, goal difficulty, and goal acceptance.

Specificity. Goal specificity refers to the preciseness with which a goal or objective is stated. Increases in goal specificity are positively related to increases in performance. Specific goals that are quantifiable reduce ambiguity and thereby help to focus employees' efforts. Therefore, it is generally a good idea to avoid developing or staging goals in broad or ambiguous terms.

Difficulty. Increasing goal difficulty can also result in superior performance. The more difficult the goal is, so the research results suggest, the more challenging the task is perceived as being. Greater task challenge, in turn, results in greater effort being put forth by an employee. One major limitation to this argument, however, is that the goals must be feasible. Setting outlandish goals or goals that are unquestionably out of the reach of the employee will more likely lead to frustration and rejection of the goal.

Acceptance. Employees must also accept the goals that are set. Goal acceptance is most likely to occur when assigned goals correspond with personal aspirations. Difficult, specific goals that are accepted by an employee will therefore result in superior performance. This line of reasoning suggests that managers must encourage employees to focus on measurable and challenging goals while trying to elicit employee commitment to the goals.

Management by objectives (MBO). Management by objectives is a practical application of the reasoning behind the notion of goal-setting theory. MBO is the process in which employees participate with management in the setting of goals or objectives. An essential feature of an MBO program is that it involves a one-on-one negotiation session between a supervisor and a direct report in order to set concrete, objective goals for the employee's performance. During the session, a deadline is set for the measurement of accomplishment, and the paths to the desired goals and the removal of possible obstacles are discussed. After an established period of time has elapsed (typically six months or a year), the supervisor and direct report meet again to review the direct report's performance using the agreed-upon measuring tool.

The ideas on how to set goals that motivate employees are voluminous. Here's a summary:

- *Be clear and specific.* Employees who are given specific goals usually perform better than those who are not.
- *Make goals measurable and verifiable.* Whenever possible, goals should be stated in quantitative terms and should include target dates or deadlines for accomplishment.
- *Make goals challenging but realistic.* Goals should be challenging but not so difficult that they appear impossible or unrealistic.
- *Set goals participatively.* Participatively setting goals usually leads to higher performance.

Lifelong Learning

Many employers today face a tremendous dilemma. On the one hand, remaining competitive requires highly committed employees who exercise self-discipline and basically do their jobs as if they owned the company. On the other hand, competitive pressures have forced many companies to continually downsize; this in turn causes employees to question whether it pays for them to work their hearts out for the company.

Lifelong learning is one method increasingly used to address both these issues simultaneously. Lifelong learning provides extensive continuing training, from basic remedial skills to advanced decision-making techniques throughout employees' careers.

The benefits of lifelong learning. Implemented properly, lifelong learning programs can achieve three things. First, the training, development, and education provide employees with the decision making and other knowledge, skills, abilities, and experiences they need to competently carry out the demanding, team-based jobs in today's organizations. Second, the opportunity for lifelong learning is inherently motivational. It enables employees to develop and to see an enhanced possibility of fulfilling their potential; it boosts employees' sense of self-efficacy; and it provides an enhanced opportunity for the employee to self-actualize and gain the sense of achievement that psychologists like Maslow, McClelland, and Herzberg correctly argue is so important. Third, although lifelong learning may not cancel out the potential negative effects of downsizing, it might at least counterbalance them to some degree by giving the employee useful and marketable new skills.

For example, one Canadian Honeywell manufacturing plant in Canada called its lifelong learning program the Honeywell–Scarborough Learning for Life Initiative. It was "a concerted effort to upgrade skill and education levels so that employees can meet workplace challenges with confidence" (Nopper, 1993). This lifelong learning program had several components. It began with adult basic education. Here the company, in partnership with the employees' union, offered courses in English as a Second Language, basic literacy, numeracy, and computer literacy.

Next, the factory formed a partnership with a local community college. Through that partnership, all factory employees—hourly, professional, and managerial—had the opportunity to earn college diplomas and certificates. Included was a 15-hour "skills for success" program designed to refresh adults in the study habits required to succeed academically. All courses took place at the factory after work.

Finally, job training was provided for two hours every other week. These sessions focused on developing skills specifically important to the job, "such as the principles of just-in-time inventory systems, team effectiveness, interpersonal communication skills, conflict resolution, problem solving and dealing with a diverse workforce" (Nopper, 1993).

It is never easy to evaluate the success of a program like this because not all employees choose to participate, and many other factors will affect factory productivity and employee motivation. However, the evidence suggests that programs like these improve commitment, skills, and motivation, and possibly productivity, too.

Motivating Yourself

Most people wait to be motivated by the manager of the organization. In terms of getting what you want, this may not be the best strategy. Your manager may not have the time, ability, or desire to ascertain the best motivational methods for you personally. Because you have a direct interest in your own motivation, it may be better for you to take an active role by following this four-step plan:

1. Apply the motivational theories to yourself.
2. Determine how best to fulfill your needs.

3. Prepare to approach your manager.
4. Approach your manager and work together on your motivation.

Remember that the organization will probably have some constraints, and they may not be able to be changed just for you. It may be all right to ask, but remember that to a degree you must work within the system or find another one where you will be happy.

The first step, then, is to apply the motivational theories to yourself and your situation. Analyze your needs. Write down a list of what it is you want or need from work and life. Then determine what it will take to motivate you to achieve these things. Remember, you must know what it is you want before you can go after it.

Not all wants and needs can be fulfilled by work. Therefore, the second step is to differentiate between the needs that work can fulfill and those that will have to be satisfied through other means. For example, if you have a need for increased status but you are working in a flat organization with little chance for promotion, you may decide to try to meet your status needs by rising through the ranks of a volunteer or charitable organization. Keep in mind that many people believe that work should satisfy all of their needs. This is often not possible, so these people end up being frustrated at work and unfulfilled outside of work. Be realistic. If your current job can't satisfy your needs, you must find another job (and perhaps another career) or try to satisfy your needs with something other than employment. Once you have identified needs that can be fulfilled at work, then try to find existing motivators that apply to you.

The third step is to prepare to meet with the manager. The meeting will go more easily if you are applying existing organizational motivators and rewards (like feedback) to yourself, but it usually doesn't hurt to ask for something different. If you plan to ask for some new motivational method, then you need to describe how this will benefit (1) your work, (2) your manager/employer, and (3) yourself. You must then provide evidence to support your case, and you must lay out your case in a logical, rational manner.

The fourth and last step is to meet with the manager. Present your case in a logical manner and remember that you may not be able to get everything you want all at once. You may have to develop a plan in which you work toward your goal gradually, but at least you will be moving in the direction you wish to go.

Zig Ziglar (1995), chairman of his own training and development company and author of *See You at the Top*, offers some suggestions for motivating yourself, even when the chips are down.

- *Give yourself a pep talk.* If you expect your employers and coworkers to believe in you, you have to believe in yourself. Write positive phrases about yourself, such as "I am honest, intelligent, and responsible," on three-by-five inch cards. Keep them where you can read them several times a day.

- *Set goals.* Be specific about the goals you want to achieve. Even create a "wild idea sheet" that lists "everything you want to be, do, or have."
- *Think positive; get positive training.* It is important to be enthusiastic about what you are doing, but you also need to *know* what you are doing. Get the training you need to support a positive attitude.
- *If necessary, get professional counseling.* There may be times in your career when you need help. Do not be afraid to ask for it from someone who has wisdom and the necessary knowledge to assist you.
- *Control your environment.* Control as many elements of your environment as you can. Exercise and eat well so you feel your best. Listen to music with positive messages, especially in the morning.
- *Use positive words to convey your message.* Learn to phrase your communications in a positive manner. For instance, try saying to an employee, "This is an important project. That's why I am assigning it to you. I know you will handle it well."
- *Leave every encounter on a positive note.* Try to end every meeting with another person on a good note. This may be difficult sometimes, but doing so will not only make you feel upbeat, it will make the other person feel good as well. That person will remember you that way.

SUMMARY

Motivation is a complex topic, yet an important one for the manager to understand. Unfortunately, still today some managers do not believe that motivation is a part of their job, believing instead that motivation is the responsibility of the individual employee.

Effective managers realize that they must understand the general patterns of individual behavior that contribute to motivation. Motivation is the process of satisfying internal needs through action and behaviors. It involves a composite of mental and physical aspects, combined with the environment and other factors that aid in explaining why people behave the way they do. The motivation process model suggests that a need (or motive) leads to action or behavior that, in turn, results in the satisfaction of the need.

A more comprehensive model of motivation involves the integration of additional factors believed to influence the process of motivation. Such factors as the environment, perception, degree of importance, personal traits, effort, ability to perform, and rewards and punishments are essential to the complete understanding of the motivation process.

We have presented the major motivational theories that are useful to improving your understanding of what it takes for managers to motivate people. Maslow, McClelland, and Herzberg suggest that managers understand what needs employees are trying to satisfy in organizations and then ensure that people receive outcomes that will satisfy these needs. An employee's thought process will also influence his or her motivation.

There are a number of methods managers and organizations can use to motivate employees. The methods based on motivational approaches like Maslow's theory and others include pay for performance, spot awards, merit pay, recognition awards, job redesign, empowerment, goal-setting, positive reinforcement, and lifelong learning.

Individuals must recognize that they must take an active role in motivating themselves and can use a four-step process to achieve this objective. Managers must also find ways to keep themselves motivated.

REFERENCES

Anderson, J.A. 1991. The bureaucracy busters. *Fortune* (June 17): 37.

Federal Express Corporation. 1998. *Blueprints for service quality*. Memphis, TN: Federal Express Corporation, pp. 34–35.

Herzberg, F. 1996. *Work and the nature of man*. Cleveland: World Publishing.

LeBoeuf, M. 1991. *The greatest management principle in the world*. New York: Putnam Publishing Group.

Ledford, G., Jr. 1991. Three case studies on skill-based pay: An overview. *Compensation & Benefits Review* 23: 11–23.

Ledford, G., Jr., and Bergel, G. 1991. Skill-based pay case no. 1: General Mills. *Compensation & Benefits Review* 23: 24–38.

Maslow, A.H. 1954. *Motivation and personality*. New York: Harper and Row.

McClelland, D.C. 1961. *The achieving society*. New York: Van Nostrand Reinhold.

McNutt, R. 1990. Sharing across the board: Dupont's achievement sharing program. *Compensation & Benefits Review* 26: 17–24.

Mitchell, T.R. 1982. Expectancy-value models in organizational psychology. In N.T. Feather (ed.), *Expectations and actions: Expectancy-value models in psychology*. Hillsdale, NJ: Erlbaum, pp. 293–312.

Nelson, B. 1994. *1,000 ways to reward employees*. New York: Workman Publishing.

Nopper, N. 1993. Reinventing the factory with lifelong learning. *Training* (May): 55–57.

Perry, N.J. 1991. The workers of the future. *Fortune* (Special Issue, Spring/Summer): 68.

Thomas, K., and Velthouse, B. 1990. Cognitive elements of empowerment: An interpretive model of intrinsic task motivation. *Academy of Management Review* 15(4): 666–681.

Tracey, D. 1990. *10 steps to empowerment*. New York: William Morrow, p. 163.

Vroom, V.H. 1964. *Work and motivation*. New York: Wiley.

Ziglar, Z. 1995. Zig Ziglar's motivation secrets. *Bottom Line* (April 15): 9–10.

Chapter 4

Performance Management

INTRODUCTION

Successfully managing organizational behavior in today's world of work means that performance must be clearly defined and understood by the employees who are expected to perform well at work. Performance in most lines of work is multidimensional. For example, a sales executive's performance may require administrative and financial skills along with the interpersonal skills needed to motivate a sales force. A medical doctor's performance may demand the positive interpersonal skills of a bedside manner to complement the necessary technical diagnostic and treatment skills for enhancing the healing process. Each specific job in an organization requires the definition of skills and behaviors essential to excellent performance on the job.

This chapter focuses on performance management systems in general and the key component, performance appraisal, in particular—the organizational activity designed to provide performance feedback to employees. This feedback serves a variety of purposes and makes potentially significant contributions to organizations and individual employees alike. Indeed, we can almost think of performance-related feedback as being like a ship's navigational system. Without such a system, the ship's captain would have no way of knowing where the ship was, where it had come from, and where it was heading. Similarly, without an effective performance management system, organizations and individual employees would have no way of knowing how well they were doing or where improvements might be needed.

Performance appraisal is the process by which an employee's contribution to the organization during a specified period of time is assessed. Some organizations actually use the term performance appraisal, whereas others prefer to use terms such as performance evaluation, performance review, annual review, employee appraisal, or employee evaluation. Regardless of the term used, this chapter is concerned with preparing managers and other employees to cope with today's workforce diversity in the management and appraisal of performance. More specifically, the purpose of this chapter is to provide an understanding of performance management in general and its key component, performance appraisal, in particular. This includes the major appraisal techniques, discussing various rating methods, identifying several performance evaluation problems, how to conduct effective performance appraisals, and how to evaluate an organization's performance appraisal system. The chapter will also outline the control process as a key driver to the performance management system and performance appraisals.

THE IMPORTANCE OF PERFORMANCE APPRAISALS IN MANAGING ORGANIZATIONAL BEHAVIOR

Strategically, it is hard to imagine a more important organizational system than performance appraisal. Organizations strive to do the following at all levels: (1) design jobs and work systems to accomplish organizational goals; (2) hire individuals with the abilities and desire to perform effectively; and (3) train, motivate and reward employees for performance and productivity. It is this sequence that allows organizations to disperse their strategic goals throughout the organization. Within this context, the evaluation of performance is a control mechanism that provides not only feedback to individuals but also an organizational assessment of how things are progressing. Without performance information, managers of an organization can only guess as to whether employees are working toward the right goals, in the correct way, and to the desired standard (Gephart, 1995).

One of the most important activities of today's organizations is maintaining and enhancing the workforce. After all the effort and costs involved in the recruiting and selection process, it is important to develop employees so that they are using their fullest capabilities, thus improving the effectiveness of the organization. The development of a standard performance appraisal process will help organizations improve their bottom-line performance, uplift motivational efforts, and resolve most morale problems.

In the future, the only successful organizations will be those that are able to increase productivity through improving the performance of their human resources. Therefore, all managers need to understand and appreciate the importance of performance appraisal as well as the various goals associated with effective performance appraisal. Moreover, HRM personnel can best serve their role as a center of expertise by ensuring that everyone in the organization has confidence in the performance appraisal systems used and that their performance appraisals fulfill their goals.

Traditionally, the organizational behavior and HRM literature has considered as separate and distinct the issues of which types of performance to measure, methods of measuring importance, who should rate performance, and methods of performance. Organizations have moved to focusing on developing a performance management system that is a broader and, more encompassing process and is the ultimate goal of performance appraisal activities. Performance management is discussed in the next section.

PERFORMANCE MANAGEMENT

Employee job performance is an important issue for all employers. However, satisfactory performance does not happen automatically; therefore, it is more likely with a good performance management system. Performance management is the integration of performance appraisal systems with broader HRM systems as a means of aligning employees' work behaviors with the organization's goals. Thus, a performance management system consists of the processes used to identify, encourage, measure, evaluate, improve, and reward employee performance at work.

There is no one best way to manage performance. Whatever system is adopted needs to be congruent with the culture and principles that pervade the organization (Ghorparde and Chen, 1995). However, most systems of performance management have several parts:

1. *Defining performance.* It is desirable to carefully define performance so that it supports the organization's strategic goals. The setting of clear goals for individual employees is a critical component of performance management.
2. *Empowering employees.* It is desirable to empower workers to deal with performance contingencies. Thus, if interaction with a supplier about timeliness of deliveries is required for an employee to achieve goals successfully, the employee is authorized to handle the situation.
3. *Measuring performance.* Measuring performance does not need to be narrowly conceived but can bring together multiple types of performance measured in various ways. The key is to measure often and use the information for midcourse corrections.
4. *Feedback and coaching.* In order to improve performance, employees need information (feedback) about their performance, along with guidance in reaching the next level of result. Without frequent feedback, employees are unlikely to know that behavior is out of synchronization with relevant goals or what to do about it. (Cardy and Dobbins, 1997)

Performance management is an outgrowth of management controls whose purpose is to ensure that work is progressing according to the organization's plans. Controls should therefore be designed to alert the organization and its managers to problems or potential problems before they become critical and to give managers time to take corrective actions. Controlling is similar to planning in many ways. The major difference between controlling and planning is that planning takes place while work is ongoing.

THE CONTROL PROCESS

Controlling is the management function concerned with monitoring performance to ensure that it conforms to plans. To ensure that their organizations are achieving expected results managers need to know what is going on in the area they manage. Do employees understand what they are supposed to do and are they able to do it? Is all the machinery and equipment—from computer-operated machines to touch-tone telephones—operating properly? Is work getting out correctly and on time?

To answer these questions, a manager could theoretically sit back and wait for disaster to strike, assuming that where there is no problem, there is no need for correction. However, managers have a responsibility to correct problems as soon as possible, which means that they need some way to detect problems quickly. Detection and correction of problems is at the heart of the control function. By controlling, the manager can take steps to ensure quality and manage costs. In many such ways, managers can benefit the organization through the control process.

Steps in the Control Process

Control is accomplished by comparing actual performance with predetermined standards or objectives and then taking action to correct any deviations from the standard. The control process has three basic requirements:

1. Establishing performance standards.
2. Monitoring performance and comparing it with those standards.
3. Taking necessary corrective actions.

The first step is part of the planning process while the other two are unique to the control process.

Establishing performance standards. Once organizational objectives have been set, they generally are used as standards that outline expectations for performance. Standards are used to set expected performance levels for machines, tasks, individuals, groups of individuals, or even the organization as a whole. Usually, standards are expressed in terms of quantity, quality, or time limitations. For example, standards may cover production output per hour, quality as reflected by customer satisfaction, or production schedule deadlines.

Performance standards attempt to answer the question, "What is a fair day's work?" or "How good is good enough?" Standards take many factors into account that may impact outcomes, such as inevitable delays and time for equipment maintenance. Several types of standards are described below:

- *Productivity standards*—designed to reflect output per unit of time. Examples: number of units produced per work hour.
- *Material standards*—designed to reflect efficiency of material usage. Examples: amount of raw material per unit, average amount of scrap produced per unit.
- *Resource usage standards*—designed to reflect how efficiently organizational resources are being used. Examples: return on investment, percent of capacity, asset usage.
- *Revenue standards*—designed to reflect the level of sales activity. Examples: dollar sales, average revenue per customer, per capital sales (i.e., sales per person).
- *Cost standards*—designed to reflect the level of costs. Examples: dollar cost of operation, cost per unit produced, cost per unit sold.

Many methods for setting standards are available. The choice of the most appropriate method depends on the type of standards in question. A common approach is to use the judgment of the manager or other recognized experts to set the standard, but his approach can be very subjective. A variation method is for the manager and the persons performing the job to jointly set the standard together, thus allowing the employees who actually perform the job to provide input. The most objective approach is to use industrial engineering methods, which usually involve detailed and scientific analysis of the work to be done.

Monitoring performance. The primary purpose of monitoring performance is to provide information on what is actually happening in the organization. Monitoring should be preventive and not punitive. In this light, the reasons for monitoring should always be fully explained to employees.

The major problem in monitoring performance is deciding when, where, and how often to monitor. Timing is important when monitoring performance. Monitoring must, therefore, be done often enough to provide adequate information. If it is overdone, however, it can become expensive and can annoy employees. The key is to view monitoring as a means of providing needed information and not as a means of checking on employees. Most control tools and techniques are primarily concerned with monitoring performance. Reports, audits, budgets, and personal observations are methods commonly used for this purpose.

Taking corrective actions. Only after the actual performance has been assessed and compared with the performance standards can managers take proper corrective action. All too often, however, managers set standards and monitor performance but do not follow up well. A major problem is determining when and why a deviation from the standard is occurring. How many mistakes should be allowed? Have the standards been set correctly? Is the poor performance due to the employee or some other factor such as a lack of proper equipment or training? The key here is the manager's timely intervention. A manager should not allow an unacceptable situation to exist for long but should promptly determine the cause and take action.

As part of the control process, the purpose of performance management is to make sure that employee goals, employee behaviors used to achieve those goals, and feedback of information about performance are all linked to the organizational strategy. It is important to note that although performance management typically relies heavily upon performance appraisals, performance management is a broader and more encompassing process and is the ultimate goal of performance appraisal activities.

THE PURPOSE OF EMPLOYEE PERFORMANCE APPRAISALS

Two decades ago, the typical manager would sit down annually with his or her employees, individually, and critique their job performance. The purpose was to review how well they did toward achieving their work goals. Those employees who failed to achieve their goals found the performance appraisal to result in little more than their supervisor documenting a list of their shortcomings. Of course, since the performance appraisal is a key determinant in pay adjustments and promotion decisions, anything to do with appraising job performance struck fear into the hearts of employees. Not surprisingly, in this climate, managers often wanted to avoid the whole appraisal process, and in many instances formal appraisal programs yielded disappointing results. Their failure was often due to a lack of top-management information and support, unclear performance standards, lack of important skills for managers, too many forms to complete, or the use of appraisal for conflicting purposes.

Today, successful organizations and managers treat the performance appraisal as an evaluation and development tool, as well as a formal legal document. Appraisals review past performance—emphasizing positive accomplishments as well as deficiencies and drafting detailed plans for development. By emphasizing the future as well as the past, documenting performance effectively, and providing feedback in a constructive manner, employees are less likely to respond defensively to feedback, and the appraisal process is more likely to motivate employees to improve where necessary. The performance evaluation also serves a vital organizational need by providing the documentation necessary for any personnel action that might be taken against an employee.

Given the importance of performance appraisal, the goals of this appraisal are almost self-evident. For example, a basic goal of any appraisal system is to provide a valid and reliable measure of employee performance along several dimensions: who is performing well and who is not, as well as to indicate the areas of specific strengths and weaknesses for each person being rated. Another goal of appraisals is to provide information in a form that is useful and appropriate for the organization with regard to HRM planning, recruiting and selection, compensation, training and development, and the legal context. But the ultimate goal for any organization using performance appraisals is to be able to improve performance on the job.

All managers need to understand and appreciate the importance of performance appraisal as well as the various goals associated with effective performance appraisal. Moreover, an organization's managers and HRM personnel must ensure that everyone in the organization has confidence in the performance appraisal system used and that the performance appraisals fulfill their goals.

When Should Appraisals Occur?

Ideally, performance appraisals should occur both formally and informally. Formal performance reviews should be conducted once a year at a minimum, but twice a year is better. Informal performance appraisals and feedback should complement the formal appraisal system. The ultimate goal is to establish an effective "performance management system" where performance is monitored and managed overall, not just appraised in a once-a-year session.

Continuous feedback is primarily important in letting employees know how they are doing. Without constructive feedback, employees tend to assume that their performance is acceptable, and problems may continue. Without positive feedback or praise, employees begin to feel that their hard work is unappreciated and may decide to stop putting forth so much effort. Employees need and expect frequent communication and feedback about their performance—not just during the formal appraisal interview session. Managers must make it a habit to get out among their employees throughout the day or week and do not wait for their employees to come to them. This type of frequent interaction also tells employees that their manager thinks they are important.

Who Performs the Performance Appraisal?

Performance appraisal can be done by anyone familiar with the performance of individual employees. Possibilities include (1) managers who rate their employees; (2) employees who rate their superiors; (3) team members who rate each other; (4) employee self-appraisal; and (5) customers.

Managers who rate their employees. Traditional rating of employees is based on the assumption that the immediate supervisor is the person most qualified to evaluate the employee's performance realistically, objectively, and fairly. An employee's immediate supervisor is usually in the best position to observe and judge how well the employee has performed on the job. There are some situations in which a "consensus" or "pooled" type of appraisal may be done by a group of managers. An example of this would be if an employee works for several managers because of rotating work-shift schedules or the organization has a matrix structure. Some organizations have implemented work team concepts that expand the manager's span of control, and some have become leaner and eliminated middle-level management positions. It is not practical for a manager to track the performance of 20, 30, or even 50 employees and evaluate their performance objectively. This restructuring of authority and responsibility could lead to grave inequities in the performance appraisal system. To ensure that employees feel that the appraisal process is fair and just, each evaluator must understand what is necessary for successful job performance and be able to apply the standards. A supervisor's appraisal typically is reviewed by the immediate boss to make sure that a proper appraisal has been done.

Employees who rate their superiors. The concept of having supervisors and managers rated by employees or group members is being used in a number of organizations today. A prime example of this type of rating takes place in colleges and universities, where students evaluate the performance of professors in the classroom. Industry also uses employee ratings for management development purposes.

Team members who rate each other. The use of peer groups as raters is another type of appraisal with potential both to help and to hurt. For example, if a group of salespersons meets as a committee to talk about one another's ratings, then they may share ideas that could be used to improve the performance of lower-rated individuals. Alternatively, the criticisms could lead to future work relationships being affected negatively. An advantage of using peers or team members in a performance appraisal process is that, by definition, they do have expert knowledge of job content, and they may have more of an opportunity than does the supervisor to observe the performance of a given worker on a day-to-day basis.

Peer ratings are especially useful when managers do not have the opportunity to observe each employee's performance, but other work group members do. Team or peer evaluations are best used for development purposes rather than for administrative purposes. However, some contend that any performance appraisal, including team/peer ratings, can affect teamwork and participative management efforts negatively.

Employee self-appraisal. In this case, the employee evaluates herself or himself with the techniques used by other evaluators. The rationale behind this approach is that, more than any other single person in the organization, an individual is in the best position to understand his or her own strengths and weaknesses and the extent to which he or she has been performing at an appropriate level. Of course, the biggest negative aspect of using self-ratings is that there is a tendency on the part of many people to inflate their own performance.

Self-appraisals seem to be used more often for developmental (as opposed to evaluative) aspects of performance evaluation. It is also used to evaluate an employee who works in physical isolation.

Customers. A final source of information in the performance appraisal system is customers. The dramatic increase in the service sector of the U.S. economy in recent years has resulted in a major push toward the use of customers as a source of information in performance appraisal. The inclusion of customers might be accomplished through such things as having customers fill out feedback forms. Some restaurants, like Chili's and Red Lobster, for example, insert brief feedback forms in their meal-check folders and ask customers to rate the server, the cook, and other restaurant personnel on various characteristics relevant to the meal. The advantage of this method is that customers are the lifeblood of an organization, and it is very helpful to managers to know the extent to which customers feel that employees are doing a good job. On the other hand, this method may be expensive to develop and reproduce and may ignore aspects of the job the customer doesn't see (e.g., cooperation with other employees).

Multisource or 360-degree feedback. One important thing for any manager to recognize is that each source of performance appraisal information is subject to various weaknesses and shortcomings. Consequently, many organizations find it appropriate and effective to rely on a variety of information sources in the conduct of a performance appraisal. That is, organizations may gather information from both supervisors and peers. Indeed, some organizations gather information from all the sources described in this section. This approach has even gained a new term in the management literature: "360-degree feedback."

Multisource feedback recognizes that the manager is no longer the sole source of performance appraisal information. For 360-degree feedback to be effective, the person managing the review process should ensure that the responses are anonymous. Employees especially may be afraid to respond honestly if they think that the person being reviewed will retaliate for negative comments. Anonymity is greater if the responses are pooled into a single report rather than presented one by one. Collecting appraisals from more than three or four people also increases the likelihood of protecting respondents' privacy.

Multisource approaches to performance appraisal are possible solutions to well-documented dissatisfaction with today's legally necessary administrative performance appraisal. But a number of questions arise as multisource appraisals become more common. One concern is whether 360-degree appraisals improve the process or simply multiply the number of problems by the total number of raters. Also, some wonder if multisource appraisals really create better decisions than conventional methods, given the additional time investment (LaMountain, 1997). It seems reasonable to assume that these issues are of less concern when the 360-degree feedback is used only for development, because the process is usually less threatening. But those concerns may negate multisource appraisals as an administrative tool in many situations (Jackson and Greller, 1998).

TYPES OF APPRAISALS

Many techniques have been developed for appraising performance. The HRM department or higher-level management usually dictate which types the organizations will use. An organization that has all managers use the same approach establishes a way to keep records showing performance over time, especially when an employee reports to more than one manager during his or her employment. Although a manager has to use the appraisal format selected for the whole organization, he or she may be able to supplement it with other helpful information. A manager can use the "Comments" section of a preprinted form or attach additional information to it, as one manager does when appraising employees.

Performance appraisals are generally conducted using a predetermined method like one or more of those described in this section.

Graphic Rating Scale

The graphic rating scale (GRS) is the simplest most popular technique for appraising performance. There are actually two types of GRSs in use today. They are sometimes both used in rating the same person. The first and most common type list a job criteria (quantity of work, quality of work, etc.). The second is more behavioral, with specific behaviors listed and the effectiveness of each rated.

The GRS presents appraisers with a list of traits assumed to be necessary to successful job performance (e.g., adaptability, maturity, cooperativeness, and motivation). Each trait is listed and accompanied by a five- or seven-point rating scale. The evaluator then goes down the list and rates each on incremental scales. The scales typically specify five points, so a factor such as job knowledge might be rated 1 ("poorly informed about work duties") to 5 ("has complete mastery of all phases of the job").

While GRSs don't provide the depth of information other performance evaluation methods do, many organizations use them because they are practical and cost little to develop. HRM staff can develop such forms quickly, and because the traits and anchors are written at a general level, a single form is applicable to all or most jobs within an organization. Another advantage of a GRS is that it is relatively easy to use. In addition, the scores provide a basis for deciding whether an employee has improved in various areas.

There are some obvious drawbacks to the GRS as well. Often, separate traits or factors are grouped together, and the rater is given only one box to check. Another drawback is that the descriptive words sometimes used in such scales may have different meanings to different raters. Terms such as initiative and cooperation are subject to many interpretations, especially if used in conjunction with words such as outstanding, average, and poor. Also, many managers tend to rate everyone at least a little above average. Some appraisal forms attempt to overcome these problems by containing descriptions of excellent or poor behavior in each area. Other rating scales pose a different problem by labeling performance in terms of how well an employee "meets requirements." Presumably, the manager wants *all* employees to meet the requirements of the job. However, scoring everyone high on this scale may be seen as a rating bias (on the assumption that not everyone can be a "top performer"), rather than successful management of human resources.

Critical Incidents

Critical incidents focus the evaluator's attention on those behaviors that are key to making the difference between executing a job effectively and executing it ineffectively. That is, the appraiser writes down anecdotes that describe what the employee did that was especially effective or ineffective. The key here is that only specific behaviors, not vaguely defined personality traits, are cited. A list of critical incidents provides a rich set of examples from which the employee can be shown those behaviors that are desirable and those that call for improvement.

To successfully conduct a critical-incident appraisal, a rating supervisor must keep a written record of incidents that show positive and negative ways an employee has acted. The record should include dates, people involved, actions taken, and any other relevant details. At the time of the appraisal, a manager reviews the record to reach an overall evaluation of an employee's behavior. During the appraisal interview, the manager should give an employee a chance to offer her or his views of each incident recorded. The critical-incident method can be used with other methods to document the reasons why an employee was rated in a certain way.

There are several disadvantages with this technique. First, what constitutes a critical incident is not defined in the same way by all supervisors. Next, keeping records of critical incidents can be time-consuming and, even if a supervisor is diligent, important incidents could be overlooked. Also, supervisors tend to record negative events more than positive ones, resulting in an overly harsh appraisal. Further, employees may become overly concerned about what the superior writes and begin to fear the manager's "black book."

Paired-Comparison Approach

The paired-comparison approach measures the relative performance of employees in a group. A manager lists the employees in the group and then ranks them. One method is to compare the performance of the first two employees on the list. A manager places a checkmark next to the name of the employee whose performance is better, then repeats the process, comparing the first employee's performance with that of the other employees. Next, the supervisor compares the second employee on the list with all the others, and so on until each pair of employees has been compared. The employee with the most checkmarks is considered the most valuable.

A manager also can compare employees in terms of several criteria, such as work quantity and quality. For each criterion, a manager ranks the employees from best to worst, assigning a 1 to the lowest-ranked employee and the highest score to the best employee in that category. Then all the scores for each employee are totaled to see who has the highest total score.

The paired-comparison approach is appropriate when a manager needs to find one outstanding employee in a group. It can be used to identify the best candidate for a promotion or special assignment. However, paired comparison makes some employees look good at the expense of others, which makes this technique less useful as a means of providing feedback to individual employees. It is especially inappropriate as a routine form of appraisal in situations calling for cooperation and teamwork.

Forced-Choice Approach

In the forced-choice approach, the appraisal form gives a manager sets of statements describing employee behavior. For each set of statements, a manager must choose one that is most characteristic and one that is least characteristic of the employee. When this approach is used by managers to appraise employees, managers deal with all their direct reports. Therefore, if a rater has 20 employees, only four can go in the top fifth and, of course, four must also be relegated to the bottom fifth.

These questionnaires tend to be set up in a way that prevents a manager from saying only positive things about employees. Thus, the forced-choice approach is used when an organization determines that managers have been rating an unbelievably high proportion of employees as above average.

Written Essays

Probably the simplest method of evaluation is to write a narrative describing an employee's strengths, weaknesses, past performance, potential, and suggestions for improvement. In short, managers answer questions such as, "What are the major strengths of this employee?" or "In what area does this employee need improvement?" The written essay requires no complex forms or extensive training to complete.

Essay or "free-form" appraisals often are used along with other types of appraisals, notably graphic rating scales. They provide an opportunity for a supervisor to describe aspects of performance that are not thoroughly covered by an appraisal questionnaire. The main drawback of essay appraisals is that their quality depends on a supervisor's writing skills.

Behaviorally Anchored Rating Scales (BARS)

Another method for appraising performance involves the use of behaviorally anchored rating scales, or BARS. BARS appraisal systems (also known as "behavioral expectation scales") represent a combination of the GRS and the critical-incident method. These scales rate employee performance in several areas, such as work quantity and quality, using a series of statements that describe effective and ineffective performance in each area. In each area, a manager selects the statement that best describes how an employee performs. Behavioral descriptions might include the following: anticipates, plans, executes, solves immediate problems, carries out orders, and handles emergency situations. The statements in the rating scales are different for each job title in the organization.

A significant advantage of BARS is that they dramatically increase reliability by providing specific behavioral examples to reflect effective and less-effective behaviors. Also, BARS can be tailored to the organization's objectives for employees. In addition, the BARS approach is less subjective than some other approaches because it uses statements describing behavior. However, developing the scales is time-consuming and therefore relatively expensive.

Behavioral Observation Scale (BOS)

The Behavioral Observation Scale (BOS) is another behavioral approach to assessing employee performance. Like BARS, a BOS is developed from critical incidents. However, rather than only use a sample of behaviors that reflect effective or ineffective behavior, a BOS uses substantially more behaviors to specifically define all the measures that are necessary for effective performance. A second difference between a BOS and BARS is that rather than assessing which behavior best describes an individual's performance, a BOS allows managers to rate the frequency with which the individual employee has exhibited each behavior during the rating period. The manager then averages these ratings to calculate an overall performance rating for the individual. Although the BOS approach avoids the limitations of the BARS approach, the BOS takes even more time and can be even more expensive to develop.

Checklist Appraisal

A checklist appraisal contains a series of questions about an employee's performance. A supervisor answers yes or no to the questions. Thus, a checklist is merely a record of performance, not an evaluation by a supervisor. The HRM department has a key for scoring the items on the checklist; the score results in a rating of an employee's performance. The following are typical checklist statements: can be expected to finish work on time; seldom agrees to work overtime; is cooperative and helpful; accepts criticism; and, strives for self-improvement.

The checklist can be modified so that varying weights are assigned to the statements or words. The results can then be quantified. Usually the weights are not known by the rating supervisor because they are tabulated by someone else, such as a member of the HRM department.

While the checklist appraisal is easy to complete, it has several disadvantages. As with the GRS, the words or statements may have different meanings to different raters. The checklist can be difficult to prepare, and each job category will probably require a different set of questions. Also, a rating supervisor has no way to adjust the answers for any special circumstances that affect performance. Additionally, raters do not assign the weights to the factors. These difficulties limit the use of the information when a rater discusses the checklist with the employee, creating a barrier to effective development counseling.

Management by Objectives (MBO)

Initially introduced in Chapter 3 in our discussion of motivation, a very popular individualized method of evaluating performance of employees (particularly managers and professionals) is management by objectives (MBO). In an MBO system an employee meets with his or her manager, and they collectively set goals for the employee for a coming period of time, usually one year. These goals are usually quantifiable, they are objective, and they are almost always written. During the year the manager and the employee periodically meet to review the employee's performance relative to attaining the goals. At the end of the year, a more formal meeting is scheduled in which the manager and employee assess the actual degree of goal attainment. The degree of goal attainment then becomes the individual's performance appraisal. That is, if an individual has attained all of his or her goals, then the person's performance is deemed to be very good. Otherwise, the individual is directly responsible for his or her performance deficiency, and the person's performance is judged to be less than adequate or acceptable.

No management tool is perfect, and certainly MBO is not appropriate for all employees or all organizations. Jobs with little or no flexibility are not compatible with MBO. For example, an assembly-line worker usually has so little job flexibility that performance standards and objectives are already determined. The MBO process seems to be most useful with managerial personnel and employees who have a fairly wide range of flexibility and control over their jobs. When imposed on a rigid and autocratic management system, MBO may fail. Extreme emphasis on penalties for not meeting objectives defeats the development and participative nature of MBO.

Which Performance Appraisal Method Is Best?

Determining the best appraisal method depends upon the objectives of the system. A combination of the methods is usually superior to any one method. For development objectives, critical incidents and MBO work well. For administrative decisions, a ranking method based on rating scales or BARS works well. The real success of performance appraisal does not lie in the method or form used; it depends upon the supervisor's interpersonal skills.

SOURCES OF BIAS IN PERFORMANCE APPRAISALS

Ideally, rating supervisors should be completely objective in their appraisals of employees. Each appraisal should directly reflect an employee's performance, not any biases of a supervisor. Of course, this is impossible to do perfectly. We all make compromises in our decision-making strategies and have biases in evaluating what other people do. Raters need to be aware of these biases, so that their effect on the appraisals can be limited or eliminated.

Unclear standards. Although the graphic rating scale seems objective, it would probably result in unfair appraisals because the traits and degrees of merit are open to interpretation. For example, different supervisors would probably define "good" performance, "fair" performance, and so on, differently. The same is true of such traits as "quality of work" or "creativity."

There are several ways to rectify this problem. The best way is to develop and include descriptive phrases that define each trait, for example, by specifying on the evaluation form what is meant by such things as "outstanding," "superior," and "good" quality of work. This specificity results in appraisals that are more consistent and more easily explained.

Harshness or leniency bias. Some managers are prone to a harshness bias, that is, rating employees more severely than their performance merits. New supervisors or managers are especially susceptible to this error, because they may feel a need to be taken seriously, Unfortunately, the harshness bias also tends to frustrate and discourage employees, who resent the unfair assessments of their performance.

At the other extreme is the leniency bias. Managers with this bias rate their employees more favorably than their performance merits. A manager who does this may want credit for developing a department full of "excellent" employees. Or the manager may simply be uncomfortable confronting employees with their shortcomings. The leniency bias may feel like an advantage to the employees who receive the favorable ratings, but it cheats the employees and department of the benefits of truly developing and coaching employees.

The harshness/leniency problem is especially serious with graphic rating scales, because supervisors aren't necessarily required to avoid giving all their employees high (or low) ratings. On the other hand, if you must rank employees, you are forced to distinguish between high and low performers. Thus, harshness/leniency is not a problem with the ranking or forced choice distribution approaches.

Central tendency. A bias that characterizes the responses to many types of questionnaires is central tendency, which is the tendency to select ratings in the middle of the scale. People seem more comfortable on middle ground than taking a strong stand at either extreme. This bias causes a manager to miss important opportunities to praise or correct employees. Ranking employees instead of using a GRS can avoid the central tendency problem, because all employees must be ranked and thus can't all be rated average.

Proximity means nearness. The proximity bias refers to the tendency to assign similar scores to items that are near each other on a questionnaire. If a manager assigns a score of 8 to one appraisal item, this bias might encourage the manager to score the next item as 6 or 7, even though a score of 3 is more accurate. Obviously, this can result in misleading appraisals.

When using a type of appraisal that requires answers to specific questions, a manager might succumb to making random choices. A rating supervisor might do this when uncertain how to answer or when the overall scoring on the test looks undesirable. For example, if a manager thinks an appraisal is scoring an employee too low, he or she might give favorable ratings in some areas where the supervisor has no strong feelings. Managers who catch themselves making random choices should slow down and try to apply objective criteria.

Similarity bias. This refers to the tendency to judge others more positively when they are like ourselves. Thus, we tend to look more favorably on people who share our interests, tastes, background, or other characteristics. For example, in appraising performance, a manager risks viewing a person's performance in a favorable light because the employee shares her or his interests in sports. Or a rating supervisor might interpret negatively the performance of an employee who is much shyer than the supervisor.

Recency syndrome. This refers to the human tendency to place the most weight on events that have occurred most recently. In a performance appraisal, a manager might give particular weight to a problem the employee caused last week or an award the employee just won whereas he or she should be careful to consider events and behaviors that occurred throughout the entire period covered by the review. The most accurate way to do this is to keep records throughout the year, as described earlier with conducting a critical-incidence appraisal.

Halo effect (also discussed in Chapter 2 in our discussion on perceptual barriers). This refers to the tendency to generalize one positive or negative aspect of a person to the person's entire performance. Thus, if a manager thinks that a pleasant telephone manner is what makes a good customer service representatives, he is apt to give high marks to a representative with a pleasant voice, no matter what the employee actually says to the customers or how reliable the performance.

Prejudices. Finally, the manager's prejudices about various types of people can unfairly influence a performance appraisal. A manager needs to remember that each employee is an individual, not merely a representative of a group. A manager who believes that African Americans generally have poor skills in using standard English needs to recognize that this is a prejudice about a group, not a fact to apply to actual employees. Thus, before recommending that a black salesperson needs to improve her speaking skills, a supervisor must consider whether the salesperson really needs improvement in that area or whether the supervisor's prejudices are interfering with an accurate assessment. Managers should try to block out the influence of factors such as previous performance, age or race.

HOW TO AVOID APPRAISAL PROBLEMS

There are at least four ways to minimize the impact of appraisal problems such as bias and central tendency. First, be sure to understand the problems as just discussed and the suggestions (like clarifying standards) given for each of them. Understanding the problem can help you avoid it.

Second, choose the right appraisal tool. Each tool, such as the GRS or the critical-incident method, has its own advantages and disadvantages as noted earlier. Third, train supervisors to eliminate rating errors such as halo, central tendency, and leniency. In a typical training program, raters are shown a videotape of jobs being performed and are asked to rate the worker. Ratings made by each participant are then placed on a flip chart, and the various errors (such as leniency and halo) are explained. Typically, the trainer gives the correct rating and then illustrates the rating errors the participants made (Hedge and Cavanaugh, 1988).

Rater training is no panacea for reducing errors or for improving appraisal accuracy. In practice, several factors including the extent to which pay is tied to performance ratings, union pressure, employee turnover, time constraints, and the need to justify ratings may be more important than training. This means that improving appraisal accuracy calls not just for training but also for reducing outside factors such as union pressure and time constraints (Athey and McIntyre, 1987).

A fourth solution—diary keeping—has been proposed and is worth the effort. A recent study illustrates this (DeNisi and Peters, 1996). The conclusion of this and other studies is that you can reduce the adverse effects of appraisal problems by having raters carefully write down positive and negative critical incidents as they occur during the period to be appraised. Maintaining such behavioral records instead of relying on long-term memories is definitely the preferred approach (Sanchez and DeLaTorre, 1996). Diary keeping isn't foolproof, as some research has shown. In one study, while raters were required to keep a diary, contrary to predictions the diary keeping actually undermined the performance appraisal's objectives (Varna, DeNisi, and Peters, 1996).

Most of the appraisal problems we have discussed reflect the fact that performance appraisal is essentially a cognitive, decision-making process. Being familiar with the potential problems, choosing the right appraisal tool, training supervisors, and keeping a diary can help diminish some of the errors that might therefore crop up.

LEGAL AND EFFECTIVE PERFORMANCE APPRAISALS

Performance appraisal plays a central role in equal employment compliance. Since the passage of Title VII, a growing number of courts have addressed issues (including promotion, layoff, and compensation decisions) in which performance appraisals play a significant role (Axline, 1994). The Equal Employment Opportunity Commission (EEOC) and other federal enforcement agencies make it clear that performance appraisal must be job-related and nondiscriminatory.

The elements of a performance appraisal system that can survive court tests can be determined from existing case law. Various cases have provided guidance. The elements of a legally defensible performance appraisal are as follows:

- Performance appraisal criteria based on job analysis
- Absence of disparate impact and evidence of validity
- Formal evaluation criteria that limit managerial validity
- Formal rating instrument
- Personal knowledge of and contact with appraised individual
- Training of supervisors in conducting appraisals
- Review process that prevents one manager acting alone from controlling an employee's career
- Counseling to help poor performers improve

Clearly, the courts are interested in fair and nondiscriminatory performance appraisals. Employers must decide how to design their appraisal systems to satisfy courts, enforcement agencies, and their employees ("Minimize performance evaluation legal risks," 1998).

In discrimination suits, the plaintiff often alleges that the performance appraisal system unjustly discriminated against the plaintiff because of race or gender. Many performance appraisal measures are subjective, and we have seen that individual biases can affect them, especially when those doing the measuring harbor racial or gender stereotypes.

It is important that organizations develop a system for archiving performance appraisal results. An organization must be able to demonstrate, beyond reasonable doubt, that a given individual was sanctioned, rewarded, punished, terminated, or remanded for training on a basis of performance-related reasons rather than nonperformance-related factors such as sex or race.

HOW TO CONDUCT A FORMAL PERFORMANCE APPRAISAL

Conducting a performance appraisal is one of the manager's most important and difficult functions. The first thing a manager can do to conduct an effective formal performance appraisal is to make sure that there are no surprises in store for employees. This means that the manager should communicate with his or her employees on a regular basis about how they are doing with their particular assignments and how well they are collaborating with others.

The formal appraisal session, therefore, should be primarily a way to summarize and continue the informal interaction that has previously taken place between the manager and the employee. It should also be a time to look at how the manager and the employee can continue to work well together in the future. The manager's job in this session is not to tell the employee all the things they think the employee did wrong over the past year. One reason employees dread these sessions is that managers feel they have to find something to criticize as well as to praise. The manager might then mention a negative comment the employee made or similar trivial points. This hypercritical approach will merely increase the employee's resentment and defensiveness and will make employees feel as though they are powerless to improve.

To make sure the session goes as well as possible and to avoid making it uncomfortable for both the manager and the employee, five general steps should be followed:

1. Refer to past feedback and documented observations of performance.
2. Describe the current performance.
3. Describe the desired performance.
4. Get a commitment to any needed change.
5. Follow up.

Specific guidelines for conducting performance appraisals are described below.

Preparing for the Appraisal Interview Session

Today's manager must recognize that failure to plan for the performance appraisal is planning to fail. Being prepared is key to making sure the discussion with each employee goes smoothly. Before the meeting, the manager needs to do some documentation and planning:

- Create and maintain logs (or documentation) on each employee that include observations of the outcomes of the employee's actions on the job and particular behaviors. Update these logs regularly. Focus on what employees are doing well, and try to understand problems from the systems perspective.
- If a rule infraction has occurred, describe in writing and have the employee sign the written record at the time of the infraction. Keep a record of all discussions that deal with problems that are directly attributable to the employee's performance.
- Review the documentation before the formal appraisal session and highlight important points.
- List the points you want to make, focusing on both strengths and areas for improvement. Be prepared to discuss problems in a manner that focuses on the behaviors that caused the problem and on solutions, not on the person. Be sure to distinguish between problems that are related to the system (e.g., too many assignments) and those that are attributable to the individual.

- Consider the follow-up actions you think might be appropriate to help the employee improve, but be prepared to take the employee's feelings into consideration.
- Think about how you have interacted with the employee and how these interactions might have affected his or her performance. Be prepared to discuss how you and the employee might improve your interactions.
- Set up an appointment with the employee about a week before the performance appraisal session.
- If the employee needs to fill out a self-assessment form, give it to him or her at the time you set up the appointment to meet.

During the Appraisal Interview Session

Here are some ways managers can make the actual session go smoothly:

- Put the employees at ease at the start of the session. Acknowledge that these sessions can be a little nerve-wracking, but that their purpose is to help everyone in the team or work group improve and to gather information on how to help these improvement efforts.
- Ask employees what they think of their total performance—not just their strong or weak areas.
- Question employees about what they think are their personal strengths. This gives employees a chance to describe what they do best, which helps them feel positive about the appraisal.
- Tell employees what you believe are their strengths. This demonstrates that you are paying attention to their performance and appreciating their good qualities.
- Describe those areas where you think employees might improve, and use documentation to demonstrate why you are making these observations. Then ask employees what they think of your assessment and listen silently to what they have to say. Consider their reasons for poor performance (e.g., lack of equipment, lack of training) in determining appropriate actions to take.
- Assuming that you identify the cause of poor performance, ask employees what you can do together to take care of it.
- Regardless of whether or not an employee receives an average or a good rating, explain why she or he did not get a higher rating. The employee should understand what needs to be done during the next performance period to get a higher rating.
- Set new goals for the next appraisal period.
- Keep a record of the meeting, including a timetable for performance improvement and what each of you will do to work toward your goals.
- Be open and honest, yet considerate of the employee's feelings. The goal is to facilitate improvement, not to make the employee feel bad.
- Be sure to give positive reinforcement to the employee during the discussion, preferably near the end. Being positive helps to motivate the employee to make any necessary change.

After the Appraisal Interview Session

It is vital to follow up on any agreements made during the appraisal session. Follow up indicates that the manager and the organization are serious about improvement. The manager should:

- make appointments to meet with employees individually to review progress;
- set up development opportunities as needed to address skill deficiencies;
- arrange for the employee to get counseling, when available, if a personal problem is involved;
- provide feedback when you see improvements in performance;
- make him or her aware of the consequences, such as demotion or dismissal, if the employee continues to perform poorly.

Follow up means more than just working with employees. Managers also have to follow up on themselves. An effective appraisal process requires an ongoing and candid self-assessment by the manager of his or her performance and its effect on employees. Managers can use the following questions to evaluate their own performance and its effect on their employees:

- Do your employees know specifically what you expect?
- Do your employees have written goals and results?
- Have you tracked your employees' performance to see if the trend is up, down, or about the same?
- Have you updated your employees recently about what you are working on and how it affects them?
- Are you maintaining performance documentation?
- Have you scheduled interim reviews with all of your employees?
- Do you frequently—even daily—discuss employee performance?
- Do you frequently "catch" your employees doing something right—and tell them about it?

EFFECTIVE PERFORMANCE MANAGEMENT

An effective performance appraisal system has a strategic importance to the organization. Clearly, the organization must monitor the extent to which it is conducting its performance appraisals effectively, adequately, and appropriately. As with selection, performance appraisal must be free from bias and discrimination.

Also, regardless of which performance appraisal approach is used, an understanding of what performance management is supposed to do is critical. When performance appraisal is used to develop employees as resources, it usually works. When management uses performance appraisal as a punishment or when raters fail to understand its limitations, it fails. The key is not which form or which method is used, but whether managers and employees understand its purposes. In its simplest form, a performance appraisal is a manager's observation: "Here are your strengths and weakness, and here is a way to shore up the weak areas." It can lead to higher employee motivation and satisfaction if done right.

But in an era of continuous improvement, an ineffective performance management system can be a huge liability (Longnecker and Fink, 1997). An effective performance management system will be:

- consistent with strategic mission of the organization,
- beneficial as a development tool,
- useful as an administrative tool,
- legal and job-related,
- viewed as generally fair by employees, and
- useful in documenting employee performance.

Most systems can be improved by training supervisors, because conducting performance appraisals is a big part of a performance management system. Training should focus on minimizing errors and providing a frame of reference on how raters observe and recall information.

Organizationally, there is a tendency to distill performance into a single number that can be used to support pay raises. Systems based on this concept reduce the complexity of each person's contribution in order to satisfy compensation-system requirements (Manzoni and Barsoux, 1998). Such systems are too simplistic to give employees useful feedback or help managers pinpoint training and development needs. In fact, use of a single numerical rating often is a barrier to performance discussions, because what is emphasized is attaching a label to a person's performance and defending or attacking that label. Effective performance management systems evolve from the recognition that human behaviors and capabilities collapsed into a single score have a limited use in shaping the necessary range of performance.

In the end, since performance appraisal feeds into the performance management process and the ultimate goal of this process is to improve performance on the job, if the process is working, managers should be able to see real improvements in organizational performance. This improvement may take the form of fewer errors in production, fewer returns in sales, higher appraisals, or lower levels of absenteeism or turnover. In the long run, however, these outcomes are not critical to the organization unless they translate into some improvement in the company's performance. That is, if performance appraisal and performance management systems are doing what they were designed to do, the organization as a whole should perform better.

EVALUATING THE PERFORMANCE APPRAISAL AND MANAGEMENT PROCESSES

Like recruitment and selection, performance appraisal must be free from bias and discrimination. This means that the organization must monitor the extent to which it is conducting its performance appraisals effectively, adequately, and appropriately.

The performance appraisal system must be doing an effective job of helping the organization identify its low performers so that their deficiencies can be remedied through training or other measures. Even more important, though, the organization must identify its strongest performers so that they can be appropriately rewarded and efforts made to retain their employment within the organization. Periodic audits of the performance appraisal system by trained professionals can be an effective method for assessing their effectiveness and appropriateness of the organization's performance appraisal process.

If the process is working, managers should be able to see real improvements in organizational performance since performance appraisal feeds into the performance management process. The improvements may take the form of lower levels of absenteeism or turnover, fewer errors in production, few returns in sales, and higher appraisals. In the long run, however, these outcomes are not critical to the organization unless they translate into some improvements in the organization's performance. That is, if performance appraisal and the broader performance management systems are doing what they were designed to do, the organization as a whole should perform better.

SPECIAL CAUSES OF PERFORMANCE PROBLEMS

Individual performance problems can harm the productivity of an organization. Some of these performance problems are due to special causes, and they arise through specific actions of the individual employees. Rather than blaming the individual for these problems, which usually does nothing to improve performance and can lower employee morale and motivation, the manager needs to deal with the underlying causes. If a manager deals effectively with performance problems due to these special causes, there is a good chance the manager will eliminate the problems and help assure that the organization operates effectively. These performance problems may include absenteeism and tardiness, disrespect or lack of cooperation, substance abuse, theft, unsafe practices, or personality problems. An effective manager will recognize these potential problems, take steps to identify the causes, and take actions toward resolving them. In some cases this may mean referring an employee to a company's employee assistance program, or taking disciplinary action if things do not improve.

Disciplining Employees

"I can't stand Fran's surly attitude any longer!" fumed Ted Tyler, her manager. "If she doesn't cut it out, she's going to be sorry." This manager is eager for the employee to experience the consequences of her behavior. Despite his anger and frustration, however, Ted needs to apply discipline in constructive ways. In many cases, effective discipline can quickly bring about a change in an employee's behavior.

Administering Discipline

Managers must exercise discretion when recommending or imposing penalties on employees. In dealing with mistakes, managers must consider what the mistakes were and under what circumstances they were made. Mistakes resulting from continued carelessness call for disciplinary action. Honest mistakes should be corrected by counseling and positive discipline, not by punishment. These corrections should help the employee learn from the mistakes and become more proficient and valuable to the organization.

The specific ways in which a manager disciplines employees may be dictated by company policies or union contracts, if any. A manager must, therefore, be familiar with all applicable policies and rules, which include respecting the rights of employees in the discipline process. Employees' rights include the following:

- The right to know job expectations and the consequences of not fulfilling those expectations.
- The right to receive consistent and predictable responses to violations of the rules.
- The right to receive fair discipline based on facts.
- The right to question management's statement of the facts and to present a defense.
- The right to receive progressive discipline.
- The right to appeal a disciplinary action.

The Discipline Process

Before administering discipline in response to problem behavior, managers need to have a clear picture of the situation. Usually managers become aware of a problem either through their own observations or from another employee. In either case, managers need to collect the facts before taking further action. Often this will result in a resolution to the problem. For example, Ted Tyler believes that one of his employees is using the office telephone for personal business. The employee has a girlfriend in another state, and Ted suspects the company is paying for the employee's long-distance calls. To solve the problem, Ted should not make hasty accusations or issue a general memo about company policy. Ted should instead ask the employee directly and privately about his telephone conversations. In getting the employee's version of the problem, Ted should use good listening practices and resist the temptation to get angry.

When a manager observes and understands the facts behind problem behavior, the discipline process takes place in four steps: verbal or written warning, suspension, demotion, and dismissal. These steps can be used one after the other in a "progressive" pattern of discipline, indicating that the steps progress from the least to the most severe action a manager can take.

In following steps in the discipline process, a manager should keep in mind that the objective is to end the problem behavior. The manager should take only as many steps as are necessary to bring about a change in that behavior. The ultimate goal is to solve the problem without dismissing the employee.

GUIDELINES FOR EFFECTIVE DISCIPLINE

The guidelines for effective discipline are:

- Act immediately.
- Focus on solving the problem.
- Keep emotions in check.
- Administer discipline in private.
- Be consistent.

These are described in greater detail below.

Act Immediately

When an employee is causing a problem—from tardiness to theft to lack of cooperation—the manager needs to act immediately. This is not always easy to do. Pointing out poor behavior and administering discipline are unpleasant tasks, but managers who ignore problem situations are effectively signaling that the problem is not serious. As a result, the problem often gets worse.

Focus on Solving the Problem

When discussing a problem with an employee, a manager should focus on learning about and resolving the issue at hand. This meeting is no time for name-calling or for dredging up instances of past misbehavior. Nor is it generally useful for a manager to dwell on how patient or compassionate he or she has been. Instead, a manager should listen to the employee and be sure he or she understands the problem, and then begin discussing how to correct it in the future. Talking about behavior instead of personalities helps the employee understand what is expected.

Keep Emotions in Check

A manager should avoid becoming emotional. Although it is appropriate to convey sincere concern about a problem, a manager's other feelings are largely irrelevant and can even stand in the way of a constructive discussion. Being calm and relaxed when administering discipline tells an employee that the manager is confident of what he or she is doing.

Administer Discipline in Private

Discipline should be a private matter. The manager should not humiliate an employee by issuing a reprimand in front of other employees. Humiliation only breeds resentment and may actually increase problem behavior in the future.

Be Consistent

A manager also should be consistent in administering discipline. One way to do this is to follow the four steps of the progressive discipline process. A manager should also respond to all instances of misbehavior equitably rather than, for example, ignoring a long-standing employee's misdeeds while punishing a newcomer.

Documentation of Disciplinary Actions

Employees who are disciplined sometimes respond by filing a grievance or suing the employer. To be able to justify their actions, therefore, managers must have a record of the disciplinary actions taken and the basis for the discipline. These records may be needed to show that the actions were not discriminatory or against company policy.

While documentation is important for any disciplinary action, it is especially important when a manager must dismiss an employee. Because the experience is so emotional, some former employees respond with lawsuits against employers. The employee's file should show the steps the manager took leading up to the termination and a record of the specific behaviors that led the manager to dismiss the employee to protect the organization against this type of legal action. The performance appraisal ratings should correspond to other documentation about problematic performance.

Positive Discipline

Ideally, discipline should not only end problem behavior, but should also prevent problems from occurring. Discipline designed to prevent problem behavior from starting is known as positive discipline, or preventive discipline. One important part of positive discipline is making sure employees know and understand the rules they must follow, and the consequences of violating those rules.

Employees may engage in problem behavior when they feel frustrated or unhappy. Therefore, a manager also can administer positive discipline by working to create positive working conditions under which employees will be unlikely to cause problems. This includes setting realistic goals, being aware of and responsive to employees' needs and ideas, and making sure employees feel that they are important to the organization.

SUMMARY

Performance management is part of an organization's effort to establish controls to ensure that work is progressing toward achieving the expected results. Control is accomplished by comparing actual performance with predetermined standards or objectives and then taking action to correct any deviations from the standards. The control process has three basic steps: (1) establishing performance standards; (2) monitoring performance and comparing it with standards; and (3) taking necessary action.

Performance appraisals are important because they help ensure that the recruiting and selection processes are adequate. They play an important role in training; they can help effectively link performance with rewards; they demonstrate that important employment-related decisions have been based on performance; and they can promote employee motivation and development. Performance appraisals also provide valuable and useful information to the organization's HRM planning process. The ultimate goal for any organization using performance appraisals is to be able to improve performance on the job.

Performance appraisals should be done by those familiar with the performance of an individual employee. Possibilities include the immediate supervisors, peers, direct reports, customers, and individuals themselves. Multisource or 360-degree feedback is increasingly used by organizations to evaluate their employees performance.

Several methods can be used to assess performance. These include written essays, critical incidents, graphic rating scales, behavioral anchored and observation scales, and multiperson comparisons like paired comparison and forced-choice approaches. All performance measurement techniques are subject to one or more weaknesses or deficiencies that are often referred to as biases. The most common are harshness bias, leniency bias, similarity bias, proximity bias, central tendency, recency syndrome, and the halo effect. Organizations should undertake efforts to reduce rating error.

Successful performance appraisals are more likely when raters do appropriate planning and preparation before the actual appraisal. Additionally, they should follow specific steps during the appraisal process and include a follow-up phase to ensure that the expected performance improvements are actually coming to fruition. Today's organizations must monitor the extent to which they are conducting performance appraisals effectively, adequately, and appropriately. Performance appraisals must be free from bias and discrimination.

Problems that a manager can attribute to individuals are special-cause problems and include absence and tardiness, disrespect and lack of cooperation, substance abuse, use of unsafe practices, and theft. One way of dealing with special-cause performance problems is discipline. Discipline is action taken by a manager to prevent employees from breaking rules.

Effective ways of administering discipline require the manager to meet with the employee(s) involved and ask for his or her version of what has happened after collecting the facts of the situation. The manager should use good listening techniques and, if necessary, let the employee experience the consequences of unsatisfactory behavior through suspension, demotion, and ultimately dismissal. The manager must take as many steps as are necessary to resolve the problem behavior.

Positive discipline focuses on preventing it from ever beginning. It can include making sure employees know and understand the rules, creating conditions under which employees are least likely to cause problems, using decision-making strategies when problems occur, and rewarding desirable behavior. Effective positive discipline results in self-discipline among employees; that is, employees voluntarily follow the rules and try to meet performance standards.

REFERENCES

Athey, T., and McIntyre, R. 1987. Effect of rater training on rater accuracy: Levels of processing theory and social facilitation theory perspectives. *Journal of Applied Psychology* 72: 567–572.

Axline, L. 1994. Ethical considerations of performance appraisals. *Management Review* 83: 62.

Cardy, R.L., and Dobbins, G.H. 1997. Performance management. In L.H. Peters,

C.R. Greer, and S.A. Youngblood (eds.), *The Blackwell encyclopedia: Dictionary of human resource management*. Malden, MA: Blackwell Publishers, pp. 255–256.

DeNisi, A., and Peters, L. 1996. Organization of information in memory and the performance appraisal process: Evidence from the field. *Journal of Applied Psychology* 81: 717–737.

Gephart, M. 1995. The road to high performance. *Training and Development* (June): 30–38.

Ghorparde, J., and Chen, M.M. 1995. Creating quality-driven performance appraisal systems. *Academy of Management Executive* 9: 32–39.

Hedge, J., and Cavanaugh, M. 1988. Improving the accuracy of performance evaluations: Comparison of three methods of performance appraiser training. *Journal of Applied Psychology* 73: 68–73.

Jackson, J.H., and Greller, M.M. 1998. Decision elements for using 360-degree feedback. *Human Resource Planning* 20: 18–28.

LaMountain, D.M. 1997. Assessing the value of multisource feedback. *Employment Relations Today* (Autumn): 75–90.

Longnecker, C.O., and Fink, L.S. 1997. Keys to designing and running an effective performance appraisal system. *Journal of Compensation and Benefits* (November/December): 28.

Manzoni, J., and Barsoux, J. 1998. The set-up-to-fail syndrome. *Harvard Business Review* (March/April): 101–114.

Minimize performance evaluation legal risks. 1998. *Journal of Accountancy* (February): 10.

Sanchez, J., and DeLaTorre, P. 1996. A second look at the relationships between rating and behavioral accuracy in performance appraisal. *Journal of Applied Psychology* 81: 7.

Varna, A., DeNisi, A.S., and Peters, L.H., 1996. Interpersonal affect and performance appraisal: A field study. *Personnel Psychology* 49: 341–360.

Chapter 5

Managing Stress

INTRODUCTION

During the past decade, stress has become a significant topic in organizational behavior, in part due to the increase in competitive pressures in many industries, increased globalization, and advances in technology. This chapter is concerned with stress and its implications for managing organizational behavior. The chapter first briefly focuses on the stress in the new environment. The discussion then examines "What stress is and is not." The next section takes a look at the General Adjustment Syndrome, an early model of stress response and then the discussion turns to predisposition to stress. Sources of stress and the consequences of stress are the focus of the next section. The discussion then turns to individual and organizational strategies for preventing, managing, and reducing stress. The chapter concludes with a look at stressors resulting from international activities or organizations and ethical issues surrounding stress in organizations.

STRESS TODAY

A leading expert on stress, cardiologist Robert Eliot, gives the following prescription for dealing with stress: "Rule No. 1 is, don't sweat the small stuff. Rule No. 2 is, it's all small stuff. And if you can't fight and you can't flee, flow" ("Stress: Can we cope?" 1983). What is happening in today's organizations, however, is that the "small stuff" is getting to employees, and they are not going with the "flow." Stress has become a major buzzword and legitimate concern of the times.

There is increasing evidence that managers and other employees are experiencing more stress, and the demands of the new environment are the cause of a lot of this stress. Globalization and strategic alliances have led to a dramatic increase in employee travel stress and relocation. The environmental impact of advanced information technology has led to a new term of technostress. Loss of privacy, information inundation, erosion of face-to-face contact and continually having to learn new skills are also problems created for today's employees at all levels by exploding technology.

Besides globalization and advanced information technology, there is also evidence that increased diversification of the workforce may lead to unique stress problems and that employees increasingly pressed into overtime work show significant higher levels of stress ("Heavy overtime," 2000; Nelson and Burke, 2000). The stress epidemic not only has a deteriorating impact on those affected and their families, but is also very costly to organizations. One quote suggests that the cost of stress in the United States "is estimated between $200 and $300 billion annually, as assessed by absenteeism, employee turnover, direct medical costs, workers' compensation and other legal costs, diminished productivity, accidents, etc., and is spread throughout the corporation, from the mailroom to the executive suite" (Dutton, 1998, p. 11). In other words, stress in the workplace seems to be getting worse, and the costs are escalating. Before getting into the details, however, the exact meaning of stress is necessary.

WHAT STRESS IS AND IS NOT

Though there is no agreement on one definition of stress, for the purpose of this chapter, stress refers to pressure, strain, or force on a system. Human stress includes physical and psychological stress. Too much of either can lead to fatigue or damage of the affected system. Hans Selye (1974), one of the foremost authorities on this subject, defines stress as follows: by stress the physician means the common results of exposure to any stimulus. For example, the bodily changes produced whether a person is exposed to nervous tension, physical injury, infection, cold, heat, X-rays, or anything else are what we call stress. The problem is not stress itself but prolonged and unchecked stress. When the body remains in an excited state after a crisis has passed, harmful effects begin to set in (p. 151).

According to Selye there are two types of stress. Believe it or not, some stress is good. Eustress is the positive type that has its foundations in meeting the challenges of a task or job. You might say it is a desirable outcome of stress. This type of stress manifests itself in achievement and accomplishment. The effects of eustress are beneficial in that they help us to overcome obstacles.

Bad or negative stress, known as distress, happens when there is too much stress and when nothing is done to eliminate, reduce, or counteract its effects. Distress is negative in that it allows us to be overpowered. Anger, loss of control, and feelings of inadequacy and insecurity are all manifestations of distress. We teeter on the edge of collapse because of these phenomena. If not restrained, serious physical and psychological health problems can result.

Technostress is a relatively new term that refers to "a computer-generated form of physical and emotional burnout" that is caused by an inability to adapt to rapidly changing technology.

Stress and tension are natural. We need them to do our best work. We need them to get the adrenalin flowing. So we cannot hope to—nor would we want to—eliminate all excitement and accompanying stress from our jobs. Too much stress and tension on or off the job, however, can have a negative effect.

It is also important to point out what stress is not.

1. Stress is not simply anxiety. Anxiety operates solely in the emotional and psychological sphere, whereas stress operates there and also in the physiological sphere.
2. Stress is not simply nervous tension. Like anxiety, nervous tension may result from stress, but the two are not the same. Unconscious people have exhibited stress, and some people may keep it "bottled up" and not reveal it through nervous tension.
3. Stress is not necessarily something damaging, bad, or to be avoided. Eustress is not damaging or bad and is something people should seek out rather than avoid. The key, of course, is how the person handles the stress. Stress is inevitable; distress may be prevented or can be effectively controlled.

VIEWS OF JOB-RELATED STRESS

The General Adaptation Syndrome has three distinct stages of a person's response to stress: alarm, resistance, and exhaustion (Selye, 1976). In the alarm stage of the stress response, muscles tense, respiration rate increases, and blood pressure and heart rate increase. Following this stage, a person experiences anxiety, anger, and fatigue. These responses indicate that the person is resisting stress. During this resistance stage, the person may make poor decisions or experience illness. Because a person cannot sustain this resistance indefinitely, exhaustion occurs. During this exhaustion stage, the individual develops such stress-induced illnesses as headaches and ulcers. Also, the capacity to respond to other work-related demands is greatly reduced. Although a person may be able to respond effectively to a threat during one of the earlier stages in this reaction, being unable to cope with a threat in the later stages can have serious detrimental effects for the individual. Selye's view suggests that all people go through the same pattern of response and that all people can tolerate only so much stress before a serious, debilitating condition of exhaustion occurs.

The preceding three-stage response to stress is sometimes termed the "fight or flight" response. It is an automatic response to threat that once served our species well when our primary concerns were finding food and protecting ourselves from wild animals. In ancient times, the powerful stress reaction was an aid in quickly responding by either fighting or swiftly fleeing from a predator. In the modern world, however, persistent forms of stress (for example, unresolved social problems) have a powerful effect on the well-being of an individual. Consider the lingering discomfort that results when an employee is harshly reprimanded by his or her supervisor. In such a situation, neither fighting with one's boss nor fleeing from the situation is an appropriate response. Nonetheless, the employee's physiological response prepares him or her to take some form of action when none may be possible. In essence, our physiological response to stress is no longer correct for many situations we currently face. Trapped in paleolithic bodies, we are not well suited for the stresses one finds in modern organizations.

Despite the drawbacks of stress, its complete or near absence may be less than ideal for performance. In situations where stress is low or absent, employees may not be sufficiently aroused or involved in their tasks. Instead, to maximize performance, low levels of stress are preferable because, in most modest amounts, stress can stimulate individuals to work harder and accomplish more. Again, a certain amount of stress may thus be beneficial (i.e., eustress).

PREDISPOSITION TO STRESS

Individuals appear to differ in the extent to which they are susceptible or tolerant to stress. For example, rates of coronary heart disease, exacerbated by stress, are higher for divorced persons than married people. Married people report higher satisfaction and less stress than unmarried people; top corporation executives have lower mortality rates than second-level executives; and people who live in suburban environments have more stress-related illness than people who live in rural environments. Some individual differences can be explained by the following factors.

Stress Personalities

Some personalities are more inclined to respond negatively to stressors. These include individuals with Type A personalities and pessimists. Others, such as Type B personalities and optimists, seem to respond more positively toward stressors.

Type A. A Type A personality is aggressive, can quickly become hostile, focuses excessively on achievement, and has a keen sense of time urgency. Type A personalities like to move fast and often do more than one activity concurrently. Some aspects of the Type A personality predict coronary heart disease, and other aspects predict high performance. Hostility is strongly associated with coronary heart disease.

Type A employees (managers, salespersons, staff specialists, secretaries, or rank-and-file operating employees) experience considerable stress. They are the ones who:

1. Work long, hard hours under constant deadline pressures and conditions for overload.
2. Often take work home at night or on weekends and are unable to relax.
3. Constantly compete with themselves, setting high standards of productivity that they seem driven to maintain.
4. Tend to become frustrated by the work situation, to be irritated with the work efforts of others, and to be misunderstood by supervisors.

Type B. By contrast, Type B personalities are very laid back, they are patient and take a very relaxed, low-key approach to life and their job. Type B personalities feel less time urgency, often stop to ponder their achievements, and reflect on where they are headed. They have high self-esteem, a characteristic that distinguishes them from Type A personalities. They are even tempered and are not bothered by everyday events.

The Type A's hurried approach to life can lead to a perception of stressors as constraints and not opportunities. Type A personalities want accomplishments and can readily perceive blockages even when no constraints are present. A Type B's more even-tempered approach lets the person see more opportunities than constraints. Type A personalities can also increase the demands made on them. In short, the Type A personality is more likely to feel distress than a Type B personality.

What do the findings on Type A and B personalities mean for today's organizations and managers? Should organizations try to choose the right person—Type A or B—for the job? No, not necessarily. In fact, this could be exactly the wrong strategy at times. One thing the results do suggest is that we probably need to become more aware of our own styles and how they may impact others (e.g., aggressiveness and hostility). Then, we can at least try to reduce these negative emotions. Some organizations have developed programs that can help Type A's or others be more realistic in what they take on and improve their planning skills. This is a difficult thing, however, since the very style of Type A's may make them unwilling or even unable to change their behavior. Perhaps this explains why at least some studies find that more top executives tend to be Type B personalities.

Pessimists and Optimists

Pessimists are negative people who don't respond appropriately to stress. They tend to ignore the problem or source of the stress, often give up on goals blocked by stress, and do not attempt to develop positive ways to deal with the problem. A pessimist in a traffic jam might think of all the negative consequences that are going to happen (e.g., "I'm going to be late so I'll have to work late tonight to finish the report on time, which means my spouse is going to yell at me and probably kick me out of the house!"). Optimists, on the other hand, deal with stress head on. In fact, they are more likely to seek proactive means of dealing with stress, such as obtaining advice from others or planning for such stressors as traffic jams by always having something to do or read in the car. They seem to recognize that it's not the end of the world if they are late for work!

Seven Types of Stress Personalities

Recently, seven types of stress personalities have been suggested by Dempcy and Tihista (1996). An individual may see himself in one or all of them because most of us have a blend of personalities that influence our behavior. These personalities can actually be a source of stress as you can see by their descriptions. The advantage to understanding and recognizing one's stress personality is being able to modify one's behavior in future stress-producing situations.

Pleasers want to make everyone happy and are usually cooperative and helpful. They tend to take on many demands and responsibilities. Under stress, which occurs when they are no longer able to meet their needs or those of others, they display resentment and perhaps anger.

Internal timekeepers also seem desirous of taking on a lot of responsibility, perhaps to please others or just because of their varied interests in many areas. Under normal situations, they are energized, efficient, and competent. Under stress, which is often caused by taking on too much, they become inefficient and anxious.

Strivers are ambitious and competitive and are usually their own source of stress. Why? Because they often place demands on themselves that they cannot meet. Their goal is to be successful at everything, even if it means to work, work, work until they burn out.

Inner con artists convince themselves not to work too hard, to avoid conflict (which usually means avoiding responsibility), and to ignore potentially stress-producing situations. This self-defeating behavior ultimately leads to even more stress in the long run as these types of people, also known as procrastinators, fall behind in both personal and work responsibilities.

Critical judges, when under stress, focus on the negative about themselves and their situation. This type of personality focuses on mistakes, not on *learning* from mistakes.

Worriers are as negative as critical judges and are highly influenced by unpredictability and unclear situations. If they don't know what is going to happen next, they predict the worst! In that sense, they are pessimists. Their constant obsessing over the future increases their stress levels. Worriers need others to tell them what they can expect from situation to situation.

Finally, *sabertooths* respond to stress with a great deal of anger, often expressed through sarcasm or humorous insults. This type of stress personality can also be the source of stress and conflict to others.

SOURCES OF STRESS

Many events and factors could be considered stressors and what is stressful for one person may not be for another. What determines whether something will be a stressor depends a great deal on its importance and the amount of perceived controllability.

Job-Related Stress

A very important thing we could pinpoint as a cause of stress is the job itself—what individuals do every day. Partially, this is just an acknowledgment that some jobs are tougher than others. Being a police officer can expose you to any number of dangers, many of them beyond your control or ability to predict. As a result, only a few of us would be surprised that police officer currently ranks as one of the most stressful jobs in the United States. The job of secretary, for example, is often among the top 10–20 most stressful jobs. Like jobs such as air traffic controller or pilot, the things that make a secretarial job stressful include a lack of control over events/timing, working with the public, managing deadlines, and more. Others claim that one of the toughest jobs might be that of the working Mom. There are still few households in which child care and domestic work are equally shared.

Beyond the jobs mentioned in the previous paragraph, however, nearly every job has characteristics about the work itself that could cause stress. For example, *role conflict* can exist in many jobs. This refers to the fact that some jobs may have built-in, but opposing, requirements. For example, a manager may find that his superior expects increased productivity from his department, while his direct reports expect his support in finding ways to reduce their daily quota. Likewise, a college faculty member may find that she is expected to devote significant amounts of time to preparing and delivering lectures, while at the same time she is expected to publish in highly competitive scholarly journals. If possible, one may resolve the conflict by devoting more time and energy to the most pressing demand in a given situation (for instance, by preparing a lecture as the time for a class approaches).

Another aspect about the job itself that may be stress-producing is something called *role ambiguity*. This refers to a lack of clear expectations about your job or role in the organization. The uncertainty associated with not knowing either what to do or how to accomplish it can be stressful. Initially, all newly hired employees experience some degree of role ambiguity when they are assigned to their tasks. However, some jobs are consistently more lacking in clarity concerning how to perform them. For example, managerial jobs generally lack a specific, well-defined set of activities that are to be routinely carried out. Project team managers are also likely to experience greater degrees of uncertainty, especially in the earlier stages of work.

Role ambiguity is closely associated with a variety of negative consequences. As with role conflict, decreased job satisfaction is thought to be a result of increased role ambiguity. In addition, lower levels of self-confidence, decreased satisfaction with life in general, and increased expression of intentions to quit have been found to be correlated with role ambiguity (Margolis, Kroes, and Quinn, 1974).

In addition to role conflict and ambiguity, role processes can play a part as a source of stress in yet a third fashion: *role overload and underload. Role overload* occurs when too many activities are expected of an employee, given the time available and the ability level of the employee. Indications of role overload include working in excess of 60 hours a week, holding down multiple jobs, and forgoing vacations. Being in a situation where one lacks the necessary time to perform required tasks has been found to be a possible cause of increased blood cholesterol levels, related to job dissatisfaction, lower self-esteem, increased heart rate, and increased cigarette consumption (Vecchio, 2000). In today's business environment where downsizing is common, fewer employees are often required to do more work than ever before. A distinction needs to be made, however, between quantitative overload—situations in which individuals are asked to do more work than they can complete in a specific period of time, and qualitative overload—employees' beliefs that they lack the required skills or abilities to perform a given job. Both types of overload are unpleasant, and research findings suggest that both can lead to high levels of stress.

Overload is only part of the total picture. Although being asked to do too much can be stressful, so can being asked to do too little. In fact, there seems to be considerable truth in the following statement: "The hardest job in the world is doing nothing—you can't take a break." Underload leads to boredom and monotony. Since these reactions are quite unpleasant, underload, too, can be stressful. Again, there is a distinction between quantitative underload and qualitative underload. Quantitative underload refers to the boredom that results when employees have so little to do that they find themselves sitting around much of the time. In contrast, qualitative overload refers to the lack of mental stimulation that accompanies many routine, repetitive jobs.

Technostress

When organizations introduce new information technology (IT), they must consider how such changes will affect human behaviors. Implementing IT systems frequently results in changes to the formal structure of an organization (such as adjustments in department boundaries, individual responsibilities, and communication channels) or to the informal structure (work relations, workgroup norms, or status).

Changes in the organization almost always meet with resistance; people fear the unknown. In addition, people may fear that change will affect their status with colleagues. For example, today's managers often type their correspondence rather than have a secretary do so. If they do not know how to type, they may feel ignorant and embarrassed in front of their colleagues.

People who work with computers for long periods of time can experience eyestrain or muscular discomfort such as carpal tunnel syndrome. This is a wrist problem directly associated with constant keyboard use.

All of these situations can create distress and resistance within a workforce. The term "technostress" addresses the physical and emotional burnout that result from a person's inability to adapt to new technology. In extreme cases people show actual symptoms of a classic phobia—nausea, dizziness, cold sweat, and high blood pressure—as a result of their fear, distrust, or hatred of computers.

Psychological Reactions to Technostress

Technostress has been linked to four major fears. First, some employees fear that as they rely more on computers and less on their job knowledge, their jobs will be "de-skilled" and they will be more easily replaceable and less secure. Second, other employees have a related fear that computers will replace people and lead to layoffs. Third, workers with low self-esteem fear that they will be unable to use computers. And fourth, some workers fear that the corporate power structure will be threatened as computers allow managers access to information that was previously jealously guarded by direct reports.

Too often, managers and information specialists address the problems of technostress or emotional resistance to IT by showing employees that such technological advances will reduce costs, increase profits, decrease decision time, permit job streamlining, and improve the flow and accuracy of information. Even though these arguments are logical and reasonable, they usually fail to address (and often in fact increase) the emotional concerns of employees. When those concerns are not properly addressed, three kinds of resistance often occur:

1. *Aggression*—attacking the information technology in an attempt to make it either inoperative or ineffective.
2. *Projection*—blaming the system for anything that goes wrong in the organization.
3. *Avoidance*—withdrawing from or avoiding interaction with the information system, often as a result of frustration.

The following four steps can be used to overcome employee fear of computers:

1. Have managers take the lead by buying and using computers to show how they can help performance.
2. Encourage and reward employees who show an interest in computers.
3. Establish a personal computer training center where employees can learn about and practice with computers.
4. Provide thorough employee computer training. (Callahan and Fleenor, 1987, pp. 78–80)

SEXUAL HARASSMENT: A PROBLEM IN TODAY'S WORK SETTINGS

There can be little doubt that sexual harassment is a source of stress found in many of today's workplaces. The stressful effects of sexual harassment stem primarily from two sources: (1) the direct affront to the victim's personal dignity and (2) the harasser's interference with the victim's capacity to do the job. It's certainly difficult to pay attention to what you're doing on your job when you have to concentrate on ways to ward off someone's unwanted attentions! Not surprisingly, sexual harassment has caused some people to experience many severe symptoms of illness, including various forms of physical illness, and led to voluntary turnover.

Unfortunately, this particular source of work-related stress is shockingly familiar. Few workplace topics have received more attention in recent years than that of sexual harassment. Sexual harassment on the job is a major problem, faced primarily by women. Needless to say, sexual harassment is legally and ethically wrong. It seriously damages both the people who are harassed and the reputation of the organization in which it occurs. It also can cost organizations large amounts of money. Managers have a legal and ethical obligation to ensure that they, their colleagues, and their employees never engage in sexual harassment, even unintentionally.

Forms of Sexual Harassment

Since 1980 U.S. courts generally have used guidelines from the Equal Employment Opportunity Commission to define sexual harassment. There are two basic forms of sexual harassment. Quid pro quo sexual harassment occurs when a harasser asks or forces an employee to perform sexual favors to receive a promotion, raise, or other work-related opportunity, or to avoid negative consequences such as demotion or dismissal. This "Sleep with me, honey, or you're fired" form of harassment is the more extreme form and is easier to identify. Hostile work-environment sexual harassment is more subtle. Hostile work-environment sexual harassment occurs when employees are faced with an intimidating, hostile, or offensive work environment because of their gender (O'Leary-Kelly, Paetzold, and Griffin, 1995). Lewd jokes, displays of pornography, displays or distribution of sexually oriented objects, and sexually oriented remarks about one's physical appearance are examples of hostile work-environment sexual harassment. A hostile work environment interferes with employees' ability to perform their jobs effectively, contributes to stress, and has been deemed illegal by the courts.

Although women are the most frequent victims of sexual harassment (particularly when working in male-dominated occupations or in positions associated with stereotypical gender relationships such as a female secretary reporting to a male boss), men also can be victims of sexual harassment. It should also be noted that while most instances of sexual harassment involve unwelcome conduct by persons of the opposite sex, allegations of harassment against members of the same sex are increasing. In a recent case, a male oil-rig worker filed and won a sexual harassment case. Managers who engage in hostile work-environment harassment or allow others to do so risk costly lawsuits for their organizations.

Eradicating Sexual Harassment

Managers have an ethical obligation to eradicate sexual harassment in their organizations. To ensure that they do not have a hostile or abusive environment, they must establish a clear and strong position against sexual harassment. There are many ways to accomplish this objective. Some steps that managers can take to deal with the problem are briefly described below (Bresler and Thacker, 1993).

Communicate policies. Clearly communicate the sexual harassment policy endorsed by top management. Senior leadership should adopt a policy against harassment that includes prohibitions against both quid pro quo and hostile work-environment sexual harassment. It should contain:

- requirements that all employees be treated with respect, giving examples of unacceptable behavior

- a procedure for employees to use to report instances of harassment
- a discussion of the disciplinary responses to harassment
- a commitment to educate and train employees about sexual harassment

Implement a fair complaint procedure. A fair complaint procedure should be used to investigate sexual harassment. A fair procedure should:

- be managed by a neutral third party
- ensure prompt and thorough management of complaints
- ensure that alleged harassers are fairly treated

Respond to complaints. Managers must take complaints of sexual harassment seriously. They must also create an environment in which employees feel comfortable making complaints to a manager, someone in HRM, or a higher level manager.

If an employee describes behavior that could be harassment, the manager should listen to the employee's concerns and assure the employee that the manager will follow up on it. The worst thing a manager can do is to pass judgment immediately or imply that the employee should put up with the behavior without complaining.

The manager's initial talk with the employee serves as the very first step of the investigation. The manager should learn all the details about what is bothering the employee. The employee should be asked if anyone else can corroborate the incidents or if anyone else may have experienced similar behavior.

Managers must then deal with complaints promptly. While there is no "bright line" measure for promptness, managers should at a minimum notify the HRM department as quickly as possible—that day or the next business day—so that the investigative process may begin. Unwarranted delay in investigating and otherwise responding to a complaint could cause the organization to be liable.

Take corrective action. When it has been determined that sexual harassment has taken place, take corrective action as soon as possible. This action can vary depending on the severity of the harassment. When harassment is extensive, prolonged over a period of time, of a quid pro quo nature, or severely objectionable in some other manner, corrective action may include firing the harasser.

Explain the duty to investigate. A manager must explain to the employee that once an allegation of harassment is raised, the company has an obligation to investigate the allegation. If the company is made aware of the allegation and fails to investigate, it could be liable for not doing all it could to prevent harassment in the workplace.

The manager should therefore inform the employee of the need to notify the HRM department of the complaint. Even if the complaint is one that both the manager and employee feel confident is just a misunderstanding that could be handled within the manager's department, HRM should be informed of the incident so that it can keep track of any repeat violations or recurring problems.

The company must investigate in the most sensitive way possible, but complete confidentiality cannot be guaranteed. Managers should stress that information about the allegations will be given only to those within the company with a need to know. Managers should let the employee know that no one in the company—including the alleged harasser—will be allowed to retaliate or treat the employee badly because of the complaint. It should be explained that if the investigation shows that harassment has occurred, appropriate disciplinary action will be taken. The employee should be thanked for coming forward, because the company cannot fix problems if it does not know they exist.

Provide training. An organization should provide sexual harassment prevention training to organizational members, including all levels of managers.

CONSEQUENCES OF STRESS

As suggested earlier, stress is a fact of life. Indeed, life would be boring without some sources of stress, and most people seek out some degree of stress. Some people even are attracted to jobs billed as challenging or exciting—those likely to be most stressful. On the job, employees tend to perform best when they are experiencing a moderate degree of stress.

However, too much stress brings problems, especially when the sources of stress are negative (e.g., a critical manager in unsafe working conditions). In a highly stressful environment, people are more apt to come down with psychological and physical illnesses. Because of illness and unhappiness, they take more time off from work. When employees are at work, the sources of stress may distract them from doing their best and may make them more prone to having accidents and producing less. Some of the consequences of stress are burnout, various health and performance effects, and aggression and violence.

Burnout

A person who cannot cope with stress over an extended period of time may experience burnout. Burnout is a feeling of physical and mental exhaustion that may start from stress at work but can extend to many parts of one's life. Burnout is the inability to function effectively as a result of ongoing stress. Employees who are burned out feel drained and lose interest in doing their job. Typically, burnout occurs in three stages: (1) The employee feels emotionally exhausted. (2) The employee's perceptions of others become calloused. (3) The employee views his or her effectiveness negatively.

Burnout is worse than just needing a vacation. Therefore, it is important to cope with stress before it leads to burnout.

People do not necessarily become burned out because they've been in a job for a long time. Career counselors are quick to point out that burnout can happen when you're at any rung of the corporate ladder, even among those who are most successful.

What can be done about burnout? Later, we'll discuss a number of general stress-reduction approaches to help prevent its occurrence, but once in the spiral it's tough to get out. However, it can be done. Since it seems to occur in phases, one strategy is to catch it early. If the early physical signs of burnout are noticed, the spiral can be stopped. Sometimes just acknowledging the problem and someone's hard work can go a long way. Clearly, however, if long and excessive work hours and work loads can be modified, a major cause of burnout can be handled. In addition, however, there are several more long-term steps that can be taken. For one organization, they could offer retraining opportunities for employees to get rid of that "dead end" feeling that accompanies burnout. Or, some organizations have gone so far as to establish sabbatical leave policies to fend off the effects of burnout. These sabbatical programs offer extended time off for employees that is above and beyond vacation time.

Health Effects

Heart disease, strokes, headaches, ulcers, back problems, and some infectious diseases have a stress-related component. In fact, the enormous cost estimates of stress to the economy mentioned earlier are in large part due to the treatment of these symptoms. However, there are also many indirect physical problems associated with stress. For example, some employees try to reduce stress with alcohol, drugs, or other forms of abuse. In increasing numbers, bigger organizations are taking aggressive steps to identify and deal with such problems. For example, many organizations whose business directly affects public safety or health (e.g., child care, transportation, etc.) are adopting drug-testing programs. Of course, some without such public concerns are also requiring drug tests of their employees. Regardless, the very presence of such programs is enough to suggest these effects are important. In conjunction with testing, some organizations have also developed programs to help employees deal with their problems.

Performance Effects

In part, decreased performance can be attributed to the psychological or physical impediments that prevent top performance. But there are indirect effects as well. For example, there seems to be at least some relationship between stress and absenteeism and turnover. Apparently, withdrawing from work temporarily or moving on to new work is a rational choice for many employees. Certainly, this approach is better than turning to alcohol or drugs as a release. Sometimes, however, the job market is not good enough to support this decision; this may account for why the stress-turnover relationship is not large. Regardless, there are high potential costs to replacing employees or dealing with underperformers who stay.

Aggression and Violence

Prior to 1980, murder at work was rare, but it is now one of the fastest growing types of murder in the United States. In addition to people being killed by work associates, thousands of people also experience other forms of violence or aggression at work. Acts such as assault, physical and verbal threats, and harassment (note our discussion on sexual harassment earlier) could actually total in the millions. It is clear that many of these acts are taken by people who might be off-base to start with, even before they experience work stress. Indeed, the common profile of a violator is someone who has very low-control, is impulsive, and has a volatile temper. Still, all this does not mean than an organization should do nothing or just throw up its hands. Beyond the critical issue of threats to employee safety, there are many other potential costs to doing nothing, including employer liability issues. Accordingly, many experts have suggested specific steps that can be taken to fend off violence in the first place; and if violence can't be prevented, they suggest what to do about it when it does occur. These suggestions go well beyond enhancing security measures, although this is extremely helpful. Some of the preventative measures include better screening of applicants, a thorough look at termination procedures, training in conflict resolution, and educating people about early warning signs.

STRESS MANAGEMENT: INDIVIDUAL AND ORGANIZATION STRATEGIES

Stress management has a goal of maintaining or reducing stress to an optimal level for both the individual and the organization. This section does not say that all stress should be reduced, because some stressors are unavoidable, and as noted earlier some amount of stress is not bad for many people.

Individual Techniques to Manage or Reduce Stress

There are many individual approaches to dealing with stressors and stress. To see this, all one need do is to visit any bookstore on site or online and look at the self-improvement section. It will be stocked with numerous how-to books for reducing stress. Below, we will briefly examine a few of the more popularly cited and frequently used approaches for individual stress prevention and management.

Use or develop better coping skills. One thing an employee can do to deal with stress is to develop better coping skills. Coping skills allow us to essentially think away the stress or overcome it once we do perceive it. For example, some people seem especially good at reconceptualizing stressful events in a more positive way—sometimes as a challenge. Research shows, for example, that happier people are more likely than depressed people to attribute negative events to temporary outside influences, rather than to a stable personality characteristic. This is not to say that happier people are more accurate. In fact, the opposite often seems to be true—depressed employees seem to perceive events more accurately (negatively). Unfortunately, this leaves them wiser, but sadder. So, we could all personally benefit by wearing rose-colored glasses, even though this may ignore the true but bleak source of events (e.g., a dysfunctional organization, bad boss, etc.).

Another coping skill seems to be the ability to adopt a "control strategy," or a take-charge attitude about a problem. For example, this coping behavior has been shown to predict how quickly a laid-off employee is able to find a new job (Leana, Feldman, and Tan, 1998). People who coped with a take-charge attitude found new jobs almost twice as fast as those with a more pessimistic attitude. This trait goes hand-in-hand with the internal control personality style. Internals are those who have a natural tendency to feel that they can master and overpower events in their lives. Interestingly, though, the better "copers" among us are also good at recognizing when they need to adopt an "escape" strategy for dealing with stress (e.g., leaving the situation, taking a vacation, seeking a new job). And many of these coping strategies can be found naturally in some people. This personality trait is often called hardiness because of the ability of these people to successfully weather stressful life events. Research shows that training can help develop at least some of those hardiness skills that come naturally to others (Smith, 1994).

Seek social support. A set of meaningful social relationships can help people deal better with stressful events. Employees are especially vulnerable to stressors that jeopardize their relations with supervisors and coworkers. Likewise, the intense stress and washout rates associated with overseas assignments can be reduced by providing social support for the expatriate. Sometimes, just knowing that social support is available, whether or not one uses it, can help people cope better. But a support network can also help out when an individual has to miss work or if he gets way behind. Of course, managers need not passively sit back and hope such support networks develop. They can encourage them by publicizing ones that do exist and maybe even allowing time at work for new ones to develop.

Other Approaches to Manage or Reduce Stress

Several other good approaches individuals can take to protect themselves against the adverse effects of stress are:

1. *Eat a healthy diet.* Growing evidence indicates that reducing intake of salt and saturated fats, and increasing consumption of fiber-rich and vitamin-rich fruits and vegetables, are steps that can greatly increase the body's ability to cope with the physiological effects of stress.
2. *Be physically fit.* People who exercise regularly obtain many benefits closely related to resistance of the adverse effects of stress. For example, fitness reduces both the incidence of cardiovascular illness and the death rate from such diseases. Similarly, physical fitness lowers blood pressure, an important factor in many aspects of personal health.
3. *Relax and meditate.* When you think of a successful leader or manager at work, what picture comes to mind? Most of us probably would conjure up an image of someone on three phones at once, surrounded by important papers in a whirlwind of activity. Probably the farthest thing from your mind would be the image of someone resting calmly in a serene setting. Yet, for a growing number of today's employees, this picture is quite common. What's going on in these organizations is designed to help people become more productive, not in the traditional, stress-inducing way, but by helping them cope more effectively with stress. One technique used in this regard is meditation, the process of learning to clear one's mind of external thoughts, often by repeating a single syllable (known as mantra) over and over again.
4. *Avoid inappropriate self-talk.* This involves telling ourselves over and over how horrible and unbearable it will be if we fail, if we are not perfect, or if everyone we meet does not like us. Such thoughts seem ludicrous when spelled out in the pages of a book, but considerable evidence indicates that most people entertain them at least occasionally. Unfortunately, such thoughts can add to personal levels of stress, as individuals imagine the horrors of not being successful, perfect, or loved. Fortunately, such thinking can be modified readily. For many people, merely recognizing that they have implicitly accepted such irrational and self-defeating beliefs is sufficient to produce beneficial change and increased resistance to stress.
5. *Learn to react differently.* When faced with stressful events, people often protect themselves from a rising tide of anxiety by adopting actions that are incompatible with such feelings. For example, instead of allowing our speech to become increasingly rapid and intense as we become upset, we can consciously modulate this aspect of our behavior. A reduction in arousal and tension may result. People who practice this skill report great success.
6. *Take a time-out.* When confronted with rising tension, people may find it useful to consciously choose to insert a brief period of delay known as time-out. This can involve taking a short break, going to the nearest restroom to splash cold water on one's face, or any other action that yields a few moments of breathing space. Such actions interrupt the cycle of ever-rising tension that accompanies

stress, and can help to restore equilibrium and the feeling of being at least partly in control of ongoing events.

7. *Enroll in a stress-management program.* A growing number of companies have introduced programs known as stress-management programs that are designed to help employees reduce and/or prevent stress. Typically, these involve systematically training employees in many of the techniques mentioned earlier (e.g., meditation, relaxation, life-style management) as well as others.

REDUCING STRESS THROUGH TIME MANAGEMENT

One especially useful strategy for coping with job-related stress is effective time management. An inability to manage time can result in overcommitment, a lack of planning, and missed deadlines. Strictly speaking, one does not manage time as such, in that time moves at its own rate and is not subject to any effort to manipulate it. In truth, effective time management is really effective self-management. Time-management specialists have developed a number of useful techniques for gaining control over one's work life and, thereby, one's sanity. Today's organizations must encourage all of their employees to improve their time management by using the following techniques.

Time Log

The first step in trying to manage one's time is to develop a time log or inventory. By jotting down the events that occur in a typical day with the time required for each activity, it is possible to learn where one's time is being spent. The results of a time log (which might be reviewed at the end of a week) can offer surprising insights. For example, some executives are amazed to find that a large percentage of each day is devoted to dealing with interruptions and pointless socializing. The results of such an inventory can help pinpoint sources of time wastage and thus help focus attention on using time more effectively.

Structuring Time

One can gain greater control over one's life by structuring the day so that time wasters are blocked or eliminated. For example, not being accessible by phone or to visitors for an hour or two in the morning provides a block of uninterrupted time during which mail can be read or writing can be done. Similarly, all visits can be arranged between 1:00 and 3:00 in the afternoon. Meetings can be strategically set one-half hour or an hour before lunch or quitting time to ensure that the participants will help complete the meeting on time.

Just Say "No"

Sometimes an employee is victimized by a desire to be accommodating to everyone. In such instances, others learn that their requests are seldom refused by such an employee and may take advantage of his or her good nature. For such individuals, an important step in gaining control of their lives is to learn how to say no to requests for their time and energy. Refusing the requests of others requires some delicacy, and should be done politely, but firmly. For people who are already heavily committed to their primary job duties, taking on the added responsibility of managing the office baseball team and the fund-raising drive will likely provide needless stress.

Make a List

One of the most useful techniques for managing time is to prepare a list of "things to do." Interviews with highly effective managers reveal that they invariably maintain a planning list of activities that aids their memories and focuses their attention and energy. A planning list contains such items as phone calls that must be returned, correspondence that must be prepared, meetings that need to be scheduled, and projects that must be monitored. In addition, the items in the list should be prioritized. The most critical items are labeled "Category A," while the next most critical items are labeled "Category B," and so on. Then, category A items are handled first, category B items are tackled if time permits, and lower-category items are put off until even later. In maintaining a "to-do" list, it is important to keep the list current, to never give in to the temptation to clean up the "small" or "easy" items first, and to scrutinize the list for items that can be reasonably delegated to subordinates.

ORGANIZATION/MANAGEMENT APPROACHES FOR COPING WITH STRESS AND BURNOUT

Organizations and their managers can reduce stress caused by the work environment in a number of ways: team meetings, using proper management techniques, establishing an effective communication system, and above all, reducing uncertainty among employees, employee assistance programs and wellness programs.

Team meetings. Talking over problems helps individuals feel better about their coworkers. This can reduce the stress they have about their ability or inability to solve problems. Team meetings allow employees to get together and discuss problems.

If employees are feeling a tremendous amount of stress, team meetings can be an effective way to reduce it. Some organizations use encounter groups to reduce stress. The members reduce strong feelings and emotions by telling others why they are upset. A professional group facilitator should lead the encounter so that people do not become too upset with what occurs.

Another approach is the deep-sensing session, in which organizational leaders meet with employees and communicate face-to-face. This approach should not be just a gripe session, but a situation where problems associated with miscommunication can be cleared up. Usually with this approach a special outside consultant must be brought in to guide and direct the meeting. The consultant can direct misunderstandings without evoking too much defensive behavior.

Good management can reduce stress. Proper management does a great deal to reduce employee stress. For example, a manager can reduce stress related to time or overwork by allowing employees enough time to plan, organize, and complete the tasks they must do.

Rest breaks during the working day can also help reduce stress. Some organizations call these rest breaks "minivacations." All people need some time during the day to sit down, to daydream, to fantasize, and to deal with feelings.

Teaching people how to cope with stress is important to management. Employees can be taught to cope with difficulties and reduce their own tensions. Managers should help employees upgrade their life goals. Working toward strong, positive life goals can help people overcome small stressful circumstances much more quickly and effectively. The organization must help employees establish life goals.

Productive communication. Effective communication within the organization and among employees is an important tool for reducing employee stress. When employees do not receive information, they wonder why, and they tend to become worried and suspicious. An effective communication system fosters openness and feedback at all levels and for all people in the organization.

One approach to increasing effective communication is to talk about the achievements of employees and to let word get out that people are doing well and that they are appreciated. This builds high employee expectations, self-esteem, and self-confidence—and reduces stress.

Also, make certain that people understand what they have been asked to do. Managers should continually ask for feedback so that they know what is happening.

Employee Assistance Programs (EAPs)

Originally conceived as alcohol abuse programs, most current EAPs are designed to deal with a wide range of stress-related problems, both work and nonwork related, including behavioral and emotional difficulties, substance abuse, family and marital discord, and other personal problems. EAPs tend to be based on the traditional medical approach to treatment. General program elements include:

- *Diagnosis.* Employee with a problem asks for help; EAP staff attempts to diagnose the problem.
- *Treatment.* Counseling or supportive therapy is provided. If in-house EAP staff are unable to help, employee may be referred to appropriate community-based professionals.
- *Screening.* Periodic examination of employees in highly stressful jobs is provided to detect early indications of problems.
- *Prevention.* Education and persuasion are used to convince employees at high risk that something must be done to assist them in effectively coping with stress.

EAPs may be internal company-run programs or external efforts in which the organization contracts with a private firm to provide services to company employees. Typical programs are concerned with prevention, treatment, and referral of employees.

Crucial to the success of any EAP is trust. Employees must trust that (1) the program can and will provide real help, (2) confidentiality will be maintained, and (3) use of the program carries no negative implications for job security or future advancement. If employees do not trust the program or company management, they will not participate. EAPs with no customers cannot have a positive effect on stress prevention and management.

Wellness Programs

Wellness programs, sometimes called Health Promotion Programs, focus on the employee's overall physical and mental health. Simply stated, any activity an organization engages in that is designed to identify and assist in preventing or correcting specific health problems, health hazards, or negative health habits can be thought of as wellness-related. Among the most prevalent examples of such programs are those emphasizing hypertension identification and control, smoking cessation, physical fitness and exercise, nutrition and diet control, and job and personal stress management.

Wellness programs are important to stress management for several reasons. First, stress prevention and management is a vital part of wellness, and, as we have already noted, it is frequently a component of wellness programs. Second, many of the concerns of wellness programs are at least partially stress related. Stress has been cited as the greatest cause of poor health habits (Randolfi, 1996), and poor health habits are what wellness programs attempt to change. Third, a major reason organizations are interested in stress management is that it contributes to healthier, more productive, and more effective employees, and consequently to healthier, more productive, and more effective organizations. Corporate wellness programs simply extend these payoffs. Fourth, it is impossible to divorce the topic of stress from health. In a sense, wellness programs represent a broad-based contemporary extension of stress programs; their focus is concern for employee health and quality-of-life issues.

Simply offering an EAP or wellness program does not guarantee positive results for either employers or the sponsoring organization. While many factors determine how successful any particular program will be, a number of recommendations, if followed, will increase the likelihood of achieving beneficial outcomes. Among the more important are:

1. Top management support, including both philosophical support and support in terms of staff and facilities, is necessary.
2. Unions should support the program and participate in it where appropriate. This can be particularly difficult to accomplish. Many unions take the position that instead of helping employees deal with stress, management should focus on eliminating those conditions that contribute to the stress in the first place.
3. The greatest payoff from stress prevention and management comes not from one-shot activities, but from ongoing and sustained effort; thus, long-term commitment is essential.
4. Extensive and continuing employee involvement would include involvement not only in the initial planning but in implementation and maintenance as well. This is one of the most critical factors for ensuring representative employee participation.
5. Clearly stated objectives lay a solid foundation for the program. Programs with no or poorly defined objectives are not likely to be effective or to achieve sufficient participation to make them worthwhile.
6. Employees must be able to participate freely, without either pressure or stigma.
7. Confidentiality must be strictly adhered to. Employees must have no concerns that participation will in any way affect their standing in the organization.

STRESS IN ORGANIZATIONS: INTERNATIONAL IMPLICATIONS

With the increase in globalization, an organization's international activities raise issues of stress for its employees in a number of areas: (1) taking business trips to other countries, (2) relocation to another country for an extended period of time, (3) working in an organization within another country, and (4) returning home from an overseas assignment. Each commonly adds to stress (Adler, 1997).

Taking business trips to another country exposes an individual to several potential stressors. Crossing time zones, adjusting sleep patterns, entering a different culture, and learning how to move about in that culture can all add to stress. People will vary, of course, in their stress response. If they perceive travel as a source of stress, they are likely to have a distress reaction and feel apprehensive. Other people may have a eustress reaction and view the experience as a challenge. Both people will have a stress response, but with different results.

A stronger and more lasting source of stress is relocation to another country for an extended time. The expatriate enters the new culture and experiences the culture shock common to traveling to any new country. The culture shock is intensified by staying longer, moving an entire family, staying in living quarters other than a hotel, and possibly having servants who do household chores. The ways and mores of a new culture cascade upon the expatriate and his family. Different rules of behavior, new relationships, and a different language all must be mastered quickly if the expatriate is to function effectively in the new environment. The immense pressure of information acts as a form of role overload and exposes the expatriate to many stressors.

Because the expatriate's family often also moves, the family unit meets new nonwork stressors early. Family members severed ties with friends and relatives back home. Spouses are left alone for extended periods as the expatriates immerse themselves in mastering the new demands of their jobs. Children must adapt to new schools and new environments. School-age children are gone during the day, leaving a spouse to master relationships with servants and to shop in unfamiliar stores. The entire family often sees big differences in its quality of life and in its social and physical environment. All these together are nonwork stressors surrounding the expatriate and his family.

The culture-shock stressors can be particularly grueling for spouses of expatriates, especially wives. Women foreigners often cannot work for pay in the host country. They may have many free daytime hours, during which they try to build relationships with servants, learn how to shop, interact with members of the local population who may be unaccustomed to foreigners, and face long periods of loneliness and boredom. If a wife left a job or a career behind to join her husband, she has lost something that gave meaning to her life. These factors are significant stressors for an expatriate's wife and can add to stress in their marriage.

After expatriates have adapted to behavioral differences in a new country, they may face a new challenge when they return to their home country to continue their career in a domestic operation of the same company. Returning to one's homeland presents the repatriate with its own set of stressors.

Repatriates often assume that nothing will have changed while they were gone. Yet, during the repatriate's time overseas, the repartiate has changed, as have family members, relatives, friends, and coworkers in the home country. While living abroad, expatriates often recall only positive features of their home culture. Returning to their home country can cause as much culture shock as entering a foreign country. Many stressors are the same. The ways and mores of the home country are different from those of the country just left and may be different from what the employee remembers. Any negative features forgotten while gone will have a particularly shocking effect.

STRESS IN ORGANIZATIONS: ETHICAL ISSUES

Many states in the United States allow work-based stress claims under worker compensation laws, raising the specter of high social and economic costs of work-based stress. The following are some ethical issues that could be raised about stress in work organizations (Grover, 1991; Harrison, 1978).

1. Organizational leaders often decide to change a work environment. The change may involve technology, organizational design, or the physical aspects of the organization. Such changes can adversely affect the person–environment fit for some, but not all employees. Do organizational leaders and managers have an ethical duty to reduce potential stress by preparing their employees for changes? Do they have an ethical duty to refrain from making changes that might be good for the organization but would cause high stress for employees?
2. An employee's work environment can present many stressors. The Occupational Safety and Health Administration (OSHA) has set standards for many stressors, including radiation, noxious fumes, and unsafe working conditions. It is unethical for leaders and managers to knowingly expose employees to such hazards to reduce operating costs.
3. An organization's selection and placement policies can affect the quality of the person–environment fit. The likelihood of a good fit can be improved if both the potential recruit and the organization have accurate information about each other. Is it unethical for an individual to knowingly distort information about himself to improve his prospects of receiving an offer of employment?
4. When harmful stress appears to result from a present poor person–environment fit, is the organization required to provide career counseling or to help the person find a better-fitting job within or outside the organization?
5. Knowledge about work and nonwork stressors can help a manager understand the total stress effects on an employee. How much should an individual reveal about his nonwork world to an organization? Should managers concern themselves with nonwork stressors when judging the total stressor exposure of an employee? To what extent is it unethical to ask about an employee's nonwork life?

SUMMARY

Although not always bad for the person, stress is still one of the most important and serious problems facing those responsible for managing organizational behavior. We need eustress—or positive stress—to help us develop personally and professionally. However, distress, or negative stress, can be dysfunctional. Stress is natural but can be our worst enemy when it leads to emotional and physical ills.

Technostress is a new type of stress that is seen as a direct result of advances in technology. Like other causes of stress, such as the job itself, responses to technostress are likely to vary from individual to individual. Type A individuals and pessimists are more prone to stress than Type B individuals and optimists.

There are a number of individual and organizational consequences of stress. Some of the consequences of stress are burnout, various health and performance effects, and aggression and violence.

Stress prevention and management strategies include individual and organizational efforts. Individual strategies include developing more coping skills, seeking social support, and other approaches like exercise, relaxation, time management, and so on. Organizational programs such as employee assistance and wellness programs are also targeted toward employees who may already be experiencing stress.

Stressors can arise from international activities of today's organizations. Business trips to other countries, relocation to another country for an extended time, working in an organization within another country, and returning home are areas in particular that contribute to stress.

Many ethical issues surround stress in organizations. The ethical issues often depend on the amount of knowledge individuals have about sources of stress in their work environments.

REFERENCES

Adler, N. 1997. *International dimensions of organizational behavior*. Cincinnati, OH: South-Western College Publishing.

Bresler, S.J., and Thacker, R. 1992. Four-point plan helps solve harassment problems. *HRMagazine* (May): 117–124.

Callahan, R.E., and Fleenor, P.C. 1987. There are ways to overcome resistance to computers. *Office* (October): 78–80.

Dempcy, M.H., and Tihista, R. 1996. *Dear job stressed*. Palo Alto, CA: Davies-Black Publishing.

Dutton, G. 1998. Cutting-edge stress busters. *HRFocus* (September): 11.

Grover, R. 1991. Say, does workers' comp cover wretched excess? *Business Week* (July 22): 23.

Harrison, R.V. 1978. Person–environment fit and job stress. In C.L. Cooper and R. Payne (eds.), *Stress at work*. Chichester, England: John Wiley & Sons, Ltd., pp. 175–205.

Heavy overtime. 2000. *The Wall Street Journal* (March 29): A1.

Leana, C.R., Feldman, D.C., and Tan, G.Y. 1998. Predictors of coping behavior after a layoff. *Journal of Organizational Behavior* 19: 85–97.

Margolis, B.L., Kroes, W.M., and Quinn, R.P. 1974. Job stress: An unlisted occupational hazard. *Journal of Occupational Medicine* 16: 659–661.

Nelson, D.L., and Burke, R.L. 2000. Women executives: Health, stress and success. *Academy of Management Executive* 14(2): 107–121.

O'Leary-Kelly, A.M., Paetzold, R.J., and Griffin, R.W. 1995. Sexual harassment as aggressive action: A framework for understanding sexual harassment. Paper presented at the annual meeting of the Academy of Management, Vancouver (August).

Randolfi, E.A. 1996. Stressed out about stress management program evaluation? Presented at Outcome of Preventive Health Programs Conference (Atlanta, GA), December 12.

Selye, H. 1974. *Stress without distress*. New York: The New American Library.

Selye, H. 1976. *The stress of life*. New York: McGraw-Hill.

Smith, L. 1994. Stamina: Who has it, why you need it, how to get it. *Fortune* (November 28): 127–139.

Stress: Can we cope? 1983. *Time* (June 6): 48.

Vecchio, R.P. 2000. *Organizational behavior*. 4th ed. Fort Worth, TX: Dryden Press.

Chapter 6

Communicating Successfully

INTRODUCTION

Few topics have commanded more time, research, and attention than communication in the entire field of organization behavior, but it is seldom clearly understood. Despite the time and effort devoted to communication, most organizational behavior experts would agree that it still remains one of the most crucial problems facing today's organizations.

In practice, effective communication is a basic prerequisite for the attainment of organizational strategies and managing behavior, but it has remained one of the biggest problems facing modern management. Ineffective communication is detrimental for organizations; it can lead to poor performance, strained interpersonal relations, and high levels of stress. Employees at all levels need to be good communicators in order for an organization to be effective in the twenty-first century.

Communication is not an easy word or process to define, nor is it an easy skill to master. However, it is an integral part of every field of endeavor. Each functional area of an organization depends on communication. Although such independent functions as marketing, production, finance, HRM receive direction from corporate goals and objectives, communication provides the necessary collective linkage that permits harmony between the functions and ultimately, results in success. In effect, the right hand must know what the left hand is doing.

Effective communication (and techniques) are essential in every job, and the importance of effective communication for today's organizations can't be overemphasized for one specific reason: Everything the organization does involves communicating. Not some things, but everything! Employees can't make a decision without information, and that information has to be communicated. Once a decision is made, communication must again take place. Otherwise, no one will know you've made a decision. The best idea, the most creative suggestion, or the finest plan cannot take form without communication. Leaders at all levels of the organization work with their direct reports, peers, immediate managers, people in other departments, vendors, customers, and others to get their own department or team's objectives accomplished; and the interaction with these various individuals all require communication of some type. The successful manager, therefore, needs effective communication skills. We are not suggesting, of course, that good communication skills alone make a successful manager. We can say, however, that ineffective communication skills can lead to a continuous stream of problems for today's supervisors, managers, and other leaders.

There seems to be little doubt that communication plays an important role in organizational effectiveness. Yet, on the other side of the same coin, ineffective communication is commonly cited as being at the root of practically all the problems in the world. It is given as the explanation for ethic prejudice, war between nations, the generation gap, lovers' quarrels, industrial disputes, and organizational conflict. These examples are only representative of the numerous problems attributed to ineffective communication. Obviously, this thinking can go too far: communication difficulties are the result of communication breakdown. Other matters discussed in this book—motivation, decision making, stress, organization structure, to name but a few—can also contribute to problems. Yet it is also true that the communication process is a central problem in most human and organizational activities.

In this chapter, we first take a look at the background of the role of communication in management and organizational behavior. This discussion is followed by offering a definition of communication, the communication process, and the role of perception in communication. Next we emphasize individual differences in communication and communication media and information richness. We then focus on the impact of technology on communication and communication networks. Before concluding the chapter with a look at linguistic styles, we describe communication skills for successfully managing organizational behavior.

THE EARLY ROLE OF COMMUNICATION IN MANAGEMENT THEORY

The earliest discussions of management gave very little attention to communication. Although communication was implicit in the managerial function of command and the structural principle of hierarchy, early management theorists never fully developed or integrated it into their theories of management. At the same time, they did generally recognize the role of informal communication in relation to the problem of supplementing the formal, hierarchical channels. But the pioneering work of theorist Charles Barnard (1938), in his classic *The Functions of the Executive*, was the first to develop the idea of the central, important role communication plays in the organization.

The Contribution of Chester Barnard

For Barnard, communication was the major shaping force in the organization. He ranked it with common purpose and willingness to serve as one of the three primary elements of the organization. To Barnard, communication both makes the organization's cooperative system dynamic and links the organization's purpose to the human participants. Communication techniques, which he considered to be written and oral language, were deemed not only necessary to attain organizational purpose but also a potential problem area for the organization. Barnard noted: "The absence of a suitable technique of communication would eliminate the possibility of adopting some purposes as a basis of organization. Communication technique shapes the form and the internal economy of the organization" (p. 90).

Barnard also interwove communication into his concept of authority. He emphasized that meaning and understanding must occur before authority can be communicated from manager to subordinate. He listed seven specific communication factors that are especially important in establishing and maintaining objective authority in an organization. He believed them, in brief, to be the following:

1. The channels of communication should be definitely known.
2. There should be a definite formal channel of communication to every member of an organization.
3. The line of communication should be direct and short as possible.
4. The complete formal line of communication should normally be used.
5. The persons serving as communication centers should be competent.
6. The line of communication should not be interrupted while the organization is functioning.
7. Every communication should be authenticated.

Contemporary Perspective

Since the early contributions by Barnard, the dynamics of communication have been one of the central concerns, if not the central concern, of management and organizational behavior theorists. Communication has been given more and more attention in management and organizational behavior textbooks. In addition, there has been a deluge of articles and books that deal specifically with interpersonal and organizational communication. A result of many of these efforts is an increased emphasis on and appreciation of how managers and others communicate on a day-to-day basis. Such a specific focus forces organizations and others to pay attention to the important role communication plays in every interaction within the organizations, interactions that when successfully managed contribute to individual, group, and organizational effectiveness and success.

WHAT IS COMMUNICATION?

The term communication is freely used by everyone in modern society, including members of the general public, organizational behavior scholars, and management practitioners. Despite its widespread usage, very few members of the general public—and not a great many more management people—can precisely define the term. Part of the problem is that communication experts have not agreed on a definition themselves.

For our purposes, communication is the sharing of information between two or more individuals or groups to reach a common understanding. The most important part of this definition is that for communication to be successful the meaning of the information or ideas conveyed must be understood. What does this definition mean in practice? First, the information shared with others must be complete. One must make sure a common understanding is reached by providing an appropriate level of information, meeting face-to-face with others, and giving them the opportunity to ask questions. Organizational members (i.e., supervisors and other managers or leaders), who are able to communicate with their employees so that a common understanding is reached, are more effective than those who do not take steps to ensure a common understanding. In fact, good communication is essential for an organization to be successful.

An important point to understand before we move on is: Good communication is often erroneously defined by the communicator as "agreement" instead of "clarity of understanding." If someone disagrees with us, many of us assume the person just didn't fully understand our position. In other words, many of us define good communication as having someone accept our views. But a person can understand very clearly what you mean and not agree with what you say. In fact, when a manager concludes that a lack of communication must exist because a conflict between two employees has continued for a prolonged time, a closer examination often reveals that there is plenty of effective communication going on. Each fully understands the other's position. The problem is one of equating effective communication with agreement.

Management Functions and the Importance of Good Communication

The success of managers depends on the effective, efficient practice of the management functions. Today's managers must be adept at and knowledgeable in all four functions: planning, organizing, leading, and controlling. The initial function of the management process involves the development of an effective plan, which serves as a guideline in achieving workflow objectives. If plans are not properly communicated, the sequence of the management process is seriously jeopardized. Consequently, the manager will be unable to adequately organize, lead, and control. However, when open lines of effective communication exist, the functions are "linked" in sequence and action.

Good communication increases the chances for organizational success by linking the management functions toward achievement of goals like increased efficiency, quality, responsiveness to customers, and innovation. In order for today's organizations to be successful, managers must strive to increase efficiency, quality, responsiveness to customers, and innovation. Good communication is essential for obtaining each of these four goals and thus is a necessity for organizational success.

Production managers, for instance, can increase efficiency by updating the production process to take advantage of new and more efficient technologies and by training members of the production unit to use the new technologies and expand their skills. Good communication is necessary for production managers to learn about new technologies, implement them in their particular units, and train team members in how to use them. Similarly, improving quality hinges on effective communication. Today's managers need to communicate to all members of their unit the meaning and importance of high quality and the routes to attaining it. Employees need to communicate quality problems and suggestions for increasing quality to their superiors, and members of self-managed teams need to share their ideas for improving quality (and efficiency) with each other.

Good communication can also help to increase responsiveness to customers. When the organizational members who are closest to customers are empowered to communicate customers' needs and desires to managers, managers are better able to respond to these needs. Managers, in turn, must communicate with other organizational members to determine how best to respond to changing customer preferences.

Innovation, which often takes place in cross-functional teams, also requires effective communications. Members of a cross-functional team developing a new kind of compact disc player, for example, must effectively communicate with each other to develop a disc player that customers will want, that will be of high quality, and that will be efficient to produce.

Members of the team also must communicate with managers to secure the resources they need to develop the disc player and keep them informed of progress on the project.

Effective communication is necessary for managers and all members of an organization to increase efficiency, quality, responsiveness to customers, and innovation and thus enhance success for the organization. Managers, therefore, must have a good understanding of the communication process if they are to perform effectively.

THE COMMUNICATION PROCESS

The communication process consists of two phases. In the transmission phase, information is shared between two or more individuals or groups. In the feedback phase, a common understanding is assured. In both phases, a number of distinct stages must occur for communication to take place.

Starting the transmission phase, the sender, the person or group wishing to share information with some other person or group, decides on the message, what information to communicate. Then the sender translates the message into symbols or language, a process called *encoding*. We encode information when we select the words we use to send an e-mail message or when we speak to someone in person.

Once encoded, a message is transmitted through a medium to the *receiver*, the person or group for which the message is intended. A medium or communication channel is simply the pathway through which an encoded message is transmitted to a receiver. There are many different pathways over which information travels, including telephone lines, radio and television signals, fiber-optic cables, mail routes, and even the airwaves that carry the vibrations of our voices. Thanks to modern technology, people sending messages have a wide variety of communication channels available to them for sending both visual and oral information. Whatever medium or channel is used, the communicator's goal is the same: to send the encoded message accurately to a desired receiver.

At the next stage, the receiver interprets and tries to make sense of the message, a process called *decoding*. This is a critical point in communication. Decoding can involve many different processes, such as comprehending spoke and written words, interpreting facial expressions, and the like. To the extent that a sender's message is accurately decoded by the receiver, the ideas understood will be the ones intended.

As you might imagine, our ability to comprehend and interpret information received from others is far from perfect. This would be the case, for example, if we were conducting business in a foreign country and lacked the language skills needed to understand the speaker. However, even when it comes to understanding one's own native language it's only too easy to imagine how we sometimes misunderstand what others intend to tell us.

The feedback phase is initiated by the receiver (who becomes a sender). The receiver decides what message to send to the original sender (who becomes a receiver), encodes it, and transmits it through a chosen medium. The message might contain a confirmation that the original message was received and understood or a restatement of the original message to make sure that it has been correctly interpreted; or it might include a request for more information. The original sender decodes the message and makes sure that a common understanding has been reached. If the original sender determines that a common understanding has not been reached, the whole process is cycled through again as many times as are needed to reach a common understanding. This cyclical nature of the communication process is an ongoing, continuous process. Feedback eliminates misunderstandings, ensures that messages are correctly interpreted, and enables senders and receivers to reach a common understanding.

Despite its apparent simplicity, it probably comes as no surprise that the communication process rarely operates as flawlessly as we have described it. As we will see, there are many potential barriers to effective communication. *Noise* is a general term that refers to anything that hampers any stage of the communication process. Whether noise results from unclear writing (i.e., poorly encoded messages), a listener's inattentiveness (i.e., poorly decoded messages), or static along a telephone line (i.e., faulty communication media), ineffective communication is inevitably the result.

Nonverbal Communication

The encoding of messages into words, written or spoken, is verbal communication We also encode messages without using written or spoken language. Nonverbal communication shares information by means of facial expressions (smiling, raising an eyebrow, frowning, dropping one's jaw), body language (posture, gestures, nods and shrugs), and even style of dress (casual, formal, conservative, trendy). When Mercedes Benz built a $300-million plant in Central Alabama, the German supervisors and middle managers agreed to wear T-shirts with their first names on them rather than suits (which is the trend in German companies) to communicate or signal that the company was interested in creating an atmosphere of cooperation and collegiality. The trend toward increasing empowerment of the workforce also led supervisors to dress informally to communicate that all employees of the organization are team members, working together to create value for customers.

Physical elements, such as buildings, office furniture, and space can also convey messages. For example, a large office with expensive draperies, plush carpeting, and elegant furniture reminds people that they are in the CEO's office, while a small metal desk located on the plant floor or in the customer service work area communicates the organizational rank of a manager. Office arrangements convey status, power, and prestige. Several forms of nonverbal communication are presented below:

- *Dress*: Communicating values and expectations through clothing and other dimensions of physical appearance.
- *Paralinguistics*: A form of language in which meaning is conveyed through variations in speech qualities, such as loudness, pitch, rate, and number of hesitations.
- *Kinetics*: The use of gestures, facial expressions, eye movements, and body postures in communicating emotions.
- *Haptics*: The use of touch in communicating, as in a handshake, a pat on the back, or an arm around the shoulder.
- *Chronemics*: Communicating status through the use of time; for example, making people wait or allowing some people to go ahead of others.
- *Iconics*: The use of physical objects or office designs to communicate status such as the display of trophies or diplomas.

Employees need to pay close attention to nonverbal behaviors when communicating. They must learn to coordinate their verbal messages with their nonverbal behavior and to be sensitive to what their employees, managers, and peers are saying nonverbally. It is easy to underestimate the impact that nonverbal communication has on the perception of others. These messages can have powerful effects and can undermine verbal or written messages with which they disagree. A manager must consider the total message and all media of communication. A message can be given meaning only in a context, and cues or signals are easy to misinterpret. Table 6.1 presents common nonverbal behaviors exhibited by managers and how employees may interpret them.

A word of caution is that nonverbal communication, like body language, does not have universal meaning. By reading others' nonverbal communication, you can often find out their feelings and attitudes toward the communication and toward you as an individual or manager. Individuals must be open to changing their communication style if they can read that it is interpreted to be negative by others, or if others tell them it is. To really improve one's interpersonal or people skills, an individual can read others' verbal and nonverbal communication, understand their preferred means of communicating, and use it when communicating with them. If anyone is interested in working at it they can improve their ability to give and interpret nonverbal communication.

Table 6.1
Common Nonverbal Cues from Manager to Employee

Nonverbal Communication	Signal Received	Reaction from Behavior
Manager looks away when talking to the employee.	Divided attention.	My manager is too busy to listen to my problem or simply does not care.
Manager fails to acknowledge greeting from fellow employee.	Unfriendliness.	The person is unapproachable.
Manager glares ominously (i.e., gives the evil eye).	Anger.	Reciprocal anger, fear, or avoidance, depending on who is sending the signal in the organization.
Manager rolls the eyes.	Not taking person seriously.	This person thinks he or she is smarter or better than I am.
Manager sighs deeply.	Disgust or displeasure.	My opinions do not count. I must be stupid or boring this person.
Manager uses heavy breathing (sometimes accompanied by hand waving).	Anger or heavy stress.	Avoid this person at all costs.
Manager does not maintain eye contact when communicating.	Suspicion or uncertainty.	What does this person have to hide?
Manager crosses arms and leans away.	Apathy and closed-mindedness.	This person already has made up his or her mind; my opinions are not important.
Manager peers over glasses.	Skepticism or distrust.	He or she does not believe what I am saying.
Manager continues to read a report when employee is speaking.	Lack of interest.	My opinions are not important enough to get the manager's undivided attention.

THE ROLE OF PERCEPTION IN COMMUNICATION

As noted in Chapter 2, perception is the process through which people select, organize, and interpret sensory input to give meaning and order to the world around them. Perception is inherently subjective and influenced by people's personalities, values, attitudes, and moods, as well as by their experience and knowledge. When senders and receivers communicate with each other, they are doing so based on their own subjective perceptions.

Perception plays a central role in communication and affects both transmission and feedback. For example, a manager might perceive that her employees would understand her message about the restructuring of her department if she communicated it in a short memo; however, this inaccurate perception about her employees might contribute to her ineffective communication. Similarly, the subjective perceptions of the manager's employees could also lead them to erroneously interpret the message in the memo as an announcement of another round of layoffs. As this example illustrates, the encoding and decoding of messages and even the choice of a medium hinges on the perceptions of senders and receivers.

In addition, as discussed in Chapter 2, perceptual biases can hamper effective communication. *Biases* are systematic tendencies to use information about others in ways that result in inaccurate perceptions. There are a number of biases that can result in diverse members of an organization being treated unfairly. These same biases also can lead to ineffective communication. For example, stereotypes, simplified and often inaccurate beliefs about the characteristics of particular groups of people, can interfere with the encoding and decoding of messages. Suppose a manager stereotypes older workers as being fearful of change. When this manager encodes a message to an older worker about an upcoming change in the organization, the individual may downplay the extent of the change so as not to make the older worker feel stressed. The older worker, however, fears change no more than his younger colleagues fear it and decodes the message to mean that hardly any changes are going to be made. The older worker fails to adequately prepare for the change and his performance subsequently suffers because of his lack of preparation for the change. Clearly, the ineffective communication was due to the manager's inaccurate assumptions about older workers. Instead of relying on stereotypes, effective managers strive to perceive other people accurately by focusing on their actual behaviors, knowledge, skills, and abilities. Accurate perceptions, in turn, contribute to effective communication.

INDIVIDUAL DIFFERENCES IN COMMUNICATION

As you know from experience, different people tend to communicate in different ways. Two people saying the same thing might do so very differently and communicate their messages in ways that may have different effects on you. In other words, there seem to be individual differences in the way people communicate. Researchers have verified that such differences are indeed real.

Personal Communication Style

Larry and Pam are two managers who are approached by a direct report, Ed, to discuss the possibility of receiving a salary increase. They both think that Ed is not deserving of the raise he requests. However, Larry and Pam each go about communicating their feelings quite differently. Pam couldn't have been more direct. "I'll be frank," she said, "a raise is out of the question." Larry's approach was far more analytical: "Well, Ed, let's look at the big picture. I see here in your file that we just gave you a raise two months ago, and that you're not scheduled for another salary review for four months. Let me share with you some of the numbers and thoroughly explain why the company will have to stick with that schedule."

Although the message was the same in both cases, Larry and Pam presented it quite differently. In other words, they appear to differ with respect to their personal communication style—the consistent ways people go about communicating with others—particularly depending on the other person involved and the situation they are in. Communication style is learned, and so it can change. But before we can consider changing how we communicate, we must first recognize the style we use. With this in mind, Linda McCallister (1994) has identified six major communication styles, one of which is likely to describe most people.

The Noble. Such individuals tend not to filter what they are thinking but come right out and say what's on their minds. Nobles use few words to get their messages across. They cut right to the bottom line.

The Socratic. These are people who believe in carefully discussing things before making decisions. Socratics enjoy the process of arguing their points and are not afraid to engage in long-winded discussions. They have a penchant for details and often "talk in footnotes."

The Reflective. These individuals are concerned with the interpersonal aspects of communication. They do not wish to offend others, and they are great listeners. Reflectives would sooner say nothing, or tell you what you want to hear (even if it's a "little white lie"), than say something that might cause conflict.

The Magistrate. A Magistrate is a person whose style is a mix of part Noble and part Socratic. Magistrates tell you exactly what they think and make their cases in great detail. These individuals tend to have an air of superiority about them, as they tend to dominate the discussion.

The Candidate. Such individuals have a style that is a mix between Socratics and Reflectives. As such, they tend to be warm and supportive, while also being analytical and chatty. They base their interactions on a great deal of information, and do so in a very likable manner.

The Senator. A Senator is an individual who has developed both the Noble style and the Reflective style. They do not mix the two styles. Rather, they move back and forth between the two of them as needed.

It is important to keep in mind that we all have the potential to use any of these styles. However, we generally tend to rely on one more than any other. Each has its strengths and weaknesses, and no one style is better than another. They are simply different. Effective communication begins with understanding your own style and that used by others. Then, when you first meet another it is advisable to attempt to match that person's style. This is because people generally expect others to communicate in the same manner as themselves. However, the better we get to know and accept another's communication style, the better we come to accept how it blends with our own. In either case, the advice is the same. Recognizing and responding to communication styles can enhance the extent to which people are able to communicate effectively with one another.

The Dangers of Ineffective Communication

Because managers must communicate with others to perform the management functions, managers spend most of their time communicating, whether in meetings, in telephone conversations, through e-mail, or in face-to-face interactions. Indeed, some experts estimate that managers spend approximately 85 percent of their time engaged in some form of communication (Adams, Todd, and Nelson, 1993).

So important is effective communication that managers cannot just be concerned that they themselves are effective communicators; they also have to help their employees be effective communicators. When all members of a team, department or organization are able to communicate effectively with each other and with people outside the team, department, or organization, they are much more likely to perform highly and be successful.

When managers and other members of the organization are ineffective communicators, organizational performance suffers, and any success they might have is likely to be lost. Moreover, poor communication sometimes can be downright dangerous and even lead to tragic and unnecessary loss of human life. For example, researchers from Harvard University recently studied the causes of mistakes, such as a patient receiving the wrong medication, in two large hospitals in the Boston area. They discovered that some mistakes in hospitals occur because of communication problems—physicians not having the information they need to correctly order medications for their patients, or nurses not having the information they need to correctly administer medications. The researchers concluded that some of the responsibility for these mistakes lies with hospital management, which has not taken active steps to improve communication (Winslow, 1995).

Communication problems in the cockpit of airplanes and between flying crews and air traffic controllers are unfortunately all too common, sometimes with deadly consequences. In the late 1970s, two jets collided in Tenerife (one of the Canary Islands) because of miscommunication between a pilot and the control tower, and 600 people were killed. The tower radioed to the pilot, "Clipper 1736 report clear of runway." The pilot mistakenly interpreted this message to mean that he was cleared for takeoff. Unfortunately, errors like this one are not a thing of the past (Newman, 1995). A safety group at NASA tracked over 6,000 unsafe flying incidents and found that approximately 529 of them were caused by communication difficulties ("Miscommunications plague pilots and air-traffic controllers," 1995).

All managers must establish goals to improve the quality of communication, especially when they recognize causes of ineffective communication like those presented above. Better communication results in increased morale, an improved work climate, better individual-team-departmental-organizational relations, and higher productivity. It also reduces mistakes and disagreements, while enhancing accuracy and understanding.

Table 6.2 presents some suggestions and techniques that managers can use to improve the quality of communication. The techniques presented in the form of guidelines, when practiced, serve to overcome barriers and obstacles that interfere with the dynamics of the communication process.

COMMUNICATION MEDIA AND INFORMATION RICHNESS

To be effective communicators, managers (and other members of an organization) need to select an appropriate communication medium for *each* message they send. Should a change in procedures be communicated to direct reports in a memo sent through e-mail? Should a congratulatory message about a major accomplishment be communicated in a letter, in a phone call, or over lunch? Should a layoff announcement be made in a memo or at a plant or organization-wide meeting? Managers deal with these questions day in and day out.

There is no one best communication medium for managers to rely on. In choosing a communication medium for any message, managers need to consider three factors. The first and most important is the level of information richness that is needed. *Information richness* is the amount of information that a communication medium can carry and the extent to which the medium enables the sender and receiver to reach a common understanding (Daft, Lengel, and Trevino, 1987). The communication media that managers use vary in their information richness (Daft, 1992). Media high

Table 6.2
Guidelines for Effective Communication

1. Clearly demonstrate the importance of communication by recognizing the opportunity to communicate (i.e., share ideas, promote feedback, and exchange points of view).
2. Learn to listen by paying attention to all verbal and nonverbal cues.
3. Keep all messages brief and as simple as possible.
4. Be selective in choosing the words to form the message.
5. Make sure your position of authority does not interfere with your ability to communicate.
6. Make sure to allow sufficient time both to plan what you are going to say and to say it.
7. When communicating, it is important to make sure that an appropriate location is selected.
8. Take the time to understand your receiver by displaying empathy and putting yourself in the receiver's place.
9. Make sure that communication receives the full attention it deserves.
10. Follow the following three-step formula for improving communication:

    Step 1: Tell them what you are going to tell them.

    Step 2: Tell them.

    Step 3: Tell them what you told them.
11. When possible, use visual aids to clarify intended meaning. A verbal description of a new house is vastly improved by the use of plans and drawings.
12. Seek feedback. For example, after conveying a message, consider asking, "What do you think?" The question conveys a desire for feedback.
13. Build a foundation for the future by taking the position that communication is an ongoing process and is part of the organization's foundation for the future.
14. Take the lead by placing a premium on communication and others will follow.

in information richness are able to carry an excessive amount of information and generally enable receivers and senders to come to a common understanding.

The second factor that managers need to take into account in selecting a communication medium is the time needed for communication, because managers' and other organizational members' time is valuable. The third factor that affects the choice of a communication medium is the need for a paper/electronic trail or some kind of written documentation that a message was sent and received. A manager may wish to document in writing, for example, that a direct report was given a formal warning about excessive lateness or to document preventive maintenance on a compressor.

Most of a manager's communication time is spent one-on-one, face-to-face with employees. Face-to-face communication provides immediate feedback and is the richest information medium because of the channels and cues of voice, eye contact, posture, blush, and body language. It is the appropriate medium for delegating tasks, coaching, disciplining, instructing, sharing information, answering questions, checking progress toward objectives, and developing and maintaining interpersonal relations. Managers also spend one-on-one, face-to-face time communicating with their supervisors, colleagues, and peers.

Telephone or spoken communication electronically transmitted lack the element of "being there" and provide only the cue of voice inflection. The amount of time spent on the telephone varies greatly with the job. No matter how much time you spend on the phone, before making a call, set an objective and write down what you plan to discuss. Use the paper to write notes during the call. The telephone is the appropriate medium for quick exchanges of information and checking up on things. It is especially useful for saving travel time. However, it is inappropriate for personal matters like discipline.

Personally addressed written communication, while personalized, convey only the cues written on paper and are slow to provide feedback. Interpersonal written (or unaddressed) communications are the lowest in richness, are not focused on a single receiver, use limited information cues, and do not permit feedback.

Research indicates that media selection is based on the message that managers wish to communicate. For example, if the message has a great potential for misunderstanding or is ambiguous, then a rich channel with immediate feedback enables managers to exchange information and ideas rapidly until a common understanding is reached. As an example, if a CEO is attempting to develop a press release with other company officials regarding an accident that has killed and injured employees, then a rich information exchange is needed. The group will meet face-to-face to consider ideas, and provide rapid feedback to resolve disagreement and convey the correct information.

On the other hand, when the message is clear, well defined, and everyone involved has similar backgrounds and understanding about an issue, then managers prefer written memos. As an example, information regarding last month's cost figures would probably be transmitted through memos.

For many managers, meetings will be the most common communication medium used in their daily work. The brief, informal get-together with two or more employees is also a common form of meeting for frontline managers. It is appropriate for coordinating employee activities, delegating a task to a group, and resolving employee conflicts.

There are certain questions managers and other employees can ask *before* sending messages inside and outside the organization. The following questions can be useful in deciding on the most appropriate communication medium for sending a message:

1. What is the nature of the information/message being sent?
2. What medium is most appropriate for acceptance of this message?
3. What are the likely consequences if the message is transmitted through an inappropriate medium?

Other questions that managers and their direct reports can ask from an information-gathering perspective that can alert them to a range of issues regarding the effectiveness of their information and communication exchanges are:

4. What information do I need to perform and complete my work successfully? What information is routine (programmed) and what is critical (unprogrammed) to my work and to the organization's work?
5. What are the sources of the information I receive and transmit? What am I expected to do with the information I receive and process?
6. Where am I in the configuration and structure of information flow? Whom do I get information from? Whom do I give it to?
7. How fast and in what form must the information be interpreted and transmitted? Does the organization structure and technology help or hinder this process?
8. What actions and results are expected of me relative to the information I receive and transmit? What effect does the information I handle have on the final product or service of the organization?

Answers to these questions provide a wide range of clues regarding the effectiveness or inadequacy of the organization's structure, the employee's roles and responsibilities, available technologies, and the quality and forms of communication used to get the work done.

THE IMPACT OF TECHNOLOGY ON COMMUNICATION

Exciting advances in information technology have dramatically increased managers' abilities to communicate with others as well as to quickly access information to make decisions. In order for today's managers to be successful they need to keep up-to-date on advances in information technology.

Computers, microchips, and digitalization are dramatically increasing a manager's communication options. Today, managers can rely on a number of sophisticated electronic media to carry their communications. These include electronic mail (e-mail), voice mail, electronic paging, cellular telephones, mode-based transmissions, video conferencing, and other forms of network-related communications.

Managers are increasingly using many of these technological advances. E-mail and voice mail allow people to transmit messages 24 hours a day. When managers are away from the office, others can leave messages for them to review on their return. For important and complex communications, a permanent record of e-mail messages can be obtained by merely printing out a hard copy. Cellular phones are dramatically changing the role of the telephone as a communication device. In the past, telephone numbers were attached to physical locations. Now, with cellular technology, the phone number attaches to mobile phones. Managers can be in constant contact with their direct reports, other managers, and key members in the organization, regardless of where they are physically located. Network-related communications also allow the manager to monitor the work of employees whose jobs are done on computers in remote locations (for example, telecommuters and maintenance workers who work in remote locations), to participate in electronic meetings, and to communicate with suppliers and customers or interorganizational members.

In order for today's managers to be successful they need to keep up-to-date on other advances in information technology such as *groupware* (i.e., computer software that enables members of groups and teams to share information with each other), *intranets* (i.e., a company-wide system of computer networks), and the *Internet* (i.e., a global system of computer networks). But managers should not adopt these or other advances without first considering carefully how the advance in question might improve communication and performance in their particular groups, teams, departments, or whole organization.

Technological advances in communications have disrupted old ways of managing in organizations. Formerly closed bureaucracies and command and control systems are being pressured to open up. It is important for managers and their direct reports to keep focused on the aim of all communication: coordination action that achieves a team, department, or organization's goals and mission.

UNDERSTANDING COMMUNICATION NETWORKS

Although various communication media are used, communication in organizations tends to flow in certain patterns. The pathways along which information flows in groups and teams and throughout an organization are called communication networks. The type of communication network that exists in a group depends on the nature of the group's tasks and the extent to which group members need to communicate with each other in order to achieve group goals.

Communication Networks in Groups and Teams

Groups or teams, whether they are cross-functional teams, top-management teams, command groups, self-managed work teams, or task forces, are the building blocks of organizations. Four kinds of communication networks that can develop in work groups and teams are the wheel, the chain, the circle, and the all-channel network.

Wheel network. In a wheel network, information flows to and from one central member of the group. Other group members do not need to communicate with each other to perform highly, and the group can accomplish its goals by directing all communication to and from the central member. Wheel networks are often found in command groups with pooled task interdependence. Picture a group of taxi cab drivers who report to the same dispatcher, who is also their supervisor. Each driver needs to communicate with the dispatcher, but the drivers do not need to communicate with each other. In groups such as this, the wheel network results in efficient communication, saving time without compromising performance. Though found in groups, wheel networks are not found in teams because they do not allow for the intense interactions characteristic of teamwork.

Chain network. In a chain network, members communicate with each other in a predetermined sequence. Chain networks are found in groups with sequential task interdependence, such as in assembly-line groups. When group work has to be performed in a predetermined order, the chain network is often found because group members need to communicate with those whose work directly precedes and follows their own. Like wheel networks, chain networks tend not to exist in teams because of the limited amount of interaction among group members.

Circle network. In a circle network, group members communicate with others who are similar to them in experiences, beliefs, areas of expertise, background, office location, or even where they sit when the group meets. Members of task forces and standing committees, for example, tend to communicate with others who have similar experiences or backgrounds. People also tend to communicate with people whose offices are next to their own. Like wheel and chain networks, circle networks are most often found in groups that are not teams.

All-channel network. An all-channel network is found in teams. It is characterized by high levels of communication: every team member communicates with every other team member. Top-management teams, cross-functional teams, and self-managed teams frequently have all-channel networks. The reciprocal task interdependence often found in such teams requires information flows in all directions. Computer software specially designed for use by work groups can help maintain effective communication in teams with all-channel networks because it provides team members with an efficient way to share information with each other.

Organizational Communication Networks

Consider the following two situations: (1) The CEO of a large organization announces plans for new products to a group of stockholders. (2) One day in the lunchroom two administrative assistants share the latest stories about someone who has been terminated. Although both examples are typical of the kind of communication that occurs in organizations, they differ in a very important way. Specifically, the first example describes a situation in which someone is sharing official information with others who need to know this information. This is referred to as formal communication. The second situation, however, involves the sharing of unofficial information about what's going on in the organization. This is referred to as informal communication. As you might imagine, both formal and informal communication occurs commonly in organizations.

An organization chart may seem to be a good summary of an organization's communication network, but often it is not. An organization chart summarizes formal reporting relationships in an organization, and the formal pathways along which communication takes place. Often, however, communication is informal and flows around issues, goals, projects, and ideas instead of moving up and down the organizational hierarchy in an orderly fashion. Thus, an organization's communication network includes not only the formal communication pathways summarized in an organizational chart but also informal communication pathways along which a great deal of communication takes place.

Communication can and should occur across departments, groups, and teams as well as within them and up and down and sideways in the organizational hierarchy. Communication up and down the organizational hierarchy is often called vertical communication and communications among employees at the same level in the hierarchy or sideways is called horizontal communication. Thus, organizations include three channels (downward, upward, and horizontal) through which "official" messages move from senders to receivers.

Formal Communication Channels: Downward, Upward, and Horizontal Communication

Managers obviously cannot determine in advance what an organization's communication network will be, nor should they try to. Instead, to accomplish goals and perform at a high level, organizational members should be free to communicate with whomever they need to contact. Because organizational goals change over time, so too do organizational communication networks. Informal communication networks can contribute to an organization's or department's success because they help ensure that organizational members have the information they need when they need it to accomplish their goals.

Downward communication. Typically, downward communication consists of instructions, directions, and orders—that is, messages telling direct reports what they should be doing. We would also expect to find feedback on past performance flowing in a downward decision. A sales manager, for example, may tell the members of his sales force what products they should be promoting.

As formal information slowly trickles down from one level of an organization to the next lowest level (as occurs when information is said to "go through channels"), it becomes less accurate. This is especially true when that information is spoken. In such cases, it is not unusual for at least part of the message to be distorted and/or omitted as it works its way down from one person to the next lowest ranking person. To avoid these problems, many organizations have introduced programs in which they communicate formal information to large numbers of people at different levels all at one time.

Upward communication. When information flows from lower levels to higher levels within an organization, such as messages from direct reports to their supervisors, it is known as upward communication. Typically, such messages involve information that managers need to do their jobs, such as data required to complete projects. This may include suggestions for improvement, status reports, reactions to work-related issues, and new ideas.

Although upward communication is the logical opposite of downward communication, there are some important differences between them. These come about because of the differences in status between the communicating parties. For example, it has been established that upward communication occurs far less frequently than downward communication. And, when people do communicate upward, their conversations tend to be far shorter than the ones they have with others at their own level.

Even more important, when upward communication does occur, the information transmitted is frequently inaccurate. Given that employees are interested in "putting their best foot forward" when communicating with their bosses, they have a tendency to highlight their accomplishments and to downplay their mistakes. As a result, negative information tends to be ignored or disguised. This tendency for people to purposely avoid communicating bad news to their supervisors is known as the *MUM effect*. We need to be concerned about this phenomenon because supervisors can only make good decisions when they have good information available to them. And, when direct reports are either withholding or distorting information so as to avoid looking bad, the accuracy of the information communicated is bound to suffer.

Horizontal communication. Within organizations, messages don't only flow up and down the organization chart but sideways as well. Horizontal communication is the term used to identify messages that flow laterally, at the same organizational level. Messages of this type are characterized by efforts at coordination, attempting to work together.

Unlike vertical communication, in which the parties are at different organizational levels, horizontal communication involves people at the same level. Therefore, it tends to be easier and friendlier. It also is more casual in tone and occurs more readily given that there are fewer social barriers between the parties. This is not to say that horizontal communication is without its potential pitfalls. Indeed, people in different departments sometimes feel that they are competing against each other for valued organizational resources, leading them to show resentment toward one another. And when an antagonistic, competitive orientation replaces a friendly, cooperative one, work is bound to suffer.

Informal Channels of Communication

Informal communications grow out of the social interactions among people who work together. Informal relationships are complex and change rapidly. A major function of informal channels is to provide communication routes for members of small groups. Every successful organization has at least one healthy, if invisible, channel to conduct the messages of its informal organization. This mysterious entity is the real heart of the organization—the means of coordinating people's energies to solve problems and get things accomplished.

Occasionally, communication channels may be structured to appear informal when in truth they are not. The so-called informal contacts that supervisors and managers are sometimes required to maintain with direct reports are an example. When supervisors and managers are ordered to associate with workers socially, a true informal channel seldom emerges, and communications remain formal and perhaps even stilted. An organizational leader's success often depends on the degree to which he or she accepts and uses the existing informal channels.

The grapevine. The grapevine is a universal method of transmitting messages of unofficial means. One informal organizational communication network along which information flows quickly if not always accurately is the grapevine. The grapevine is an informal network along which unofficial information flows. Every organization has its grapevine. This is a perfectly natural activity since it fulfills the employees' desires to know the latest information and to socialize with other people. The grapevine offers members of an organization an outlet for their imaginations and an opportunity to express their apprehensions in the form of rumors.

Rumors. Rumors are unofficial pieces of information of interest to organizational members but with no identifiable source. Rumors spread quickly once they are started and usually concern topics that organizational members think are important, interesting, or amusing. Rumors, however, can be misleading and can cause harm to individual employees and their organizations when they are false, malicious, or unfounded.

An amazing amount of information may be transmitted through the grapevine. Employees often know about major decisions before managers have been officially notified. The grapevine carries various types of information, including which employees might be looking for other jobs, compensation paid to individual employees, and information concerning sexual harassment or a union's organizing efforts. The grapevine is also likely to convey information about your leadership style, the quality of your decisions, and your integrity as a manager.

Information passed through the grapevine often gets exaggerated as it travels from employee to employee. This is particularly true for organizations that fail to distribute information openly. Given the absence of open and honest information from management, employees try to fill the vacuum by providing bits of information to each other, even if these are based on speculation rather than facts.

The pervasiveness of the grapevine has two major implications for managers. As a manager, recognize that your organization has a grapevine and use it to your advantage. If you gain the trust of employees, they will share with you the information they hear on the grapevine. With access to this information, you can then correct or further explain, as appropriate. The grapevine can also help you learn about the basic attitudes and thoughts of employees and whether they regard the company in a positive or negative light. This is useful for you to know because attitude affects employee motivation to perform.

Think of the grapevine as one means of taking the pulse of your organization. If you can monitor it, you will be able to identify problem areas and assertively counteract inaccurate rumors before they adversely affect employee morale and performance. Also, if you develop trusting relationship with your employees, they will speak positively about you to others, making it easier to get everyone working together to achieve organizational goals.

The best prescription to dealing with rumors is to state the facts openly and honestly. If the manager does not have all the necessary information available, the individual should frankly admit this and then try to find out what the situation actually is. One of the best ways to stop a rumor is to expose its untruthfulness. The manager should bear in mind that the receptiveness of a group of employees to rumors is directly related to the quality of the manager's communications and leadership. If employees believe that their supervisor is concerned about them and will make every effort to keep them informed, they will tend to disregard rumors and look to the manager for proper answers to their questions.

There is no way to eliminate the grapevine, even with the best efforts made through all formal channels of communication. The manager, therefore, should listen to the grapevine and develop skills in dealing with it. For example, an alert manager might know that certain events will cause undue anxiety. In this case, the manager should explain immediately why such events will take place. When emergencies occur, changes introduced, and policies modified, the manager should explain why and answer all employee questions as openly as possible. Otherwise, employees will make up their own explanations and often these will be incorrect. There are situations, however, when the manager does not have the facts either. Here the manager should seek out the appropriate higher-level manager to explain what is bothering the employees and to ask for specific instructions as to what information may be given, how much may be told, and when. Also, when something happens that might cause rumors, it is helpful for managers to meet with their most influential employees to give them the real story. Then the employees can spread the facts before anyone else can spread the rumors.

Managers should be extremely careful not to criticize everything communicated through the grapevine because doing so can damage their credibility. This is especially true if the information communicated or even a portion of it is accurate. The following suggestions for dealing with the grapevine and rumors should also be followed:

1. The grapevine should be viewed as a permanent part of the formal organization structure and should be used to improve communication within the organization.
2. Managers should know what information the grapevine is communicating and why that information is being communicated.
3. Managers should seek and provide accurate information so that the messages communicated through the grapevine are correct.
4. False information in the grapevine should be corrected by the manager by calling a meeting of employees and providing the accurate information.

COMMUNICATION SKILLS FOR SUCCESSFULLY MANAGING ORGANIZATIONAL BEHAVIOR

Just how important is communication in the manager's daily life? If you are a typical manager (or employee), you are constantly faced with communication challenges. These challenges may include interacting with others, transacting business on the telephone, inputting and accessing messages via the computer, and breaking down barriers to promote understanding. Communication is a vital link in achieving personal and career success. Without good communication today's manager cannot expect to build successful relationships.

This section discusses communication skills for managers today. More specifically, this section will discuss various kinds of barriers to effective communication in organizations (i.e., some have their origin in senders and receivers) and what managers can do to overcome these barriers.

Managers as Senders

There are various kinds of barriers to effective communication in organizations. Some have their origins in senders. When messages are unclear, incomplete, or difficult to understand, when they are sent over an inappropriate medium, or when no provision for feedback is made, communication suffers. Other communication barriers have their origins in receivers. When receivers pay no attention to or do not listen to a message or when they make no effort to understand the meaning of a message, communication is likely to be ineffective.

To overcome these barriers and effectively communicate with others, managers (as well as other organization members) must possess or develop certain communication skills. Some of these skills are particularly important when managers send messages; others are critical when managers receive messages. These skills help ensure that managers will be able to share information, will have the information they need to make good decisions and take action, and will be able to reach a common understanding with others.

Organizational effectiveness depends on managers (as well as other organizational members) being able to effectively send messages to people both inside and outside an organization. The following are some of the communication skills that help ensure that when managers send messages, they are properly understood and the transmission phase of the communication process is effective. Let's see what each skill entails.

Send clear and complete messages. Managers need to learn how to send a message that is clear and complete. A message is clear when it is easy for the receiver to understand and interpret, and it is complete when it contains all the information that the sender and receiver need to reach a common understanding. In striving to send messages that are both clear and complete, managers must learn to anticipate how receivers will interpret messages and adjust messages to eliminate sources of misunderstanding or confusion.

Encode messages in symbols the receiver understands. Manages need to appreciate that when they encode messages, they should use symbols or language that the receiver understands. When sending messages in English to receivers whose native language is not English, for example, it is important to use commonplace vocabulary and to avoid using clichés that, when translated, may make little sense and sometimes are either comical or insulting.

Jargon—specialized language that members of an occupation, group, or organization develop to facilitate communication among themselves—should never be used when communicating with people outside the occupation, group, or organization. For example, truck drivers refer to senior-citizen drivers as "double-knits," compact cars as "roller skates," highway dividing lines as "paints," double or triple freight trailers as "pups," and orange barrels around road construction areas as "Schneider eggs." Using this jargon among themselves results in effective communication because they know precisely what is being referred to. But if a truck driver used this language to send a message to a receiver who did not drive trucks (such as "That roller skate can't stay off the paint"), the receiver would be without a clue about what the message meant.

Select a medium appropriate for the message. As you have learned, when relying on verbal communication, managers can choose from a variety of communication media, including face-to-face communication, written letters, memos, newsletters, phone conversations, e-mail, voice mail, faxes, and video conferences. When choosing among these media, managers need to take into account the level of information richness required, time constraints, and the need for a paper/electronic trail. A primary concern in choosing an appropriate medium is the nature of the message. Is it personal, important, nonroutine and likely to be misunderstood and in need of further clarification? If it is, face-to-face communication is likely to be in order.

Select a medium that the receiver monitors. Another factor that managers need to take into account when selecting a communication medium is whether the medium is one that the receiver monitors. Managers differ in the communication media they pay attention to. Many managers simply select the communication medium that they themselves use the most and are most comfortable with, but doing this can often lead to ineffective communication. Managers who dislike telephone conversations and too many face-to-face interactions may prefer to use e-mail, send many e-mail messages per day, and check their own e-mail every few hours. Managers who prefer to communicate with people in person or over the telephone may have e-mail addresses but rarely use them and forget to check for messages. No matter how much a manager likes e-mail, sending messages to an individual who does not check his or her e-mail is futile. Learning which managers like things in writing and which prefer face-to-face interactions and then using the appropriate medium enhances the chance that receivers will actually receive and pay attention to messages.

A related consideration is whether receivers have disabilities that hamper their ability to decode certain kinds of messages. A blind receiver, for example, will not be able to read a written message. Managers should ensure that their employees with disabilities have resources available to communicate effectively with others.

Avoid filtering and information distortion. Filtering occurs when senders withhold part of a message because they (mistakenly) think that the receiver does not need the information or will not want to receive it. For example, managers should avoid mistakenly filtering the information they give their direct reports.

Filtering can occur at all levels in an organization and in both vertical and horizontal communication. For example, many operating employees may filter messages they send to managers, managers may filter messages to middle managers, and middle managers may filter messages to top managers. Such filtering is most likely to take place when messages contain bad news or problems that direct reports are afraid they will be blamed for.

Information distortion occurs when the meaning of a message changes as the message passes through a series of senders and receivers. Some information distortion is accidental due to faulty encoding and decoding or to a lack of feedback. Other information distortion is deliberate. Senders may alter a message to make themselves or their groups look good and to receive special treatment.

Managers themselves should avoid filtering and distorting information. But how can they eliminate these barriers to effective communication throughout their team or organization? Direct reports who trust their managers believe that they will not be blamed for things beyond their control and will be treated fairly. Managers who trust their direct reports provide them with clear and complete information and do not hold things back.

Include a feedback mechanism in messages. Because feedback is essential for effective communication, managers should build a feedback mechanism into the messages they send. They either should include a request for feedback or indicate when and how they will follow up on the message to make sure that it was received and understood. When managers write letters and memos or send faxes, they can request that the receiver respond with comments and suggestions in a letter, memo, or fax; schedule a meeting to discuss the issue; or follow up with a phone call. By building feedback mechanisms such as these into their messages, managers insure that they get heard and are understood.

Managers as Receivers

Managers receive as many messages as they send. Thus, managers must possess or develop communication skills that allow them to be effective receivers of messages. Three of these important skills are: pay attention, be a good listener, and be empathetic. These are examined in greater detail below.

Pay attention. Because of their multiple roles and tasks, managers often are overloaded and forced to think about several things at once. Torn in many different directions, they sometimes do not pay sufficient attention to the messages they receive. To be effective, however, managers should always pay attention to messages they receive, no matter how busy they are. When discussing a project with a direct report, an effective manager focuses on the project and not on an upcoming meeting with his or her own boss. Similarly, when managers are reading written forms of communication, they should focus their attention on understanding what they are reading; they should not be sidetracked into thinking about other issues.

Be a good listener. Managers (and all other members of an organization) can do several things to be good listeners. First, managers should refrain from interrupting senders in the middle of a message so that senders do not lose their train of thought and managers do not jump to erroneous conclusions based on incomplete information. Second, managers should maintain good eye contact with senders so that senders feel their listeners are paying attention; doing this also helps managers focus on what they are hearing. Third, after receiving a message, managers should ask questions to clarify points of ambiguity or confusion. Fourth, managers should paraphrase, or restate in their own words, points senders make that are important, complex, or open to alternative interpretations; this is the feedback component so critical to successful communication.

Managers, like most people, often like to hear themselves talk rather than listen to others. Part of being a good communicator, however, is being a good listener, an essential communication skill for managers as receivers of messages transmitted face-to-face and over the telephone. Table 6.3 lists a number of keys to effective listening.

Be empathetic. Receivers are empathetic when they try to understand how the sender feels and try to interpret a message from the sender's perspective, rather than viewing a message from only their own point of view. Consider the following example: Serena Martinez, the chief psychologist in a university counseling center in the Midwest, recently learned this lesson after interacting with a new psychologist on her staff. The new psychologist, Karla Graham, was distraught after meeting with the parent of a student she had been working with extensively. The parent was difficult to talk to and argumentative and was not supportive of her own child. Graham told Martinez how upset she was, and Martinez responded by reminding Graham that she was a professional and that dealing with such a situation was part of her job. This feedback upset Graham further and caused her to storm out of the room.

In hindsight, Martinez realized that her response had been inappropriate. She had failed to empathize with Graham who had spent so much time with the student in question and was deeply concerned about the student's well-being. Rather than dismissing Graham's concerns, Martinez realized, she should have tried to understand how Graham felt and given her some support and advice for dealing positively with the situation.

Table 6.3
The Keys to Effective Listening

Keys to Effective Listening	The Bad Listener	The Good Listener
1. Capitalize on thought speed	Tends to daydream mentally	Stays with the speaker, summarizes the speaker, weighs evidence, and listens between the lines
2. Listen for ideas	Listens to facts	Listens for central or overall ideas
3. Find an area of interest	Tunes out dry speakers or subjects	Listens for any useful information
4. Judge content, not delivery	Tunes out dry or monotone speakers	Assesses content by listening to entire message before making judgments
5. Hold your fire	Gets too emotional or worked up by something said by the speaker and enters into an argument	Withholds judgment until comprehension is complete
6. Work at listening	Does not expend energy on listening	Gives the speaker full attention
7. Resist distractions	Is easily distracted	Fights distractions and concentrates on the speaker
8. Hear what is said	Shuts out or denies unfavorable information	Listens to both favorable and unfavorable information
9. Challenge yourself	Resists listening to presentations of difficult subject matter	Treats complex presentations as exercise for the mind
10. Use handouts, overheads, or other visual aids	Does not take notes or pay attention to visual aids	Takes notes as required and uses aids to enhance understanding of the presentation

Source: Derived from Manning, Curtis, and McMillan (1996), pp. 125–154; Slizewski (1995), p. 7.

UNDERSTANDING LINGUISTIC STYLES

Consider the following scenarios:

A manager from New Jersey is having a conversation with a manager from Des Moines, Iowa. The Des Moines manager never seems to get a chance to talk. He keeps waiting for a pause to signal his turn to talk, but the New Jersey manager never pauses long enough. The New Jersey manager wonders why the Des Moines manager does not say much. He feels uncomfortable when he pauses and the Des Moines manager says nothing, so he starts talking again.

Sally compliments Aaron on his presentation to upper management and asks Aaron what he thought of her presentation. Aaron launches into a lengthy critique of Sally's presentation and describes how he would have handled it differently. This is hardly the response Sally expected.

Sieya shares with fellow members of a self-managed work team a new way to cut costs. Malik, another team member, thinks her idea is a good one and encourages the rest of the team to support it. Sieya is quietly pleased by Malik's support. The group implements Malik's suggestion, and it is written up as such in the company newsletter.

Terrence was recently promoted and transferred from his company's Nebraska office to its headquarters in New York. Terrence is perplexed because he never seems to get a chance to talk in management meetings; someone else always seems to get the floor. Terrence's new boss wonders whether Terrence's new responsibilities are too much for him, although Terrence's supervisor in Nebraska rated him highly and said he is a real "go-getter." Terrence is timid in management meetings and rarely says a word.

Linguistic Styles

What do these scenarios have in common? Essentially, they all describe situations in which a misunderstanding of linguistic styles leads to a breakdown in communication. The scenarios are based on the work of linguist Deborah Tannen (1990), who describes *linguistic style* as a person's characteristic way of speaking. Elements of linguistic style include tone of voice, speed, volume, use of pauses, directness or indirectness, choice of words, credit-taking, and use of questions, jokes, and other manners of speech. When people's linguistic styles differ and these differences are not understood, ineffective communication is likely.

The first and last scenarios illustrate regional differences in linguistic style. The Des Moines manager and Terrence from Nebraska expect the pauses that signal turn-taking in conversations to be longer than the pauses made by their colleagues in New Jersey and New York. This difference causes communication problems. The Iowan and transplanted Nebraskan think that their Eastern colleagues never let them get a word in edgewise, and the Easterners cannot figure out why their colleagues from the Midwest and Southwest do not get more actively involved in conversations.

Differences in linguistic style can be a particularly insidious source of communication problems because linguistic style is often taken for granted. People rarely think about their own linguistic styles and often are unaware of how linguistic styles can differ. In the example above, Terrence never realized that when dealing with his New York colleagues, he could and should jump into conversations more quickly than he used to do in Nebraska, and his boss never realized that he felt that he was not being given a chance to speak in meetings.

The aspect of linguistic style just described, length of pauses, differs by region in the United States. Much more dramatic communication differences occur cross-culturally.

Cross-Cultural Differences

It's important to recognize that communication isn't conducted in the same way around the world. For example, compare countries that place a high value on individualism (such as the United States) with countries where the emphasis is on collectivism (such as Japan) (Larkey, 1996; Lindahl, 1996).

Owing to the emphasis on the individual in countries such as the United States, communication patterns are individual-oriented and rather clearly spelled out. For instance, U.S. managers rely heavily on memoranda, announcements, position papers, and other formal forms of communication to stake out their positions in the organization. They also often hoard secret information in an attempt to promote their own advancement and as a way of inducing their employees to accept decisions and plans. For their own protection, lower-level employees also engage in this practice.

In collectivist countries such as Japan, there is more interaction for its own sake and a more informal manner of interpersonal contact. The Japanese manager, in contrast to U.S. managers, will engage in extensive verbal consultation over an issue first and will draw up a formal document later only to outline the agreement that was made. Face-to-face communication is encouraged. Additionally, open communication is an inherent part of the Japanese work setting. Work spaces are open and crowded with individuals at different levels in the work hierarchy. In contrast, U.S. organizations emphasize authority, hierarchy, and formal lines of communication.

Today's managers must make themselves familiar with cross-cultural communication differences. Before managers communicate with people from abroad, they should try to find out as much as they can about the aspects of communication that are specific to the country or culture in question.

SUMMARY

Good communication is necessary for successfully managing organization behavior. To be successful, communicators must understand that communication occurs in a cyclical process that entails two phases, transmission and feedback.

Communication by organizations and all of their employees is impacted by information richness (i.e., the amount of information a communication medium can carry and the extent to which the medium enables the sender and receiver to reach a common understanding) and advances in technology, like the Internet, intranets, and groupware software continue to allow managers and their organizations to improve communication, performance, and customer service.

Communication networks are the pathways along which information flows in an organization. Four communication networks found in groups and teams are the wheel, the chain, the circle, and the all-channel network.

There are also various barriers to effective communication in organizations. To overcome these barriers and effectively communicate with others, managers must possess or develop communication skills as senders and receivers of messages. For example, managers should send messages that are clear and complete, encode messages in symbols the receiver understands, choose a medium appropriate for the message and monitored by the receiver, avoid filtering and information distortion, include a feedback mechanism in the message, provide accurate information to ensure that misleading rumors are not spread, pay attention, be a good listener, and be empathetic. Understanding linguistic styles is also an essential communication skill for managers.

REFERENCES

Adams, D.A., Todd, P.A., and Nelson, R.R. 1993. A comparative evaluation of the impact of electronic and voice mail on organizational communication. *Information & Management* 24: 9–21.

Barnard, C.I. 1938. *The functions of the executive*. Cambridge, MA: Harvard University Press.

Daft, R.L. 1992. *Organization theory and design*. St. Paul, MN: West.

Daft, R.L., Lengel, R.H., and Trevino, L.K. 1987. Message equivocality, media selection, and manager performance: Implications for information systems. *MIS Quarterly* 11: 355–366.

Larkey, L.K. 1996. Toward a theory of communicative interactions in culturally diverse workgroups. *Academy of Management Review* (June): 463–491.

Lindahl, R.V. 1996. Automation breaks the language barrier. *HRMagazine* (March): 79–82.

Manning, G., Curtis, K., and McMillan, S. 1996. *Building the human side of work community*. Cincinnati, OH: Thomson Executive Press.

McCallister, L. 1994. *I wish I'd said that! How to talk your way out of trouble and into success*. New York: Wiley.

Miscommunications plague pilots and air-traffic controllers. 1995. *Wall Street Journal* (August 25): A1.

Newman, G. 1995. Global chatter. *Wall Street Journal* (March 22): A1.
Slizewski, P. 1995. Tips for active listening. *HRFocus* (May): 7.
Tannen, D. 1990. *You just don't understand: Women and men in conversation.* New York: Ballantine Books.
Winslow, R. 1995. Hospital's weak systems hurt patients, study says. *Wall Street Journal* (July 5): B1, B6.

Chapter 7

Groups and Teamwork

INTRODUCTION

Groups and teams are critical to organizational success. And such success means that managers must increasingly get things done with and through others. The job is simply too big to do alone.

Let us begin by defining the term group as a prelude to examining types of groups, functions of group members, and group formation and development. The discussion then focuses on group structure and its consequences. The latter part of the chapter then describes the nature and types of teams, and compares low-performing and high-performing teams. We conclude the chapter with a look at building high-performing teams.

WHAT IS A GROUP?

Groups and teams are inescapable features of modern life. We all serve on various types of groups be they at work, school, or in our community. Modern managers need a solid understanding of groups and group processes so as to both avoid their pitfalls and tap their vast potential. Moreover, the huge and growing presence of the Internet—with its own unique network of informal and formal social relationships—is a major challenge for profit-minded business managers.

We use the word "group" rather casually in everyday discourse—special-interest groups, ethnic groups, and others. Although other definitions of groups exist, define a group as two or more freely interacting individuals who share collective norms and goals and have a common identity.

Interaction is the most basic aspect of a group—it suggests who is in the group and who is not. The interaction of group members need not be face-to-face, and it need not be verbal. For example, employees who "telecommute" can be part of their work group at the office even though they live miles away and communicate with a modem. Also, the impromptu group that forms to pass water buckets to fight a fire need not speak to meet the requirement of interaction. Interdependence simply means that group members rely to some degree on each other to accomplish goals. Ten individuals who independently throw buckets of water on a fire do not constitute a true group. Finally, all groups have one or more goals that their members seek to achieve. These goals can range from having fun to marketing a new product or achieving world peace.

Group memberships are important for two reasons. First, groups exert a tremendous influence on us. They are social mechanisms by which we acquire many beliefs, values, attitudes, and behaviors. Group membership is also important because groups provide a context in which we are able to exert influence on others.

Formal and Informal Groups

Individuals join groups, or are assigned to groups, to accomplish various purposes. Formal groups are groups that organizations establish to facilitate the achievement of organizational goals. They are intentionally designed to channel individual effort in an appropriate direction. Formal groups typically wear such labels as work group, team, committee, quality circle, or task force.

The most common formal group consists of a superior and direct reports who report to that superior. In a manufacturing company, one such group might consist of a production manager and the six shift supervisors who report to her. In turn, the shift supervisors head work groups composed of themselves and their respective direct reports. Thus, the hierarchy of most organizations is a series of formal interlocked work groups.

Task forces are temporary groups that meet to achieve particular goals or to solve particular problems, such as suggesting productivity improvements. Committees are usually permanent groups that handle recurrent assignments outside the usual work group structures. For example, an organization might have a standing committee on equal employment opportunity.

It was safe to say that early writers about management and organizations felt that their work was done when they had described an organization's formal groups. After all, such groups had management's seal of approval and could be illustrated in black and white on an organizational chart. What more was there to say about grouping? In fact, you probably recognize how incomplete this view is. In addition to formal groups sanctioned by management to achieve organizational goals, informal grouping occurs

Table 7.1
Organizational and Individual Functions Fulfilled by Formal Groups

Organizational Functions	**Individual Functions**
• Accomplish complex, interdependent tasks that are beyond the capabilities of individuals. • Generate new or creative ideas and solutions. • Coordinate interdepartmental efforts. • Provide a problem-solving mechanism for complex problems requiring varied information and assessment. • Implement complex decisions. • Socialize and train newcomers.	• Satisfy the individual's need for affiliation. • Develop, enhance, and confirm the individual's self-esteem and sense of identity. • Give individuals an opportunity to test and share their perceptions of social reality. • Reduce the individual's anxieties and feelings of insecurity and powerlessness. • Provide a problem-solving mechanism for personal and interpersonal problems.

in all organizations. An informal group emerges naturally in response to the common interests of organizational members. They seldom are sanctioned by the organization, and their membership cuts across formal groups. Informal groups can either help or hurt an organization, depending on their norms for behavior.

Functions of Formal Groups

Over the years, researchers have suggested that formal groups fulfill two basic functions: organizational and individual. The various functions are listed in Table 7.1 (Schein, 1980). Complex combinations of these functions can be found in formal groups at any given time. For example, consider what Mazda's new American employees expected when they spent a month working in Japan before the opening of the firm's Flat Rock, Michigan, plant:

> After a month of training in Mazda's factory methods, whipping their new Japanese buddies at softball and sampling local watering holes, the Americans were fired up. . . . [A maintenance manager] even faintly praised the Japanese practice of holding group calisthenics at the start of each working day: "I didn't think I'd like doing exercises every morning, but I kind of like it." (Castro, 1986, p. 65)

While Mazda pursued the organizational functions it wanted—interdependent teamwork, creativity, coordination, problem solving, and training—the American workers benefited from the individual functions of formal groups. Among those benefits were affiliation with new friends, enhanced self-esteem, exposure to the Japanese societal reality, and reduction of anxieties about working for a foreign-owned company. In short, Mazda created a workable blend of organizational and individual group functions by training its newly hired American employees in Japan.

HOW ARE GROUPS FORMED?

It is important to recognize that there are various factors that lead to group formation. In the case of informal groups, we are concerned with the factors that prompt their emergence in the formal work setting. In the case of formal groups, we are interested in factors that lead organizations to form such groups and the ease with which the groups can be maintained and managed. The formation of both types of groups is affected by opportunity for interaction, potential for goal accomplishment, and members' personal characteristics.

Opportunity for Interaction

One obvious prerequisite for group formation is opportunity for interaction. When people are able to interact with one another, they are able to recognize that they might have common goals that they can achieve through dependence on each other. For example, "inside" employees (such as headquarters' technical advisors) often develop more informal solidarity than "outside" employees (such as technicians who visit clients) because they are in more constant interaction. Similarly, organizations are adept at using open-plan offices, face-to-face meetings, and electronic networks to bolster formal work groups.

Potential for Goal Accomplishment

Potential for goal accomplishment is another factor that contributes to group formation and maintenance. Physical goals (such as building a bridge) or intellectual goals (such as designing a bridge) are often accomplished more efficiently by the careful division of labor among groups. Groups can also achieve social-emotional goals, such as self-esteem and security. Informally, strangers might band together during a natural disaster, or employees might band together to protect the firing of a coworker. Formally, organizations might use decision-making groups to spread the risk associated with a tough decision.

Members' Personal Characteristics

Finally, personal characteristics can influence group formation and maintenance. When it comes to attitudes, there is plenty of evidence that "birds of a feather flock together," that is, people with similar attitudes (such as satisfaction with their job) tend to gravitate together. When it comes to personality characteristics similar people are often attracted to each other, but opposites sometimes also attract. For example, dominant people might seek the company of submissive people. We are speaking here mainly of informal attraction and grouping. When organizations staff formal working groups, they often assign people with different but complementary skills, attitudes, or personalities to the group. A tight-fisted practical accountant might be inclined to offset an impulsive, creative marketer.

The Group Formation Process

Groups and teams in the workplace go through a maturation process, such as one would find in any life-cycle situation (e.g., humans, organizations, products). While there is general agreement among theorists that the group formation or development process occurs in identifiable stages, they disagree about the exact number, sequence, length, and nature of those stages (see Wanous, Reichers, and Malik, 1984). We will focus on two systematic models of group development that appear to be most descriptive of how all groups or teams form: the five-stage model and the punctuated-equilibrium model.

The five-stage model. Just as infants develop in certain ways during their first months of life, groups also show relatively stable signs of maturation and development (Long, 1984). The five-stage model identifies five distinct stages through which groups develop (Tuckman and Jensen, 1977). The stages are as follows:

1. *Forming.* During this stage of group development, the members get acquainted with each other. They also establish the ground rules by finding out what behaviors are acceptable regarding the job (e.g., how productive they are expected to be) and interpersonal relations (e.g., who is really in charge). During the forming stage, people tend to be a bit confused and uncertain about how to act in the group and how beneficial membership will be. Once the individuals come to think of themselves as members of a group, the forming stage is complete.
2. *Storming.* As the name implies, this stage is characterized by a high degree of conflict within the group. Members often resist the control of the group's leaders, and they show hostility toward each other. If these conflicts are not resolved and group members withdraw, the group may disband. Otherwise, as conflicts are resolved and the group's leadership is accepted, the storming stage is complete.

3. *Norming.* During this stage, the group becomes more cohesive, and identification as a member becomes greater. Close relationships develop, and shared feelings become common. A keen interest in finding mutually agreeable solutions also develops. Feelings of camaraderie and shared responsibility for the group's activities are heightened as well. The norming stage is complete when the members accept a common set of expectations constituting an acceptable way of doing things.
4. *Performing.* During this stage, questions about group relationships and leadership have been resolved—and the group is ready to work. Having fully developed, the group may now devote its energy to getting the job done. The members' good relations and acceptance of the leadership helps the group to perform well.
5. *Adjourning.* Groups may cease to exist because they have met their goals and no longer are needed (e.g., an ad hoc group created to raise money for a charity project), in which case the end is abrupt. Other groups may adjourn gradually, as the group disintegrates either because members leave or the norms no longer are effective.

The stage model is a good tool for monitoring and troubleshooting how groups are developing. However, it is very important to understand that not all groups go through these stages of development. The process applies mainly to new groups that have never met before. Well-acquainted task forces and committees can short-circuit these stages when they have a new problem to work out. Also, some organizational settings are so structured that storming and norming are unnecessary for even strangers to coalesce into a team. For example, most commercial airline cockpit crews perform effectively even though they can be made up of virtual strangers who meet just before takeoff.

Punctuated-equilibrium model. When groups have a specific deadline by which to complete some problem-solving task, we can often observe a very different development sequence from that described above. This sequence is described in the punctuated-equilibrium model of group development (Gersick, 1989). Equilibrium means stability, and the research revealed apparent stretches of group stability punctuated by a critical first meeting, a midpoint change in group activity, and a rush to task completion. This approach recognizes that members working together to meet a deadline approach their task differently in the first half of their time together than they do in the second half.

Phase 1 begins with the first meeting and continues until the midpoint in the group's existence. The very first meeting is critical to setting the agenda for what will happen in the remainder of this phase. Assumptions, approaches, and precedents that members develop in the first meeting end up dominating the first half of the group's life. Although it gathers information and holds meetings, the group makes little visible progress toward its goal.

Interestingly, once groups reach the midpoint of their lives (whether this is just a few hours or several months), something curious happens. Almost as if an alarm goes off, groups at this point experience a sort of "midlife crisis"—a time when they recognize they must change how they operate if they are going to meet their goals. This begins Phase 2 of their existence, which is a time when groups drop old ways of thinking and adopt new perspectives. Groups then carry out these missions until they reach the end of Phase 2, when they show bursts of activity needed to complete their work.

The idea is straightforward. Groups develop inertia, which keeps time going (i.e., an "equilibrium") until the midpoint, when they realize that deadlines loom. This stimulates them to confront important issues and to initiate changes, beginning (i.e., "punctuation") a new equilibrium phase. This new phase lasts until the group kicks into a final push, just before the deadline.

What advice does the punctuated equilibrium model offer managers for understanding group formation and dynamics (Gersick, 1988)?

- Prepare carefully for the first meeting. What is decided here will strongly determine what happens in the rest of Phase 1.
- As long as people are working, do not look for radical progress during Phase 1.
- Manage the midpoint transition carefully. Evaluate the strengths and weaknesses of the ideas that people generated in Phase 1. Clarify any questions with whoever is commissioning your work. Recognize that a fundamental change in approach must occur here for progress to occur. Essential issues are not likely to "work themselves out" during Phase 2.
- Be sure adequate resources are available to actually execute the Phase 2 plan.
- Resist deadline changes. These could damage the midpoint transition.

GROUP STRUCTURE AND ITS CONSEQUENCES

We are all no doubt aware that groups frequently seem to differ from one another. The differences that are most obvious might include the way members interact with one another, how members feel about the group, and how the group performs. Group structure refers to the characteristics of the stable social organization of the group, the way a group is "put together." In this section we will examine the way groups influence individuals and the way individuals influence groups.

Social Facilitation: Performing in the Presence of Others

Perhaps the most fundamental feature of groups is the presence of other people. Imagine that you have been taking piano lessons for 10 years, and you are now about to go on stage for your first major solo concert performance. You have been practicing diligently for several months, getting ready for the right night. But now, you are no longer alone in your own living room but on stage in front of hundreds of people. Your name is announced, and silence breaks the applause as you take a seat in front of the concert grand. How will you perform now that you are before an audience? Will the audience spur you on to your best performance yet? In other words, what impact will the presence of the audience have on your behavior?

After studying this question for a century, using a wide variety of tasks and situations, social scientists found that the answer to this question is not straightforward (Geen, 1989). Sometimes people were found to perform better in the presence of others than when alone, and sometimes they were found to perform better alone than in the presence of others. Results of such studies indicate that having others nearby tends to facilitate performance on relatively simple and well-rehearsed tasks. However, for fairly complex tasks, the presence of others can have a detrimental effect. The positive effect of others being present is called the social facilitation effect, while the detrimental effect is termed the social inhibition effect.

You may have noticed such effects greatly magnified if you have ever been asked to perform in front of an audience. If your assigned task was relatively simple, such as spelling your name or reciting other well-rehearsed information, you probably had little difficulty. But if you were asked to solve a problem that you had never encountered before, you probably did poorly. The reasons for these effects are twofold. First, when we expect others to evaluate us, we feel apprehensive (regardless of whether we are actually being judged). Second, the presence of others can increase arousal because of greater self-evaluation of performance. Such self-evaluation can aid performance of a simple task, but impair performance of a difficult task. The implications of this line of research are fairly direct: For tasks that are simple and repetitive, the presence of coworkers can have positive effects, while for complex and novel tasks, working in isolation is preferable.

Group Size

Group size has detectable effects on group performance. In larger groups, the potential impact and contribution of each individual are somewhat diminished, but the total resources of the group are increased. Administering a larger group also creates unique problems for managers.

Although most organizations settle on groups of five to seven persons to handle most problem-solving tasks, some organizations use much larger "spans of control" for simple tasks. Hard evidence about an ideal size for groups is sparse, yet several conclusions seem possible.

First, members appear to become more tolerant of authoritarian and directive leadership as group size increases. Apparently, group members recognize and concede the administrative difficulties that can arise in a larger work unit. In addition, as unit size increases, it becomes more difficult for a handful of direct reports to be influential, and members may feel inhibited about participating in group activities.

Second, larger groups are more likely to have formalized rules and set procedures for dealing with problems. Despite this greater formality, larger groups require more time to reach decisions than smaller groups. Additionally, subgroups are not committed to the full group's formal goals and prefer instead to pursue the more selfish interests of a few members.

Third, job satisfaction is lower in larger groups. This probably occurs because people receive less personal attention and fewer opportunities to participate. It is also likely that employees in smaller work units feel that their presence is more crucial to the group and therefore are inclined to be more involved. For blue-collar workers, absenteeism and turnover also increase in larger work units. Cohesion and communication diminish with increased group size, making a job inherently less attractive and lessening the worker's desire to attend. In white-collar jobs, on the other hand, employees may have other sources of satisfaction to draw on.

Fourth, as group size increases, productivity reaches a point of diminishing returns because of the rising difficulties of coordination and member involvement. This may be a primary reason that five-member groups are so popular. Groups of five have several advantages. The group size is not intimidating, so that a member disagreeing with the majority is less inclined to remain silent. Having an odd number of members means that a tie or split decision can be avoided when voting. Members of such a group also have less difficulty in shifting roles within the group.

Group Composition

How well a group performs a task depends in large part on the task-relevant resources of its members. The diversity versus redundancy of members' traits and abilities, then, is an important factor in explaining group performance. Groups composed of highly similar individuals who hold common beliefs and have much the same abilities are likely to view a task from a single perspective. Such solidarity can be productive, but it may also mean that members will lack a critical ingredient for unraveling certain kinds of problems. In a comparison of group versus individual problem solving, one of a group's greatest assets in comparison to individuals acting alone is the likelihood of achieving higher-quality solutions. Carrying this logic a step further, we can reasonably expect that diversified groups tend to do better on many problem-solving tasks than do homogeneous groups of highly similar individuals.

The diverse abilities and experiences of the members of a heterogeneous group offer an advantage for generating innovative solutions, provided the skills and experiences are relevant to the task. Thus, merely adding more people to a problem-solving group to broaden the pool of skills and experience will not guarantee a better job. Attention must be paid to the relevance of the members' attributes and the mix of these attributes within the group. Additionally, the more competent members of a work group must also be the most influential members. If the people who are the least informed are the most influential group members, the quality of the decision will be diminished.

Group Member Roles

Every member of a group has a differentiated set of activities to perform. The set of expected behaviors relating to an individual's position within a group is called a role. Although the term role seems familiar enough (we can each easily define the roles of school teachers, managers, and others), it can be viewed in several different ways.

A person's expected role is the formal role that is defined in a job description and the signals that other members of a work unit send as they teach newcomers how to perform their jobs. An individual's expected role, however, may differ from his or her perceived role. A perceived role is the set of activities that an individual believes he or she is expected to perform. The perceived role may or may not greatly overlap with the expected role that originates with other members of the organization. Finally, an enacted role is a person's actual conduct in his or her position. It is more likely to reflect the individual's perceived role than the expected role.

The process of how individuals receive information about their role and adjust their behavior accordingly generally begins with the standards that are held by evaluators, such as managers, supervisors, peers, and direct reports. These standards or expectations are then communicated to the individual. Because communication is often imprecise, the expected (or set) role may not be identical to the perceived (or received) role. Furthermore, due to constraints on actual behavior, the enacted role is observed by the evaluators, who then compare it to the standards they have set. This feedback then completes a single role episode. If the individual's behavior does not come sufficiently close to the standards, another role episode may be initiated.

Many things can go wrong in a role episode. Sometimes the evaluators do not send consistent signals. For example, your supervisor may assign you a task, while his or her boss, in turn, may later tell you that you should not perform that duty, perhaps because it is not your responsibility or not included in your job description. Different groups sometimes send different signals, as when a supervisor's direct reports indicate that they would like less pressure for production, while his or her superiors simultaneously insist on higher levels of output. Differing signals from evaluating groups and individuals result in role conflict. On occasion, the messages that evaluators send are not clear, or they give incomplete information, which leads to role ambiguity. Poor communication and other obstacles may interfere with the role episode process.

Although role conflict and role ambiguity seem to be undesirable, there are some indications that in modest amounts and under the right conditions, they may actually have positive effects. In fact, a work setting that is totally devoid of conflict and ambiguity can be dull and uninspiring. Thus, in order to avoid stagnation and encourage innovation, managers should perhaps seek to create a productive level of conflict and ambiguity.

Status Hierarchy

Status is the social ranking or social worth accorded an individual because of the position he or she occupies in a group. Status and position are so similar that the terms are often interchangeable. The status assigned to a particular position is typically a consequence of certain characteristics that differentiate one position from other positions. In some cases, a person is assigned status because of such factors as job seniority, age, or ability. For example, the oldest worker may be perceived as being more technically proficient and is, therefore, attributed status by a group of technicians. Thus, assigned status may have nothing to do with the formal status hierarchy.

Norms

Norms are standards shared by the membership of a group. They have certain characteristics that are important to group members. First, norms are formed only with respect to things that have significance for the group. They may be written, but they're often verbally communicated to members. In many cases, they are never formally stated but somehow are known by group members. Second, norms are accepted in various degrees by group members. Some are accepted completely, others only partially. And third, norms may apply to every group member or to only some group members.

Both formal and informal groups may have a variety of norms. For example, most groups have loyalty norms fostering the development of a strong degree of loyalty and commitment from their members. Members are expected to do certain things (e.g., work late, accept transfers, help out other members) to prove they are loyal. Other groups have formal or informal dress norms. Company sales force members may all dress similarly to present the company's desired image to customers; people working in the operations center of a bank away from customers, however, may come

Table 7.2
Examples of Positive and Negative Norms

Positive Norms	Negative Norms
1. It's tradition around here for people to stand up for the company when others criticize it unfairly.	1. In our company, they are always trying to take advantage of us.
2. In our company, people always try to improve, even when they are doing well.	2. Around here, there's no point in trying harder; nobody else does.
3. Around here, people are good listeners and actively seek out the ideas and opinions of others.	3. Around here, its dog-eat-dog and save your own skin.
4. Around here, managers and supervisors really care about the people they supervise.	4. In our company, it's best to hide your problems and avoid your supervisor.

to work in very casual clothing. Finally, groups have resource allocation norms and performance norms. Resource allocation norms of a formal organization relate to how status symbols, pay, and promotions should be allocated. Informal groups may also have allocation norms regarding such informal rewards as who works with whom or who gets helped and who does the helping. Performance norms relate to evaluating satisfactory performance. In formal groups, this may be made relatively clear by management; but performance norms may not be accepted by the informal group. In fact, informal groups may have performance norms of their own. Table 7.2 contains some examples of some positive and negative norms, as expressed in one study (Allen and Plotnick, 1973). Managers must take into account both formal and informal norms when they try to assemble high-performance groups.

Cohesiveness

Formal and informal groups seem to possess a closeness or commonness of attitude, behavior, and performance. This closeness, referred to as cohesiveness, is generally regarded as a force acting on the members to remain in a group that is greater than the forces pulling the member away from the group. Joining a group allows an individual to have a sense of belonging and feelings of morale. A cohesive group, then, involves individuals who are attracted to one another. A group that is low in cohesiveness doesn't possess interpersonal attractiveness for the members.

There are of course, numerous sources of attraction to a group. A group may be attractive to an individual because

1. The goals of the group and the members are compatible and clearly specified.
2. The group has a charismatic leader.
3. The reputation of the group indicates that the group successfully accomplishes its tasks.
4. The group is small enough to permit members to have their opinions heard and evaluated by others.
5. The members are attractive in that they support one another and help each other overcome obstacles and barriers to personal growth and development. (Cartwright and Zander, 1968)

Since highly cohesive groups consist of individuals who are motivated to be together, there's a tendency to expect effective group performance. This logic isn't supported conclusively by research evidence. In general, as the cohesiveness of a work group increases, the level of conformity or group norms also increases. But the group norms may be inconsistent with those of the organization.

Groupthink

Highly cohesive groups are important forces in organizational behavior. In other words, the organization should place people with many similarities in an isolated setting, give them a common goal, and reward them for performance. On the surface, this may look like a good idea. However, one author has provided a provocative analysis of highly cohesive groups (Janis, 1973). Janis defines groupthink as the "deterioration of mental efficiency, reality testing, and moral judgment" in the interest of group solidarity. Janis described the following characteristics associated with groupthink:

1. *Illusion of invulnerability.* Members of groups believe that they are invincible.
2. *Tendency to moralize.* Any opposition to group views is characterized by members as weak, evil, or unintelligent.
3. *Feeling of unanimity.* Each member of the group supports the leader's decisions. Members may have reservations about decisions but do not share their views. Rather than appearing weak, members keep views to themselves. This indicates how pressure toward group solidarity can distort individual members' judgments.
4. *Pressure to conform.* Formal and informal attempts are made to discourage discussion of divergent views. Groups exert great pressure on individual members to conform.
5. *Opposing ideas dismissed.* Any individual or outside group that criticizes or opposes a decision receives little or no attention from the group. Group members tend to show strong favoritism toward their own ideas in the manner by which

information is processed and evaluated, thus guaranteeing that their ideas will win out.

Certainly, some level of group cohesiveness is necessary for a group to tackle a problem. If seven individuals from seven different organizational units are assigned a task, the task may never be completed effectively. The point, however, is that when it comes to cohesiveness, more may not necessarily be better. When members of task groups may redefine solving a problem to mean reaching agreement rather than making the best decision, members of cohesive groups may redefine it to mean preserving relations among group members and preserving the image of the group. Groupthink illustrates the impact of group dynamics and cohesiveness on group performance.

THE NATURE AND TYPES OF TEAMS

So far, the chapter's discussion has focused on issues related to all types of groups. Now attention is turned to one special type of group, a team. The use of teams has become an increasingly popular work design in all types of organizations, both on a domestic and foreign basis.

How do we explain the current popularity of teams? The evidence suggests that teams typically outperform individuals when the tasks being done require multiple skills, judgment, and experience. As organizations have restructured themselves to compete effectively and efficiently, they have turned to teams as a way to better utilize employee talents. Managers and organizations have found that teams are more flexible and responsive to changing events than are traditional departments or other forms of permanent groupings. Teams have the capability to quickly assemble, deploy, refocus, and disband.

Managers should not overlook the motivational properties of teams. Consistent with the role of employee involvement as a motivator, teams facilitate employee participation in operating decisions. For instance, some assembly-line workers at John Deere are part of sales teams that call on customers. These workers know the products better than any traditional salesperson; and by traveling and speaking with farmers, these hourly workers develop new skills and become more involved in their jobs. Teams are an effective means for managers to democratize their organizations and increase employee motivation.

Teams are just like any other tool. They can be very powerful if used correctly, and they can be complete time wasters if used inappropriately. There is no doubt that teams have the potential to drastically improve performance. Yet teams alone are not enough. Strong leadership and organizational vision, mission, and goals must guide the use of teams.

To effectively guide the use of teams, managers must understand what teams are and when teams are appropriate. A team is a small number of people with complementary skills who are committed to a common purpose, set of performance goals, and approach for which they hold themselves mutually accountable.

Because of this shared accountability, teams are most appropriate when coordination of various steps, skills, or individuals is necessary. Tasks that do not require coordination are better left to individuals.

Problem-Solving Teams

Problem-solving teams are formed on a temporary basis to address a specific problem that is confronting the organization. For example, a manufacturing manager may form a team to study space and equipment requirements needed to reconfigure production space to accommodate a new product. Likewise, a marketing manager may assemble a team to evaluate the effects a competitor's new advertising campaign may have on company sales. As seen by the examples, the duration of a problem-solving team's existence is usually short in nature. For the most part, problem-solving teams are composed of individuals from the same department or area of an organization who meet together to address and solve a specific problem. Once the problem is solved, the team disbands.

Self-Managed Teams

While problem-solving teams were on the right track they did not go far enough in getting employees involved in work-related decisions and processes. This led to experimentation with truly autonomous teams that could not only solve problems but implement solutions and take full responsibility for outcomes.

Self-managed teams, otherwise known as self-directed work teams, autonomous work groups, high-commitment teams, or empowered employees, represent an entire change in organizational structure or design. The traditional hierarchy of managers, supervisors, and operating employees is replaced by a working team entirely responsible for its own operations. The team members are individually and jointly accountable for performance and results. To build this accountability, team membership is full-time, mandatory, and part of the job itself.

In this "supervisor-free," more personally rewarding environment, employees are exposed to all of the team's operations and skills. This exposure not only forces learning on the job but constantly challenges members to evaluate more productive ways to work. Importantly, today's supervisors and managers should realize that self-managed teams do not eliminate the need for all supervisory or managerial control. Self-managed teams represent a balance between management and group control.

Cross-Functional Teams

Cross-functional teams are composed of employees from different areas from about the same hierarchical level of the organization who are brought together to work on the same project. Ideally, a cross-functional team has all the expertise needed to complete even the most complex projects. The Boeing Company used cross-functional teams to develop its 777 jet.

Many organizations have used horizontal, boundary-spanning groups for years. For example, IBM created a large task force in the 1960s—made up of employees from across departments in the company—to develop the highly successful System 360. And a task force is really nothing more than a temporary cross-functional team. Similarly, committees composed of members from across departmental lines are another example of cross-functional teams.

Cross-functional teams are an effective means for allowing people from different areas within an organization (or even between organizations) to exchange information, develop new ideas and solve problems, and coordinate complex projects. Of course, cross-functional teams are no picnic to manage. It takes time to build trust and teamwork, especially among people from different backgrounds, with different experiences and perspectives.

Virtual Teams

With continuing developments in computer networking and electronic communication, information technology is bringing a new type of group into the workplace. This is the virtual team, a team whose members convene and work together electronically via networked computers. Also called "distributed work groups," these teams are a fairly recent phenomenon. In this new age of the Internet, intranets, the World Wide Web, and more, there is no doubt but that more and more virtual teams will operate in organizations of all types.

Members of virtual teams typically do the same things as members of face-to-face teams. They share information, make decisions, and complete tasks.

Although technology can help to overcome great distances in making communication possible among a group of people, it may also create teams whose members do not share much, if any, direct "personal" contact. Whereas this may have an advantage of focusing interaction and decision making on facts and objective information rather than emotional considerations, it also may increase risks as decisions are made in a limited social context. Virtual teams may suffer from less social rapport and less direct interaction among members. Finally, the high cost of supporting technology and training to bring virtual teams online can be high.

WHY SOME TEAMS FAIL

Although there are many success stories reported about teams, there are also several possible problems and difficulties in implementing them. After all, working in a team demands a great deal, and not everyone may be ready for the challenge. Fortunately, we can learn from these experiences. Analyses of failed attempts at introducing teams into the workplace suggest several obstacles to team success, and pitfalls that can be avoided if you know about them.

First, some teams fail because their members are unwilling to cooperate with each other. A second reason why some teams are not effective is that they fail to receive support from management. A third obstacle to group success, and a relatively common one, is that some managers are unwilling to relinquish control. Good managers work their way up from the plant floor by giving orders and having them followed. Finally, teams might fail not only because their members do not cooperate with each other, but also because they fail to cooperate with other teams. Without close cooperation between teams (as well as within them), organizations are not likely to reap the benefits they hoped for when creating teams in the first place.

Managers and organizations should understand that advocates of the team approach to management paint a very optimistic and bright picture. Yet there is a dark side to teams. While exact statistics are not available, they can and often do fail. If teams are to be effective, managers must make a concerted effort to understand the characteristics of low-performing and high-performing teams as discussed in the next section.

LOW-PERFORMING AND HIGH-PERFORMING TEAMS

Requiring several people to work together does not make the group a team, and certainly not a high-performing one. An underperforming or unproductive team might simply lack the sort of initiative and sense of urgency that coaches traditionally try to ignite during halftime breaks. But a lack of initiative is often just one of the problems with which teams must cope as highlighted in the symptoms of low-performing teams and the characteristics of high-performing teams.

Symptoms of Low-Performing Teams

Obviously, many problems can lead to low-performing teams. For example, all the things that contribute to a cohesive team—trust, complementary goals, and a clear mission—can determine a team's productiveness if absent. Various symptoms make it easy to recognize low-performing teams.

Cautious or guarded communication. When people fear some form of punishment, ridicule, or negative reaction, they may say nothing or be guarded in what they do say.

Lack of disagreement. Lack of disagreement among team members may reflect an unwillingness to share members' true feelings and ideas.

Use of personal criticism. Personal criticism, such as "If you can't come up with a better idea than that, you better keep quiet," is a sign of unhealthy team–member relations.

Ineffective meetings. Low-performing teams often have ineffective meetings characterized by boredom, lack of enthusiastic participation, failure to reach decisions, and dominance by one or two people.

Unclear goals. High-performing teams have a clear sense of mission, whereas members of low-performing teams are often unable to recite their own team's objectives.

Low commitment. Without a clear sense of purpose, low-performing teams tend to have low commitment, because it's not clear what they should be committed to.

Destructive conflict within the team. Low-performing teams are often characterized by a suspicious, combative environment and by conflict among team members.

Characteristics of High-Performing Teams

Of course, it is not low-performing teams that organizations want but high-performing or productive ones. Remember, a team is "a small number of people with complementary skills who are committed to a common purpose, set of performance goals, and approach for which they hold themselves mutually accountable." The characteristics of high-performing teams are implicit in this definition. Specifically, high-performing teams have five characteristics.

Commitment to a mission. The essence of a team is a common commitment. Without it, groups perform as individuals; with it, they become a powerful unit of collective performance. Teams must, therefore, have a clear mission to which to be committed, such as Saturn's "Let's beat the Japanese by producing a world-class quality car."

Specific performance goals. High-performing teams translate their common purpose (such as "build world-class quality cars") into specific performance goals (such as "reduce new-car defects to no more than four per vehicle"). In fact, transforming broad directives into specific and measurable performance goals is the surest first step for a team trying to shape a purpose meaningful to its members.

Right size, right mix. Best-performing teams generally have fewer than 25 people, and usually between 7 and 14 people. Team members also complement each other in terms of their skills. For example, accomplishing the team's mission usually calls for people strong in technical expertise as well as those skilled in problem solving, decision making, and interpersonal relationships.

A common approach. High-performing teams also agree on a common approach with respect to the way they will work together to accomplish their mission. For example, team members agree about: who will do particular jobs; how schedules will be set and followed; what skills need to be developed; what members will have to do to earn continuing membership in the team; and how decisions will be made and modified.

Mutual accountability. The most productive teams also develop a sense of mutual accountability. They believe "we are all in this together" and that "we all have to hold ourselves accountable for doing whatever is needed to help the team achieve its mission." Such mutual accountability cannot be coerced. Instead, it emerges from the commitment and trust that come from working together toward a common purpose.

BUILDING HIGH-PERFORMING TEAMS

The ability to build effective teams is increasingly considered an essential managerial capability; the ability to contribute successfully to team performance is increasingly considered an essential capability of any employee. All teams need members who are motivated to actively work with others to accomplish important tasks—whether those tasks involve recommending things, making or doing things, or running things. As suggested in our definition of teams the members of true teams feel "collectively accountable" for what they accomplish through "teamwork." Formally stated, teamwork occurs when team members work together in such a way that their respective skills are utilized to achieve a common purpose. A commitment to teamwork is found in the willingness of every member to listen and respond constructively to views expressed by others, give others the benefit of the doubt, provide support, and recognize the interests and achievements of others.

Making teams work effectively is no easy task and building a high-performance or successful team is not automatic. Rather, teams must be cared for and maintained carefully for them to accomplish their missions. As one expert put it, "Teams are the Ferraris of work design. They're high performance but high maintenance and expensive" (Dumaine, 1994). What, then, can be done to make teams as effective as possible? Based on analyses of successful teams, we can identify several suggestions (Dumaine, 1994):

1. *Diversify team membership.* Teams function most effectively when composed of highly skilled individuals who can bring a variety of different skills and experiences to the task at hand (Campion and Higgs, 1995).

2. *Keep teams small in size.* Effective teams consist of the smallest number of people needed to do the work. Coordination is difficult when teams are too large, and overload is likely when teams are too small. Generally, 10 to 12 members are ideal (Campion, Medsker, and Higgs, 1993).
3. *Select the right team members.* Some individuals enjoy working in teams, and others prefer to work alone. Thus, problems can be eliminated by not forcing loners into teams. Similarly, it is important to select team members based on their skills (or potential skills). Because the success of teams demands the members work together closely on may tasks, it is essential for them to have complementary skills. This includes not only job skills but interpersonal skills as well, especially because getting along with one's teammates is so important.
4. *Train, train, train.* For teams to function effectively, members must have all the technical skills needed for their jobs. This may involve cross-training on key aspects of others' specialty areas. It also is essential for them to be well-trained in the interpersonal skills needed to get along with each other. Given the great responsibilities team members have, they should be trained in the most effective ways to make decisions as well.
5. *Clarify goals.* When team members have a well-defined mission, they are likely to pull in the same direction and attempt to reach the same goals. Therefore, team goals must be articulated clearly.
6. *Link individual rewards to team performance.* To the extent team members are rewarded for the group's success by getting to share in the financial rewards, they are likely to be highly committed to striving for success.
7. *Use appropriate performance measures.* Teams work best when they develop their own measures of success. Furthermore, these measures should be based on processes rather than on outcomes. For example, instead of measuring profitability, which is a traditional measure of success, a manufacturing team may concentrate on measures with diagnostic value, such as the average time per service call or the number of late service calls. After all, team members who are aware of these indices may be able to do something about them.
8. *Promote trust.* For teams to operate successfully, members must trust each other to support their mutual interests. People can demonstrate trustworthiness by showing they are concerned for the welfare of the team and all its members.
9. *Encourage participation.* The more team members participate in making decisions, the more likely they are to feel committed to those decisions. Thus, for teams to be committed to their work, all team members must be involved.
10. *Cultivate team spirit and social support.* Teams work most effectively with a "can-do" attitude—that is, when they believe they can succeed. This often is encouraged when team members lend interpersonal and task support to teammates, but support also must come from top management. To the extent team members suspect management is not fully behind them, they will be unlikely to dedicate themselves to the task at hand.
11. *Foster communication and cooperation.* Naturally, team members must communicate and cooperate with each other so they can coordinate their efforts toward the common goal. At the same time, however, they must communicate

and cooperate with other teams as well. Doing so fosters the overall success of the parent organization.

12. *Emphasize the urgency of the team's task.* Team members tend to rally around challenges that compel them to meet high-performance standards.
13. *Clarify the rules of behavior.* Effective teams have clear rules about what behaviors are and are not expected. Rules about good attendance, giving only constructive criticism, and maintaining confidentiality are examples of such rules of behavior.
14. *Regularly confront teams with new facts.* Fresh approaches are likely to be prompted by fresh information, and introducing new facts may present the challenges teams need to stay innovative.
15. *Acknowledge and reward vital contributions to the team.* Rewarding desired behavior is a way of ensuring that behavior is repeated in the future.

After reading this list, if you are thinking it is no easy matter to make teams work effectively, you have reached the same conclusions as countless practicing managers. Indeed, you do not form teams and then just sit back and watch the results. Teams can be very useful tools, but using them effectively requires work. It also is important to caution that although these suggestions are important, they will not ensure the success of work teams. Many other factors such as the economy, competitors, and the organization's financial picture, are important determinants of organizational success as well. In view of the considerable gains found to occur, however, the effort is worth making.

SUMMARY

Groups and teams are inescapable features of modern life. We define a group as two or more freely interacting individuals who share collective norms and goals and have a common identity. Some groups go through a series of developmental stages: forming, storming, norming, performing, and adjourning. However, the punctuated equilibrium model stresses an important first meeting, a period of little apparent progress, a critical midpoint transition, and a phase of goal-directed activity.

Characteristics of or factors that affect groups and their performance include the presence of others, size, status hierarchy, composition, roles, norms, and cohesiveness. These characteristics pervade all groups.

Teams are a common occurrence in today's organizations as many herald their success. Problem-solving, self-managed, cross-functional, and virtual teams are examples of various teams used in organizations. Not all teams function effectively, and managers will find a number of symptoms of low-performing teams. These include cautious or guarded communication, lack of disagreement, use of personal criticism, malfunctioning meetings, unclear goals, low commitment, and conflict within the team. On the other hand, characteristics of high-performing or productive teams include commitment to a mission, specific performance goals, the right size and mix, a common approach, and mutual accountability. With some effort, organizations can build high-performance teams by following the suggestions outlined in this chapter.

REFERENCES

Allen, R.F., and Plotnick, S. 1973. Confronting the shadow organization: How to detect and defeat negative norms. *Organizational Dynamics* (Spring): 6–10.

Campion, M.A., and Higgs, A.C. 1995. Design work teams to increase productivity and satisfaction. *HRMagazine* (October): 101–102, 104, 107.

Campion, M.A., Medsker, R., and Higgs, A.C. 1993. Relations between work group characteristics and effectiveness: Implications for designing effective work groups. *Personnel Psychology* 46: 823–850.

Cartwright, C., and Zander, A. 1968. *Group dynamics: Research and theory*. New York: Harper & Row.

Castro, J. 1986. Mazda U. *Time* (October 20): 65.

Dumaine, B. 1994. The trouble with teams. *Fortune* (September 5): 86–88, 90, 92.

Geen, R. 1989. Alternative conceptualizations of social facilitation. In P.B. Paulus (ed.), *Psychology of group influence*. 2nd ed. Hillsdale, NJ: Lawrence Erlbaum Associates, pp. 15–51.

Gersick, C. 1988. Time and transition in work teams: Toward a new model of group development. *Academy of Management Journal* 31: 9–41.

Gersick, C. 1989. Making time: Predictable transitions in task groups. *Academy of Management Journal* 32: 274–309.

Janis, I. 1973. *Victims of groupthink: A psychological study of foreign policy decision and fiascos*. Boston: Houghton Mifflin.

Long, S. 1984. Early integration in groups: A group to join and a group to create. *Human Relations* 37: 311–332.

Schein, E.H. 1980. *Organizational psychology*. 3rd ed. Englewood Cliffs, NJ: Prentice-Hall.

Tuckman, B.W., and Jensen, M.A. 1977. Stages of small group development revisited. *Group and Organization Studies* 2: 41–47.

Wanous, J.P., Reichers, A.E., and Malik, S.D. 1984. Organizational socialization and group development: Toward an integrative perspective. *Academy of Management Review* (October): 670–683.

Chapter 8

Decision Making

INTRODUCTION

Life is full of decisions. Each day, people are faced with different problems requiring answers and solutions. At early stages in life, decisions about which school to attend and what career to pursue must be answered. At later stages in life, when employment is sought, individuals must decide what organization is the best vehicle for career advancement.

Among the primary factors that distinguish managers from other employees are the level and types of decisions that they must make. Managers must be concerned with how a decision might affect their employees and the organization. An operating employee, in contrast, is primarily concerned with how a decision affects him or her individually.

The quality of the decisions that managers make is the yardstick of their effectiveness. In fact, a manager's skill in making decisions is often a key factor in the kind of evaluation and rewards (promotion, money, assignments, etc.) that he or she receives. Moreover, a manager's decision-making ability will ultimately contribute to the success or failure of the organization.

The focus of this chapter is on decision making. This chapter describes and analyzes decision making in terms that reflect the ways in which managers and others make decisions based on their understanding of individual, group, and organizational goals and objectives. After first defining decision making, the chapter discusses types and levels of decision making in organizations, the decision-making process, a comparison of individual and group decision making, and pitfalls that managers should avoid in making decisions.

WHAT IS DECISION MAKING?

All human activities involve decision making. Everyone has problems at home, at work, and in social groups for which decisions must be made. Thus, decision making is a normal human requirement that begins in childhood and continues throughout life.

In work settings, when asked to define their major responsibilities, many managers respond that "solving problems" and "making decisions" are the most important components of what they do on a daily basis and throughout their ongoing management tasks. *Decision making* is the process of defining problems and choosing a course of action from among alternatives. The term decision making often is associated with the term *problem solving*, since many management decisions focus on solving problems that have occurred or are anticipated. However, the term problem solving should not be construed as being limited only to making decisions about problem areas. Problem solving also includes making decisions about realistic opportunities that are present or available if planned for appropriately.

Many of the problems that confront managers in their daily activities are recurring and familiar; for these problems, most managers have developed routine answers. But when managers are confronted with new and unfamiliar problems, many find it difficult to decide on a course of action.

Managers at all levels are constantly required to find solutions to problems that are caused by changing situations and unusual circumstances. Regardless of their managerial level, they should use a similar, logical, and systematic process of decision making. Although decisions that are made at the senior management level usually are of a wider scope and magnitude than decisions made at the lower management levels, the decision-making process should be fundamentally the same throughout the entire management hierarchy.

Decision making is an important skill for all of today's managers and employees. It is a skill that can be developed—just as the skills involved in playing golf are developed—by learning the steps, practicing, and exerting effort. By doing this, today's employees can learn how to make more thoughtful decisions and improve the quality of their decisions.

At the same time, managers should ensure that their employees learn to make their own decisions more effectively. A manager cannot make all the decisions necessary to run a department. Many daily decisions in a department are made by the employees who do the work. For example, what materials to use, and how a job is to be done, when it is to be done, and how to achieve coordination with other departments are decisions that employees often have to make without their supervisor. As evidenced in our discussion of teams in Chapter 7, organizations are giving employees a more active role in decision making. Therefore, training employees in the process of making decisions should be a high priority for all managers.

TYPES OF DECISIONS AND LEVELS OF MANAGEMENT

Clearly, all managers must make decisions. Even when the decision-making process is highly participative in nature, with full employee involvement, it is the manager who ultimately is responsible for the outcomes. Regardless of whether the manager makes the decision unilaterally or in consultation with employees, decisions may be classified into two categories: programmed or nonprogrammed, though most decisions fall somewhere between these two extremes.

Programmed decisions produce solutions to repetitive, well-structured, and routine problems. When making a programmed decision, there is a specific procedure, or program, that can be applied to the problem at hand. Many daily problems that confront managers are not difficult to solve because a more or less set answer is available. Usually the organization has already developed procedures and rules that deal with these problems. Managers can delegate these kinds of decisions to employees and be confident that the decisions will be made in an acceptable and timely manner.

Nonprogrammed decisions are made to address new, unusual, or unstructured problems that are unlikely to reoccur. Nonprogrammed decisions tend to be more important, demanding, and strategic than programmed decisions. There are no set answers or guidelines for making these decisions. Managers are called on to use intelligence, good judgment, intuition, and creativity in attempting to solve these problems. They should apply a decision-making process that is consistent and logical, but also adaptable.

THE DECISION-MAKING PROCESS

In making nonprogrammed managerial decisions, managers can follow the steps of the decision-making process. First, they must define the problem. Second, they must analyze the problem using available information. Third, they need to establish decision criteria—factors that will be used to evaluate alternatives. Fourth, after thorough analysis, they should develop alternative solutions. After these steps have been taken, the manager should carefully evaluate the alternatives and select the solution that appears to be the "best" or most feasible under the circumstances. The concluding step in this process is follow-up and appraisal of the consequences of the decision.

Step 1: Define the Problem

Before seeking answers, the manager should identify what the real problem is. Nothing is as useless as the right answer to the wrong question. Defining the problem is not an easy task. What appears to be the problem might be merely a symptom that shows on the surface. It usually is necessary to delve deeper to locate the real problem and define it.

Consider the following scenario: The manager of a computer maintenance department believes that a problem of conflicting personalities exists within the department. Two employees are continually bickering and cannot get along together. Because of this lack of cooperation a number of jobs are not being done in a timely manner. The manager needs to develop a clear, accurate problem statement. The problem statement should be brief, specific, and easily understood by others. A good problem statement should address the following questions:

- What is the problem?
- How do you know there is a problem?
- Where has the problem occurred?
- When has it occurred?
- Who is involved in or affected by the problem?

Expressing a problem through a problem statement can help the manager understand it. A careful review of answers to the key questions can lead to a problem statement like the one below, which reveals that the major problem is that the work is not getting done in a timely manner. When checking into this situation, the manager should focus on why the work is not getting done.

> *Problem statement*: "The bickering between Dan and Sylvia detracts from the completion of work assignments. Last Monday and Tuesday, neither of them completed assigned work. Customers, coworkers, and other departments are all affected."

Defining a problem can often become a time-consuming task, but it is time well spent. A manager should not go any further in the decision-making process until the problem relevant to the situation has been specifically determined. Remember, a problem exists when there is a difference between the way things are and the way they should be. The effective manager will use problem solving not only to take corrective action but also as a means to make improvements in the organization.

Step 2: Analyze the Problem Using Available Information

After the problem has been defined, the next step is to analyze it. The manager begins by assembling the facts and other pertinent information. This is sometimes viewed as being the first step in decision making, but until the real problem has been defined, the manager does not know what information is needed. Only after gaining a clear understanding of the situation can the manager decide how important certain data are and what additional information to seek. Information is a fuel that drives organizations. Information is vital to the survival of the organization, but to be useful it must be at the right place at the right time, and it must be used efficiently and effectively.

A major job of a manager is to convert information into action through the process of decision making. The manager is either helped or hindered by the availability of information. Making decisions without knowing enough about a situation is risky and sometimes even dangerous. Having too much information can also be a problem. Simple decisions do not require exhaustive information; but specific information is necessary to decide how to handle a complex problem. The quality of a decision depends greatly on understanding the circumstances surrounding an issue and selecting the appropriate strategy. The better the information, the better the resulting decision is likely to be because there is less risk and uncertainty about the facts.

Managers can stay informed by actively keeping up with everything related to their areas of responsibility and paying careful attention to all kinds of communications. Time spent reading equipment manuals and other technical materials may be helpful. Discussing potential problems with employees and getting their input on possible solutions could eventually lead to a stroke of genius when a problem arises.

Many managers often complain that they must base their everyday decisions on insufficient or irrelevant information. Managers complain that they have too much of the wrong kind of information, information is difficult to locate and/or suppressed by employees, or other managers did not have to deal with an overabundance of information; instead they gathered a bare minimum of information and hoped that their decisions would be reasonably good. By contrast, today's managers often feel buried by the deluge of information and data, much of it useless, confronting them on a regular basis. It is essential that they learn to manage this deluge of information.

How information is used depends greatly on its quality (accuracy), presentation (form), and timeliness (available when needed). Effective use of information is possible only if the right questions are asked by managers and their employees to determine information needs. The goal is to have the right information at the right time. To this end, timeliness may take precedence over accuracy. If information is not available when it is needed, then its accuracy is not important. In most cases, however, both accuracy and timeliness are critical. Additionally, information should be formally cataloged in some manner to ensure its availability. Managers cannot remember everything. Critical information should be put where it can be found quickly and easily. Personal computers offer a handy way to maintain ready access to a vast body of information.

After gathering information, the manager needs to analyze the problem. In our manager's example presented earlier, the manager needs to find out why the work is not getting done. When he or she gathered information, it was discovered that the expectations for each employee were not clearly outlined—where their duties begin and where they end. What appeared on the surface to be a problem arising from a personality conflict was actually a problem caused by the manager. The chances are good that once the activities and responsibilities of the two employees are clarified, the friction will end. The manager needs to monitor the situation closely to ensure that the new definition of duties results in a more timely completion of work.

A manager will find that personal opinions are likely to creep into decision making. This is particularly true when employees are involved in the problem. For example, if a problem involves an employee who performs well, the manager may be inclined to show this person greater consideration than would be afforded a poor performer. The manager should, therefore, try to be as objective as possible in gathering and analyzing information.

In the process of analysis the manager should also try to think of intangible factors that play a significant role in the problem, such as reputation, morale, discipline, and personal biases. It is difficult to be specific about these factors; nevertheless, they should be considered. As a general rule, written and objective information is more reliable than opinions and hearsay.

Step 3: Establish Decision Criteria

Decision criteria are the standards or measures to use in evaluating alternatives. They typically express what the manager wants to accomplish with the decision and can also be used to evaluate whether the implementation phase of the decision is producing the expected results. To illustrate, suppose the manager's initial actions do not remedy the conflict between the two employees. A criteria needs to be established that can be used to evaluate other courses of action, as in the following six criteria. The decision:

- should result in timely completion of assignments;
- should incur no additional costs;
- must not impede quality of service to the customer;
- should not put either employee's job in jeopardy;
- should not have a negative impact on other employees;
- must alleviate the problem within one week.

Once the decision criteria are established, the manager must determine which criteria are absolutely necessary and their order of priority. Because it is likely that no solution alternative will meet all the criteria, the manager needs to know which criteria are most important so that alternatives can be judged by how many of the important criteria they meet. The manager may want to consult with upper-level managers, peers, or employees to assist in prioritizing the criteria.

Step 4: Develop Alternatives

After the manager has defined and analyzed the problem and established the decision criteria, the next step is to develop various alternative solutions. By formulating and considering many alternatives, the manager is less apt to overlook the best course of action. Stating this another way, a decision will only be as good as the best alternative. Almost all problem situations have a number of alternatives, which may not always be obvious. Managers must work to develop alternatives rather than fall into an "either/or" kind of thinking. They must stretch their minds to develop alternatives even in the most discouraging situations, although none of the alternatives may be attractive.

Suppose that a manager had been ordered to make a 20-percent reduction in employment because the organization is experiencing financial problems. After careful study, the following feasible alternatives exist:

- Lay off employees who have the least seniority, regardless of their jobs or performance, until the overall 20-percent reduction is reached.
- Lay off employees who have the lower performance ratings until the overall 20-percent reduction is reached.
- Analyze department duties and decide which jobs are essential. Keep the employees who are best qualified to perform those jobs, and lay off the least qualified until the 20-percent reduction is reached.
- Without laying off anyone, develop a schedule of reduced work hours for every employee that would be equivalent to a 20-percent overall reduction.
- Develop proactive alternatives to increase the organization's performance so that no employee has to be laid off.

While the last alternative may be most attractive, it is not realistic, given the economic situation. Although none of the other alternatives may be an ideal solution to this unpleasant problem, at least the manager has considered several alternatives before making a decision. This "no-win" situation unfortunately portrays the realities of organizational life.

When enough time is available, a manager should get together with a group of other managers or employees to brainstorm alternative solutions to a perplexing problem. Brainstorming is a free flow of ideas within a group, with judgment suspended, in order to come up with as many alternatives as possible. Using this technique, the manager presents the problem and the participants offer as many alternative solutions as they can develop in the time available. It is understood that any idea is acceptable at this point—even those that may at first appear to be wild or unusual. Evaluation of ideas is suspended so that participants can give free rein to their creativity. Creative approaches and brainstorming meetings are particularly adaptable to nonprogrammed decisions, especially if the problem is new, important, or strategic. One authority on creativity and brainstorming (Osborn, 1979; see also Caggiano, 1999) has suggested the following four major guidelines for effective brainstorming by both individuals and groups:

Defer all judgment of ideas. During the brainstorming period, do not allow criticism by anyone in the group. Although it is natural for people to suppress new ideas both consciously and unconsciously, this tendency must be avoided. Even if an idea seems impractical and useless at first, it should not be rejected by quick initial judgments because the rejection itself could inhibit the free flow of more ideas. Managers should understand that how people respond to creative ideas affects individual and group actions.

Seek quantity of ideas. Idea fluency is the key to creative problem solving, and fluency means quantity. The greater the number of ideas, the greater the likelihood that some of them will be viable solutions.

Encourage "free wheeling." Being creative calls for a free-flowing mental process in which all ideas, no matter how extreme, are welcome. Even the wildest idea may, on further analysis, have a germ of usefulness, and should be encouraged.

"Hitchhike" on existing ideas. Combining, adding to, and rearranging ideas often can produce new approaches that are superior to any one original idea. When creative thought processes slow or stop, review some of the ideas already produced and try to combine them, considering additions or revisions.

When a fairly large group of people are brainstorming, an unstructured session can become rather long, tedious, and unproductive because many of the ideas are simply not feasible, and conflicts may develop within the group due to individual biases. For this reason, the so-called nominal group technique (NGT) is more useful, as it allows group members to generate ideas more efficiently. Typically under NGT, individual members of the group develop and write down a list of ideas and alternatives to solve the problem at hand. Afterward, the group members share their ideas, discussing, evaluating, and refining them. The group's final choice may be made by a series of confidential votes in which the list of ideas is narrowed until a consensus is reached. More will be said about NGT later in this chapter.

Both in the development and the evaluation of alternatives, a manager should consider only lawful options that fall within the organization's ethical guidelines. More organizations are encouraging their managers and employees to make ethical decisions because they recognize that good ethics is good business in the long term. Consequently, many organizations have developed handbooks, policies, and official statements that specify the ethical standards and practices expected. The following list of guidelines or ethical tests for decision making is not totally comprehensive, but these considerations are relevant in addressing the ethical aspects of most problem situations.

Legal-compliance test. Legal compliance should be only a starting point in most ethical decision making. Laws, regulations, and policies should be followed, not broken or ignored. The rationale and explanation that "everybody's doing it" or "everybody's getting away with it" are poor excuses if you are caught in an illegal or unethical act. If in doubt, ask for guidance from someone who understands the particular law or regulation.

Public-knowledge test. Decisions should be made as if they were going to be publicized. You should ask, "what the consequences would be if a part of a particular decision became known to the public, your family, the media, or a government agency?"

Long-term consequences test. The long-term and short-term consequences of a decision should be weighed against each other. This test helps avoid decisions that are expedient but could have negative long-term effects.

Examine-your-motives test. You should be sure that your decision benefits the organization and others. It should not be primarily selfish in nature or designed to harm other people and their interests.

Inner-voice test. This is the test of conscience and moral values that have been instilled in most of us since childhood. If something inside you says that the choice being contemplated is or may be wrong, it usually is.

It cannot be stressed enough that if a manager believes that a particular alternative is questionable or might not be acceptable within the organization's ethical policies, the manager should consult with his or her manager or with a staff specialist who is knowledgeable in the area for guidance in how to proceed. More will be said about ethics in Chapter 12.

Step 5: Evaluate the Alternatives and Select the Best Solution

The ultimate purpose of decision making is to choose the specific course of action that will provide the greatest number of wanted and the smallest number of unwanted consequences. After developing alternatives, managers can mentally test each of them by imagining that each has already been put into effect. They should try to foresee the probable desirable and undesirable consequences of each alternative. By thinking the alternatives through and appraising their consequences, the managers will be in a position to compare the desirability of the various choices. The usual way to begin is to eliminate alternatives that do not meet the supervisor's previously established decision criteria. The manager should evaluate how many of the most important criteria each remaining alternative meets. The final choice is the one that satisfies or meets the most criteria at the highest priority levels. More often than not, there is no clear choice.

Nonprogrammed decisions usually require the decision maker to choose a course of action without complete information about the situation. In making a decision, therefore, also consider the degree of risk and uncertainty involved in each alternative. No decision will be completely without risk; one alternative may simply involve less risk than the others.

The issue of time may make one alternative preferable, particularly if there is a difference between how much time is available and how much time is required to carry out one alternative in comparison with another. The manager should consider the facilities, records, tools, and other resources that are available. It is also critically important to judge different alternatives in terms of economy of effort and resources. In other words, managers should consider which action will give the greatest benefits and results for the least cost and effort.

In making a selection from among various alternatives, the manager should be guided by experience. Chances are that certain situations will reoccur, allowing managers to make wise decisions based on personal experience or the experience of another manager. Knowledge gained from experience is a helpful guide, the importance of which should not be underestimated; on the other hand, it is dangerous to follow experience blindly. When examining an earlier decision as a basis for choosing among alternatives, the manager should examine the situation and the conditions that prevailed at that time. It may be that conditions remain nearly identical, implying that the current decision should be similar to the previous one. More often than not, however, conditions have changed considerably and the underlying assumptions are no longer the same, indicating that the new decision probably should differ from the earlier one.

Managers admit that at times they base their decisions on intuition, defined as the ability to recognize quickly and instinctively the possibilities of a given situation. Some managers appear to have an unusual "intuitive" ability to solve problems satisfactorily by subjective means. A closer look, however, usually reveals that the so-called "intuition" is really experience or knowledge of similar situations that has been stored in the manager's memory.

Intuition may be particularly helpful in situations in which other solutions have not worked. If the risks are not too great, a manager may choose a new alternative because of an intuitive feeling that a fresh approach might bring positive results. Even if the hunch does not work out well, the manager benefits from trying something different. The manager will remember the new approach as part of his or her experience and can draw upon it in reaching future decisions.

Although a manager cannot shift personal responsibility for making decisions, the burden of decision making often can be eased by seeking the advice of others. The ideas and suggestions of employees, other managers, staff experts, technical authorities, and the manager's manager can be of great help in weighing facts and information. Seeking advice does not mean avoiding a decision, however; ultimately the manager decides what advice to accept and remains responsible for the outcome.

Many people believe that input from others can improve decision making. The following guidelines can help managers decide whether to include groups in the decision-making process:

- If additional information would increase the quality of the decision, involve those who can provide that information.
- If acceptance of the decision is critical, involve those whose acceptance is important.
- If employee's skills can be developed through participation in decision making, involve those who need the development opportunity.
- If the situation is not life threatening and does not require immediate action, involve others because generally their varied perspectives and experiences will enhance the decision-making process.

In the scientific world, laboratory experimentation is essential and accepted. In management, however, experimentation to see what happens often is too costly in terms of people, time, and money. Nevertheless, sometimes a limited amount of testing and experimentation is advisable before making a final decision. For example, there are some instances in testing that provides employees with an opportunity to try out new ideas or approaches, perhaps of their own design. While experimentation may be valid from a motivational standpoint, it can, however, be a slow and relatively expensive method of reaching a decision.

When one alternative clearly appears to provide a greater number of desirable consequences and fewer unwanted consequences than any other alternative, the decision is fairly easy. However, the "best" alternative is not always so obvious. When two or more alternatives seem equally desirable, the choice may become a matter of personal preference. When no single alternative seems to be significantly stronger than any other, it might be possible to combine the positive aspects of the better alternative into a composite solution. Sometimes none of the alternatives is satisfactory; all of them have too many undesirable effects and none will bring about the desirable effects. In this case, the manager should begin to think of new alternative solutions or perhaps even start all over again by attempting to redefine the problem.

A situation might arise in which the undesirable consequences of all the alternatives appear to be so overwhelmingly unfavorable that the manager feels that the best available solution is to take no action at all. This solution may be deceptive, however, as the problem will continue to exist if no action is taken. Taking no action is as much a decision as is taking a specific action, even though the manager may believe that an unpleasant choice has been avoided. The manager should visualize the consequences that are likely to result from taking action. Only if the consequences of inaction are more desirable should it be selected as the best solution.

Selecting the alternative that seems to be the best is known as optimizing. However, sometimes the manager makes a satisficing decision—selecting an alternative that minimally meets the decision criteria. A famous management theorist, Herbert Simon, once compared the process to the difference between finding a needle in a haystack (satisficing) and finding the biggest, sharpest needle in the haystack (optimizing). A manager will rarely make a decision that is equally pleasing to everyone.

Step 6: Follow Up and Appraise the Consequences of the Decision

After a decision has been made and implemented, managers should evaluate the consequences. Follow-up and appraisal of the outcome of a decision are actually part of the decision-making process. Managers should ask: "Did the decision achieve the desired results? If not, what went wrong, and why?" The answers to these questions can be of great help in similar future situations.

Follow-up and appraisal of a decision can take many forms, depending on the nature of the decision, timing, costs, standards expected, personnel, and other factors. For example, a minor project-scheduling decision could easily be evaluated through a short written report or perhaps even by the manager's observation or a discussion with employees. A major decision involving the maintenance of some complex equipment, however, will require close and time-consuming follow-up by the manager, technical or other employees, and higher-level managers. This type of decision usually requires the manager to prepare numerous detailed written reports on equipment performance under varying conditions, which are compared closely with plans or expected standards for equipment maintenance.

The important point to recognize is that the task of decision making is not complete without some form of follow-up and appraisal of the actions taken. If the manager has established decision criteria or specific objectives that the decision should accomplish, it will be easier to evaluate the effects of the decision. If the results meet the objectives, the manager can feel reasonably confident that the decision was sound.

If the follow-up indicates that something has gone wrong or that the results have not been achieved, then the manager's decision-making process must begin all over again. This may even mean going back over each of the various steps of the decision-making process in detail. The manager's definition and analysis of the problem and the development of alternatives may have to be completely revised in view of new circumstances surrounding the problem. In other words, when follow-up and appraisal indicate that the problem has not been resolved satisfactorily, the manager will find it advisable to treat the situation as a brand-new problem and go through the decision-making process from a completely fresh perspective.

In some situations, managers may feel they do not have enough time to go through the decision-making process outlined here. Frequently, a manager, a coworker, or an employee approaches the manager, says "Here's the problem," and looks to the manager for an immediate answer. Most problems do not require an immediate answer, however, and managers cannot afford to make decisions without considering the steps outlined here. Many managers get themselves into trouble by making hasty decisions.

When an employee brings up a problem, the manager should usually ask questions such as those listed below:

- How extensive is the problem? Does it need an immediate response? Is it safety related?
- Who else is affected by the problem? Should they be involved in this discussion?
- Have you (the employee) thought through the problem, and do you have an idea of what the end result should be?
- What do you recommend? Why?

This approach is a form of participative management that can help to develop employees' analytical skills. With the additional information gained from the process, the manager can think through the problem, apply the decision-making steps, and make a decision.

A word of caution here: During any stage of the process, managers should identify a specific time and then follow through when they tell other people that they "will get back to them." When managers fail to make a decision or give feedback by the specified time, they incur a serious breach of trust.

OBSTACLES TO SOUND DECISION MAKING

It is always tempting to take the easy way out when making decisions. Sometimes, you may not be as thoughtful as necessary and may make decisions based on impressions or habit rather than on data, information, and a sound understanding of the situation. And you may be unaware of doing this. The purpose of this section is to bring to your attention some of the obstacles that may compromise the quality of your decisions and subsequent actions. Knowing about these obstacles will allow you to deal with them more effectively.

Personal Biases

People have biases—preconceived notions of what is best to do in any situation that are not based on realistic assumptions about the situation. These biases can influence what people decide to do when they face different problems. Biases are often based on limited experience or on what people have learned from others as the appropriate way to respond in different situations. An obvious example of an unacceptable bias is the refusal to hire women to do certain types of jobs. While it is natural to have biases, they keep you from considering other alternatives that might yield better results. It's important, therefore, to make sure you avoid letting your prejudices undermine the quality of your decisions.

Taking the Easy Way Out

When people face decisions where there is a seemingly easy solution to the problem as opposed to one that may take more effort, they are tempted to take the easy way out. This often creates consequences that are far more costly and time-consuming than would have been the case had the more effortful solution been pursued. The reason for this is that the easy way out usually involves dealing with some *symptom* of the problem rather than its *causes*.

For example, if there is a conflict between two employees, the easy way out may be to have them work with other people. However, if the two do not deal with the causes of the conflict or resolve it, it will remain a problem. How these people work with others, as well as their motivation to do a good job, can be affected. Because everyone's work affects that of others, the unresolved problem can affect the entire group and its work quality. An alternative and better decision is to get the two people together and have each person explain his or her side. Each can begin to understand the assumptions behind the other's position. The manager can then work with the two individuals to resolve the conflict in a way that maintains their self-respect, fosters respect for each other, and prevents the problems that might have arisen from not taking this approach.

Pleasing the Boss

Employees sometimes have a tendency to make a decision they think will please the boss. If the boss is against overtime, managers are likely to refrain from keeping people beyond normal working hours, even if there is a need. Instead, they may try to take care of a problem during regular hours—an approach that may, if it involves a crucial process, negatively affect the work of many other people and be more costly than paying overtime.

Certainly, employees need to listen to their managers. However, they also must be able to communicate honestly about what needs to be done, even if it is contrary to the manager's normal approach to a situation. A manager should appreciate, as well, that their job is about adding value not for their boss, but for customers. When there is agreement between employee and manager on this crucial point, pleasing the boss will not be an obstacle to sound decisions.

Escalation

Another common tendency in decision making is escalation, or continuing to commit to a previous decision when a "rational" decision maker would withdraw. Escalation occurs when the decision maker focuses on the amount of time and resources already invested in a project and fails to focus on future costs and benefits.

An example of escalation is when managers decide to develop a new process for delivering a particular product. When things go awry with the process or unanticipated problems crop up, they stick with it, even though it will probably never pay off. It may be better to return to the previous process or to go back to the drawing board and come up with something else. You may think of personal examples. Do you put more money into the repair of an old car than it's worth? How long do you wait on the phone after you have been put on hold by a receptionist? By following a decision-making process, you can better face the facts and avoid the mental mistake of escalation, where the cost of a particular action will exceed the derived benefits.

Groupthink

As discussed in Chapter 7, Irving Janis has identified a fascinating phenomenon that can lead groups to commit serious errors in decision making. In describing this situation, which he called groupthink, Janis proposed that highly cohesive working groups (that is, groups whose members enjoy a high degree of interpersonal attraction) are in danger of taking a distorted view of situations that confront them. As a result, the group's decision-making processes may be slanted toward seeking consensus rather than exploring alternative courses of action. Because dissent and critical analysis are not encouraged in discussion sessions, the group may select a course of action that ignores potential dangers and pitfalls.

DECISION-MAKING STYLES

There are three basic decision-making styles: reflexive, reflective, and consistent (Lancaster, 1997). Let's take a closer look at each of these styles.

Reflexive Style

Reflexive decision makers like to make quick decisions—"to shoot from the hip"—without taking the time to get all the information that may be needed and without considering all alternatives. On the positive side, reflexive decision makers are decisive; they do not procrastinate. On the negative side, making quick decisions can lead to waste and duplication when a decision is not the best possible alternative. Reflexive decision makers may be viewed by employees as poor managers if they consistently make bad decisions. If you use a reflexive style, you may want to slow down and spend more time gathering information and analyzing alternatives. Following the steps in the decision-making process can help you develop those skills.

Reflective Style

Reflective decision makers like to take plenty of time to make decisions, taking into account considerable information and an analysis of several alternatives. On the positive side, the reflective type does not make quick decisions that are rushed. On the negative side, the person may procrastinate and waste valuable time and other resources. The reflective decision maker may be viewed as wishy-washy and indecisive. If you use a reflective style, you may want to speed up your decision making.

Consistent Style

Consistent decision makers tend to make decisions without rushing or wasting time. They seem to know when they have enough information and alternatives to make a sound decision. Compared to decision makers using other styles, these decision makers tend to have the most consistent record of good decisions. They usually follow the decision-making steps discussed earlier.

In reality, there is no right or universal way to make decisions. Although the reflexive, reflective, and consistent styles are distinct, most managers possess characteristics of more than one style. It is important that managers avoid relying on one style exclusively and recognize the strengths and weaknesses of each style. For example, the reflexive style is great if the person is well informed and intimate with the subject matter. Very often, missed opportunities happen when the decision-making process is prolonged. On the other hand, the reflective style works well if you have plenty of time to act, but it is detrimental when decisions are needed right away. Today's managers must be flexible in making decisions, feel comfortable in shifting their style depending on the situation, and learn when to make quick decisions and when to take their time.

GROUP DECISION MAKING

Decisions in organizations are increasingly being made by groups rather than by individuals. There seem to be at least two primary reasons for this. First, a group is likely to develop more and better alternatives than a single person, as indicated by the adage "two heads are better than one." Second, organizations are relying less on the historical idea that departments should be separate and independent decision units. To produce the best ideas and to improve their implementation, organizations are increasingly turning to teams that cut across traditional departmental lines. This requires the use of group decision-making techniques.

Advantages of Group Decisions

Individual and group decisions each have their own set of strengths. Neither is ideal for all situations. Let's review the advantages that group decisions have over individuals.

More complete information. A group will bring a range of experience and diverse perspectives to the decision-making process that an individual, acting alone, cannot.

More alternatives. Because groups have a greater quantity and diversity of information, they can identify more alternatives than can an individual.

Acceptance of a solution. Many decisions fail because people do not accept the solution. If the people who will implement or be affected by a certain decision could participate in the decision-making process, they would be more likely to accept the decision and to encourage others to accept it.

Legitimacy. The group decision-making process is consistent with democratic ideals and therefore may be perceived as more legitimate than decision making by a single person.

Disadvantages of Group Decision Making

If groups are so good, how did the phrase "A camel is a racehorse put together by a committee" originate? The answer, of course, is that group decision making has drawbacks. The major disadvantages of group decision making are described below.

Time consuming. It takes time to assemble a group. In addition, the interaction that takes place once the group is in place is frequently inefficient. The result is that a group almost always takes more time to reach a decision than does one individual.

Minority domination. Members of a group are never perfectly equal. They may differ in terms of rank in the organization, experience, knowledge about the problem, influence with other members, verbal skills, assertiveness, and the like. This creates the opportunity for one or more members to use their advantages to dominate others and impose undue influence on the final decision.

Pressures to conform. There are social pressures in groups. The desire of group members to be accepted and considered assets to the group can quash any overt disagreement and encourage conformity among viewpoints. The withholding by group members of different views in order to appear in agreement is called *groupthink* and as suggested previously can result in bad decisions.

Ambiguous responsibility. Group members share responsibility for making decisions, but no one person is actually responsible for the final outcome. In an individual decision, it is clear who is responsible, but in a group decision, the responsibility of any single member is diluted.

When to Use Group Decision Making

In making decisions, when are groups better than individuals and vice versa? That depends on what you mean by "better." There are four criteria frequently associated with good decisions. First, the evidence indicates that, on average, groups make more accurate decisions than individuals. This does not mean, of course, that every group outperforms every individual. Rather, group decisions have been found to be more effective than those of the average member of the group; however, they seldom are as good as those of the best group member. Next, individual decision makers are faster than groups. Group decision processes are characterized by give and take, which consumes time.

Groups tend to do better than individuals in reaching creative decisions. This requires, however, that groups must avoid groupthink. They must encourage doubts about the group's shared views and challenges to favored arguments; they must avoid an excessive desire to give an appearance of consensus; and they must not assume that silence or abstention by members is a "yes" vote. Finally, group decisions typically result in greater acceptance. Because group decisions are made using input from more people, they are likely to result in solutions that more people will accept.

ENHANCING GROUP DECISION MAKING

Just as individuals can improve the quality of their decisions, so can groups. The basic idea underlying these techniques is identical: Structure the group experience to experience its benefits without also experiencing its weaknesses.

The Delphi Technique: Decisions by Expert Consensus

According to Greek mythology, to see what fate the future held for them, people could seek the counsel of the Oracle of Delphi. Today, organizational decision makers sometimes consult experts to help them make the best decisions as well. Developed by the Rand Corporation, the Delphi technique represents a systematic way of collecting and organizing the opinions of several experts into a single decision (Dalkey, 1969).

The Delphi process begins by enlisting the cooperation of experts and presenting the problem to them, usually in a letter. Each expert then proposes what he or she believes is the most appropriate solution. The group leader compiles these individual responses, reproduces them, and shares them with all the other experts in a second mailing. At this point, each expert comments on the other experts' ideas and then compiles them again and looks for a consensus of opinions. If a consensus is reached, the decision is made; if not, the process of sharing reactions with others is repeated until a consensus eventually is obtained.

The obvious advantage of the Delphi technique is that it allows the collecting of expert judgments without the great costs and logistical difficulties of scheduling a face-to-face meeting. The technique is not without limitations, however. For example, the Delphi process can be very time-consuming. Mailing letters, waiting for responses, transcribing and disseminating those responses, and then repeating the process until a consensus is reached can take quite some time. In fact, the minimum time required for the Delphi technique is estimated to be more than 44 days. In one case, the process took five months to complete (Van de Ven and Delbecq, 1971). Obviously, the Delphi approach is not appropriate for crisis situations—or for whenever time is of the essence. The approach has been employed successfully, however, to make decisions such as what items to put on a conference agenda and what the potential effect of implementing new land-use policies would be (Van de Ven and Delbecq, 1971).

The Nominal Group Technique (NGT)

When only a few hours are available to make a decision, group discussion sessions can be held in which members interact with each other in an orderly, focused fashion. The nominal group technique (NGT) brings together a small number of individuals (usually seven to ten) who systematically offer their individual solutions to a problem and share their personal reactions to those solutions (Gustafson, Shulka, Delbecq, and Walster, 1975). The technique is referred to as nominal because the individuals involved form a group in name only. The participants do not attempt to agree on any one solution but rather vote on all the solutions proposed.

The NGT begins by gathering the group members together around a table and identifying the problem at hand. Each member then writes his or her solutions. Next, each member presents his or her solutions to the group, and the leader writes those solutions on a chart. This process continues until all the ideas have been expressed. Each solution then is discussed, clarified, and evaluated by the group. Each member is given a change to voice his or her reactions to each idea as well. After all the ideas have been evaluated, the group members privately rank-order their preferred solutions. The idea with the highest rank is taken as the group's decisions.

The NGT has several advantages and disadvantages (Ulshak, Nathanson, and Gillan, 1981). As noted, this approach can arrive at a group decision in only a few hours. It also discourages any pressure to conform to the wishes of a high-status group member, because all ideas are evaluated and all preferences expressed in private balloting. The technique does require a trained group leader, however, and using it successfully requires that only one narrowly defined problem can be considered at a time. Thus, for complex problems, many NGT sessions would be needed—and only if the problem under consideration could be broken into smaller parts.

Traditionally, nominal groups meet in face-to-face meetings, but modern technology enables such groups to meet even when the members are far away from each other. Specifically, electronic meeting systems allow individuals in different locations to participate in a group conference via telephone lines or direct satellite transmission (Harmon, Schneer, and Hoffman, 1995). Messages may be sent by characters on a computer monitor or by images viewed during a teleconference. Despite their high-tech look, automated decision conferences really are just nominal groups meeting in a manner that approximates face-to-face contact.

It is important to consider the relative effectiveness of nominal groups and Delphi groups compared with face-to-face interacting groups. In general, research has shown the superiority of these special approaches to decision making (Willis, 1979). Overall, members of nominal groups tend to be the most satisfied with their work and to make the best-quality judgments. In addition both nominal and Delphi groups are more productive than face-to-face interacting groups.

As noted, however, there is one potential benefit from face-to-face interaction that cannot be realized in nominal or Delphi groups: acceptance of the decision. Groups are likely to accept their decisions and be committed to them if the members have been actively involved in making them. Thus, the more detached and impersonal atmosphere of nominal and Delphi groups sometimes makes their members less likely to accept decisions. Thus, there is no one best type of group with which to make decisions. The most appropriate type depends on the trade-offs decision makers are willing to accept in terms of speed, quality, and commitment (Stumpf, Zand, and Freedman, 1979).

The Stepladder Technique: Systematically Incorporating New Members

Another way of structuring group interaction is known as the stepladder technique (Rogelberg, Barnes-Farrell, and Love, 1992). This approach minimizes the tendency for group members to be unwilling to present their ideas. This is accomplished by adding new members one at a time and requiring each to present his or her ideas independently to a group that already has discussed the problem at hand. To begin, each of two people works on a problem independently. Then, they come together to present their ideas and to discuss solutions jointly. While the two-person group is working, a third person working alone also considers the problem. This individual then presents his or her ideas to the two-person group and joins in a three-person discussion of a possible solution. During this period, a fourth person works on the problem alone, then presents his or her ideas to the three-person group, and then joins in a four-person group discussion. After each new person has been added to the group, the entire group works together at finding a solution.

In following this procedure, each individual must be given enough time to work on the problem before joining the group. Then, each person must be given enough time to present thoroughly his or her ideas to the group. In turn, groups must have sufficient time to discuss the problem and to reach a preliminary decision before the next person is added. The final decision is made only after all individuals have been added to the group.

The rationale is that by forcing each person to present independent ideas—without knowing what the group had decided so far—the new person will not be influenced by the group. In turn, the group is required to consider a constant infusion of new ideas. If this is so, then groups solving problems using the stepladder technique should make better decisions than conventional groups meeting all at once to discuss the same problem. This is exactly what happens, too. Moreover, members of stepladder groups report feeling more positive about their group experiences than their counterparts in conventional groups. The stepladder technique is new, but evidence suggests it holds promise for enhancing the decision-making capacity of groups.

Training Discussion Leaders

When organizations utilize group decision making, an appointed leader often convenes the group and guides the discussion. The actions of this leader can "make or break" the decision. On the one hand, if the leader behaves autocratically, trying to "sell" a preconceived decision, the advantages of using a group are obliterated, and decision acceptance can suffer. If the leader fails to exert any influence, however, the group might develop a low-quality solution that does not meet the needs of the organization. The use of role-playing training to develop these leadership skills has increased the quality and acceptance of group decisions. The following are examples of the skills that people learn in discussion leader training (Maier, 1973).

- State the problem in a nondefensive, objective manner. Do not suggest solutions or preferences.
- Supply essential facts and clarify any constraints on solutions (e.g., "We can't spend more than $5,000").
- Draw out all group members. Prevent domination by one person, and protect members from being attacked or severely criticized.
- Wait out pauses. Do not make suggestions or ask leading questions.
- Ask stimulating questions that move the discussion forward.
- Summarize and clarify at several points to mark progress.

INCREASING EMPLOYEE INVOLVEMENT IN DECISION MAKING

The traditional view of decision making placed the manager in the eminent position of primary decision maker. In today's complex work environment, it is unrealistic to expect one person to know all the answers. In addition, as employees continue to grow and take advantage of educational opportunities, it is smart to draw on their knowledge, creativity and experience. When employees are involved effectively in decision making, the quality of decisions can be improved and an increased commitment to the organization can be achieved. By no means is this process meant to interfere with the authority of the manager. On the contrary, it is designed to promote teamwork, improve creativity, increase interaction, expand communication, and enhance overall organizational efficiency. By the same token, it is conceivable that the manager may earn even greater respect by including employees in the process.

A manager's decision-making ability can be improved if more employee ideas and suggestions are collected at the outset. The following two techniques can greatly increase the level of employee involvement.

Technique 1: Delegate—Learn to Be a Guardian of Decisions Instead of the Maker of Decisions

When possible, decisions should be delegated to employees at lower levels. Employees have a right to participate in decisions directly affecting them. The rationale is that employees possess valuable day-to-day knowledge of the job, and therefore, the organization benefits by allowing them to make certain decisions. The manager serves as a guardian—making sure that the group's decisions are in keeping with departmental goals and organizational objectives.

When employees make decisions, the organization gains because the most knowledgeable people make the decisions, and the group gains by being included in the process. Individuals grow as a result of the technique, increasing their potential and their long-term contributions to the organization.

Technique 2: Use Participative Approaches to Decision Making

Many managers have implemented participative decision-making techniques to boost productivity, improve employee relations, and increase the quality of decisions.

Participative approaches invite decision sharing. Employees are made responsible for contributing opinions and information, and they are expected to participate in the decision-making process as much as possible. Participative managers do not disguise their power to make the final decision, particularly when faced with crises. They do, however, request and expect constant feedback, a practice that provides them with the best available information, ideas, suggestions, talent, and experience.

As suggested at various points in this book, the move toward participation is increasingly popular. Some organizations prefer traditional authoritarian methods for decision making; however, many organizations find themselves in transition and may wish to consider the many benefits of a participative approach. When employees participate in making decisions that affect them, they support those decisions more enthusiastically and try harder to make them work.

PRACTICAL PITFALLS TO AVOID WHEN MAKING DECISIONS

Many managers have a tendency to encounter one or more of a number of problems when making decisions. Some managers make all decisions into big or crisis decisions.

Pitfall 1: Making All Decisions into Big or Crisis Decisions

Everyone has run into the manager who treats every decision as if it were a life-and-death issue. These managers may spend two hours deciding whether to order one or two boxes of rubber bands. Some managers seem to delight in turning all decision situations into crisis situations. These approaches keep the employees confused; they have a hard time distinguishing between the important and less important issues, crisis and non-crisis situations. As a result of this approach, the really important problems may not receive proper attention because the manager wastes time and becomes bogged down in unimportant matters. This type of manager must learn to allocate an appropriate amount of time to each decision, based on its relative significance. Even when a true crisis does occur, such as the breakdown of a major piece of equipment or an accident, the manager must learn to remain calm and think clearly.

Pitfall 2: Failing to Consult with Others

The advantage of consulting others in the decision-making process was discussed earlier in this chapter. Yet some managers are reluctant to seek advice, fearing it will make them look incompetent. Many managers, especially new ones, are under the impression that they should know all the answers and that to ask someone else for advice would be admitting a weakness. Successful managers place good sense and their reasoning ability ahead of their egos.

Pitfall 3: Never Admitting a Mistake

No one makes the best decision every time. If a manager makes a bad decision, it is best to admit this and do what is necessary to correct the mistake. The worst possible course is to try to force a bad decision into being a good decision.

Pitfall 4: Constantly Regretting Decisions

Some managers always want to change the unchangeable. Once a decision has been made and is final, don't brood over it. Remember, very few decisions are totally bad; some are just better than others. A manager who spends all of his or her time dreaming about "what if" will not have enough time to implement decisions already made.

Pitfall 5: Failing to Utilize Precedents and Policies

Why reinvent the wheel? If a similar problem has arisen in the past, managers should draw on that experience. If a situation seems to recur constantly, it is usually useful to implement a policy covering it. For example, it is wise to have a policy covering priorities for vacation time. Managers should also keep abreast of current organizational policies, which can often help solve problems.

Pitfall 6: Failing to Gather and Examine Available Data

Some managers often ignore or fail to utilize available factual information. One common reason for this is that some degree of effort is normally required to gather and analyze data—it is easier to utilize only the data already on hand. A related problem is the need to separate the facts from gossip and rumor. The general tendency is to believe only what you want to believe and not to consider the facts.

Pitfall 7: Promising What Cannot Be Delivered

Managers sometimes make promises they know they can't keep and commitments when they don't have the necessary authority to do so. Managers may view such commitments and promises as ways of getting employees to go along with decisions. Failed commitments almost always come back to haunt the manager. The best approach is to promise no more than can be delivered.

Pitfall 8: Delaying Decisions Too Long

Many managers tend to put off making a decision "until we have more information." A time line is often critical and even good decisions can be ineffective if delayed too long. Managers rarely ever have all the information they would like. Good managers know when they have adequate information and then make decisions promptly.

SUMMARY

Managers confront many decision situations, which can vary from the programmed type at one extreme to the nonprogrammed at the other. Decisions for routine, repetitive-type problems are usually made easier by the use of policies, procedures, standard practices, and the like. However, nonroutine decisions are usually one-time, unusual, or unique problems that require sound judgment and systematic thinking. Better decisions are more likely to occur when managers follow the guidelines for making decisions, get input from others, use group decision-making strategies when appropriate, and take steps to avoid decision-making pitfalls.

REFERENCES

Caggiano, C. 1999. The right way to brainstorm. *Inc.* (July): 94.

Dalkey, N. 1969. *The Delphi method: An experimental study of group decisions.* Santa Monica, CA: Rand Corporation.

Gustafson, D.H., Shulka, R.K., Delbecq, A., and Walster, W.G. 1973. A comparative study of differences in subjective likelihood estimates made by individuals, interacting groups, Delphi groups, and nominal groups. *Organizational Behavior and Human Performance* 9: 280–291.

Harmon, J., Schneer, J.A., and Hoffman, L.R. 1995. Electronic meetings and established decision groups: Audioconferencing effects on performance and structural stability. *Organizational Behavior and Human Processes* 61: 138–147.

Lancaster, H. 1997. Managing your career: That team spirit can lead your career to new victories. *Wall Street Journal* (January 14): B1.

Maier, N.R.F. 1973. *Psychology in industrial organizations*. 4th ed. Boston: Houghton Mifflin.

Osborn, A.F. 1979. *Applied imagination: Principles and procedures of creative thinking*. 3rd ed. New York: Scribner.

Rogelber, S.G., Barnes-Farrell, J.L., and Love, C.A. 1992. The stepladder technique: An alternative group structure facilitating effective group decision making. *Journal of Applied Psychology* 77: 730–737.

Stumpf, S.A., Zand, D.E., and Freedman, R.D. 1979. Designing groups for judgmental decisions. *Academy of Management Review* 4: 589–600.

Ulshak, F.L., Nathanson, L., and Gillan, P.B. 1981. *Small group problem solving: An aid to organizational effectiveness*. Reading, MA: Addison-Wesley.

Van de Ven, A.H., and Delbecq, A.L. 1971. Nominal versus interacting group processes for committee decision making effectiveness. *Academy of Management Journal* 14: 203–212.

Willis, R.E. 1979. A simulation of multiple selection using nominal group procedures. *Management Science* 23: 171–181.

Chapter 9

Leading in the New Economy

INTRODUCTION

As we settle into the new millennium, organizations are challenged to compete in changing domestic and global environments using diverse workforces. Leadership styles that were practical in traditional hierarchies and that relied on authoritarian controls are no longer appropriate in today's world of work. Today's organizational leaders will have to practice different styles appropriate to the situation. They have to increasingly inspire trust, gain credibility, and implement innovations through their followers. Moreover, leaders are increasingly challenged to balance task and relationship (people) styles and to assume not only the roles of monitors and controllers, but also the roles of cheerleaders, orchestrators, conductors, coaches, and mentors. As effective leaders in the twenty-first century, managers and other organizational leaders must recognize that concepts like "empowerment," "workout," "quality," and "excellence" are important leadership factors.

Those who can demonstrate flexibility and a variety of competent leadership styles will most likely be effective in managing organizational behavior. In this chapter, we define and present new and traditional leadership skills, competencies, and approaches. We begin by defining leadership and the difference between leaders and managers. We next define followership before describing the foundations of leadership. Then we look at traditional and contemporary theories of leadership. We end the chapter with an examination of issues related to leading effectively in the new economy (i.e., obstacles to effective leadership, myths of leadership, and suggestions for improving leadership skills).

WHAT IS LEADERSHIP?

For our purposes, leadership is both a process and a set of distinct abilities. Leaders cannot reach organizational goals by themselves; they need followers. However, leaders are also held individually accountable. For instance, today's team leader bears responsibility for the team's performance at the end of each day, week, month, and year. Leaders as individuals are, therefore, responsible for providing direction in the form of vision and strategies for the organization and their teams.

Leadership—the very word brings to mind names like George Washington, Thomas Jefferson, Abraham Lincoln, and in recent times, Colin Powell, Nelson Mandela, and Lee Iacocca. But what exactly is leadership? Are successful leaders only those who achieve national recognition? Can leaders be developed, or is leadership a trait people must inherit from their parents? All of these issues and others will be discussed in the remainder of this chapter. First, however, we want you to expand your thinking about what leadership is and who leaders are. While there are probably hundreds of accurate definitions of leadership, the one by Vance Packard is a pointed, succinct definition.

Leadership is the art of getting others to want to do something that the individual is convinced should be done (Kouzes and Posner, 1987, p. 1).

There are several key words in this definition that should be noted. The first is "art"—leadership clearly is not an exact science, a set of skills, or attributes. Organizations spend millions of training dollars giving their current and future leaders skills to become successful leaders. Yet there is a certain characteristic of leadership that is an art, and thus it is difficult to measure or develop in people. A second key in this definition is the phrase "others"—leaders can only be successful if they can, through whatever means, such as their position, power, charisma, and so on, convince others to follow a course of action. A third key in the definition is "want"—not order, direct, or force—but want. Leaders are able to convince others to internally desire to achieve an objective: such as meet a deadline, win a ballgame, or simply work harder. If a leader only relies on external force, such as a manager giving direct orders, will his employees contribute their best efforts in the long-run? The final key in the definition is "should be done." Leaders clearly communicate the organization's goals and objectives, both long-run and immediate (or short-term).

Who are the leaders of an organization? They are people who decide what are the goals and objectives of an organization or group and then direct the activities needed to achieve these goals. They are people who, by their own behavior, beliefs, and words affect the actions of others. In our society leaders are not only presidents, corporate executives, and owners, they are also team captains, teachers, civic activists, and parents—everyone who inspires and directs others in work, leisure, religious, political, or other activities.

In today's organizations leaders must be able to motivate and bring together members of a different type of workforce—one which is increasingly diverse, less loyal to the organization, has been downsized, and often disenfranchised. Today's leaders, thus, must lead a workforce at a time when confidence in leadership is low and there are never-ending new developments and challenges in the industry.

MANAGEMENT AND LEADERSHIP

Observers, scholars, and historians have often distinguished between management and leadership. To some, "management" is a pejorative term associated with everything that's wrong with organizations. Nevertheless, managing and leading aren't mutually exclusive terms, nor is the distinction between them all that clear. However, managers and leaders play different roles in an organization.

Managers sustain and control organizations; leaders try to change them. Organizations also have different needs for each of those roles at different levels and at different times in their development or history.

Leaders are more likely to focus on creating a vision for the future, developing strategies to achieve the vision, and inspiring followers to pursue that vision to overcome technical, bureaucratic, and personnel hurdles, and embrace change. Leaders take risks, especially if they perceive high payoffs from a course of action. They readily use power for influence, pulling people along instead of using punishment to coerce followers into compliance. Leaders actively seek opposing views to identify options to a course of action.

In contrast, managers follow the present vision for the organization, are more likely to focus on allocating resources, organizing and controlling other followers, and measuring results against preset expectations. Managers solve problems and try to bring order to the workplace while ensuring the commitment of others to the organization's goals. Managers take fewer risks than leaders. They use available rewards and sanctions, coupled with their knowledge of human motivation, to get predictable behavior. In sum, while many leaders are managers, and many managers are leaders, *managers* are people who develop budgets and plans, organize personnel by reporting structures, and execute by monitoring results against the plan.

The supervisory, management, and senior leader positions in organizations can have different requirements for management and leadership. Some positions require only management. Other positions require large amounts of leadership with little need for management. Still others need a mixture of leadership and management.

An organization's requirement for management and leadership will change as the factors affecting the organization change. Because leaders are important change agents, they play key roles when the external environment is changing fast as is the case with the new economy. An organization has little need for a strong change agent if little is changing around it.

In today's world of work it is important to recognize that most of all, people cannot be managed—they must be led. One management consultant probably best sums up the difference between managers and leaders, distinguishing between management and leadership: "Management's about arranging and telling. Leadership's about growing and enhancing" (Peters, 1988). The workplace of the new millennium is rapidly changing and needs leaders who can successfully lead their followers.

To be successful under the conditions resulting from the changes, developments, and challenges in today's world of work, leaders must move away from a style of "managing" to a style of "leadership." What does this leadership entail? First, a leader's primary role will be to coach and develop people, not simply give orders. Second, leaders need to provide autonomy to employees so they become self-managed. Third, leaders should participate in and encourage teamwork where reasonable. Fourth, leaders should encourage fast decision making by those employees closest to the situation. Fifth, leaders should encourage innovation and risk taking to meet the ever-changing challenges facing organizations. Finally, leaders must treat employees as assets, not expenses, and they will need to invest more time and resources in the training and development of their human resources.

Management, while most important, is about practices and procedures needed to cope with complexity. Leadership, also important, but different, is about coping with change. One leadership theorist emphasizes that the need to shift from "managing" to "leading" means that today's organizations don't just need effective leadership from the CEO but from "hundreds of individuals below the plant manager level" (Kotter 1990, p. 7). It is easy for organizations today to be overmanaged and underled, because many of today's leaders were trained to keep things on time and under budget. Leaders today, however, realize the rapid changes in technology, globalization, and the diversity of the workforce require a leader who can develop a vision of how to compete with these changes, a strategy to implement the vision, and the ability to communicate and inspire others to participate in that strategy.

The demand for more leaders does not mean that good managers are not also needed or that being a leader is better than being a manager. Organizations, without question, need both good leaders and good managers. In fact, balancing both types of activities—without losing sight of either—may be the key to leadership and organizational success.

The Leader's Role in Providing a Vision

Showing the way out of the wilderness—providing direction—has always been a crucial task for leaders. Each year during one executive training program the instructor polls the executives to compile what he calls a list of conditions for effective leadership. "Clarify the mission, purposes, or objectives of your employees' assignments" and "describe assignments clearly" head the list.

More than ever before, today's leaders must provide a direction that their followers can work toward. Whether that "direction" is a statement of vision, mission, or objectives depends largely on what the leader wants to achieve and the level at which he or she is acting.

Sometimes what's required is a *vision*, a general statement of the organization's intended direction that evokes positive emotional feelings in organization members. An individual leader's vision of a more efficient, effective, and customer responsive organization will help provide the sense of direction employees, upper management, and customers all require, and around which they can rally.

Setting Direction: Vision, Missions, and Objectives

Many experts believe that communicating a vision is especially important in today's rapidly changing environment, where business conditions are "volatile and carry in them the seeds of rapid and potentially hostile change" (El-Namaki 1992, p. 25). Here, the faster senior leadership can conceive (and frontline supervisors and managers can implement) a future vision where new products and services are positioned within a rapidly changing environment the greater is the ability of the organization to control its destiny and affirm a sense of direction.

The organization implements top management's vision. A *mission statement* "broadly outlines the organization's or a department's future course and serves to communicate who we are, what we do, where we're headed" (El-Namaki 1992, p. 25). Mission statements like one elevator firm's ("Our mission is to provide any customers a means of moving people and things up, down, and sideward over short distances") are meant to communicate a specific sense of direction. It specifies the purpose of the company, department, or team.

The leader's task might require providing objectives, which are specific results an organization, department, or group needs to achieve. Setting a direction with a vision, mission, or goal is one area in which the roles of leader and manager clearly converge. Planning, the process of establishing objectives and courses of action, prior to taking action, is the first of the manager's functions. But in providing direction and showing the way, the frontline manager is wearing his or her leadership hat, too. Leading means influencing others to work toward some aim, and the first step in doing so is to show the way. However, showing the way is only effective if there are individuals who are willing to follow the direction or vision of the leader. They must not only be willing to follow but they must also be effective followers.

What about Followership?

When someone was once asked what it took to be a great leader, he responded, "Great followers!" While the response may have seemed sarcastic, it has some truth. We have long known that many individuals can't lead a horse to water. But, then again many employees can't follow a parade.

Only recently have we begun to recognize that in addition to having leaders who can lead, successful organizations need followers who can follow them (Challeff, 1995; Kelley, 1988). In fact, it's probably fair to say that all organizations have far more followers than leaders, so ineffective followers may be more of a handicap to an organization than ineffective leaders.

What qualities do effective followers have? One writer focuses on four.

1. They manage themselves well. They are able to think for themselves. They can work independently and without close supervision or monitoring.
2. They are committed to a purpose outside themselves. Effective followers are committed to something—a cause, a product, a work team, an organization, an idea—in addition to the care of their own lives. Most people like working with colleagues who are emotionally, as well as physically, committed to their work.
3. They build their competence and focus their efforts for maximum impact. Effective followers master skills that will be useful to their organizations, and they hold higher performance standards than their job or work group requires.
4. They are courageous, honest, and credible. Effective followers establish themselves as independent critical thinkers whose knowledge and judgment can be trusted. They hold high ethical standards, give credit where credit is due and aren't afraid to own up to their mistakes. (Kelley, 1988)

Due to the increased use of teams and horizontal organizational structures, today's organizational leaders must also be followers and be able to successfully move back and forth between the two roles (Challeff, 1995; Kelley, 1988). It is, in fact, common for a person in a leadership position within one unit of an organization to serve as a member of project teams, task forces, and committees that require them to be effective or successful followers.

It is important to understand that leadership and followership are related in several important ways: (1) leaders cannot be successful without followers that implement their vision; (2) leaders, themselves, must be successful followers in various roles within the organizations; (3) leaders must recognize the need for followers to exhibit the traits discussed previously and reward them accordingly; and (4) leaders must provide an organizational climate that supports and serves followers rather than one in which followers serve leaders.

There are a number of strategies followers can use to develop effective, respectful relationships with their leaders. These strategies are (1) be a resource for the leader, (2) help the leader be a good leader, (3) build a relationship with the leader, and (4) view the leader realistically.

FOUNDATIONS OF LEADERSHIP: POWER, INFLUENCE, AND DECISION MAKING

In most organizations there are many leaders—people in positions of authority, people whom others seek out when they have technical problems, people who have the support of others on internal political issues, and so on. All are leaders because they can influence the thoughts and behaviors of others. This gives them leadership power and influence within the organization.

What Are Power and Influence?

Effective leadership begins with an understanding of power. Leadership also depends on the responsible use of power and influence with followers and external constituencies. Power and influence are interrelated. Power is defined as the ability to get someone to do something you want done or the ability to make things happen in the way you want them to. The essence of power is control over the behavior of others. One of the interesting things about power is that it has no verb form. You do not "power" something. You can, however, *influence* something. Power is the force you use to make things happen in an intended way, whereas influence is what you have when you exercise power and is expressed by others' behavioral response to your exercise of power. Influence depends on the followers' acceptance of the influencer and on the types of influence used. Influence is related, in this sense, to authority (i.e., the power granted to a leader by followers).

Sources and Types of Leadership Power

Organizational leaders at various levels in the organization derive power from both organizational and individual sources. These sources are called position power and personal power, respectively (French and Raven, 1960). Three bases of power are available to the leader solely as a result of his or her position in the organization: legitimate, reward, and coercive power.

Legitimate power. Perhaps the most common source of power is that given by the organization itself. Thus, positions that are allocated formal power of authority by the organization have legitimate power. For example, various leadership positions usually receive legitimate power from the organizations and accept the power of the individual occupying such a position.

Reward power. When an individual has the ability to grant rewards to others, they have a source of power. This reward power may be due to the leader's position in the organization, such as a mid-level manager giving a merit pay raise or a more desirable work schedule. However, praise received from highly respected senior colleagues can be a valued reward as well—thus giving the colleagues an informal source of power and ability to influence others who desire their recognition.

Coercive power. Some leaders have the authority to punish others by not granting a desired scheduled vacation, pay raise, or promotion recommendation. Other leaders are not directly in a position to decide such punishments, but have the ability to convince the person in the position of authority to use such coercive power. Employees, for example, may quickly learn "who the boss listens to" and thus try to keep in favor of those who possess coercive power.

Personal power resides in the individual and is independent of the position the individual holds. Personal power is important in many well-led organizations. Two bases of personal power are expert and referent.

Expert power. Some leaders become known to be experts within technical areas, or are known to be effective in getting things accomplished. This ability or knowledge gives them expert power, because others will seek their assistance or advice.

Referent power. A leader whose personality enables him or her to affect the behavior of others may be said to possess referent power. This personality characteristic may be charm, attraction, wit, or charisma.

How can an individual develop one of these bases of leadership power? The most common, direct method is to be appointed to a position of authority that has legitimate power in an organization. However, to achieve that first position of legitimate authority often requires a person to develop another basis of power. The most likely source is expert power. People who develop expert knowledge or skill in a particular field can continually build that knowledge base and are often then given the opportunity to occupy a position of legitimate power within the organization. Steps that can build such a power base are:

1. Develop a reputation as an expert in a certain aspect of the organization.
2. Spend more time in critical relationships (supervisor, key clients, etc.) instead of social relationships.
3. Develop a network of resource people who can provide career assistance.
4. Develop an arsenal of effective communication skills—including written and oral presentation methods, humor, and public speaking—and learn to use them effectively according to the situation.
5. Determine methods to utilize developed expertise and skills to achieve organizational goals, not personal goals.

Thus, a person who develops expert knowledge or skill in a field, continually builds on that knowledge base, concentrates time where that knowledge can be utilized to achieve organizational goals, and develops a network of contacts. The individual utilizes effective communication skills to convince others and to ultimately achieve organizational goals to gain leadership power.

Decision making (i.e., choosing between two or more alternatives) discussed in Chapter 8 represents another part of the foundation of leadership. When a position of responsibility is accepted, the need to make decisions naturally follows. Reduced to simple terms, the style and effectiveness of a leader are largely determined by power and decision making.

When an individual accepts a leadership position solely for power, the position is accepted for the wrong reason. Effective leadership is based not on having power, but rather on how the leader uses the power. As Abraham Lincoln said, "Nearly all men can stand adversity, but if you want to test a man's character, give him power." Effective leaders learn when to be coercive. They learn when and how to use reward—based on the individual and the situation. With experience, the effective leader can apply the essence of all the power bases so as to benefit the individual, the department, and the organization.

Leadership demands making decisions on a daily basis. As problems develop, employees look to the organization's leaders for direction. The way that direction is provided, via decision making, largely determines the manner in which employees perceive the leadership style of the manager. Hence, today's organizational leaders must learn when to make an independent decision and when to use participative methods, based on the situation, the nature of the problem, and the philosophy of the organization.

Key Leadership Behaviors

Although power, influence, and decision making serve as important foundations, they represent only part of the leadership process. Leadership is also characterized by five key behavioral functions:

1. *Coaching*: providing specific direction, advice, and guidance to employees on tasks and assignments.
2. *Counseling*: interviewing employees and aiding them in finding their own answers.
3. *Evaluating*: controlling, reviewing, and appraising employees in order to give feedback on job performance.
4. *Delegating*: assigning tasks, responsibilities, and authority to employees who have been deemed competent and mature.
5. *Rewarding*: providing tangible and intangible recognition to employees who have successfully accomplished tasks and assignments.

The five behaviors, when coupled with the foundations of leadership, enable leaders to perform successfully.

A BRIEF HISTORY OF MODERN LEADERSHIP THEORY

The roots of the modern theories of leadership can be traced to the industrial revolution that took place in the Western world at the end of the nineteenth century. During the industrial revolution, the study of leadership, much like research in other aspects of organizations, became more rigorous. Scientific methods were used to understand and predict leadership effectiveness and specific attempts to identify and measure leadership characteristics were made. The history of modern leadership can be divided into three general areas: the trait era, the behavioral era, and the contingency era. Each era is characterized by distinct contributions to our understanding of leadership and each continues to influence our thinking about the process.

The Trait Era: Late 1800s to Mid-1940s

People often describe those in leadership and management positions as having certain traits, such as initiative and drive. It is not surprising that the earliest studies of leadership in organizations focused on the psychological and personal characteristics that distinguish leaders from nonleaders.

Much of the late nineteenth century and the early part of the twentieth century were dominated by the belief that leaders are born. Consequently, leaders were assumed by virtue of their birth to have special qualities that allowed them to lead others. Their special characteristics were assumed to push them toward leadership regardless of the context. By providing limited opportunities for common people to become social, political, and industrial leaders, the social structure of that period further reinforced such beliefs. The belief in the power of personality, and other innate characteristics strongly influenced leadership researchers and sent them on a massive hunt for leadership traits.

Variables such as age, physical characteristics, intelligence, motivation, initiative, and self-confidence were only a few of the hundreds of characteristics studied during this era and more recently in the 1960s and 1970s. Many of the contemporary leadership theories show the influence of the trait approach. The findings regarding leadership traits clearly indicate that leadership is much more than a combination of traits. However, the leadership research community is becoming increasingly aware that traits play an important role in leadership.

The Behavioral Era: Mid-1940s to Early 1960s

As the trait approach did not yield expected results and the need for identification and training of leaders came to the forefront with the advent of World War II, researchers turned to behaviors, rather than traits, as the source of leader effectiveness. Instead of trying to identify who would be an effective leader, the behavioral approach focuses on trying to identify effective leadership behaviors. Focusing on behaviors provides several advantages over the trait approach. First, behaviors can be observed objectively. Second, they can be measured precisely and accurately. Finally, as opposed to traits which are either innate or develop very early in life, behaviors can be taught. These three factors provided the military and various other organizations with an applied interest in leadership with a clear benefit. They did not have to identify leaders who had particular personality traits, rather they could train people to perform effective leadership behaviors.

Two complementary behavioral theories of leadership were designed to describe the behavior that distinguished leaders of effective and ineffective work groups. One set of researchers was at the University of Michigan; the other set was at Ohio State University.

Armed with results of early work on leadership behaviors, a number of researchers (the Ohio State and University of Michigan studies) (Coons, 1957) developed a list of close to 2,000 leadership behaviors which were later reduced and became the Leader Behavior Description Questionnaire (LBDQ). The LBDQ, which continues to be used today, focuses mostly on the behaviors of consideration (or employee-centered) and initiation structure (or job-centered). The consideration factor encompasses behaviors that are generally people oriented and deal with helping and looking out for employees. On the other hand, the initiation structure factor includes a variety of task-related behaviors such as setting deadlines and clarifying roles. The behaviors are suggested to be two different dimensions rather than two ends of the same continuum. As such, a leader is assumed to be able to perform both sets of behaviors to varying degrees.

Although these studies clearly identified a number of leader behaviors, the links between those behaviors and leadership effectiveness were not clearly established. Overall, the behavior approach has increased our understanding of leadership by successfully identifying several categories of behaviors. Considering leadership to be an acquired behavior rather than a personality trait has also focused attention on leadership training. As had been the case with the trait approach, the behavioral approach to leadership, by concentrating on only behaviors and disregarding powerful situational elements, provides a simplistic view of a very complex process and, therefore, fails to reach a thorough understanding of the leadership phenomenon.

The Contingency Era: Early 1960s to Present

Neither the trait nor behavioral approaches offered completely satisfactory explanations of leadership in organizations, causing researchers to develop contingency theories of leadership. However, even before the lack of success of the behavioral approach in explaining and predicting leadership effectiveness became evident, a number of researchers were calling for a more comprehensive approach to leadership (Stodgill, 1948). Specifically, it was suggested that situational factors such as the type of task and the type of work group needed to be taken into consideration. However, it wasn't until the 1960s that this suggestion was applied. Leadership research, spearheaded by Fred Fiedler (1967), moved from simplistic models based solely on the leader to more complex models that take a contingency point of view. Such views are still dominant in current leadership research (a more detailed discussion of several contingency models will be presented later in this chapter). The primary assumption of the contingency view is that the personality, style, or behavior of leaders that is effective will depend upon the requirements of the situation in which the leaders find themselves.

Overall, the contingency approach holds the following assumptions. First, there is no one best way to lead. Different leadership traits, styles, or behaviors can all be effective; it is the situation and the various relevant contextual factors that will help determine which style or behavior is most effective. Second, people can learn to become good leaders. Few of us will become a Joan of Arc, Mahatma Gandhi, or Martin Luther King, Jr., but there are many areas where we can improve and become better leaders. Third, leadership makes a difference in the effectiveness of groups and organizations. There are many factors that affect the course an organization, department, or team takes and the decisions that are made. Many such factors are as important, if not more important, than a leader; for example, the style of the leader's immediate supervisor, group norms, time demands, and the organization's culture. However, in spite of the influence of other factors, the leader can have either a positive or negative impact on the process or outcome. Fourth, both the personal and situational characteristics affect leadership effectiveness. Neither the leader's traits nor the demands of the situation in and of themselves will determine leadership effectiveness; there is an interactive role. Therefore, we need to understand both the leader and the leadership situation.

In spite of somewhat general agreement over the assumptions just presented, there is still little agreement over what constitutes effectiveness, whether leadership style is a trait or a learned behavior, or which situational characteristics are relevant. In spite of all the disagreements about leadership, the existing research and theory have much to offer today's leaders. The following section takes a look at several contingency theories in more detail.

CONTINGENCY LEADERSHIP THEORIES

Advocates of the contingency approach (i.e., the leadership style is dependent upon the situation, the task, the employees, and the leader) believe that leaders must adjust their leadership style and emphasis based on the total environment.

Several approaches to isolating key situational variables have proven more successful than others and, as a result, have gained wider recognition. We shall consider two: the Fiedler model and path-goal theory.

How Does the Fiedler Model Operate?

One of the most intuitive leadership models is based on Fred Fiedler's Contingency Theory (1967). Fiedler studied leadership in widely varying groups, such as manufacturing groups, boards of directors, managers, and military combat teams. Fiedler proposed that effective leadership is a function of a proper match between the leader's style of interacting with followers and the degree to which the situation gives control and influence to the leader. According to Fiedler, a leader's style could be identified based on how the leader describes an individual he or she last enjoyed working with. When a leader describes this person in favorable terms, this indicates that the leader is interested in good relationships. Accordingly, that leader's style would tend to be more people-centered. On the other hand, describing the least-preferred individual in unfavorable terms indicates more of a task-centered style. Fiedler felt that one's style is fixed. Using three situational factors (degree of respect for employees; structured jobs; and influence over the employment process) he identified eight situations where either the task-centered or people-centered styles would work best. That is, these situational factors would dictate which leadership style would be more effective. Fiedler developed the least-preferred coworker (LPC) questionnaire, which claims to measure whether a person is task-oriented or relationship-oriented.

Leader-member relations refers to the degree of employee confidence, loyalty, respect, and trust in the leader. Acceptance leads to commitment and loyalty, a rating of unacceptable leads to friction and tension. This dimension is measured on a continuum ranging from good to poor. Obviously, the better the relationship, the easier it is to lead people. When the relationship is characterized as poor, the leader is at a great disadvantage.

Leader position power refers to the authority that is granted based on coercive, reward, and legitimate power. According to Fiedler, the more position power possessed, the easier it is to lead others.

Fiedler classifies leadership styles into task-oriented and relationship-oriented categories using the LPC. Respondents describe the person they are least able to work with in either favorable or unfavorable terms. The leadership style of the person is judged relationship-oriented if the person is favorably evaluated, and task-oriented if unfavorably judged.

To determine whether task or relationship is appropriate, the user answers three questions pertaining to situational favorableness, using the Fiedler model. After a leader's style is determined through the LPC, a match can be determined through the other major contingency variables: leader-member relations, task structure, and position power. Organizations, Fiedler claims, should match tasks and work environments with an individual's leadership style to ensure high group performance.

Fiedler's Contingency Theory in Perspective

Overall, there seems little question that Fiedler has provided one of the major breakthroughs for leadership theory, research, and practice. Although some criticism is justified, there are several reasons that Fiedler's model has made a contribution:

1. It was the first highly visible leadership theory to present the contingency approach.
2. It emphasized the importance of both the situation and the leader's characteristics in determining leader effectiveness.
3. It stimulated a great deal of research, including tests of its predictions and attempts to improve on the model, and inspired the formulation of alternative contingency theories.

At the very least, Fiedler conducted considerable empirical research, and more recently he proposed another contingency theory (Fiedler and Garcia, 1987).

In Fiedler's recent cognitive resource theory (CRT), he identifies the situations under which a leader's cognitive resources, such as intelligence, experience, and technical expertise, relate to group and organizational performance. Based on Fiedler and his colleagues' research, CRT predicts the following:

1. More intelligent leaders develop better plans, decisions, and action strategies than less intelligent leaders.
2. Intelligence contributes more strongly to group performance if the leader is directive and the group members are motivated and supportive of the leader.
3. Interpersonal stress distracts the leader from the task and the leader's intelligence will contribute more highly if the leader has relatively stress-free relationships with superiors and subordinates. (Fiedler, Murphy, and Gibson, 1992)

As is the case with his original contingency model, CRT has been criticized (Vecchio, 1992), but it also will generate more research and, one hopes, make meaningful linkages to practice.

How Does the Path-Goal Model Operate?

The other widely recognized theoretical development from a contingency approach is the path-goal theory derived from the expectancy framework of motivation theory. House's path-goal theory is one of the most promising approaches for determining leadership effectiveness (House, 1971). Essentially, this approach posits that leaders motivate people successfully by communicating how desired goals, such as merit pay raises, promotions, and recognition can be achieved if people achieve higher performance standards (paths). That is, leaders can help followers by showing them how their performance directly relates to the organization's goals and to obtaining their rewards. Effective followers' performance occurs if the leader clearly defines the employees' jobs and the path to reach their work goals. The leader can assist by providing training, coaching, and guidance, and by removing obstacles to goal attainment.

According to House, leaders are effective when their styles enable employees to accomplish their work goals and thus achieve the organization's aims. This happens when the appropriate leadership style matches and complements follower characteristics, taking other environmental factors into consideration. When leadership style fits with these other factors, followers' perceptions of the leader are likely to be positive, and followers are likely to be motivated, reach their work goals, perform well, and be satisfied.

House proposes and defines four leadership styles (i.e., directive, supportive, participative, and achievement-oriented), which he believes could be adapted (any or all) by leaders, depending on the situation. The four styles are:

1. *Directive leadership.* This style focuses on what must be done, when it must be done, and how it must be done. Subordinates know exactly what is expected of them, and the leader gives specific directions. There is no participation by subordinates.
2. *Supportive leadership.* The leader is friendly and approachable and shows a genuine concern for subordinates.
3. *Participative leadership.* The leader asks for and uses suggestions from subordinates but still makes the decisions.
4. *Achievement-oriented leadership.* The leader sets challenging goals for subordinates and shows confidence that they will attain these goals and perform well.

The environmental factors that moderate leadership behavior and style include tasks, formal authority of the organization, and the work group. The contingency factors that also affect a leader's choice of style are the characteristics of the followers: locus of control (internal or external) and their experience and ability. Environmental factors can also influence followers' motivation.

Similar to Fiedler's contingency model, the path-goal theory emphasizes the utilization of different leadership styles depending on the situation. The path-goal theory, however, allows more than one style to be engaged at any one time. Two of the situational factors that have been identified are the personal characteristics of subordinates and the environmental pressures and demands facing subordinates.

Research to validate path-goal predictions is generally encouraging, although not every study found positive support. House (1996) has reformulated and expanded the theory after 25 years of research by himself and others. The theory describes leader behaviors and relationships that not only affect subordinate performance but also help work unit performance. Instead of four behaviors, the new version features eight behaviors. The new behaviors focus on path-goal clarification, social interaction within the work group, the political behavior necessary to increase the group's power, and the leader's charismatic behavior. These behaviors add to the behavior repertoire noted earlier. This expanded version of path-goal theory has not yet been empirically tested. However, House's contributions to contingency leadership theory overall include his approach's practicality and conceptually appealing diagnostic method.

What Is the Situational Model?

Over the years, organizational leaders and managers have often complained that esoteric theories don't help them do a better job on the production line, in the office, or in a research and development lab. They request something they can apply and use. Hersey and Blanchard developed a situational leadership theory that has appealed to organizational leaders and managers. Hersey and Blanchard's situational leadership theory is based on the premise that effective leadership styles depend on two factors: the followers' level of readiness or maturity and situational demands. A leader should be able to adapt his or her style to meet these contingencies. *Follower readiness* indicates the extent to which followers have the ability and willingness to perform a task. Leadership style (*situational leadership*) centers around task and relationship behaviors. As in the early behavioral studies, task behavior signals the giving of instruction and direction; relationship behavior indicates the giving of emotional and human support. The leader offers the type of behavior that suits the followers' readiness to perform tasks.

Hersey and Blanchard used the Ohio State studies to further develop four leadership styles available to managers:

1. *Telling.* The leader defines the roles needed to do the job and tells followers what, where, how, and when to do the tasks. In short, leaders provide specific instructions and closely supervise performance.
2. *Selling.* The leader provides followers with structured instructions, but is also supportive. The leader explains decisions and provides opportunities for clarification.
3. *Participating.* The leader and followers share in decisions about how best to complete a high-quality job.
4. *Delegating.* The leader provides little specific, close direction or personal support to followers.

A leader should use the telling style when followers are unable and unwilling to perform a task. A leader should use a selling style when followers have low ability and are moderately willing to perform tasks. A participating style should be used when followers have moderate to high ability and readiness. A delegating style should be used when followers show a high ability and readiness to perform.

Although a number of managers find this model attractive, there are some serious unanswered questions. The most important may be, does it really work? On the basis of research to date, conclusions must be guarded. Some researchers provide partial support for the theory (Norris and Vecchio, 1992; Vecchio, 1987), while others find no support for its assumptions (Norris and Vecchio, 1992). As a result, any enthusiastic endorsement should be cautioned against.

The enduring contribution of the contingency theory models is their message that no one best leadership style exists for all situations. Each approach is valuable because it adds insight into our understanding of leadership. Leadership style depends on the situation and the followers. Effective leaders can and do change and adapt their style to accommodate follower readiness and situational contingencies.

Charismatic Leadership: Trait Theories Updated

Most of the leadership theories discussed in this chapter have involved transactional leaders. These people guide or motivate their followers in the direction of established goals by clarifying role and task requirements. There is another type of leader who inspires followers to transcend their own self-interests for the good of the organization and who is capable of having a profound and extraordinary effect on his or her followers. These are transformational, or charismatic leaders. Ted Turner, Mother Theresa, General Douglas MacArthur, and Franklin D. Roosevelt are of this latter type. By the force of their personal abilities they transform their followers by raising the sense of the importance and value of their tasks. "I'd walk through fire if my boss asked" is the kind of support that charismatic leaders inspire.

The charismatic, or charisma, goes as far back as the ancient Greeks and is cited in the Bible. What characteristics differentiate charismatic leaders from noncharismatic ones? Studies on charismatic leadership have, for the most part, been directed at identifying those behaviors that differentiate charismatic leaders. Such individuals have high amounts of self-confidence, present a clearly articulated vision, behave in extraordinary ways, are recognized as change agents, and are sensitive to the environmental constraints they face (Conger and Kanungo, 1988).

What can we say about charismatic leaders' impact on their followers' attitudes and behavior? There is an increasing body of research that shows positive relationships between charismatic leadership and high performance and satisfaction among followers (House, Wyocke, and Fodor, 1988). Charismatic leaders attract devoted followers who energetically pursue the leader's vision. People working for charismatic leaders are motivated to exert extra work effort and, because they like their leader, express greater satisfaction.

Which Leadership Style Is Best?

Given that many approaches to leadership are learned in the process of becoming an effective leader, the desire for a single best leadership style is understandable. However, as we have already seen, there is no single best answer.

Most of the theorists agree that a model must accommodate the differences between situations and the differences between leaders in order to be useful. Factors affecting the choice of leadership style include the leader's philosophy of human nature, experience, training, and professional and technical competence. Similarly, the followers' belief systems, attitudes toward work and authority, maturity levels, experience, and knowledge and skill levels will determine the leadership style that is most effective.

Imagine how these additional factors will affect an individual's leadership style:

- The number of people in the workgroup
- The type of tasks
- Situational stress
- Objectives of the unit
- The presence or absence of a union
- The leadership style of the manager or leader's boss
- The overall relationship of the leader with the followers.

Contemporary Thoughts on Leadership

Contemporary writings concerning leadership are replete with many findings and some contradictions. However, there are several areas of agreement. One of the most noted writers on leadership, Warren Bennis (1994), reported from his extensive research four things people want from their leaders.

1. *Direction.* People want leaders to have a purpose. Leaders have a clear idea of what they want to do. The leaders love what they do and love doing it. Followers want passion and conviction from a strong point of view.
2. *Trust.* The ability to trust a leader is perhaps more important today than any time in recent history. Integrity, maturity, and candor are essential elements of building a relationship of mutual trust.
3. *Hope.* Leaders believe, and they kindle the fire of optimism in followers.
4. *Results.* Accomplishment of difficult tasks. Success breeds success.

Stephen R. Covey (1991), author of *Principle-Centered Leadership*, notes that:

> Leadership is influence, and we influence by modeling, mentoring and teaching—walking our talk. If organizational values include such principles as the worth of people and the need for cooperative synergy, be sure that you practice habits of seeking win-win mutual benefit, seeking first to understand in communications and a willingness to consider contrary opinions in the spirit of genuine synergy.
>
> Trust bonds management to labor, employees to each other, customers to suppliers, and strengthens all other stakeholder relationships. With low trust, developing performance is exhausting. With high trust it is exhilarating. The principle of alignment means working together in harmony, going in the same direction, supporting each other. Alignment develops the organizational trustworthiness required for trust. And if personal trustworthiness and interpersonal trust are to mature, hiring, promoting, training and other systems must foster character development as well as competence.

Noted leadership researchers James M. Kouzes and Barry Z. Posner (1987) contend that "leadership is an observable, learnable set of practices. Given the opportunity for feedback and practice, those with desire and persistence to lead can substantially improve their abilities to do so" (p. 33). After examining the experiences of managers who were leading others to outstanding accomplishments, Kouzes and Posner identified five practices and ten specific behaviors that can be learned and used by managers at all levels. The practices and corresponding behaviors include:

- Challenging the process (searching for opportunities, experimenting, and taking risks)
- Inspiring a shared vision (envisioning the future, enlisting the support of others)
- Enabling others to act (fostering collaboration, strengthening others)
- Modeling the way (setting an example, planning small wins)
- Encouraging the heart (recognizing contributions, celebrating accomplishments)

They also emphasize the notion that credibility is one of the major qualities that employees look for in their leaders.

Jack Welch, former CEO of General Electric, wanted a special kind of person to be a part of the GE team: "I want someone with incredible energy who can excite others, who can define their vision, who finds change fun and doesn't get paralyzed by it. I want somebody who feels comfortable in Delphi or Denver, I mean, somebody who really feels comfortable and can talk to all kinds of people. I don't know what the world's going to be; all I know is it's going to be nothing like it is today. It's going to be faster; information's going to be everywhere" ("A Conversation with Roberto Goizueta and Jack Welch," 1995).

Stretch targets are one example of Welch's philosophy. A stretch target is an extremely ambitious goal that by definition is one you don't know how to reach. Stretch targets are artificial stimulants for finding ways to work more efficiently. They force you to work smarter, get out of the box, and be creative.

CONTEMPORARY LEADERSHIP CHALLENGES

Now that we have looked at contemporary leadership theories, we turn our attention to important challenges that effective leaders in the twenty-first century will continue to be concerned about. Specifically, how does participative leadership provide new challenges for today's leaders? What are the special considerations of leading teams? And, what is leading through empowerment?

Participative Leaders Share Authority

The participative model requires leaders to share their leadership authority with others rather than making decisions alone. Leaders with substantial egos are not likely to be successful in the new millennium where participatory style is prevalent. They may find it difficult to relinquish a portion of their authority, because they perceive it to be a reduction of their role in the organization. The new economy leader must recognize the immense benefits of participative leadership.

- Workers know their job better than anyone else.
- People can and will accept the responsibility for managing their own work if that responsibility is given to them in the proper way.
- Intelligence, perspective, and creativity exist among people at all levels of the organization.

In practice, participative leadership generally follows one of two styles:

- The leader involves other employees in the decision-making process but retains the authority to take independent action when necessary.
- The leader allows the employees to form autonomous teams or workgroups that are given a few specific objectives and allowed to determine their own leaders and make their own decisions (see Chapter 7 for discussion on this point).

In the first style, the leader generally follows a four-step process: ask, listen, involve, and provide feedback (Hackett, 1990).

1. *Ask* their opinion and delegate authority. One of the greatest compliments one may bestow upon followers is to ask their opinion and delegate to them the authority to make decisions about work. This will build their self-esteem and make them feel a part of the problem-solving process. They will then be more likely to support the company's objectives. Methods for soliciting employee input include ad hoc committees, department meetings, suggestion systems, and voluntary employee-advisory committees.
2. *Listen* to them and build concern. The leader must be an effective listener. This individual must learn to gain an understanding of not only the employee's ideas but also the employee's feelings about the issue. When asking a question, leaders should take the time to listen without interruption. They should never invite employee input if they have already made a decision on the issue and are only trying to "sell" their decision. Allow the employees themselves, through discussion and consensus, to make decisions whenever possible.
3. *Involve* everyone. To truly be committed to the participative process, a leader must demonstrate to employees that their decision-making ability is trusted. Allow them autonomy. This doesn't mean leaders are obligated to use all ideas. But a timely, factual explanation of why a suggestion was not adopted should

be provided. In circumstances where an employee's idea is used in its entirety or in part, it is important to give proper credit or recognition to the employee(s) involved.

4. *Provide* feedback and demonstrate interest. Where leaders spend their time sends a clear message to employees as to what is important. Don't "micro-manage" (review every employee action and decision)—let employees make day-to-day decisions. If leaders delay providing employees feedback on the success of a project, they are saying the project is not important. A simple, clear, periodic method of feedback is essential to the success of the project and future employee motivation.

The most effective method of utilizing the four-step process of participative leadership is to simply practice it every day in all situations, not just when employees ask for the opportunity to participate. The effects can be tremendous.

The second common form of participative leadership is the formation of self-managed teams. Such teams highlight special considerations in leading teams for those in leadership positions.

Leadership and Self-Managing Teams

As suggested in Chapter 7 managers in organizations are increasingly using self-managing teams to get work done. The use of self-managing teams changes the traditional distribution of decision authority in an organization as its teams take on much of the decision authority formerly exercised by middle managers and supervisors.

When most people think of leaders, they think of individuals who make strategic decisions on behalf of followers, and who are responsible for carrying them out. In many of today's organizations, however, where the movement toward self-managed teams predominates, it is less likely than ever that supervisors and managers as leaders are responsible for getting others to implement orders to help fulfill their visions. And the role of team leader is different from the traditional leadership role performed by many supervisors and managers.

Today's team leaders may be called upon to provide special resources to groups empowered to implement their own missions in their own ways. They don't call all the shots but help employees take responsibility for their own work. This suggests that the role of team leader is clearly very different than the "command and control" leadership role we have traditionally seen in organizations. Today's supervisors and managers delegate almost all authority and responsibility to a team of employees, and usually serve as their coach, advisor, or administrator, depending on what type of organizational support the team requires to work effectively.

The role of traits in the leadership process and the different leader behaviors described earlier in this chapter also apply to team leaders. For example, a team member who rotates into the team leader role might not have leadership traits, or other team members might not attribute those traits to the person. Leaders of self-managing teams could benefit from viewing the team leader role from the different perspectives offered by the various theories.

Managers outside the team do not cease to be leaders or managers. The nature of their work shifts from close, day-to-day supervision to long-range planning, team guidance, team development, resource support, and political support from more senior management. The behavior of external leaders and managers should focus on developing the self-managing part of self-managing teams.

The challenge for many of today's organizational leaders is to learn how to become an effective team leader. They have to learn skills such as the patience to share information, to trust others, to give up authority, and to understand when to intervene. Effective team leaders have mastered the difficult balancing act of knowing when to leave their teams alone and when to intercede. New team leaders may try to retain too much control at a time when team members need more autonomy, or they may abandon their teams at times when the teams need support and help.

In conclusion, leading teams in the new millennium is a far cry from leading individuals in the traditional directive (or even participative) manner. The special nature of teams makes the leader's job very different. Although appreciating these differences is easy, making the appropriate adjustments may be extremely challenging, especially for today's leaders, who are well practiced in the ways of traditional leadership. However, given the prevalence of teams in today's work environment, the importance of making the adjustments cannot be overstated. Leading new teams using old methods is a surefire formula for leadership failure.

THE MYTHS OF LEADERSHIP

The subject of leadership has always been permeated with myths. The following is a list of some of these myths:

1. Leadership is a rare skill. In reality, nothing could be farther from the truth; everyone has leadership potential. There are millions of leadership roles throughout the world, and many are filled by capable leaders. People may be leaders in one organization and followers in another. Leadership opportunities are plentiful and within the reach of most people.
2. Leaders are born, not made. Biographies mislead by sometimes portraying great leaders as unpredictable superhumans with unique charisma and almost mystical genius. Leadership is not a gift of grace too abstract to be defined, much less learned. Because the title of leader is often attributed to those whose actions

take place in the most dramatic realms of human endeavor (for example, Winston Churchill, Mahatma Gandhi, Nelson Mandela, Joan of Arc), we sometimes assume they were destined to lead. This myth perpetuates myth 3.

3. Leaders are created by extraordinary circumstances and great events. This myth would have us believe that leaders emerge suddenly during times of great conflict and chaos, as did Martin Luther King, Jr. This is true only sometimes. This myth limits the opportunities for leadership still further. It indicates that leadership is only associated with some sort of grand cataclysm or rise and fall of power; we have no opportunity to exercise leadership skills under normal circumstances. But leadership is exercised by all kinds of people in all kinds of situations every day.
4. Leadership exists only at the top of an organization. We feed this myth by focusing on top leadership when organizations have thousands of leadership roles available to employees. Corporations are moving in the direction of creating more leadership roles through empowerment and self-directed or managed teams within the organization.
5. The leader controls, directs, prods, manipulates. This is perhaps the most damaging myth of all. Leadership is not so much the exercise of power itself as the ability to empower others. Leaders align their energies with others: they pull, rather than push; they inspire, rather than command. Managers may command people, use a system of rewards and punishments, and maintain control through intimidation—but a leader's tools are very different. Some managers try to substitute management for leadership. Often organizations are overmanaged and underled. Management is never a substitute for leadership.
6. Leaders are charismatic. Some are, but most are not. There are always a few leaders who correspond to our fantasies of "divine inspiration" and "grace under pressure" (for example, John F. Kennedy), but most leaders are all too human—fallible, flawed, with no particular charm that separates them externally from their followers. Charisma is the result of effective leadership—not the other way around. It is often the ability to articulate the felt needs of an emerging group of people.
7. It is immoral to seek power. Those who recognize that power is a key requisite for change may feel revulsion toward it. Power has been maligned and misunderstood. Power is often associated with greed and selfish ambition. Power is associated with those who abuse and misuse it, rather than with those who use it wisely. We confuse power with subjugation and control. In doing so, we reject power, whether consciously or unconsciously, and thereby restrict our own opportunities for leadership. Power is a means to an end. Power is energy, and as with any form of energy, its value lies in how we use it. Until used, power is neutral—it is neither benign nor corrupting.

We all have opportunities to be leaders. All that's really required is that we work to avoid some of the mistakes that individuals in leadership positions make and continuously try to improve our leadership skills as discussed in the last part of this chapter.

OBSTACLES TO LEADERSHIP EFFECTIVENESS

J.K. Van Fleet (1973) has compiled a list of the biggest mistakes that managers make. Any one of these mistakes can be fatal to their career, and many of these principles are not readily deductible from any theory. Following is a selected list of the top 10 mistakes:

1. Failing to stay abreast of developments in your field and limiting yourself to your own specialty area.
2. Refusing to seek higher responsibility or to take responsibility for your own actions.
3. Failing to make sure that assignments are understood, supervised, and accomplished.
4. Refusing to assess your own performance and abilities realistically.
5. Using your position for personal gain or failing to tell the truth.
6. Not setting a positive, personal example for direct reports.
7. Trying to be liked rather than respected.
8. Emphasizing rules rather than skill.
9. Failing to keep criticism in a constructive vein.
10. Not attending to employee gripes and complaints.

Other factors tied to leadership or management failure have also been identified by the Center for Creative Leadership in Greensboro, North Carolina. The four sets of individual factors associated with failure (McCall and Lombardo, 1983) are:

1. *Defensiveness*: trying to hide mistakes or fix blame on others, rather than taking responsibility and seeking to remedy errors.
2. *Emotional instability*: engaging in emotional outbursts or displaying moodiness, rather than projecting confidence and a calm demeanor.
3. *Poor interpersonal skills*: lacking sensitivity and tact, and being arrogant or abrasive.
4. *Weak technical and cognitive skills*: lacking technical know-how for upper-level jobs, possessing a narrow perspective based on a single specialty, or trying to micromanage the work of subordinates who possess substantial technical competence.

It is particularly difficult to state precisely the level of flawed leadership in organizational positions. However, it has been estimated that the base rate for seriously flawed leadership exceeds 50 percent (Church, 1998). This suggests that the majority of employed adults work for someone who is not capable of exercising adequate leadership skills. The downside consequence of this state of affairs is that employees often retaliate against their immediate bosses in subtle ways (such as withholding loyalty, reducing output or customer service, and engaging in theft, sabotage, and vandalism).

IMPROVING YOUR LEADERSHIP SKILLS

Today's organizations realize the critical importance of developing leadership abilities among all levels of employees. Top and middle managers, supervisors, technicians, and hourly workers can all learn to share the vision for the future of the organization and develop one for themselves and their position.

How can you improve your leadership skills? Basically, there are four alternatives: (1) trial and error, (2) formal education and training, (3) mentoring or coaching and guided practice, and (4) analysis of feedback from others. We recommend that you use all four; to get you going, here's a systematic approach to self-improvement.

Step 1: Examine your goals and your status. Do you have a vision of what your company and your department should be doing? Do you have clear and realistic long-term goals and midrange objectives, and have you communicated them to your people? Do you have the interpersonal, conceptual, technical, and analytical skills that your position requires? Do you have a plan to shore up your deficiencies?

Step 2: Analyze your leadership style. What style of leadership do you now practice? Has your style changed over the last two or three years? Does your style take into account the vision, mission, and culture of your organization? What are the maturity, skills, and expectations of your people?

Step 3: Get feedback. What kind of feedback have you received from your people, from colleagues, and from managers? What specifically did the feedback reveal? What specific suggestions has your boss made to improve your leadership? How can you get better and more frequent feedback from all your constituencies (superiors, peers, and employees)?

Step 4: Develop an improvement plan. What is your plan to improve your leadership skills? Have you identified specific improvement objectives, a time frame, and a way of accomplishing them?

No matter which of the approaches to leadership an individual uses, effective leadership is the result of planned behavior based on learning. To reinforce this belief, the following guidelines are offered as a foundation for the practice of effective leadership:

1. *Learn from the past.* Many times, past experiences serve as lessons for life. It is important to learn from past successes and failures and to use the knowledge gained as a positive foundation for the future.

2. *Learn to set an example.* Frequently, direct reports assume the personality of the leader. Learn to set a productive example. Learn to be enthusiastic—it becomes contagious. Be a "doer."
3. *Learn to inspire others.* An effective leader does not drive others, but rather inspires others by instilling a belief that success is attainable. Building teamwork is a vital component.
4. *Learn to know yourself and your people.* Everyone has limitations. It is imperative to learn personal and direct report limitations. Build on strengths. Develop a plan to correct weaknesses.
5. *Learn to exhibit confidence, trust, and support.* Don't try to push employees. Learn to pull them by confidence, trust, and support. When a positive climate is built, direct reports will not only believe in themselves, they will believe in the leader.
6. *Learn to communicate and ask questions.* Learn to place a premium on communication. Show employees that they count. Learn to ask questions—it will have surprising results.
7. *Learn to be positive and optimistic.* A positive attitude adds to a positive climate. Be optimistic. Be positive about the things that can happen and then work hard to make them happen.
8. *Learn to take charge.* Leadership involves accepting responsibility. Don't be afraid. Leaders take charge of themselves, their direct reports, and the situation.
9. *Learn to take risks.* Don't be afraid to take a chance. On occasion, take calculated risks. Leadership is an action-oriented role and people admire risk takers.
10. *Learn to delegate.* It is impossible to do everything. Learn to delegate and train people to develop individual skills. Part of leadership involves being a teacher. Facilitate the learning process effectively through delegation.
11. *Learn to accept criticism.* Leadership involves taking risks, making decisions, and being a focal point. When actions generate criticism, exhibit discipline—and learn from it. It will promote better leadership.
12. *Learn to learn.* Learning is a lifelong process. Effective leaders continue to learn—and keep getting better. The same holds true for direct reports. Encourage them to continually learn and seek ways to improve job skills and knowledge.
13. *Learn human relations.* Effective human relations serve as the foundation for effective leadership. Positive human relations skills are the common thread in all leadership situations. People skills are an essential for leadership because leadership involves people.

As organizations change they will continue to demand more from their leaders—and this means individuals at all levels of the organization. The lesson for new economy leaders is clear: Their efforts to succeed will be greatly enhanced if they accept that they must be leaders each day, week, and year.

SUMMARY

In the currently evolving workplace, traditional methods and styles of leadership must change to meet the changing environment. Leadership styles must be flexible and adaptable to the situation at hand. Today's successful organizations must ensure that those individuals in leadership positions learn to be both a leader and a manager if they are going to be successful. This means they must understand that there is a difference between leading and managing. By definition, leadership is the ability to get others to want to do something that the leader is convinced should be done, and to follow directions. Managers are people who develop budgets and plans, organize personnel, and execute by monitoring results against the plan.

Power, influence, and decision making are the foundation components of leadership that allow leaders to successfully perform their roles. Additionally, today's leaders must be able to interpret and develop visions, missions, and objectives that are central to their own and the organization's success. Interpreting and developing visions, missions, and objectives puts individuals in leadership positions in both the role of a follower and leader. They must be able to balance both the role of an effective follower and leader for themselves while encouraging similar behavior from their employees.

A number of major theorists have contributed valuable research to the process of leadership. Major theorists include Fiedler, House, Hersey, and Blanchard.

The charismatic approach to leadership provides additional ideas for improving the effectiveness of today's leaders as they respond to challenges to learn to share their leadership authority with others, respond to special considerations of self-managed teams, and lead through empowerment.

The study of leadership has been permeated with many myths. An understanding of these myths can increase our understanding of what is and is not leadership. People in leadership roles fail for a variety of reasons. Along with external influences, failure can arise from such personal factors as defensiveness, emotional instability, poor interpersonal skills, and weak technological and cognitive skills.

Leadership can be learned through the successful practice of the 13 guidelines. Learn to be an effective leader.

REFERENCES

Bennis, W. 1994. *On becoming a leader*. Reading, MA: Addison-Wesley.

Challeff, I. 1995. *The courageous follower: Standing up to and for our leaders*. San Francisco: Berrett-Koehler.

Church, A.H. 1998. From both sides now: Leadership—So close and yet so far. *The Industrial Psychologist* 35: 57–69.

Conger, J.A., and Kanungo, R.N. 1988. Behavioral dimensions of charismatic leadership. In J.A. Conger and R.N. Kanungo (eds.), *Charismatic leadership*. San Francisco: Jossey-Bass, pp. 78–97.

A conversation with Roberto Goizueta and Jack Welch. 1995. *Fortune* (December 11): 99–101.

Coons, A.E. 1957. Development of leader behavior description questionnaire. In R.M. Stodgill and A.E. Coons (eds.), *Leader behavior: Its description and measurement*. Columbus: Ohio State University, Bureau of Business Research, pp. 28–51.

Covey, S.R. 1991. *Principle-centered leadership*. New York: Summit Books.

El-Namaki, M.S. 1992. Creating a corporate vision. *Long-Range Planning* 25(6): 25–29.

Fiedler, F.E. 1967. A path-goal theory of leadership effectiveness. *Administrative Science Quarterly* (September): 321–328.

Fiedler, F.E., and Garcia, J.E. 1987. *New approaches to leadership: Cognitive resources and organizational performance*. New York: Wiley.

Fiedler, F.E., Murphy, S.E., and Gibson, F.W. 1992. Inaccurate reporting and inappropriate variables: A reply to Vecchio's examination of cognitive resource theory. *Journal of Applied Psychology* 77: 372–374.

French, J.B., and Raven, B. 1960. The bases of social power. In D. Cartwright and A.F. Zanders (eds.), *Group dynamics*. Evanston, IL: Row, Peterson, pp. 607–623.

Hackett, M.E. 1990. A worm's eye view of leadership. *Supervision Management* (September): 8–9.

House, R.J. 1971. A path-goal theory of leadership effectiveness. *Administrative Science Quarterly* (September): 321–328.

House, R.J. 1996. Path-goal theory of leadership: Lessons, legacy and a reformulated theory. *The Leadership Quarterly* 7: 323–352.

House, R.J., Woycke, J., and Fodor, E.M. 1988. Charismatic and noncharismatic leaders: Differences in behavior and effectiveness. In J.A. Conger and R.N. Kanungo (eds.), *Charismatic leadership*. San Francisco: Jossey-Bass, pp. 103–104.

Kelley, R.W. 1988. In praise of followers. *Harvard Business Review* (November/December): 143.

Kotter, J. 1990. *A force for change: How leadership differs from management*. New York: Free Press.

Kouzes, J.M., and Posner, B.Z. 1987. *The leadership challenge*. San Francisco: Jossey-Bass.

McCall, M., and Lombardo, M. 1983. *Off the track: Why and how successful executives get derailed—Technical report No. 21*. Greensboro, NC: Center for Creative Leadership.

Norris, W.R., and Vecchio, R.P. 1992. Situational leadership theory: A replication. *Group & Organization Management* (September): 331–342.

Peters, T. 1988. In search of excellence—A talk with Tom Peters. *NASSP Bulletin* 73: 37.

Stodgill, R.M. 1948. Personal factors associated with leadership: A survey of the literature. *Journal of Psychology* 25: 35–71.

Van Fleet, J.K. 1973. *The 22 biggest mistakes managers make.* West Nyack, NY: Parker.

Vecchio, R.P. 1987. Situational leadership theory: An examination of a prescriptive theory. *Journal of Applied Psychology* (August): 444–521.

Vecchio, R.P. 1992. Cognitive resource theory: Issues for specifying a test of the theory. *Journal of Applied Psychology* 77: 325–376.

Chapter 10

Conflict and Negotiation at Work

INTRODUCTION

We have all experienced conflict of various types, yet we probably fail to recognize the variety of conflict that occur in organizations. Conflict may be defined as a difference of opinion between two or more individuals or groups.

Today's organizations may face greater potential for conflict than ever before in history. The marketplace, with its increasing competition and globalization, magnifies differences among people in terms of personality, values, attitudes, perceptions, languages, cultures, and national backgrounds. With the increasing diversity of the workforce, furthermore, comes potential incompatibility and conflict.

In this chapter we examine conflict and negotiation from several viewpoints. First, we compare functional versus dysfunctional conflict. Next, we identify what causes conflict to include various types and sources of conflict. We examine workplace violence and aggression before turning to a discussion of factors that make jobs especially prone to coworker conflict. Then we present various reactions to the frustration that accompanies conflict along with effective and ineffective techniques for coping with difficult behavior and conflict. We focus on major conflict resolution approaches. The chapter concludes with an examination of negotiation and mediation, two types of conflict management.

FUNCTIONAL VERSUS DYSFUNCTIONAL CONFLICT

Not all conflict is bad. In fact, some types of conflict encourage new solutions to problems and enhance the creativity in the organization. In

Table 10.1
Consequences of Conflict

Positive Consequences	Negative Consequences
• Leads to new ideas • Stimulates creativity and innovation • Motivates change and consideration of new approaches and ideas • Promotes organizational vitality • Helps individuals and groups establish identities • Increases loyalty and performance within each of the groups in conflict • Serves as a safety valve to indicate problems by bringing them out into the open	• Diverts energy from work • Threatens psychological well-being • Wastes resources • Creates a negative climate • Interferes with communication • Breaks down group cohesion • Can increase hostility and aggressive behaviors • Leads to an increase in politics (i.e., individual efforts to acquire power to advance their own efforts) • Leads groups to stereotype each other • Reduces the organization's capacity to complete in the marketplace

these cases, managers will want to encourage the conflicts. Therefore, managers should stimulate functional conflict and prevent or resolve dysfunctional conflict. This is the key to conflict management. However, the difficulty lies in trying to tell the difference between dysfunctional and functional conflicts. The consequences of conflict can be positive or negative, as shown in Table 10.1. Functional conflict is healthy, constructive disagreement between two or more people or groups. Functional conflict can improve an individual's or group's performance. Functional conflict can bring about a greater awareness of problems, enhance the search for solutions, release innovations, and motivate employees to change and adapt when advisable. In addition, it can improve working relationships, because when two parties work through their disagreements, they feel they have accomplished something together. By releasing tensions and solving problems in working together, morale is improved. A key for recognizing functional conflict is that it is often cognitive in origin; that is, it arises from someone challenging old policies or thinking of new ways to approach problems.

Dysfunctional conflict is an unhealthy, destructive disagreement between two or more people or groups. Its danger is that it takes the focus away from the work to be done and places the focus on the conflict itself and the parties involved. Dysfunctional conflict can create distorted perceptions, negative stereotyping, poor communication, decreased productivity, and can even result in sabotage. A key for recognizing a dysfunctional conflict is that its origin is often emotional or behavioral. Disagreements that involve personalized anger and resentment directed at specific individuals rather than specific ideas are dysfunctional. With individuals involved in dysfunctional conflict, the losses to both parties may exceed any potential gain from that conflict.

Conflict can be viewed as a bell curve. A moderate level of healthy conflict can enhance achievement. Too much or too little conflict, on the other hand, can lead to negative and even destructive behaviors, especially if unreasonable pressures and tensions are present. One responsibility of today's managers is to decide how much functional conflict is needed to create, enhance, and sustain the productivity of employees and to make sure it does not degenerate into dysfunctional conflict.

Diagnosing conflict as good or bad is not easy. The manager must look at the issue, the context of the conflict, and the parties involved. The following questions can be used to diagnose the nature of the conflict a manager faces:

- Are the parties approaching the conflict from a hostile standpoint?
- Is the outcome likely to be a negative one for the organization?
- Do the potential losses of the parties exceed any potential gains?
- Is energy being diverted from goal accomplishment?

If the majority of the answers to these questions are yes, then the conflict is probably dysfunctional.

Other questions that managers and employees can also use to diagnose the sources and types of conflict include:

- Where is the conflict in the system? Is it at the leadership, individual, group/team, intergroup, organizational, or organization-environment level?
- What is the nature of the conflict?
- Is the conflict "functional" or "dysfunctional." For whom?
- How is the individual, team, or department that is experiencing the conflict related to other parts of the organization?
- How high up and how far down the organizational chart does the conflict extend?
- Which people experiencing the conflict are ready for change?
- Do we have an approved conflict resolution method for solving the problem?

Once the manager has diagnosed the type of conflict and understands its sources, he or she can either work to resolve it (if it is dysfunctional) or to stimulate it (if it is functional). Effective conflict-resolution techniques that can be used by managers and employees and organizations as well as individuals and teams are discussed later in the chapter.

CAUSES OF WORK CONFLICTS

Before managers can respond effectively to a particular conflict, they need to understand it. They need to ask, "Who is involved?" "What is the source of the conflict?" Managers are likely to respond differently to a conflict that results from a clash of opinions than to one stemming from frustration over limited resources. Conflict may occur between or within organizations, within departments, and even between an individual and the organization. There are four types of conflict a manager is likely to have to deal with: structural, intrapersonal, interpersonal, and interorganizational.

Structural Conflict

In traditionally structured companies, employees are organized by functional areas and departments: marketing and sales, research and development (R&D), maintenance, production, finance, legal, and human resources. (See Chapter 11 for a discussion of various types of organizational structures and designs.) These groups have different goals, different cultures, and different approaches and resources; and conflicts can naturally be expected to arise between them. These structural conflicts occur because of cross-functional departmental differences over goals, time horizons, rewards, authority, line and staff activities, status, or resources.

When structural conflict arises between two groups of employees a manager may be able to help minimize or resolve it. Managers can provide opportunities for the two groups to communicate and get to know each other's viewpoints, ask them to collaborate to achieve a mutually desirable goal, or give each group training in the role of the other group.

Because managers do not establish an organization's structure, they have limited impact on the sources of structural conflict. If they are able to recognize that a conflict is structural, however, they will know not to take the issue personally and will be alerted to situations that require extra diplomacy. Managers also may be better able to understand the other party's point of view and communicate it to their employees.

Interpersonal conflict occurs between two or more individuals. Interpersonal conflicts may arise from differing opinions, misunderstandings of a situation, or differences in value or beliefs. Sometimes two people just rub each other the wrong way.

Managers may be involved in interpersonal conflicts with a manager, an employee, a peer, or even a customer. In addition, managers may have to manage conflicts between two or more of their employees. Solving and managing interpersonal conflict requires knowledge about the nature of the conflict and skills for dealing with it. Practice will help you to build those skills.

Intrapersonal Conflict

Intrapersonal conflict is an internal struggle within an individual. This type of conflict often results from problems with a person's role in the organization—that is, conflict between the person's expectations about the role and the expectations of others. These role conflicts can cause considerable stress on individuals.

Learning to manage intrapersonal conflict involves first identifying the nature and extent of the conflict and then selecting the appropriate conflict-management approach. In many cases, a manager lacks the expertise to resolve an intrapersonal conflict. When managers notice that an employee is struggling with such a conflict, they should identify someone who can help. People with skills in handling various types of intrapersonal conflicts include psychologists, religious advisors, and career counselors.

There are three types of role conflict an individual can experience: intra-role, inter-role, and person-role conflict.

Intra-role conflict occurs when a person receives conflicting information from others concerning a particular role. For example, Jenny James, a member of a production maintenance team, received a bonus from management for her outstanding performance record. But two hours later, she and her manager, Kevin, are called into Kevin's boss's office and told that one of the company's oldest clients is complaining about the slow response to his request to fix the building's HVAC system. Jenny believes her team's response time was appropriate. Who is right? This type of conflicting expectation can lead to confusion and disagreements. Jenny may begin to question whether she understands and can effectively perform her role.

Managers should consider whether they or their organizations are contributing unnecessarily to intrapersonal conflicts. For example, does the training program emphasize ethical behavior, while the company rewards unethical behavior? If so, the employer is creating conflicts between employees' values and their desire to be rewarded.

Inter-role conflict occurs when a person receives conflicting information from others concerning a particular role. For example, a working mother may experience conflict between her desire to care for her children and her need to meet the same work standards as her male counterparts in order to perform well. This type of conflict has become increasingly common. Another example is an employee who cannot perform two separate tasks quickly enough for both to be completed on time.

Person-role conflict occurs when individuals find their values clashing with job requirements. For example, a maintenance specialist who is a perfectionist is required to speed up his completion of work assignments under a "right-the-first-time" maintenance policy. This person may experience conflict when pressured to follow standards other than his own.

Interpersonal Conflict

Interpersonal conflict occurs between two or more individuals. Interpersonal conflicts may arise from differing opinions, misunderstandings of a situation, or differences in values or beliefs. Sometimes two people just rub each other the wrong way.

Managers may be involved in interpersonal conflicts with another manager, an employee, a peer, or even a customer. In addition, managers may have to manage conflicts between two or more of their employees. Solving and managing interpersonal conflict requires knowledge about the nature of the conflict and skills for dealing with it. Practice will help you to build those skills. A manager is not exercising enough leadership when employees are engaged in constant interpersonal conflict such as bickering and complaining about one another. In some instances, a manager might be listening to complaints with too much sympathy, or might be watching disruptive conduct too passively. Instead, a manager should establish, communicate, and enforce guidelines for acceptable behavior and set an example by living up to them.

Interorganizational Conflict

The fourth type of conflict, interorganizational, occurs between one organization and another organization or group. Mergers and acquisitions often create interorganizational disaccord. Situations that pit unions or employees against management often lead to significant hostility. The resolution of such large conflicts usually requires the help of outside professional negotiators. Sometimes, interorganizational conflict can be resolved only through litigation.

WORKPLACE VIOLENCE AND AGGRESSION

Dramatic incidents of workplace violence have been much in the news recently. While large numbers of persons are killed at work, however, most of these deaths result from robberies and other crimes, not assault by organization members. Efforts by individuals to harm others with whom they work—workplace aggression—can take many forms other than direct physical attacks. Such behavior may be passive as well as active, and indirect as well as direct. Many factors influence the occurrence of workplace aggression, including personal characteristics, friction in interpersonal relations, and unpleasant physical conditions. In addition, downsizing, increased workforce diversity, increased use of part-time employees may contribute to such behavior.

Regardless of the forms or causes of workplace aggression, supervisors must be aware of the potential threat of such behavior directed at themselves and others in the organization. For example, Robert Earl Mack wounded his supervisor and killed another manager after a termination hearing at a General Dynamics plant in San Diego. Another example is the kidnapping and murder of an Exxon Corporation executive. Investigators say that the person who is charged with these crimes was obsessed with retaliating against Exxon because he had been fired.

Workplace aggression and other kinds of conflict put additional pressure on supervisors to develop their own and their employees' abilities to manage and resolve conflicts. Efforts to reduce workplace aggression include screening for "high-risk" employees, clear disapproval of such behavior coupled with appropriate disciplinary procedures, assuring high levels of organizational justice, and training employees on how to deal with such behavior.

A CLOSER LOOK AT JOBS AND COWORKER CONFLICT

With the above in mind, managers often blame work conflicts on the people involved. Certainly all of us have had experiences with people who are simply argumentative and disagreeable. However, it is much more productive to think about the causes of conflict as being difficult situations as opposed to difficult people. Some jobs and departments simply have high levels of conflict built into them. Even the most cooperative team player would not be able to serve in those jobs and departments without experience with the conflicts. This is important to bear in mind for two reasons: (1) it is easier to change the work situation than it is to change the workers, and (2) managers typically have little authority to unilaterally hire and fire. Below are some of the factors that make jobs especially prone to coworker conflict:

Employees Must Deal with Coworkers Whose Duties Are Much Different from Their Own

Employees in jobs that require them to interact with a diversity of people have a more conflict-ridden experience. Consider the work experience of a custodian or a clerical person assigned to several specialists. These individuals must interact with a large array of employees. What makes this diversity so potentially conflict ridden is that it creates multiple different demands. If employees are required to deal with a wide array of different individuals, then chances are the manager will have to contend with conflicts no matter how good the manager is or how good the employees are at staying out of trouble.

Employees Need to Share Limited Resources

Work conflicts are also caused by employees having to share such things as work space, funds, raw materials, tools, and equipment. Sharing one kind or another is common to every organization, but when resources are particularly tight, the potential for coworker conflict is significantly enhanced. This is the reason that there are often problems between people who work at the same work station on different shifts. It is also the reason that budget cutbacks often cause conflicts between coworkers.

Employees Must Work with Other People in Complicated Ways

One of the most important causes of conflict is work interdependence. This refers to the situation where workers are required to work together in ways requiring complicated interactions or cooperation. Such complications arise when direct reports have to (a) rely on others for their inputs, (b) rely on others for feedback on how well they have done their work, and (c) interact with others face to face to complete their work.

If the work generates interdependence, workers have to rely on what others do. Such mutual dependence is a chief factor in causing conflict, for example, between sales and production personnel. Since the work between such individuals is highly intertwined or interdependent, it has greater conflict potential.

Knowing the typical kinds of conflicts that arise in various relationships and work situations can help a manager diagnose conflicts and devise appropriate ways to manage them.

DEFENSE MECHANISMS

When individuals are involved in conflict with another individual, frustration often results. Conflicts can often arise within the context of a performance appraisal. Most people do not react well to negative feedback.

When people are frustrated, as they often are in interpersonal conflict, they respond by exhibiting defense mechanisms. Defense mechanisms are common reactions to the frustration that accompanies conflict. Several mechanisms seen in organizations are aggression, compromise, and withdrawal.

Aggressive mechanisms are aimed at attacking the source of the conflict. Some of these are fixation, displacement, and negativism. In fixation, an individual fixates on the conflict, or keeps up a dysfunctional behavior that obviously will not solve the conflict. An example of fixation occurred in a university, where a faculty member became embroiled in a battle with the dean because the faculty member felt he had not received a large enough salary increase. He persisted in writing angry letters to the dean, whose hands were tied because of a low budget allocation to the college. Displacement means directing anger toward someone who is not the source of the conflict. For example, a manager may respond harshly to an employee after a telephone confrontation with an angry customer. Another aggressive defense mechanism is negativism, which is active or passive resistance. Negativism is illustrated by a manager who, when appointed to a committee on which she did not want to serve, made negative comments throughout the meeting.

Compromise mechanisms are used by individuals to make the best of a conflict situation. Three compromise mechanisms include compensation, identification, and rationalization. Compensation occurs when an individual tries to make up for an inadequacy by putting increased energy into another activity. Compensation can be seen when a person makes up for a bad relationship at home by spending more time at the office. Identification occurs when one individual patterns his or her behavior after another's. One manager at a construction company, not wanting to acknowledge consciously that she was not likely to be promoted, mimicked the behavior of her boss, even going so far as to buy a car just like the boss's. Rationalization is trying to justify one's behavior by constructing bogus reasons for it. Employees may rationalize unethical behavior like padding their expense accounts because "everyone else does it."

Withdrawal mechanisms are exhibited when frustrated individuals try to flee from a conflict using either physical or psychological means. Managers often withdraw psychologically by distancing themselves from employees during layoffs. Flight, conversion, and fantasy are examples of withdrawal mechanisms. Physically escaping a conflict is flight. An employee who takes a day off after a blowup with the boss is an example. Withdrawal may take the form of emotionally leaving a conflict, such as exhibiting an "I don't care anymore" attitude. Conversion is a process whereby emotional conflicts become expressed in physical symptoms. Most of us have experienced the conversion reaction of a headache following an emotional exchange with another person. Fantasy is an escape by daydreaming. An excellent example of fantasy was shown in the movie *9 to 5*, in which Dolly Parton, Lily Tomlin, and Jane Fonda played characters who fantasized about torturing their boss because he was such a tyrant.

Knowledge of these defense mechanisms can be extremely beneficial to a manager. By understanding the ways in which people typically react to interpersonal conflict, managers can be prepared for employees' reactions and help them uncover their feelings about a conflict.

COPING WITH DIFFICULT BEHAVIOR

Many interpersonal conflicts arise when one person finds another person's behavior uncomfortable, irritating, or bothersome in one way or another. Robert Bramson (1981) has identified seven basic types of difficult behavior that may cause interpersonal conflict at work. The difficult behavior types are: hostile-aggressives, complainers, clams, superagreeables, negativists, know-it-alls, and indecisive stallers.

Hostile-aggressive behavior occurs when individuals bully other people by bombarding them with cutting remarks, or by throwing a tantrum when things do not go their way. Their focus is on attacking the other party in a conflict. Often emotional, they use these displays to create discomfort or surprise in their adversaries. Underlying their behavior is a strong sense of "shoulds"—internal rules about the way things ought to be. A key to dealing with hostile-aggressive behavior is to recognize the behavior and not to be drawn into it yourself.

Complainers gripe constantly but never take action about what they complain about, usually because they feel powerless or they do not want to take responsibility. You may want to hear complainers out and let them know you understand their feelings, but do not get drawn into pitying them. Use a problem-solving stance. For instance, a manager might say, "Dangaia, what do you want the outcome of our meeting to be? What action needs to be taken?" This focuses the complainer on solutions, not complaints.

Clams are silent and unresponsive when asked for opinions. They react to conflict by closing up (like their namesakes) and refusing to discuss problems. The challenge in coping with clams is getting them to open up and talk. Open-ended questions are invaluable, as is patience in allowing them their silence for a reasonable time. If a coworker is avoiding you and has refused to talk, "Are you angry with me?" may not be a good question. "Why are you avoiding me?" may be better. If no response is forthcoming, you might try direct action. "Since you won't discuss this, I'm going to assume that there's nothing wrong and sign us both up for the company volleyball team."

Superagreeable behavior is often exhibited by charming individuals who are sincere and helpful to our face, but fail to do what they promise when you leave. A service manager at an auto dealership may listen attentively to the problems you report with your new car, dutifully write them down, and assure you that they will be taken care of. When you pick up the car, however, none of the problems are resolved. Does this sound familiar? These people are often conflict avoiders and make unrealistic promises to avoid a confrontation. Be prepared to compromise on a solution, and make sure it is workable. Finally, if you get a humorous response from a superagreeable, look for the hidden meaning in it.

Negativists respond to any attempts to solve a problem with pessimism. Their behavior is dangerous, because their negativism is contagious, and you may lose your optimism about solving the problem in interacting with them. A problem-solving mode is appropriate in the case; let the negativist bring up alternative solutions. Play devil's advocate, bringing up the negative aspects yourself. You may also want to ask, "What is the worst that might happen?" When the negativists are convinced that they can handle even the worst-case scenarios, they may feel more in control.

Know-it-alls display superior attitudes, wanting you to know that they know everything there is to know about everything. If they really know what they are talking about, they are bulldozers. Bulldozers overrun individuals with their blustery style, and they are most aggravating because they are always right. To cope with bulldozers, you need to be prepared. They will respect you if you have done your homework. Phony experts are known as balloons. Balloons only think they know everything. To deal with balloon behavior, state your position as your own perception of the situation. It is also important to allow the balloon to save face when deflated, so confront the balloon in private.

Indecisive stallers put off decisions until they have no choice, or they fail to come to a decision at all. Stallers often are genuinely concerned about others and are afraid that no matter what they decide, they will alienate or fail to please someone. The key in coping with stallers is to uncover the reasons for their hesitation. You must take responsibility to ensure that the staller follows through. If stallers are too disruptive, you may want to remove them from the decision situation.

In dealing with difficult behavior, it is important to identify the reasons you perceive the behavior as difficult. Bramson's framework helps accomplish this. In addition, you should analyze your response to the difficult person.

Ineffective Techniques

There are many specific techniques for dealing with conflict. Before turning to techniques that work, it should be recognized that some actions commonly taken in organizations to deal with conflict are not effective (Miles 1980; Steers 1991).

Nonreaction is doing nothing in hopes that the conflict will disappear. This is not generally a good technique, because most conflicts do not go away, and the individuals involved in the conflict react with frustration.

Secrecy, or trying to keep a conflict out of view of most people, only creates suspicion. An example is an organizational policy of pay secrecy. In some organizations, discussion of salary is grounds for dismissal. When this is the case, employees suspect that the company has something to hide.

Administrative orbiting is delaying action on a conflict by buying time, usually by telling the individuals involved that the problem is being worked on or that the boss is still thinking about the issue. Like nonaction, this technique leads to frustration and resentment.

Due process nonaction is a procedure set up to address conflicts that is so costly, time consuming, or personally risky that no one will use it. Some companies' sexual harassment policies are examples of this technique. To file a sexual harassment complaint, detailed paperwork is required, the accuser must go through appropriate channels, and the accuser risks being branded a troublemaker. Thus, the company has a procedure for handling complaints (due process), but no one uses it (nonaction).

Character assassination is an attempt to label or discredit an opponent. In the confirmation hearings of Supreme Court Justice Clarence Thomas, for example, attempts at a character assassination were made upon Anita Hill by referring to her as a spurned woman and by saying she lived in fantasy. Justice Thomas was also a victim of character assassination; he was portrayed as a womanizer and a perpetrator of sexual harassment. Character assassination can backfire and make the individual who uses it appear dishonest and cruel.

MANAGING CONFLICT AND ENCOURAGING RESOLUTION

The goal of conflict management is primarily to prevent negative or dysfunctional conflict from occurring, while at the same time encouraging healthy conflict that stimulates individual and team innovation and performance. If dysfunctional conflict cannot be prevented, then the goal is to eliminate it, or at least minimize or decrease it. This section will provide the manager with tools to encourage functional conflict and discourage dysfunctional conflict.

A major goal of managers is to channel potential conflict into a positive, functional framework, making it productive rather than destructive. Programmed conflict is conflict that allows the expression of different opinions in a structured setting, so that personal feelings are not involved. It encourages open dialogue and constructive debate among potentially conflicting parties.

The two approaches we discuss next identify methods for managing conflict. The first approach classifies various approaches to conflict management based on the needs and interests of the parties. The optimal approach is to strive for "win-win" outcomes in which both parties' needs are met. The second approach describes two methods for promoting functional conflict.

Thomas's Conflict-Resolution Approach

The first direct conflict-resolution approach, developed by Kenneth Thomas (1976) identifies five possible styles of conflict resolution used by every party (individual or group) to a conflict. These five styles are each based on two factors: the degree of assertiveness and the degree of cooperativeness of the parties. The assertiveness factor is the extent to which a party wants to satisfy its own needs and concerns. The cooperativeness factor is the extent to which a party is willing to meet the needs and concerns of the other party. The five conflict-resolution styles resulting from combinations of these factors are: avoiding, competing, compromising, collaborating, and accommodating.

Table 10.2 lists the appropriate conditions for using the different styles. Note that no one style is always appropriate. A competing style may be necessary in emergencies or against those who take advantage of noncompetitive behavior. Although an avoiding style is unassertive, it may be necessary to use it to allow people to calm down, or when potential disruption outweighs the benefits of resolving dispute. Collaborative approaches are generally the most effective approaches for stimulating new, creative ideas and getting the positive results associated with high productivity and performance, because they meet both parties' needs.

Cosier and Schwank's Methods of Promoting Programmed Conflict

A major goal of managers is to channel potential conflict into a positive, functional framework, making it productive rather than destructive. Programmed conflict allows the expression of different opinions in a structured setting, so that personal feelings are not involved. It encourages open dialogue and constructive debate among potentially conflicting parties.

Cosier and Schwank (1990) propose two programmed approaches for stimulating functional conflict: a "devil's advocate decision method" and a "dialectic decision method." Both approaches require the participants to submit proposals for debate and engage in structured role playing.

The devil's advocate decision program includes the following steps:

1. A proposed course of action is generated.
2. A devil's advocate (individual or group) is assigned to criticize the proposal.
3. The critique is presented to key decision makers and additional information is gathered.
4. The decision to adopt, modify, or discontinue the proposed course of action is taken and the decision is monitored.

The dialectic decision method includes the following steps:

1. A proposed course of action is generated.
2. Assumptions underlying the proposal are identified.
3. A conflicting counterproposal is generated based on different assumptions.

Table 10.2
Five Styles of Conflict Management

Conflict-Handling Style and Appropriate Conditions

Competing

1. When quick, decisive action is vital (e.g., emergencies).
2. On important issues where unpopular actions need implementing (cost cutting, enforcing unpopular rules, discipline).
3. On issues vital to company welfare when you know you are right.
4. Against people who take advantage of noncompetitive behavior.

Collaborating

1. To find an integrative solution when both sets of concerns are too important to be compromised.
2. When your objective is to learn.
3. To merge insights from people with different perspectives.
4. To gain commitment by incorporating concerns into a consensus.
5. To work through feelings that have interfered with a relationship.

Compromising

1. When goals are important, but not worth the effort or potential disruption of more assertive modes.
2. When opponents with equal power are committed to mutually exclusive goals.
3. To achieve temporary settlements to complex issues.
4. To arrive at expedient solutions under time pressure.
5. As a backdrop when collaboration or competition is unsuccessful.

Avoiding

1. When an issue is trivial, or more important issues are pressing.
2. When you perceive no chance of satisfying your concerns.
3. When potential disruption outweighs the benefits of resolution.
4. To let people cool down and regain perspective.
5. When gathering information supersedes immediate decision.
6. When others can resolve the conflict more effectively.
7. When issues seem tangential or symptomatic of other issues.

Accommodating

1. When you find you are wrong—to allow a better position to be heard, to learn, and to show your reasonableness.
2. When issues are more important to others than to yourself—to satisfy others and maintain cooperation.
3. To build social credits for later issues.
4. To minimize loss when you are outmatched and losing.
5. When harmony and stability are especially important.
6. To allow employees to develop by learning from mistakes.

Source: K.W. Thomas, "Toward Multi-Dimensional Values in Teaching: The Example of Conflict Behaviors," *Academy of Management Review* 21 (1977): 484–490.

4. Advocates of each position present and debate the merits of their proposals before key decision makers.
5. The decision to adopt either position, or some other position (e.g., a compromise), is taken.
6. The decision is monitored.

The primary difference in the two processes is the fact that with the devil's advocate approach, one proposal is being critiqued while with the dialectic model two competing proposals are considered.

Royal Dutch Shell Group, General Electric, and Anheuser-Busch have built devil's advocates into their decision-making processes. For instance, when the policy committee at Anheuser-Busch considers a major move, such as getting into or out of a business or making a major capital expenditure, it often assigns teams to make the case for each side of the question. This process frequently results in decisions using alternatives that previously had not been considered.

While it is vital that managers encourage functional conflict, or disagreement with the "status quo," it can be a real challenge for managers to hear unwelcome news. The news may make their blood boil or their hopes collapse, but they can't show it. They have to learn to take bad news without flinching: no tirades, no tight-lipped sarcasm, no rolling eyes, no gritted teeth. Managers should instead ask calm, even-tempered questions: "Can you tell me more about what happened? What do you think we ought to do?" A sincere, "Thank you for bringing this to my attention," will increase the probability of similar communications in the future.

Other Approaches to Managing Conflict

Managers have a variety of approaches they can use to address conflict. They may have to intervene as the person to resolve conflict among the work group as well. Some of these are described below. Managers can:

- divide up the conflict by reducing a large conflict into smaller parts and working on each part separately.
- contain the conflict, by limiting discussion to the present problem, not the past; refraining from labeling the conflict as the "fault" of one party; and describing the problem in objective terms.
- allow the griping to set the agenda for problem solving, and cooperate to solve those problems.
- look for areas of "common ground" where both parties might agree.

Managers should prepare for conflict resolution by understanding the reasons for the conflict. They should focus on behavior, which people can change, and not on personalities, which they cannot change. It also is important to determine what actions cause the problem, and how that action affects the manager and others. For example, if you are receiving weekly reports late from another manager, you can describe the problem and why it is difficult for you. You might say, "I haven't been getting the weekly production reports until late Friday afternoon. That means I have to give up precious family time to review them over the weekend, or else I embarrass myself by being unprepared at the Monday-morning production team meetings."

After you have stated the problem, listen to how the other person responds and attempt to understand their point of view. If the other person does not acknowledge there is a problem, restate your concern until the other person understands it or until it is clear that you cannot make any progress on your own. Often a conflict exists simply because the other person has not understood your point of view or your situation. Or, you may not understand their point of view. When you have begun communicating about the problem, the two of you can work together to find a solution. Restate your solution to be sure that you both agree on what you are going to do next.

NEGOTIATION AND MEDIATION (FORMS OF CONFLICT MANAGEMENT)

Negotiation is only one of the many ways we have to deal with differences. And being able to confront differences productively through negotiation can turn conflict into a creative and innovative force. In today's organizations it is important to recognize and understand the importance of negotiation—which, after all, is a method of settling conflict rather than resolving it.

Negotiation refers to the process by which two or more interdependent parties use bargaining to reconcile their differences. Most people have had the experience of negotiating an increase in salary or the price of a car. Many managers or teams negotiate resources while many workers negotiate their job assignments. Negotiations regularly play a role in organizations. Negotiations typically have four key elements:

- A degree of interdependence between the parties.
- A perceived conflict between the parties.
- An opportunistic interaction between parties (i.e., parties looking for opportunities to influence one another; each individual or team cares about and pursues its own interests and tries to influence decisions to its advantage).
- The possibility of agreement (each party expects to come to some agreement).

We examine these elements in more detail below by looking first at the distributive and integrative bargaining. Then we trace the four steps of the negotiation process.

Distributive versus Integrative Bargaining

The negotiating process shows a fundamental tension between the claiming and creating of value. Value claimers view negotiations purely as an adversarial process. Each side tries to claim as much of a limited pie, such as financial or other resources, as possible by giving the other side as little as possible. Each party claims value through the use of manipulation, arguments, limited concessions, and hard bargaining.

Value creators, in contrast, participate in a process that results in joint gains to each party. They try to create additional benefits for each side in the negotiations. They emphasize shared interests, develop a collaborative relationship, and negotiate in a pleasant, cooperative manner.

A negotiator incorporates these strategies singly or in combination in one of two basic paradigms. Distributive bargaining takes an adversarial or win-lose approach. Integrative bargaining takes a problem-solving or win-win approach.

Distributive bargaining. The classical view considers bargaining as a win-lose situation, where one party's gain is the other party's loss. Known also as a *zero-sum* type of negotiation (because one party's gain equals the other party's loss for a net gain of zero), this approach typifies the purchase of used cars, property, and other material goods in organizations. It has also been applied to salary negotiation and labor-management negotiation.

Distributive bargaining emphasizes the claiming of value. Negotiators carefully make their opening offers, as well as later offers and counteroffers, so they can successfully claim value and "win" the negotiation. Power plays a key role in successful distributive bargaining because it increases a party's leverage and ability to shape perceptions.

Integrative bargaining. Recently negotiators have been encouraged to transform the bargaining into a win-win situation. Here both parties gain as a result of the negotiations. Known as a positive-sum type of negotiation, because the gains of each party yield a positive sum, this approach has recently described international negotiations, labor-management negotiations, and specific job-related bargaining.

Although the negotiation process described in the next section can result in both distributive and integrative bargaining, it more often helps individuals, managers, or teams take a win-win approach that will result in mutual gains for both parties.

The Steps in Negotiation

People can follow four basic steps for an effective negotiation.

Step 1: Prepare. Preparation for negotiations should begin long before the formal negotiation begins. Each party gathers information about the other side—its history, likely behavior, previous interactions, and previous agreements reached by the party. Each side must also make sure it understands the issues or matters over which the parties disagree and seek to reach agreement on. Use the following questions to assist you in your preparation.

- Who are the relevant parties? Who makes the decisions? Who will actually negotiate? Who are their relevant constituencies?
- What do I/we want from the other party(ies)? How do they see their choices? What problems will meeting my/our needs create for them? Their boss(es)? Their colleagues? Other constituencies?
- What organizational considerations are relevant? What negotiating behaviors are rewarded?
- How does the culture view negotiations? What organization constraints exist for them? For me (us)?
- What kinds of behavior should I/we expect? How do they usually negotiate? How do I/we react to their negotiating style? What should I/we do to prepare myself/ourselves? Should I/we expect that gender, race, and/or culture will be issues in the negotiation?
- What are the *issues* we need to negotiate? Try to be as clear as possible.
- Are the issues separate or can they be linked in the current situation or over time?
- Are there other ways to frame the issue?

Step 2: Evaluate Alternatives. The two sides attempt to identify the *bargaining range*, that is, the range in which both parties would find an agreement acceptable. In determining this range, each party asks questions such as the following, known as the mix-max strategy:

- What is the minimum I/we can accept to resolve the conflict?
- What is the maximum I/we can ask for without appearing outrageous?
- What is the maximum I/we can give away?
- What is the least I/we can offer without appearing outrageous?
- What is the minimum the other party can accept to resolve the conflict?
- What is the maximum the other party can ask for without appearing outrageous?
- What is the maximum the other party can give away?
- What is the least the other party can offer without appearing outrageous?

The bargainers determine the alternatives acceptable to them. The more alternatives they have, the more leverage they typically have in the negotiation.

Negotiators also identify their best alternative if a negotiated settlement is not reached, known as their BATNA. Identifying a set of alternatives, including the best one, helps individuals determine whether to continue the negotiation or seek another course of action.

Step 3: Identify Each Party's Interests. Interests are what parties seek to advance in negotiations. If the issues are the matters over which parties disagree, then interests are the wants, needs, goals, and desires parties have relative to the issues. Negotiators act to satisfy their own interests, which may be substantive, relationship, personal, or organizational ones. Managers' interests, for example, can include their reputation, their relationship with other parties, the organization's goals, or the bottom line. Workers' interests might include an improved standard of living, a positive working relationship with management, or improved status as compared to workers in other companies.

In focusing on their own interests, a party often ignores or simplifies the interests of the other party, particularly when uncertain future events play a role in each party's interests. The person or group must assess the other party's interests and then decide how to respond to those interests in their offers.

In assessing what interests are at stake, use the following advice and questions:

- Consider both intangible interests and subtler interests, such as reputation, fairness, and precedent.
- Separate interests from issues and positions (i.e., positions are the stands we take about an issue).
- "I demand a 10-percent salary increase this year." Interests are the reasons we take a position. The idea is that we focus on interests, there is more bargaining room to find agreement than if we just stick with position).
- Recognize that interests may have either intrinsic or instrumental value. Increased autonomy may have value by itself or may help accomplish other personal goals.
- Understand that interests depend on perceptions, which are subjective.
- Note that interests and issues can change intentionally or accidentally.
- Why are the parties at the table?
- What are my/our underlying concerns? What are theirs? What are their goals? Mine/Ours?
- What interests are of higher priority? Are their differences priorities?
- What would they consider a good outcome? What would it be for me/us?
- What kinds of questions can I/we ask to learn about interests?

Step 4: Make Trade-offs and Create Joint Gains. Bargainers use trade-offs to satisfy their own and others' interests. In labor negotiations, the union side may trade wage increases for job-security provisions or vice versa.

People can assess trade-offs by first identifying the best and worst possible outcomes. Then they can specify what impact trade-offs will have on these outcomes. Finally, they can consider whether the changed outcomes will better meet the parties' interests.

In addition to making trade-offs as a way of reaching a satisfactory negotiating outcome, integrative bargaining attempts to create gains for both parties. A party may offer something of relatively less value to them but of more value to the other party. Or the parties may build on shared interests. They may also use economies of scale to create joint gains. Negotiators need to overcome the idea that a fixed amount of outcome exists. They also should try not to escalate conflict unnecessarily. Negotiators can create joint gains in a variety of circumstances:

- They can consider interests separately, rather than bundling them into a single, comprehensive, and complex interest.
- They can create contingent agreements where outcomes depend on the particular circumstances as they arise.
- They can create agreements where both parties share the risk.
- They can alter the pattern of payment or actions over time rather than requiring a consistent set of behaviors from either party.
- They can use a variety of criteria, such as precedence, substance, and fairness to create joint gains.
- They can use economies of scale to create increased value.

Negotiators can reach either explicit or implicit agreements; both can be satisfactory. An explicit written agreement covers all contingencies and binds the parties by an external enforcement mechanism. An implicit, or oral agreement, offers flexibility for responding to unforeseen circumstances and binds the parties by the nature of their personal relationship.

NEGOTIATION STRATEGIES AND TACTICS

In effective bargaining situations, the negotiators attack the problem, not the people, and treat negotiation as joint problem-solving. They remain open to persuasion and explore interests rather than positions. They also create multiple options and try to improve their alternatives in case they do not reach an agreement. In addition, successful negotiators draw upon a variety of negotiation strategies, tactics, and styles, keeping in mind cross-cultural issues.

Strategies

Three common negotiation strategies exist as described below:

- *Competitive.* This strategy frequently accompanies distributive bargaining. It focuses on achieving a party's goals at the expense of the other party's goals. The group (or individual) may use secrecy, threats, or bluffs as a way of hiding its own goals and uncovering the other party's goals.
- *Collaborative.* This strategy, typically used with integrative bargaining, emphasizes pursuing common goals held by the two parties. It calls on each party to accurately communicate its needs to the other. It takes a problem-solving approach and looks for solutions that satisfy both parties.
- *Subordinate.* This strategy has one party put its goals after the other party's to avoid conflict. This party becomes overly concerned with the other's goals rather than its own or both parties' goals.

Choosing a strategy depends on the desired relationship between the negotiating parties and the importance of substantive (content) outcomes to the individual or group.

Tactics

Negotiators use a variety of short-term, focused maneuvers, known as tactics, to accomplish their objectives. For example, the negotiator can choose to wait out the other party. She can take a unilateral action and treat the negotiation outcome as a fait accompli. Or, the negotiator can suddenly shift his or her approach and do the reverse of what is expected, thereby, catching the other party unprepared. She or he can withdraw from the negotiation or impose time, dollar, or deadline limits. Finally, the negotiator can grant or withhold favors or show anger, intimidating the other party.

Negotiating Styles

Negotiators can use a variety of styles which they fine tune for the particular situation. They may take a domineering and aggressive approach or may act more collaboratively.

Women may conduct negotiations differently from men. They may use different styles in searching for agreement and have traditionally faired as well as men. They differ in a number of ways.

- Women think of their interests within a relational context, that is, within existing responsibilities and commitments.
- Women may need to create a climate in which they know the other parties by sharing their feelings and ways of interacting.
- Women expect others to act consistently with previous and future behaviors and tend not to see negotiating as discrete events.

- Women use empowerment rather than power through domination or superiority as a way to control the situation.
- Women rely on problem solving through dialogue to reach an agreement.

Cross-Cultural Issues in Negotiation

The assumptions that underlie effective negotiations differ significantly in various parts of the world. Consider this situation:

Your company has just received confirmation that a high-level delegation from the People's Republic of China will visit your office. Since the Chinese have already received a sample of your product, the purpose of their visit is probably to (1) sign an agreement to act as your local distributor in China; (2) establish a firm relationship with the company management; (3) learn more about your company's technological advancements; or (4) visit your country as a reward for their hard work at home.

If you chose (2), you answered correctly. Most Chinese begin by establishing rapport and acquiring commitment. Lower-level managers handle technical details.

The general approach to negotiation varies in different cultures, although exceptions exist in every culture. In addition, people in different cultures may have different perceptions of the appropriateness of specific negotiating tactics. In Asia, negotiators focus on saving face for all parties. Being too frank, critical, insincere, impatient, and unadaptable will result in ineffective negotiations. They ask questions indirectly: "I've developed a short-cut for manufacturing these garments in lower cost with higher quality and would appreciate any suggestions you have for improving it," not "Can you make this garment more cheaply but improve its quality?"

Negotiating with Russians has historically posed different challenges. The Russians emphasize building arguments on asserted ideals and deemphasize relationship-building. They make few concessions. An opponent's concessions are viewed as weaknesses and are almost never reciprocated. They have been described as making no effort to build continuing relationships, often offering an extreme initial position and ignoring any deadlines.

Arabs, on the other hand, use primarily an emotional rather than an ideological or factual negotiating style. They request and make concessions throughout the negotiating process and almost always reciprocate an opponent's concessions. They start with extreme initial positions but rarely enforce deadlines. They focus on building a long-term relationship; thus the business climate and personal relationship are critical.

North Americans, in contrast, appeal to logic and counter opponents' arguments with objective facts rather than with subjective feelings or asserted ideals. They may make small concessions early and then usually reciprocate an opponent's concessions. But they take a moderate initial position, build only a short-term relationship, and value deadlines greatly.

While these generalities may not always apply, they should suggest that all managers or workers who work in cross-cultural situations think carefully about the context of any negotiations. They should be aware of differences in negotiators' styles and the way negotiators view the process itself.

Developing Effective Negotiation Skills

The essence of effective negotiation can be summarized in the following six recommendations:

- *Research your opponent.* Acquire as much information as you can about your opponent's interests and goals. What people must he or she appease? What is his or her strategy? This information will help you to better understand your opponent's behavior, to predict his or her responses to your offers, and to frame solutions in terms of his or her interests.
- *Begin with a positive overture.* Research shows that concessions tend to be reciprocated and lead to agreements. As a result, begin bargaining with a positive overture—perhaps a small concession—and then reciprocate your opponent's concessions.
- *Address problems, not personalities.* Concentrate on the negotiation issues, not on the personal characteristics of your opponent. When negotiations get tough, avoid the tendency to attack your opponent. It's your opponent's ideas or position that you disagree with, not him or her personally. Separate people from the problem, and don't personalize differences.
- *Pay little attention to initial offers.* Treat an initial offer as merely a point of departure. Everyone has to have an initial position, and initial positions tend to be extreme and idealistic. Treat them as such.
- *Emphasize win-win solutions.* If conditions are supportive, look for an integrative solution. Frame options in terms of your opponent's interests and look for solutions that can allow your opponent, as well as yourself, to declare a victory.
- *Be open to accepting third-party assistance.* When stalemates are reached, consider the use of a neutral third party—a mediator, an arbitrator, or a conciliator. Mediators can help parties come to an agreement, but they don't impose a settlement. Arbitrators hear both sides of the dispute, then impose a solution. Conciliators are more informal and act as a communication conduit, passing information between parties, interpreting messages, and clarifying misunderstandings.

MEDIATION

Mediation is a process by which a third party helps two or more individuals resolve one or more conflicts. Most of the actual negotiations occur directly between the involved individuals. But, when the parties appear likely to become locked in win-lose conflict, a mediator, acting as a neutral party, may be able to help them resolve their differences.

As noted thus far in this chapter, there are proven ways to manage work conflicts that have positive results both for employees and for the organization. However, much depends on the particular circumstances involved. For this reason, it is critical that the manager knows both the people who work for him or her and the culture of the organization. This is important for several reasons. First, knowing direct reports allows a manager to understand something about the history of the relationship between the parties. Conflicts are often the result of unresolved problems in the past or merely a form of some long-standing issue in the relationship. It is also important for the manager to know the people in order to tell whether individuals in the situation are speaking for themselves or are representing others. Sometimes people speak for others in conflicts, either by fighting another person's battles or by joining the side of a popular coworker.

It is also important that a manager appreciate how the culture of an organization affects expectations about conflict. Some organizations have cultures that suppress the expression of disagreement. Other organizational cultures are more uninhibited. Some companies have unwritten rules against going to higher authorities with unresolved conflicts and some do not. If a manager is not aware of these unwritten rules about conflict, it is easy to misjudge the importance of a particular conflict or to handle it in a fashion that others are not used to. The following are some steps managers can take to mediate problems between their direct reports.

Step 1: Meet with Each Employee Separately to Define the Conflict and Create the Proper Atmosphere. Once a manager knows that there is a conflict and has decided that it is serious enough to act on, the first step should be to find out how the conflicting parties see the issue. The best way to do this is to talk with the individuals separately and privately. During this meeting, the manager should keep several things in mind.

During the interview the manager should try to separate information and emotion. The initial view is often emotionally charged. Clearly, overheated situations require cool heads, and the manager must take the lead. First, it is imperative that the supervisor be an attentive, nonjudgmental listener. One technique is for the manager to respond to emotionally charged statements by restating them in a form that strips away the strong feelings. Second, it is important for the manager to appear initially neutral, to avoid taking sides. The conflicting parties will often press the manager into making some sort of statement about how the situation will be resolved, but he or she should remain neutral. Third, the manager should begin to depersonalize the issue. Statements made against the personal character of one's "opponent" should immediately be ruled out of bounds. Fourth, during the interview the manager should try to change the way the parties are viewing the conflict.

Resolution is easier if:

1. each party appreciates the other's point of view.
2. each knows why the other has taken his or her position.
3. the issue is seen as a problem between the two of them.
4. the issue can be defined in simple concrete terms.
5. each has hope that the conflict can be worked out.

The initial meeting is an ideal time to work on these perspectives. If an employee expresses an opinion that losing is inevitable, the manager should immediately challenge that opinion. If a person believes that he will never have to work again with a coworker after the conflict is settled, again the manager should make it clear that they will be expected to work together in the future. Essentially then, the manager should not only listen during this first meeting, but should try to shape the way the issue is seen.

Fifth, the manager should begin to distinguish between the demands of the parties and their interests. People in a conflict often state their demands clearly and forcefully. They do not, however, state the interests they have that underlie their demands.

Finally, the manager should make it clear to each how he or she plans to deal with the conflict as a third party.

Step 2: Get the Parties Together for an Initial Meeting. Sometime very soon after the first separate meetings the manager should get the parties together. This meeting will likely be tense. It is useful for the meeting to be conducted on "neutral" ground, with the manager sitting across from (not between) the two individuals and close to a chalkboard or easel. This reinforces the notion that the session is devoted to solving the problem rather than the conflict with one another.

It is useful for the manager to take the employees through the following process: (1) ask each employee to state the problem, (2) ask each employee to state the other's view of the problem, (3) ask each to confirm the accuracy of the other's repetition.

Step 3: Ask Each to Suggest Solutions. Once positions have been laid out and understood, it is then possible to generate alternative solutions. It may be useful to use a structured idea generating technique like brainstorming here. (A rule of thumb if a manager is dealing with an important conflict, at least a half-hour should be devoted to the idea-generating phase.)

Step 4: Use Recesses Strategically. Recess is one of the most powerful tools a manager has to deal with conflicts. Recesses can do several things:

1. They can be used to call off emotionally charged episodes.
2. They can be called to conduct further private inquiries about interests.
3. They can be used to de-escalate the conflict by breaking the cycle of strong statements and creating an opportunity to refocus energy from the people to the problem.

Step 5: Focus on Objective Facts, Areas of Mutual Need, or Mutual Goals. Excellent win-win settlements are sometimes illuminated during solution-generating activities. However, the manager must be prepared to develop win-win options if they do not come from the parties. The following are questions to consider that might help develop such options:

1. Is it possible to expand the pie, to expand the resources to the parties?
2. Is it possible for one party to offer the other some "compensation" for giving in (i.e., for each to get something that they want)?
3. Is it possible to rank the interests of each party, and for parties to concede some interests in order to gain others?

Structural Solutions

As noted earlier in this chapter, not all conflicts have win-win resolutions. And, it makes little sense to explore the situation endlessly until one is found. Before settling on a win-lose alternative, however, a manager should consider the feasibility of resolving the conflict in a structural way. Basically, structural options act on the causes of work conflicts: job diversity, resource sharing, and interdependence. If a win-win settlement does not seem possible, one of the structural options listed below may be suitable:

1. Move employees between jobs to develop an appreciation of each other's point of view.
2. Use rules to regularize resource sharing.
3. Separate parties to the conflict and reduce the complexity of their required work interactions.

Step 6: Bring Both Parties to Agreement of Specific Steps to Resolve Conflict. Once solutions are uncovered, the rest of the process is simple. All that needs to be done is to work out the implementation plan and agree on some sort of follow through.

It is important, however, that the manager always be alert to the importance of intangibles. Some important intangibles might include appearing tough to coworkers, having the settlement implemented quietly or in a piece-by-piece fashion, or guaranteeing that the settlement will not serve as a precedent in the future. Intangibles can become a major stumbling block because parties are reluctant to admit just how important they are.

INCREASING CONFLICT

In concluding this chapter it is important to emphasize that conflict management includes increasing conflict when it becomes dysfunctionally low. The goal of increasing conflict is to get the functional qualities of conflict, such as more information and decisions and creative solutions to problems.

Increasing conflict must be done skillfully and cautiously so conflict levels do not become dysfunctionally high. The manager's role is to structure situations as described below and not express opinions or take positions on issues. This role is especially important because it can encourage direct reports to express their views.

Groups with members of different social backgrounds, education, expertise, organization positions, and opinions have high-conflict potential. By deliberately forming heterogeneous groups to find creative solutions to problems, a manager tries to use the functional qualities of conflict. Organizations with a diverse workforce have an especially rich resource for forming groups with high-conflict potential.

A manager of a decision-making group can ask one member of the group to play the role of devil's advocate. As suggested in our discussion of this approach earlier, this person deliberately criticizes a position that has emerged as dominant within the group. Alternatively, the manager can ask each person in the group to critique the alternatives under consideration. Each approach recognizes the information-generating function of conflict.

Managers can also try to develop an organizational culture with a set of values and norms that support openness about debate and opinions. They must devote time to building this type of culture. Searching for quick solutions to problems can lead to pressure to reduce differences and emphasize similarities.

SUMMARY

Conflict is an integral part of organizational life and occurs because of disagreements or incompatibilities between individuals, or within groups and entire organizations. Conflict can be functional or dysfunctional—even destructive. Two approaches are especially appropriate for stimulating and managing conflict in organizations. The first approach is aimed at directing attention and solutions to the emotional and substantive causes of conflict. The second approach encourages functional or healthy conflict.

Negotiation describes a process in which two or more parties attempt to reach an agreement. In distributive bargaining, one party's gain is the other's loss. In integrative bargaining, mutual gains for both parties occur.

Effective negotiation includes preparation, evaluation of alternatives, identifying interests, and making trade-offs and creating joint gains. Negotiators may pursue competitive, collaborative, or subordinate strategies.

They may use an array of tactics to supplement these strategies. When negotiating in different cultures you should diagnose the effect of culture on the process and people involved in the negotiations so they can bargain effectively. Finally, managers can follow the six recommendations for developing negotiation strategies. Mediation can be helpful when the negotiating parties anticipate or experience difficulties in reaching agreement.

REFERENCES

Bramson, R. 1981. *Coping with difficult people*. New York: Dell.

Cosier, R.A., and Schwank, C.R. 1990. Agreement and thinking alike: Ingredients for poor decisions. *Academy of Management Executive* (February): 72–73.

Miles, R. 1980. *Macro organizational behaviour*. Glenview, IL: Scott, Foresman.

Nelson, D.L., and Quick, J.C. 2000. *Organizational behavior: Foundations, realities, and challenges*. 3rd ed. Cincinnati, OH: South-Western College Publishing.

Steers, R. 1991. *Introduction to organizational behaviour*. New York: HarperCollins.

Thomas, K. 1976. Conflict and conflict management. In M. Dunnette (ed.), *Handbook of industrial and organizational psychology*. New York: John Wiley & Sons, p. 900.

Chapter 11

Designing Effective Organizations

INTRODUCTION

How should companies organize themselves into separate units so as to be most effective? This question is a challenging and very important one for today's organizations. Experts in the field of organizational behavior have provided insight into the matter by studying what is called organizational structure—the way individuals and groups are arranged with respect to the tasks they perform—and organizational design—the process of coordinating these structural elements in the most effective manner. As you may suspect, finding the best way to structure and design organizations is no simple matter. However, because understanding the structure and design of organizations is so key to fully appreciating their functioning, organizational scientists have devoted considerable energy to this topic.

To begin, we will describe why structure and design matter in organizations. We will then note how various factors influence the design of an organization. Then, we introduce and compare mechanistic and organic systems and show how each type reflects a basic design decision. Next, we describe some of the traditional ways organizations have structured themselves. Finally, we discuss new forms of organizing that are highly adaptive and cost efficient and intended to respond to the demands of a changing world of work.

WHY STRUCTURE AND DESIGN MATTER

As suggested earlier, organizational structure refers to how an organization is put together. But it isn't only about how jobs or departments are arranged (e.g., production, human resource management [HRM], or accounting). Structure reflects some of the underlying ways that people interact with one another in and across jobs or departments. For example, organizations can be very formal and even bureaucratic in how they deal with one another, or they can be very loose and laissez-faire in their interactions. Likewise, it's important to look at how power is arranged in an organization; some organizations concentrate power in the hands of a few people, whereas others share much of the power and decision making, even down to the lowest levels.

Choosing among these various ways of arranging an organization and determining the ideal pattern for a particular industry are issues that managers must address. Managers must structure their organization to reach the organization's goals. The allocation of duties, tasks, and responsibilities between departments and individuals is an element of organizational design. Reporting relationships and the number of levels in the organization's hierarchy are other structural elements that managers must agree on.

Managers must develop organizational charts to show the formal design of an organization. Organizational charts show the configuration of the organization as it is or as the organization's managers would like it to be. Such charts typically use boxes to show positions in the organization and lines connecting the boxes to show reporting relationships. An organizational chart can quickly give you an image of how managers have divided the major tasks of the organization and the major reporting relationships. An organizational chart may be considered a representation of an organization's internal structure.

Organizational charts are incomplete pictures of an organization's division of labor. They do not show all communication links, integrating mechanisms, behavior processes, and informal arrangements within the organization. Nevertheless, organizational charts are useful for showing the basic intended design of an organization.

It is important to note that organizational structure seems to serve a number of purposes. First, people choose a particular structural design because they think it's going to work. So, decisions about what departments to put together, how to coordinate international operations, and how "tall" to make an organization's hierarchy are either consciously made or evolve somewhat automatically from the process of doing business. Regardless, structure makes things work better by minimizing the large amount of variation that's possible in a relatively unstructured environment. In other words, one effect of structure is to produce regularity in the pattern of people's behavior. Thus, organizational structure provides some constancy in the way the organization treats people and frees up the time that might otherwise be spent hashing out territories or interpersonal issues.

To be effective the structural design managers agree on must get information to the right places for effective decision making, and it must help coordinate the interdependent parts of the organization. When the organization's design is not right for what it's doing, managers may not get the information they need to predict problems and make effective decisions. They also may not react quickly enough to problems because the existing organizational design blocks needed information. The existing structure may not do an effective job of monitoring changes in the external environment. It may fail to signal managers that a decision is needed now because of such environmental changes.

THE CONTINGENCY FACTORS OF ORGANIZATIONAL DESIGN

Managers often assess four factors before deciding to design or redesign an organization. The factors are the organization's strategy, its external environment, its technical process, and its size. Each factor alone can affect design decisions, or they can act as a collection of forces that both constrain design choices and drive them.

Strategy

Many of top management's strategic choices affect organization design decisions. An organization's strategy describes the organization's long-term goals and the way it plans to reach those goals. Strategy also specifies how managers should allocate resources to reach the long-term goals of their organization. An organization's strategy may need to change as changes occur in its external environment.

According to Michael Porter, organizations need to distinguish and position themselves differently from their competitors in order to build and sustain a competitive advantage (Porter, 1980; Surowiecki, 1999). Organizations have attempted to build competitive advantages in various ways, but three underlying strategies appear to be essential in doing so: cost leadership, differentiation, and focused.

Under cost leadership, an organization provides the same services or products as its competitors, but produces them at a lower cost. An organization that chooses this strategy seeks to gain a significant cost advantage over other competitors and pass the savings on to consumers in order to gain a large market chare. Such a strategy aims at selling a standardized product that appeals to an "average" customer in a broad market. Organizations that use this strategy earn a better return on their investment in capital and human resources and attain significant economies of scale in key business activities (e.g., purchasing and logistics). Because the environment is uniform and stable, few product modifications are needed to satisfy customers. The organization's design is functional, with accountability and responsibility clearly assigned to various departments (see the later discussion to learn more about this design). Organizations that have successfully used this strategy include Wal-Mart in discount stores, Whirpool in washers and dryers, BIC in ballpoint pins, Black & Decker in power tools, and Procter-Silex in coffeemakers.

Differentiation is a second example of a competitive strategy. In a differentiation strategy, an organization seeks to be unique in its industry along dimensions that are widely valued or preferred by buyers. An organization that chooses a differentiation strategy typically uses a product organization design whereby each product has its own manufacturing, marketing, and research and development (R&D) departments (see the later discussion to learn more about this design). Like Mercedes Benz, organizations can usually charge a premium price if they successfully stake out their claim to being substantially different from their competition in some covered way. Rolex in watches, American Express in credit cares, Nordstrom in department stores, Krups in coffeemakers and espresso makers, and BMW in automobiles are other organizations that have successfully used a differentiation strategy.

Focused is a third example of a competitive strategy. A focused strategy is designed to help an organization target a specific niche within an industry, unlike both the cost leadership and differentiation strategies, which are designed to target industrywide markets. An organization that chooses a focused strategy may utilize any of a variety of organization designs, ranging from functional to product to matrix, to satisfy their customers' preferences (see the later discussion for a description of these designs). The choice of organization design reflects the niches of a particular buyer group, a regional market, or customers that have special tastes, preferences, or requirements. The basic idea is to specialize in ways that other organizations can't match effectively. These organizations generally operate in either varied–stable or uniform–unstable environments. Organizations that have successfully used a focused strategy include Karsten Manufacturing, Southwest Airlines, Nucor, and Chapparal Steel.

External Environment

An organization's environment is composed of those institutions or forces that are outside the organization and potentially affect the organization's performance. These typically include suppliers, customers, competitors, government regulatory agencies, public pressure groups, and the like.

Why should managerial decisions about an organization's structural design be affected by its environment? Because of environmental uncertainty. Some organizations face relatively stable environments—few forces in their environment are changing. There are, for example, no competitors, no new technological breakthroughs by current competitors, or little activity by public pressure groups to influence the organization. Other organizations face very dynamic environments—rapidly changing government regulations affecting their business, new competitors, difficulties in acquiring raw materials, continually changing product preferences by customers, and so on. Static environments create significantly less uncertainty for managers than do dynamic ones. And since uncertainty is a threat to an organization's effectiveness, management will try to minimize it. One way to reduce environmental uncertainty is through adjustments in the organization's structure.

The environment also needs to be assessed in terms of complexity, that is, the degree of heterogeneity and concentration among environmental elements. Simple environments are homogeneous and concentrated or simply have a few similar elements. A complex environment has many different elements that managers must monitor. It is useful to think of environmental complexity as a continuum ranging from simple to complex.

Four possible states of the external environment have varying degrees of uncertainty. A simple-static environment has the lowest uncertainty; a complex-dynamic environment has the highest uncertainty. Both simple-dynamic and complex-static environments are about midway between the other two. The unexpected explosive growth in Internet commerce has created a complex-dynamic environment for much of the retail industry.

Organization Size

Organizations usually develop more formal written rules and procedures as they increase in size. Large organizations have more management levels and more structured work activities than small organizations and use a decentralized form.

Small organizations can have an informal decision process and a simpler design than large organizations. Small organizations also have fewer diverse activities, fewer formal written procedures, and narrower spans of control. Large organizations can have more diverse activities that need more coordination than small organizations. Managers in large organizations make decisions guided by written rules and procedures.

Technology

Technology influences organization design in terms of job design and the creation of teams and departments, the delegation of authority and responsibility, and the need for formal integrating mechanisms. Technology refers to how an organization transfers the inputs into outputs. Every organization has at least one technology for converting financial, human, and physical resources into products or services.

The common theme that differentiates technologies is their degree of routineness. By this we mean that technologies tend toward either routine or nonroutine activities. The former are characterized by automated and standardized operations. Nonroutine activities are customized. They include such varied operations as furniture restoring, genetic research, and custom shoemaking.

Organizations must increasingly respond to technological change. The organization must be structured to accommodate the daily advances of new product development and improved production systems. The twenty-first century will continue to be characterized by dynamic technological development. To remain competitive, it is imperative for organizations, management, and other employees to be aware of this phenomenon. Rapid technological change causes organizations to re-examine and re-evaluate their structures as is evident by the number of downsizing and restructurings that have taken place over the past decade or so.

MECHANISTIC AND ORGANIC SYSTEMS

A mechanistic system is characterized by reliance on formal rules and regulations, centralization of decision making, narrowly defined job responsibilities, and a rigid hierarchy of authority. The emphasis is on following procedures and rules. In contrast, an organic system is characterized by low to moderate use of formal rules and regulations, decentralized and shared decision making, broadly defined job responsibilities, and a flexible authority structure with fewer levels in the hierarchy.

Top management typically makes decisions that determine the extent to which an organization will operate as a mechanistic system or an organic system. A mechanistic system is essentially a bureaucracy. Bureaucracy is characterized by principles that include:

1. specialization
2. hierarchy (chain of command)
3. rules and regulations
4. rational decision making
5. selection and promotion based on technical competence

All organizations must rely to some extent on these principles, which should be used as guidelines, not rules. The concept of bureaucracy, however, usually is associated with a number of negative attributes. The word often brings to mind rigidity, incompetence, red tape, inefficiency, and ridiculous rules. In principle though, the basic characteristics of a mechanistic system may make a bureaucratic organizational design feasible or even desirable in some situations. Any discussion of a mechanistic system must distinguish between the way it should ideally function and the way some large-scale organizations actually operate.

The degree to which an organization emphasizes a mechanistic or an organic system can vary substantially. Radio Shack, McDonald's, and Target are organizations that have relatively mechanistic systems in terms of dimensions like hierarchy of authority, centralization, rules, procedures, impersonality, chain of command, and span of control. The organic system emphasizes employee competence, rather than the employee's formal position in the hierarchy, and empowers employees to deal with uncertainties in the environment. Cisco Systems, Solectron Corporation, Apple, and Microsoft are organizations that place more emphasis on the dimensions that represent an organic system.

Hierarchy of Authority

Hierarchy of authority represents the extent to which decision-making processes are prescribed and where formal power resides. In a mechanistic system, higher level departments set or approve goals and detailed budgets for lower level departments and issue directives to them. A mechanistic system has as many levels in its hierarchy as necessary to achieve tight control. An organic system has few levels in its hierarchy, which makes coordination and communication easier and fosters innovation.

The hierarchy of authority is closely related to centralization. Centralization means that all major, and oftentimes many minor, decisions are made only at the top levels of the organization. Centralization is common in mechanistic systems, whereas decentralization and shared decision making between and across levels are common in an organic system. At McDonald's, Jiffy Lube, and Pier 1 Imports, top executives make nearly all decisions affecting store operations. Rules and regulations are sent from headquarters to each store, and reports from the stores are sent up the hierarchy.

In recent years, organizations have downsized and attempted to restructure themselves. The underlying assumption behind these changes is that fewer layers reduce waste and enable people to make better decisions (by moving them closer to the problems at hand), thereby leading to greater profitability. Management experts claim that although some layers of hierarchy are necessary, too many can be needlessly expensive. Moreover, as technology advances, fewer people are needed to carry out traditional management roles.

Division of Labor

Division of labor refers to the various ways of dividing up tasks and labor to achieve goals. The more that tasks are divided into separate jobs, the more those jobs are specialized and the narrower the range of activities job incumbents are required to perform.

The mechanistic system follows the view that the greater the division of labor in organizations, the greater will be the efficiency of organizations and the amount of wealth created. However, a continued increase in the division of labor may eventually become counterproductive. Employees who perform only very routine and simple jobs that require few skills may become bored and frustrated. The results may be low quality and low productivity, high turnover, and high absenteeism. The organic system takes advantage of the benefits from the division of labor, but it is sensitive to the negative results of carrying the division of labor too far.

Rules and Procedures

Rules are formal statements specifying acceptable behaviors and decisions by employees. One of the paradoxes of rules that attempt to reduce individual autonomy is that someone must still decide which rules apply to specific situations. Rules are an integral part of both mechanistic and organic systems. In a mechanistic system, the tendency is to create detailed uniform rules to cover tasks and decisions whenever possible. In an organic system, the tendency is to create rules only when necessary (e.g., safety rules to protect life and property). Managers and employees alike tend to question the need for new rules, as well as existing rules that no longer seem to have any validity. In a mechanistic system, the tendency is to accept the need for extensive rules and to formulate new rules in response to new situations.

Procedures refer to present sequences of steps that managers and employees must follow in performing tasks and dealing with problems. Procedures often comprise rules that are to be used in a particular sequence. Procedures have many of the same positive and negative features that characterize rules, and they often proliferate in a mechanistic system. Managers in organic systems usually know that rules and procedures can make the organization too rigid and thus dampen employee motivation, stymie innovation, and inhibit creativity. In a mechanistic system, rules and procedures tend to be developed at the top and issued via memoranda. Such memos may convey the expectation of strict compliance and the adverse consequences of not complying. In an organic system, employee input is likely to be sought on changes in current rules and procedures or on proposed rules and procedures when they are absolutely necessary. In an organic system employees at all levels are expected to question, evaluate, and make suggestions about such proposals, with an emphasis on collaboration and interdependence.

Impersonality

Impersonality is the extent to which organizations treat their employees, customers, and others according to objective, detached, and rigid characteristics. Managers in a highly mechanistic system are likely to emphasize matter-of-fact indicators (college degrees, certificates earned, test scores, training programs completed, length of service, and the like) when making hiring, salary, and promotion decisions. Although managers may consider these factors in an organic system, the emphasis is likely to be on the actual achievements and professional judgments of individuals rather than on rigid quantitative indicators.

Chain of Command

Chain of command is the formal flow of authority in an organization. It depicts the authority relationship existing between managers and direct reports. Chain of command is a hierarchical concept essential in all organizations.

A sign of a well-structured or well-designed organization is the presence of clear lines of authority, from top to bottom, throughout the organization. It is important that individuals know to whom they report. Confusion can be costly. Besides, it is impossible to be loyal to more than one boss. To avoid potential conflicts, managers must make sure the chain of command is clear, accurate, and understood.

Span of Control

Span of control refers to the number of employees reporting directly to one manager. When the span of control is broad, relatively few levels exist between the top and bottom of the organization. Conversely, when the span of control is narrow, more levels are required for the same number of employees. Although there is no "correct" number of direct reports that a manger can supervise effectively, the competencies of both the manager and employees, the similarity of tasks being supervised, and the extent of rules and operating standards all influence a manager's span of control.

In both mechanistic and organic systems, well-defined rules and procedures may have to be developed and applied through a relatively impersonal process in certain instances. For example, laws, court rulings, and regulatory agency decisions may even mandate impersonality, extensive rules, and rigid procedures.

Figure 11.1
The Functional Organization

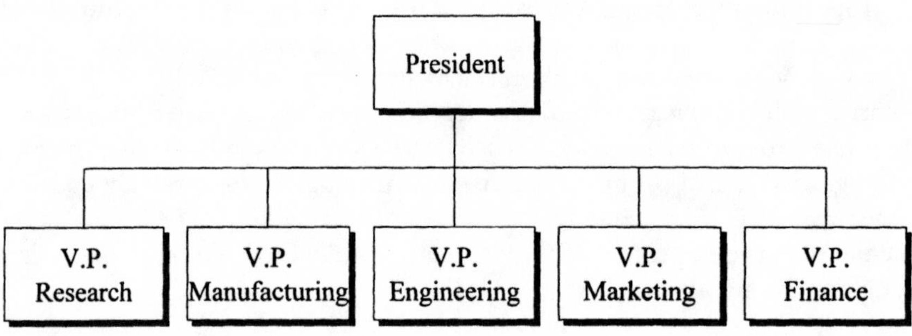

FORMS OF STRUCTURING OR DESIGNING ORGANIZATIONS

Organizations have traditionally structured themselves into three forms: (1) functional departments that are task specialized, (2) self-contained units that are oriented to specific products, customers, or regions, and (3) matrix structures that combine both functional specialization and self-containment. Faced with accelerating changes in competitive environments and technologies, however, organizations have increasingly redesigned their structures into more integrative and flexible forms. These more recent innovations include process-based structures that design subunits around the organization's core work processes and network-based structures that link the organization to other, interdependent organizations. The advantages, disadvantages, and contingencies of the different structures are described below.

The Functional Organization

Perhaps the most widely used organizational structure in the world today is the basic hierarchical structure, as shown in Figure 11.1. This is the standard pyramid, with senior management at the top, middle and lower managers spread out directly below, and workers at the bottom. The organization is usually subdivided into different functional units, such as engineering, research, operations, human resources, finance, and marketing. This organizational structure is based on early management theories regarding specialization, line and staff relations, span of control, authority, and responsibility. The major functional subunits are staffed by specialists in such disciplines as engineering and accounting. It is considered easier to manage specialists if they are grouped together under the same head and if the head of the department has training and experience in that particular discipline.

Table 11.1
Advantages, Disadvantages, and Contingencies of the Functional Organization

Advantages

- Provides a logical method for grouping activities
- Promotes skill specialization
- Results in more efficient use of resources and facilities; duplication of work is minimized
- Permits clear identification and assignment of responsibilities
- Enhances career development for specialists within large departments
- Facilitates communication and performance because managers share expertise with their direct reports
- Exposes specialists to others within the same specialty

Disadvantages

- Emphasizes routine tasks, which encourages short time horizons
- Fosters parochial perspectives by managers, which limit their capacities for top-management positions
- Reduces communication and cooperation between departments
- Could result in a slower decision-making process
- Multiplies the interdepartmental dependencies, which can make coordination and scheduling difficult
- Employees may lose site of the organization as a whole
- Obscures accountability for overall outcomes and may cause employees to lose touch with the need to meet or exceed customer expectations

Contingencies

- Stable and certain environment
- Small to medium size
- Routine technology, interdependence within functions
- Goals of efficiency and technical quality

A paper route serves as an example of functional departmentalization in its simplest form. The newspaper is printed (production), customers are sought (marketing), and the papers are distributed and money collected (finance). Oil companies serve an excellent example of a functional design in its more complex form because functional activities include exploration, research, drilling, production, refining, marketing, advertising, and distribution.

Table 11.1 lists the advantages, disadvantages, and contingencies of functional structures. On the positive side, functional structures promote specialization of skills and resources. People are grouped together who perform similar work and face similar problems. This facilitates communication within departments and allows specialists to share their expertise. It permits clear identification and assignment of responsibilities, and employees easily understand it. It also enhances career development within the specialty, whether it be accounting, finance, engineering, or sales. The functional structure reduces duplication of services because it makes the best use of people and resources.

On the negative side, functional structures tend to promote routine tasks with a limited orientation. Departmental members focus on their own tasks, rather than the organization's total task. This can lead to conflict across functional departments when each group attempts to maximize its own performance without considering the performances of other units. Coordination and scheduling among the departments can be difficult when each emphasizes its own perspective.

As shown in Table 11.1, the functional structure tends to work best in small to medium-sized firms facing environments that are relatively stable and certain. These organizations typically have a small number of products or services, and coordination across specialized units is relatively easy. This structure is also best suited to routine technologies in which there is interdependence within functions and to organizational goals emphasizing efficiency and technical quality.

The Division (Self-Contained-Unit) Organization

The self-contained-unit structure represents a fundamentally different way of organizing. Also known as a product or divisional structure, it was developed at about the same time by General Motors, Sears, Standard Oil of New Jersey (Exxon), and DuPont. It groups organizational activities on the basis of products, services, customers, programs, technical processes, or geography. All or most of the resources necessary for the accomplishment of specific objectives are set up as a self-contained unit headed by a product or division manager. General Motors gives a classic example of product departmentalization in its purest form, with its Pontiac, Chevrolet, Cadillac, Buick, Oldsmobile, Saturn, and GMC truck divisions. In another example, General Electric has plants that specialize in making jet engines and others that specialize in household appliances. Each plant manager reports to a particular division or product vice-president, rather than a manufacturing vice-president. In effect, a large organization that may set up smaller (sometimes temporary) special-purpose organizations, each geared to a specific product, service, customer, or region. A typical product structure is shown in Figure 11.2. Interestingly, the formal structure within a self-contained unit is often functional in nature.

Table 11.2 provides a list of the advantages, disadvantages, and contin-

Figure 11.2
The Division (Self-Contained-Unit) Organization

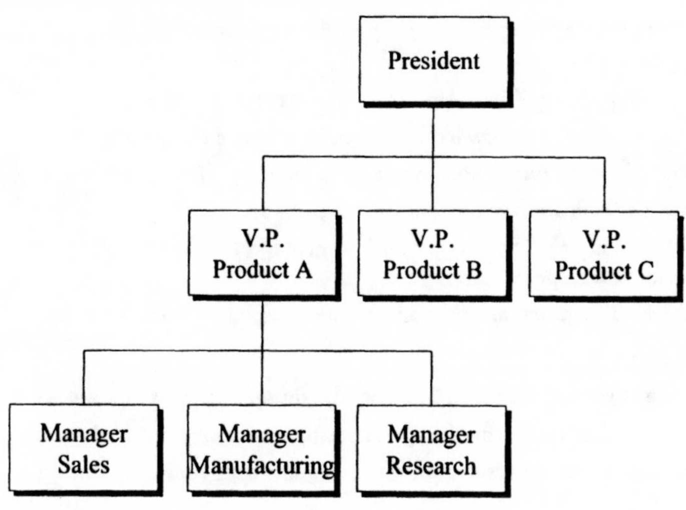

gencies of divisional or self-contained-unit structures. These organizations recognize key interdependencies and promote coordination of resources toward an overall outcome. This strong outcome orientation ensures departmental accountability and promotes cohesion among those contributing to the product. These structures provide employees with opportunities for learning new skills and expanding knowledge because they can more easily move among the different specialties contributing to the product. As a result, self-contained-unit structures are well-suited for developing general managers.

Self-contained-unit organizations have certain problems, however. They may not have enough specialized work to fully use people's skills and abilities. Specialists may feel isolated from their professional colleagues and may fail to advance in their career specialty. These structures may promote allegiance to departmental goals, rather than to organizational objectives. They also place multiple demands on people, which may create stress.

The self-contained-unit structure works best in conditions almost the opposite of those favoring a functional organization, as shown in Table 11.2. The organization needs to be relatively large to support the duplication of resources assigned to the units. Because each unit is designed to fit a particular niche, the structure adapts well to uncertain conditions. Self-contained units also help to coordinate technical interdependencies falling across functions and are suited to goals promoting product or service specialization and innovation.

Table 11.2
Advantages, Disadvantages, and Contingencies of the Self-Contained-Unit Form

---

Advantages

- Recognizes sources of interdepartmental interdependencies
- Fosters an orientation toward overall outcomes and clients
- It easily adapts to differences in products, services, clients, location, and the like
- Allows diversification and expansion of skills and training
- Ensures accountability by departmental managers and so promotes delegation of authority and responsibility
- Heightens departmental cohesion and involvement in work

Disadvantages

- May use skills and resources inefficiently; thus, economies of scale are lost
- Limits career advancement by specialists to movements out of their departments
- Specialists in one division cannot talk readily with similar specialists in another division
- Puts multiple-role demands upon people and so creates stress
- May promote departmental objectives, as opposed to overall organizational objectives

Contingencies

- Complex, unstable and has moderate to high uncertain environments
- Common management reaction to large size
- Technological interdependence across functions (e.g., technical processes often are nonroutine and interdependent with other parts of the organization)
- Goals of product specialization and innovation

The Matrix Organization

Some organizations have focused on maximizing the strengths and minimizing the weaknesses of both the function and the self-contained-unit structures. This has resulted in the matrix organization. It superimposes the lateral structure of a product or project coordinator on the vertical functional structure, as shown in Figure 11.3. The word matrix evolved during the 1950s within the aerospace industry to describe the grid-like organizational design used in project management. Changing customer demands and technological conditions caused managers to focus on lateral relationships between functions in order to develop a flexible and adaptable system of resources and procedures, and to achieve a series of project objectives. Matrix organizations are now used widely in manufacturing, service, nonprofit, governmental, and professional organizations.

Figure 11.3
The Matrix Organization

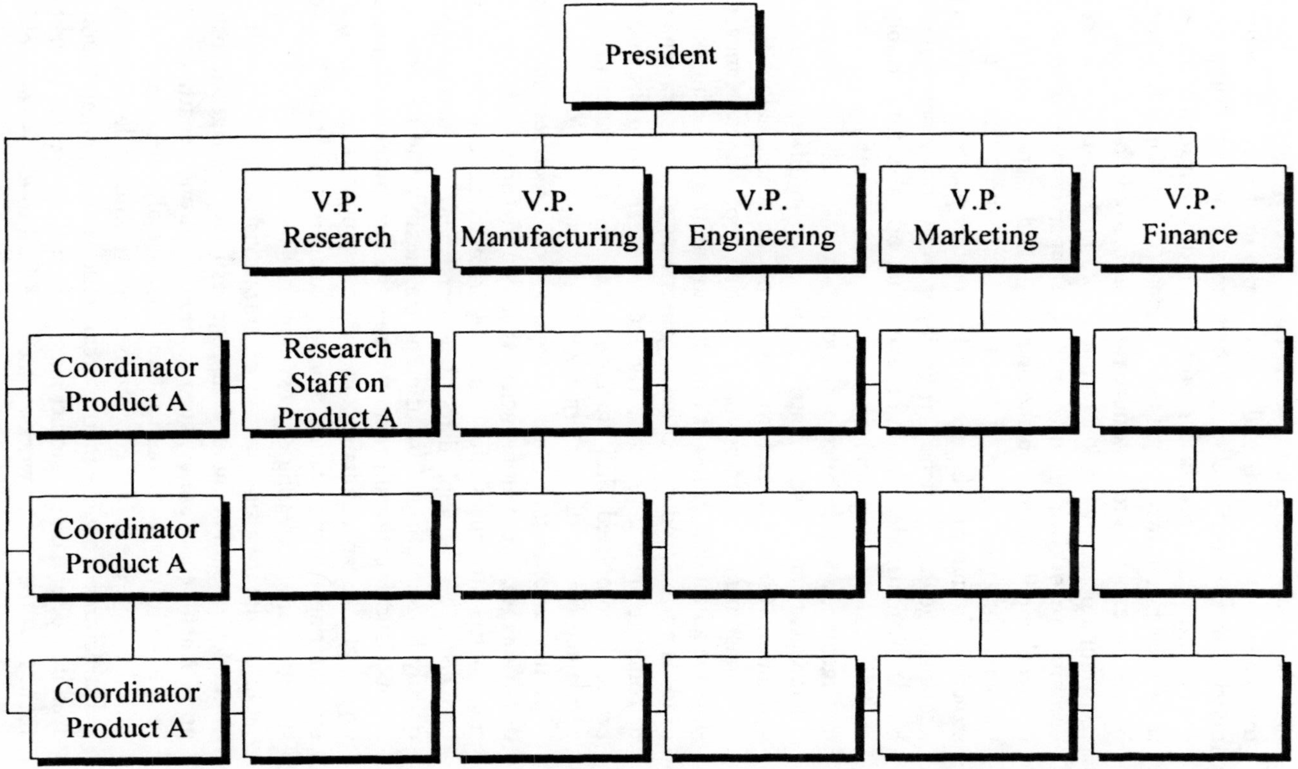

President

V.P. Research

V.P. Manufacturing

V.P. Engineering

V.P. Marketing

V.P. Finance

Coordinator Product A

Research Staff on Product A

Coordinator Product A

Coordinator Product A

A matrix design is based on multiple support systems and authority relationships, whereby some employees report to two supervisors rather than one. Every matrix organization contains three unique and critical roles: the top manager who heads and balances the dual chains of command; the matrix bosses (functional, product, or area) who share subordinates; and the two-boss managers who report to two different matrix bosses. Each of these roles has it own unique requirements. For example, functional matrix bosses are expected to maximize their respective technical expertise within constraints posed by market realities. Two-boss managers, however, must accomplish work within the demands of supervisors who want to achieve technical sophistication on the one hand, and to meet customer expectations on the other. Thus, a matrix organization is more than a matrix structure. It must also be reinforced by matrix processes, such as performance management systems that get input from both functional and project bosses, by matrix leadership behavior that operates comfortably with lateral decision making, and by a matrix culture that fosters open conflict management and a balance of power.

Managers can design a matrix organization in different ways. Some organizations use a matrix form within specific functional areas only. Such an arrangement is common in a marketing department. Managers responsible for a brand or group of brands bring all the marketing skills together to focus on the products. Other organizations use temporary matrix forms to complete specific projects. The matrix organization disbands after the project is completed. Still other organizations have the matrix form as a permanent feature of their organizational design.

Matrix organizations, like all organization structures, have advantages, disadvantages, and contingencies, as shown in Table 11.3. On the positive side, matrix structures allow multiple orientations. Specialized, functional knowledge can be applied to all projects. New products or projects can quickly be implemented by using people flexibly and by moving between product and functional orientations as the circumstances demand. Matrix organizations can maintain consistency among departments and projects by requiring communication among managers. For many people, matrix structures are motivating and exciting.

On the negative side, matrix organizations can be difficult to manage. To implement and maintain them requires heavy managerial costs and support. When people are assigned to more than one department, there may be role ambiguity and conflict. Similarly, overall performance may be sacrificed if there are power conflicts between functional departments and project structures. To make matrix organizations work, organization members need interpersonal and conflict management skills. People can get confused about how the matrix works, which can lead to chaos and inefficiencies.

As shown in Table 11.3, matrix structures are appropriate under three important conditions. First, there must be outside pressures for a dual fo-

Table 11.3
Advantages, Disadvantages, and Contingencies of the Matrix Organization

Advantages

- Makes specialized, functional knowledge available to all projects
- Uses people flexibly, since departments maintain reservoirs of specialists
- Maintains consistency between different departments and projects by forcing communication between managers
- The dual focus of matrix organizations lets management respond quickly to changes in market or product demand by shifting emphasis between project and functional aspects
- Recognizes and provides mechanisms for dealing with legitimate, multiple sources of power in the organization
- Individuals can get information about a total project, not only about their particular specialty

Disadvantages

- Can be very difficult to introduce without a pre-existing supportive management climate
- Ambiguity in authority relationships can encourage power struggles among managers who compete for dominance
- People reporting to both a functional and a project manager can experience opposing demands from the two managers
- Without power balancing between product and functional forms, lowers overall performance
- Makes inconsistent demands, which may result in unproductive conflicts and short-term crisis management
- May reward political skills as opposed to technical skills
- All the disadvantages can act as significant stressors for people in such organizations

Contingencies

- Dual focus on unique product demands and technical specialization
- Pressure for high information processing capacity
- Pressure for shared resources

cus. That is, a matrix structure works best when there are many customers with unique demands on the one hand and strong requirements for technical sophistication on the other hand. Second, there must be pressures for high information-processing capacity. A matrix organization is appropriate when the organization must process a large amount of information. There tend to be a few conditions that produce the need for high information-processing capacity. When external environmental demands change unpredictably, there is considerable uncertainty in decision making. When the organization produces a broad range of products or services, or offers those outputs to a large number of different markets, there is considerable complexity in decision making. And when there is reciprocal interdependence among the tasks in the organization's technical core, there is considerable pressure on communication and coordination systems. Third, and finally, there must be pressures for shared resources. When customer demands vary greatly and technological requirements are strict, valuable human and physical resources are likely to be scarce. Thus, the matrix works well under these conditions because it facilitates the sharing of these scarce resources. If any of these conditions are not met, a matrix organization is likely to fail.

Process-Based Organization Design

A radically new logic for structuring organizations is to form multidisciplinary teams around core processes, such as product development, sales generation, and customer support. As shown in Figure 11.4, process-based structures emphasize lateral rather than vertical relationships. They group all related functions that are necessary to produce a product or service into a common unit usually managed by someone called a "process owner." There are few hierarchical levels, and the senior executive team is relatively small, typically consisting of the chairperson, the chief operating officer, and the heads of a few key support services, such as strategic planning, HRM, and finance.

Process-based organizational designs eliminate many of the hierarchical and departmental boundaries that can impede task coordination and slow decision making and task performance. They reduce the enormous costs of managing across departments and up and down the hierarchy. Process-based structures enable organizations to focus most of their resources on serving customers, both inside and outside the firm.

The application of process-based structures is growing rapidly in a variety of manufacturing and service companies. Typically referred to as "horizontal," "boundaryless," or "team-based" organizations, they have been used to enhance customer service at such organizations as AT&T, Pratt and Whitney, Honeywell, Lexmark International, Motorola, Eastman Chemical, Pfizer, Hewlett-Packard, and Xerox. Although there is no one right way to design process-based structures, the following features characterize this new form of organizing.

- *Processes drive structural design.* Process-based structures are organized around the three to five key processes that define the work of the organization. Rather than products or functions, processes define the structure and are governed by a

Figure 11.4
The Process-Based Organization

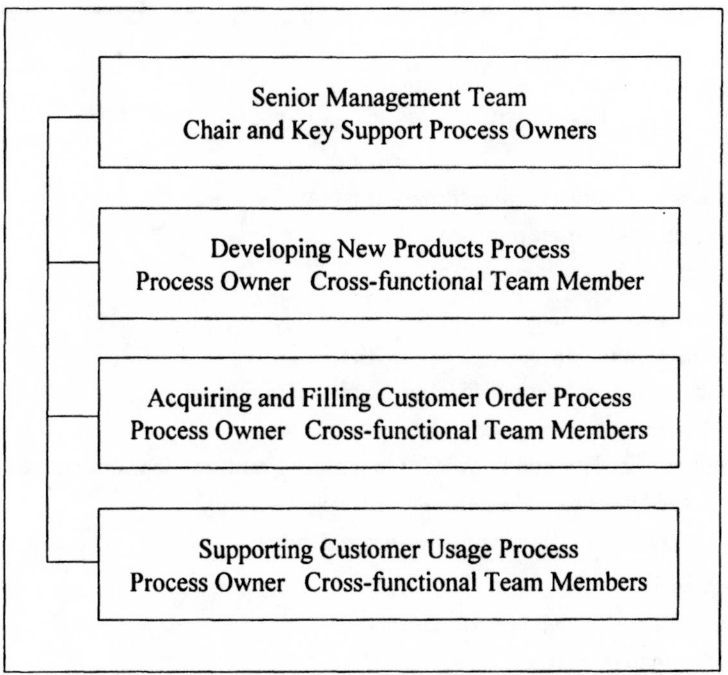

"process owner." Each process has clear performance goals that drive task execution.

- *Work adds value.* To increase efficiency, process-based structures simplify and enrich work processes. Work is simplified by eliminating nonessential tasks and reducing layers of management. It is enriched by combining tasks so that teams perform whole processes.
- *Teams are fundamental.* The key organizing feature in a process-based design is teams. They are used to manage everything from task execution to strategic planning; they are typically self-managing; and they are responsible for goal achievement.
- *Customers define performance.* The key goal of any team in a process-based structure is customer satisfaction. Defining customer expectations and designing team functions to meet these expectations command much of the team's attention. The organization must value this orientation as the primary path to financial performance.
- *Teams are rewarded for performance.* Appraisal systems focus on measuring team performance against customer satisfaction and other goals and then provide real recognition for achievement. Team-based rewards are given as much, if not more, weight than individual recognition.

Table 11.4
Advantages, Disadvantages, and Contingencies of the Process-Based Organization

Advantages

- Focuses resources on customer satisfaction
- Improves speed and efficiency, often dramatically
- Adapts to environmental change rapidly
- Reduces boundaries between departments
- Increases ability to see total work flow
- Enhances employee involvement

Disadvantages

- Can threaten middle managers and staff specialists
- Requires changes in command-and-control mind-sets
- Duplicates scarce resources
- Requires new skills and knowledge to manage lateral relationships and teams
- May take longer to make decisions in teams
- Can be ineffective if wrong processes are identified

Contingencies

- Uncertain and changing environments
- Moderate to large size
- Nonroutine and highly independent technologies
- Customer-oriented goals

- *Teams are tightly linked to suppliers and customers.* Teams, through designated members, have timely and direct relationships with vendors and customers to understand and respond to emerging concerns.
- *Team members are well informed and trained.* Successful implementation of a process-based structure required team members who can work with a broad range of information, including customer and market data, financial information, and personnel and policy matters. Team members also need problem-solving and decision-making skills and abilities to address and implement solutions.

Table 11.4 lists the advantages, disadvantages, and contingencies of process-based structures. The most frequently mentioned advantage is intense focus on meeting customer needs, which can result in dramatic improvements in speed, efficiency, and customer satisfaction. Process-based structures remove layers of management, and consequently information flows more quickly and accurately throughout the organization. Because process teams are composed of different functional specialties, boundaries between departments are removed, thus affording organization members a broad view of the work flow and a clear line of sight between team performance and organization effectiveness. Process-based designs are also more flexible and adaptable to change than traditional structures.

A major disadvantage of process-based structures is the difficulty of changing to this new organizational form. Process-based structures typically require radical shifts in mindsets, skills, and managerial roles. These changes involve considerable time and resources and can be resisted by functional managers and staff specialists. Moreover, process-based structures may result in expensive duplication of scarce resources and, if team skills are not present, in slower decision making as teams struggle to define and reach consensus. Finally, implementation of process-based structures relies on proper identification of key processes needed to satisfy customer needs. If critical processes are misidentified or ignored altogether, performance and customer satisfaction are likely to suffer.

Table 11.4 shows that process-based structural designs are particularly appropriate for highly uncertain environments where customer demands and market conditions are changing rapidly. They enable organizations to manage nonroutine technologies and to coordinate work flows that are highly interdependent. Process-based designs generally appear in medium- to large-sized organizations having several products or projects. They focus heavily on customer-oriented goals and are found in both domestic and worldwide organizations.

Network Designs

Many of the organization designs discussed so far have limitations that often hinder organizations in coping with turbulent environments and technologies. Increasingly today's organizations face two important trends. First is the shift from traditional mechanistic systems to more organic systems. This shift is accompanied by the realization that an organization's competitive advantage lies in its ability to manage its knowledge assets, or human capital, more effectively. Doing so requires sharing and shifting power and decision making away form top management toward employees at all levels. Second, as multinational organizations become larger, subsidiaries within these are becoming geographically dispersed. There is a need to take into account and act on ideas of managers in foreign lands. General Electric sees itself as a "boundaryless" organization, noting that it wants people to behave entrepreneurially and share ideas across organizational lines.

A network design is intended to overcome those limitations and facilitate the management of highly diverse and complex organizations involving multiple departments and many people. A network design manages the diverse, complex, and dynamic relationships among multiple organizations, each specializing in a particular business function or task. A network design focuses on sharing authority, responsibility, and resources among people

Figure 11.5
The Network Organization

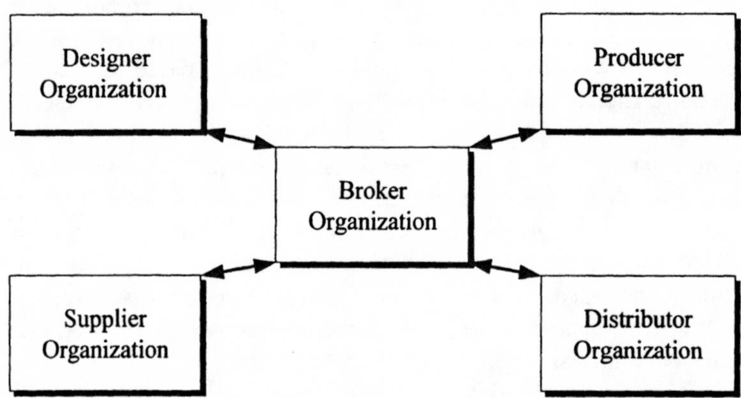

and departments that must cooperate and communicate frequently to achieve common goals. Various designs (functional, product, or place) must be applied in a network organization as the tasks to be performed and the goals to be achieved change.

As shown in Figure 11.5, the network structure redraws organizational boundaries and links separate organizations to facilitate task interaction. The essence of networks is the relationship between organizations that perform different aspects of work. In this way, organizations do the things that they do well; manufacturing expertise is applied to production and logistical expertise is applied to distribution, for example. Examples of network organizations include joint ventures to design, manufacture, and market advanced products; research and development consortia; subcontracting and licensing arrangements across national borders; and wholly owned subsidiaries selling products and services to one another.

Network-based structures are called by a variety of names, including virtual corporations, modular corporations, or Shamrock organizations. Less formally, they have been described as "pizza" structures, spiderwebs, starbursts, and cluster organizations. Organizations such as Eastman Chemical, Apple Computers, Bennetton, Sun Microsystems, MCI WorldCom, and Merck have implemented fairly sophisticated network structures. They are also found in the construction, fashion, and entertainment industries, as well as in the public sector.

Network structures typically have the following characteristics:

- *Vertical disaggregation.* This means that different business functions, such as production, marketing, and distribution, that are traditionally performed within a single organization, are performed by different network members. In the film industry, for example, separate organizations providing transportation, cinematography, music, actors, and catering work together under a broker organization, the studio. The organizations making up the network represent an important factor in determining its success.

- *Brokers.* Networks are often managed by broker organizations that locate and assemble member organizations. The broker may play a central role and subcontract for needed products or services, or it might specialize in linking equal partners into a network. In the construction industry, the general contractor typically assembles and manages drywall, mechanical, electrical, plumbing, and other specialties to erect a building.
- *Coordinating mechanisms.* Network organizations are not generally controlled by hierarchical arrangements or plans. Rather, coordination of the work in a network falls into three categories: informal relationships, contracts, and market mechanisms. First, coordination patterns can depend heavily on interpersonal relationships between individuals who have a well-developed partnership. Conflicts are resolved through reciprocity; network members recognize that each will likely have to compromise at some time. Trust is built and nurtured over time by these reciprocal arrangements. Second, coordination can be achieved through formal contracts, such as ownership control, licensing arrangements, or purchase agreements. Finally, market mechanisms, such as spot payments, performance accountability, and information systems, ensure that all parties are aware of each other's activities.

Network structures have a number of advantages, disadvantages, and contingencies, as shown in Table 11.5. They are highly flexible and adaptable to changing conditions. The ability to form partnerships with different organizations permits the creation of a "best of the best" company to exploit opportunities, often global in nature. They allow each member to exploit its distinctive competence. They can enable sufficient resources and expertise to be applied to large, complex tasks that single organizations cannot perform. Perhaps most important is the fact that network organizations can have synergistic effects, allowing members to build on each other's strengths and competencies.

The major problems with network organizations are in managing such complex structures. Network structures have been described as matrix organizations extending beyond the boundaries of single firms but lacking the ability to appeal to a higher authority to resolve conflicts. Thus, matrix skills of managing lateral relations across organizational boundaries are critical to administering network structures. Most organizations, because they are managed hierarchically, can be expected to have difficulties managing lateral relations. Other disadvantages of network organizations include the difficulties of motivating organizations to join such structures and of sustaining commitment over time. Potential members may not want to give up their autonomy to link with other organizations. Once linked, they may have problems sustaining the benefits of joining together. This is especially true if the network consists of organizations that are not the "best

Table 11.5
Advantages, Disadvantages, and Contingencies of the Network Organization

Advantages

- Enables highly flexible and adaptive response to dynamic environments
- Creates a "best of the bet" organization to focus resources on customer and market needs
- Each organization can leverage a distinctive competency
- Permits rapid global expansion
- Can produce synergistic results

Disadvantages

- Managing lateral relations across autonomous organizations is difficult
- Motivating members to relinquish autonomy to join the network is troublesome
- Sustaining membership and benefits can be problematic
- May give partners access to proprietary knowledge/technology

Contingencies

- Highly complex and uncertain environments
- All size organizations
- Goals of organizational specialization and innovation
- Highly uncertain technologies
- Worldwide operations

in breed." Finally, joining in a network may expose the organization's proprietary knowledge and skills to others.

As shown in Table 11.5, network organizations are best suited to highly complex and uncertain environments where multiple competencies and flexible responses are needed. They seem to apply to organizations of all sizes, and they deal with complex tasks or problems involving high interdependencies across organizations. Network structures fit with goals emphasizing organization specialization and innovation. They also fit well in organizations with worldwide operations.

Virtual Organization

The principal developments in information technologies over the past 10 years have both pushed and enabled organizations to move toward more cooperative relationships with their suppliers, distributors, and even competitors. These cooperative relationships are referred to as virtual organizations. A virtual organization is a network of companies or individuals that focus on reaching a specific target or responding to new opportunities (see Figure 11.6). These networks of relationships enable organizations to

Figure 11.6
The Virtual Organization

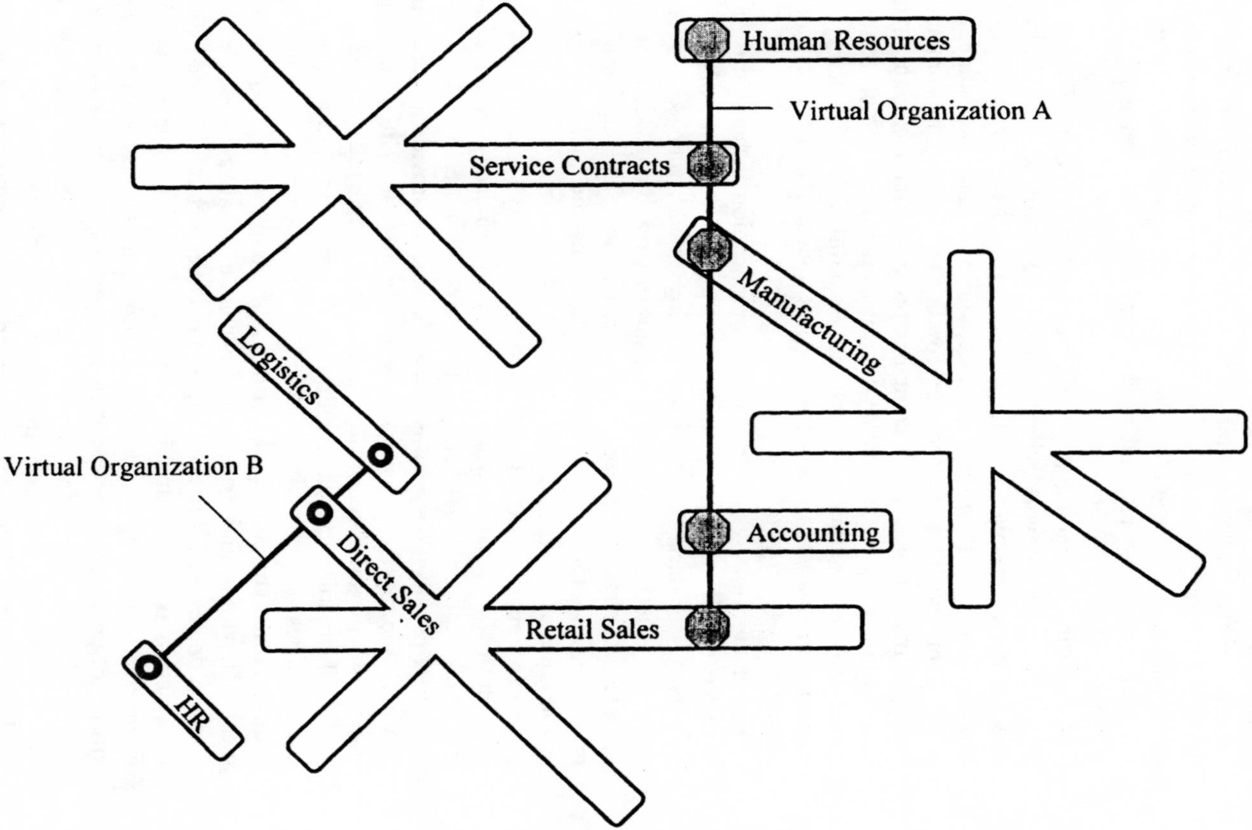

achieve both efficiency and flexibility to exploit advantages of the mechanistic and organic organization designs.

The networks can be temporary or permanent. They also are flexible in response to fast environmental changes. The cooperative relationships between these organizations enable the principal organization to rely upon the smaller, closer-to-the market partner to sense impending changes in the environment and to respond at the local level, thus relieving the parent organization of that necessity.

Information technology, the Internet, and the World Wide Web link members of the network wherever they are in the world. The computer network allows people to work cooperatively and share knowledge quickly and easily regardless of time, distance, and organizational boundaries.

The term virtual organization borrows its metaphor from computer technology. Virtual memory is a computer programming technique that lets a programmer have more memory than is available on the computer. Software simulates memory by using space on a disk drive. When the program runs, it is unaware that the software gives it virtual memory instead of real memory.

The metaphor carries to the virtual organization. Any organization that lacks a particular skill or resource enters an agreement with an organization or person (consultant or contract employee) with that skill or resource. Information technology links the organizations and individuals so they can operate as though they were a single organization. The number of elements in a virtual organization network is defined by the skills, talents, and resources needed to reach the goal.

An example of a virtual organization is Barclay's global bank. The organization is a global network created by electronically linking extant networks of small, regional banks. Customers of the regional banks feel like they are a part of a large entity, because they are provided with worldwide services. The feeling of being a part of a worldwide entity exists, as customers remain members of their local community banks as well.

Virtual organizations have a number of advantages, disadvantages, and contingencies as identified in Table 11.6. Virtual organizations have a faster response time, autonomy, greater flexibility, and more efficient use of technical, behavioral, and professional expertise. Disadvantages are increased conflict, decreased loyalty, a lack of any coherence in plans and strategies, information overload, and no social interaction fulfillment. Work in e-commerce, consulting, marketing, and job searching seems best suited for virtual organizations. These jobs are service-oriented, require extensive communication, are dynamic, and are knowledge-based. There is also the issue of whether an organization has the managerial competence suited to lead, coordinate, facilitate, and provide constructive feedback to virtual organization workers. These and similar issues should be carefully evaluated before taking a plunge into virtual organization discussions, plans, or implementation.

Table 11.6
Advantages, Disadvantages, and Contingencies of the Virtual Organization

Advantages

- Faster response time
- Economic gains of acquiring goals and services from specialized firms
- Autonomy
- Greater flexibility
- More efficient use of technical, behavioral, and professional expertise
- Concentrate all effort on performing one or just a few functions extremely well
- Lower transaction costs associated with buying from an external supplier

Disadvantages

- Increased conflict
- Decreased loyalty
- Depend upon others for key elements needed to make the entire virtual corporation work
- A lack of coherence in plans and strategies
- Constantly forming and reforming with different partners
- Information overload
- May lack the size needed to launch products on a national or global scale
- No social interaction fulfillment
- Success is highly dependent on the ability to find partners and to find partners that are dependable

Contingencies

- Uncertain and changing environments
- All size organizations
- Goals of organizational flexibility
- Highly uncertain technologies
- Customer-oriented goals and broad operations

SUMMARY

The environment facing an organization consists of all those stakeholders that are external to the organization, including customers, suppliers, competitors, and regulators, among others. Organizations must be sensitive to their environment in making organizational design decisions. The choice of business strategy—cost, focused, differentiation—also has a direct impact on an organization's design. Organization size and technology also are dimensions that must be considered in making decisions about structural design.

If management supports tight, centralized control of day-to-day decisions, a mechanistic system is more likely to be used than an organic one. Mechanistic systems are effective in stable environments, whereas organic systems are more effective in unstable environments.

Several basic structural designs, such as the functional, the divisional or self-contained unit, and the matrix configuration, dominate most organizations. Two newer forms, process-based and network structures, were also described. Each of these structures has corresponding strengths and weaknesses, and contingency guidelines must be used to determine which structure is an appropriate fit with the organization's environment.

Virtual organizations have become important ways of getting work done. A virtual organization uses technology to connect far-flung parts of the organization. Managers are using these new designs to build organizations that respond faster and more effectively to shifting constraints and opportunities.

REFERENCES

Porter, M.E. 1980. *Competitive strategy*. New York: Free Press.

Surowiecki, J. 1999. The return of Michael Porter. *Fortune* (February 1): 135–136.

Chapter 12

Organizational Culture and Ethics

INTRODUCTION

Many organizations create a culture that gives them a competitive advantage. They may focus on customer service, emphasize employee involvement, or incorporate technological innovation in their product development or service delivery. In this chapter we first explore the nature, levels, and functions of organizational culture. Next, we investigate how to create, maintain, and change a culture. The discussion then turns to business ethics in the workplace that influences how a business functions, such as individual and corporate ethics and includes an emphasis on ethical standards managers can use to decide on the proper way to behave toward organizational stakeholders. Social responsibility and the institutionalization of ethics within an organization are described before concluding the chapter with a look at the issue of diversity.

ORGANIZATIONAL CULTURE

At the outset, we can say that organizational culture is not the easiest concept to define. It is a complex and deep aspect of organizations that can strongly affect organization members. Informally, culture might be thought of as an organization's style, atmosphere, or personality. This style, atmosphere, or personality is most obvious when we contrast what it must be like to work in various organizations such as General Electric, Nordstrom's, the U.S. Marine Corps, or the New York Yankees. Even from their mention in the popular press, we can imagine that these organizations provide very different work environments. Thus, culture provides uniqueness and social identity to organizations.

More formally, organizational culture includes the values, norms, rites, rituals, ceremonies, heroes, and scoundrels in the history of the organization (Deal and Kennedy, 1982). Organizational culture defines what a new employee needs to learn to be accepted as a member of the organization.

Organizational cultures are similar to cultures of different countries. Your entry into a new organizational culture is like entering the culture of another country. Key aspects of these culture include a sharing of values and a structuring of experiences in an organization. Different sets of values can coexist among different groups of people throughout the organization. Although values differ from group to group, members of each group can share a set of values. The term *share* does not necessarily mean that members are in close agreement on these matters, although they might well be. Rather, it means that they have had uniform exposure to the values and have some minimum common understanding of them. Thus, not all people in an organization will fully agree about the dominant values and norms (Martin, 1992).

The specific content of an organization's culture develops from the experiences of a group adapting to its external environment and building a system of internal coordination. Each of the different human systems within which we interact has a culture. Our family, our employer, and any leisure-time organization such as clubs or religious groups all have their own cultures. These cultures can make different—and sometimes conflicting—demands on us.

Each organizational culture divides into multiple subcultures. An organization's structural design creates varying subcultures and processes within the organization. Subcultures grow readily within these differentiated parts of the total organization. They also grow readily within departments, divisions, and different operating locations of an organization.

Different occupational groups within an organization often form different subcultures. Specialists in manufacturing, accounting, information systems and finance often have their own jargon that helps them talk to each other. That jargon becomes an integral part of an occupational subculture and often cannot be understood by those outside the subculture. An information systems specialist easily understands terms like upload, download, and token-ring networks, which often are a foreign language to people outside that occupation.

The global environment and workforce diversity also help build subcultures in organizations. Global operations often require organizations to hire people from the host country. Those employees often will bring values into the organizations that differ from those of the organization's home country. People who come from different social backgrounds and have different values will infuse organizations with a variety of values and viewpoints. Effective organizations will develop an overarching culture that manages differences that might exist between the various subcultures.

LEVELS OF ORGANIZATIONAL CULTURE

Organizational cultures are revealed at three different but related levels: artifacts, values, and basic assumptions. These levels vary in their visibility to an outsider, with the first being easiest to see and the last the most difficult.

Artifacts are the most visible parts of an organization's culture. They are the obvious features of an organization that are immediately visible to a new employee. Artifacts consist of the physical manifestation of an organization's culture. Artifacts include sounds, architecture, smells, behavior, attire, language, products, awards, observable rituals and ceremonies, myths and stories told about the organization, published lists of values, special parking places, decorations, and so on.

Organizations differ in the layout of their interior space and the formality of their working relationships. Do people work in an open office space or behind closed doors? Do people dress formally or informally? Does the interior design give the impression of a cheerful or a somber work environment? Do people refer to each other by first names or do they use formal titles such as Mr., Ms., Doctor, Captain? These factors are clues to an organization's culture. You can infer some values, norms, and required behavior from such factors. A new employee must first attend to messages from the physical characteristics of the organization and then watch the behavior of veteran organizational members.

Artifacts are easier to change than the less visible aspects of organizational culture. At the less visible level, culture reflects the values and basic assumptions shared among organizational members. These values tend to persist over time and are more resistant to change.

At the next level of awareness are the values embedded in the culture. Values tell organization members what they "ought" to do in various situations. Values are hard for the newcomer to see, but he can discover and learn them. The newcomer must be aware of espoused values that guide what veteran members say in a given situation. More important are the in-use or enacted values that really guide the behavior of organization members.

Espoused values represent the explicitly stated values and norms that are preferred by an organization. They are generally established by the founder of a new or small company and by the top management team in a larger organization.

Each level of culture influences the other. For example, if an organization truly values providing high-quality service, employees are more likely to adopt the behavior of responding faster to customer complaints. Similarly, causality can flow in the other direction. Employees can come to value high-quality service based on their experiences as they interact with customers.

FUNCTIONS OF ORGANIZATIONAL CULTURE

Organizational culture plays several important roles in organizations. The two major roles of culture are (1) adaptation to the organization's external environment, and (2) coordination of internal systems and processes (Schein, 1992; Trice and Beyer, 1993).

An organization that has adapted successfully to its internal environment can develop a culture with a consensus among members about the organization's mission. Specific goals derived from the mission and the means to reach those goals will be part of the culture. A consensus about a mission among veteran members lets the organization move forward smoothly toward those goals. Members agree about what needs to be done and how it will be done. In short, an organization's culture can help its members develop a sense of identity with the organization and a clear vision of the organization's direction.

People sometimes have difficulty in thinking beyond their own interests (i.e., how will this affect me?). When there is a strong, overarching culture, however, people feel part of that larger, well-defined whole and are involved in the entire organization's work. Bigger than any one individual's interests, culture reminds people what their organization is all about.

An organizational culture that gives its members a clear vision of the organization's mission also presents a consistent image to its markets, customers, and clients. Over time, that image can give an organization a competitive advantage by building commitment to its products and services.

Employees of developed organizational cultures agree about how results will be measured and what remedial action will be taken if something goes wrong. Long-term employees know almost automatically when things are not going right and how to take corrective action. If there was no consensus about those matters, conflict levels could be dysfunctionally high. With so much conflict among its members, the organization would have difficulty responding rapidly in situations requiring quick action.

Organizational cultures define the rewards and sanctions that managers can use. Rules develop about how good performance will be rewarded and about what sanctions will be levied for poor performance. Some cultures respond to poor performance by saying the individual is not properly matched to the task. Those organizations reassign the person to a new task and let her or him try again. Other cultures develop specific sanctions that include demotions and terminations.

Organizational cultures differ in the way they use reward systems (Kerr and Slocum, 1987). Some reward systems emphasize total organization performance, leading to feeling that members are part of a fraternal group. Other cultures reward individual performance, ignoring the larger system. Members of the latter cultures develop a strong sense of individuality and independence.

Culture also helps integrate an organization's subsystems and processes. The integration lets the organization coordinate its various actions effectively. Common language develops within a culture, helping communication. Conceptual categories develop that filter unimportant detail and focus attention on important matters. Perceptual filtration reduces the likelihood that an individual will become overloaded by stimuli defined as unimportant by the culture.

The culture defines boundaries of groups and criteria for inclusion in the group. Well-defined group boundaries enhance member identification with the group and the group's work. Strong groups support and help members get their work done.

Organizational cultures define rules for power, rules for social stratification, and the ways in which social status is determined. Some accord social status and power to people of high achievement. Others base status and power on seniority.

The nature and quality of peer relationships and interpersonal interactions are defined by the organization's culture. Are interactions characterized by cooperation among peers at any cost or by confrontation and debate?

The last organizational culture function is the development and communication of an ideology that defines what the organization is all about. An ideology is a set of overarching values that collect all the basic assumptions embedded in the organization's culture (Deal and Kennedy, 1982). The ideology appears in stories about past successes or descriptions or organizational heroes. The heroes may still be with the organization, may have left it long go, or passed on. In either case, what each hero represents stays in the ideology and becomes part of the organization's folklore. The ideology is a strong and sometimes overwhelming guide to action. As such, the ideology is an important element of an organization's culture that must be communicated to and discovered by the newcomer. By serving these important roles, culture clearly is an important force in influencing behavior in organizations.

DYSFUNCTIONS OF ORGANIZATIONAL CULTURE

Dysfunctions of organizational culture are also created by the same functional features of an organization's culture (Schein, 1992; Trice and Beyer, 1993). Changes in an organization's external environment often require changes in an organization's strategy. The existing organizational culture, though, has developed from a particular strategy, and members of the organization who are accustomed to that culture may resist changing the strategy. They may feel that such change will require changes in existing values and basic assumptions. When considering a change in strategy, managers must either dramatically change the existing culture or learn how to manage within its constraints (Schein, 1992).

The existing organizational culture can lead to dysfunctional results when the organization tries product or market diversification, acquires a new company, or engages in a merger. Analyses of any of these changes ordinarily include financial, physical, and technical aspects of the proposed action, but rarely consider the culture of the target organization. A merger may result in merging incompatible cultures producing conflict and inefficiencies (Trice and Beyer, 1993). Moving into new markets brings the organization into new subcultures that may not respond in the usual ways to its product or service.

Organizations that introduce technologies to gain efficiency in manufacturing or provide service often experience latent dysfunctions. New technology can change familiar ways of acting that have become an accepted part of the existing organizational culture. Power and status may shift to those who know, understand, and can use the new technology. Such shifts undermine the position of those who had power and status in the culture before the new technology arrived. All those factors can lead to conflict, inefficiency, and possible sabotage of the new technology.

Cultures produce different ways of looking at the world and interpreting language and events. People from different subcultures may distrust those from other subcultures because of their different worldviews (Trice and Beyer, 1993). Conflict can erupt between people from different subcultures, especially when they passionately hold to different views.

CREATING, MAINTAINING, AND CHANGING ORGANIZATIONAL CULTURE

Three important issues besides understanding how culture operates are (1) how culture is initially created, (2) how it is sustained—that is, what keeps it going once it is created, and (3) how it is changed. Since our knowledge of organizational culture is limited, it is difficult to state with firm confidence detailed prescriptions for creating and maintaining organizational cultures.

How Is Organizational Culture Created?

Based on the available understanding of organizational culture, it appears that there are at least four major influences on the origins of this culture (Kilman, 1985).

1. The beliefs and values of the organization's founder can be strong influences in the creation of organizational culture. During her or his tenure, these beliefs and values can become embedded in the organization's policies, programs, and in-

formal statements perpetuated by continuing members of the organization (akin to the oral tradition of storytelling). For example, James Cash Penney infused his organization with "the Penney idea," consisting of such principles as "treat everyone as an individual" and "value loyalty."

2. The societal norms of the organization's native or host country can also play a role in determining an organization's culture. That is, the culture of the surrounding society influences the culture of firms existing within it.
3. Problems of external adaptation and survival pose challenges for organizations that its members must meet via the creation of organizational culture (that is, norms). For example, the development of strategies and goals and the selection of methods to achieve goals require the creation of norms.
4. Problems of internal integration can lead to the formation of organizational culture. For example, setting rules for social relations and the distribution of status, and establishing criteria for group and organizational membership require the development of norms and the acceptance of a set of beliefs.

How Is Culture Sustained?

How do employees come to learn about their organizations' cultures? Several key mechanisms are involved in the maintenance and reinforcement of organizational culture: symbols, stories, jargon, ceremonies, and statements of principle.

Symbols. Objects that say more than meets the eye. First, organizations often rely on symbols—material objects that connote meanings that extend beyond their intrinsic content. For example, some organizations use impressive buildings to convey their organization's strength and importance, signifying that it is a large, stable place. Other organizations rely on slogans to symbolize their values, including such classic examples as General Electric's "Progress is our most important product," or Ford's "Quality is job one." Corporate cars (or even jets!) also are used to convey information about certain aspects of an organization's culture, such as who wields power.

Stories. "In the old days, we used to. . . ." Organizations also transmit information about culture by virtue of the stories that are told in them, both formally and informally. Stories illustrate key aspects of an organization's culture, and telling them can effectively introduce or reaffirm those values to employees (Martin, 1982). It is important to note that stories need not involve some great event, such as someone who saved the company with a single wise decision, but may be small tales that become legends because they so effectively communicate a message. For example, employees at the British confectionery firm, Cadbury, are purposefully told stories about the company's founding on Quaker traditions to get them to appreciate and accept the basic Quaker value of hard work.

Jargon. The special language that defines a culture. Even without telling stories, the everyday language used in organizations helps sustain culture. For example, the slang or jargon that is used in a company helps its members define their identities as members of an organization. For instance, for many years employees at IBM referred to disk drives as "hard files" and circuit boards as "planar boards," terms that defined the insulated nature of IBM's corporate culture. Over time, as organizations—or departments within them—develop unique language to describe their work, their terms, although strange to newcomers, serve as a common factor that brings together individuals belonging to a corporate culture or subculture.

Ceremonies. Special events that commemorate corporate values. Organizations also do a great deal to sustain their cultures by conducting various types of ceremonies. Indeed, ceremonies may be seen as celebrations of an organization's basic values and assumptions. Just as a wedding ceremony symbolizes a couple's mutual commitment and a presidential inauguration ceremony marks the beginning of a new presidential term, various organizational ceremonies also celebrate some important accomplishment. Ceremonies convey meaning to people inside and outside the organization.

Statements of principle. Defining cultures in writing. A fifth way in which culture is reinforced is via the direct statements of principle. Some organizations have explicitly written their principles for all to see. For example, Forest Mars, the founder of the candy company M&M Mars developed his "Five Principles of Mars," which still guide his company today: quality (everyone is responsible for maintaining quality), responsibility (all employees are responsible for their own actions and decisions), mutuality (creating a situation in which everyone can win), efficiency (most of the company's 41 factories operate continuously), and freedom (giving employees opportunities to shape their future).

Some organizations have chosen to make explicit the moral aspects of their cultures, by publishing codes of ethics—explicit statements of a company's ethical values. More will be said about codes of ethics later in this chapter.

Maintaining organizational culture does not mean that managers passively and uncritically accept the values and basic assumptions of the present culture. Organizations must recognize that maintenance of a culture presents managers with a dilemma. They want to hold on to the values that were successful in the past, but they also need to question whether those values are right for the environment the organization now faces.

The maintenance or reinforcement of an organization's culture can be best understood by knowing (1) what managers consider important (what they measure and control); (2) the manner in which top management reacts to crises and critical events; (3) what types of deliberate role modeling are provided by managers; (4) criteria for distributing rewards and status; and (5) criteria for hiring, firing, and promotion (Schein, 1985; Smith and Vecchio, 1993).

How Is Culture Influenced or Changed?

There is a limited amount of research done on culture change. The difficulty in creating a culture is made even more complex when attempting to bring about a significant change. The themes that appear in discussing change are these:

- Cultures are so elusive and hidden that they cannot be adequately diagnosed, managed, or changed.
- Because it takes difficult techniques, rater skills, and considerable time to understand a culture and then additional time to change it, deliberate attempts at culture change are not really practical.
- Cultures sustain people throughout periods of difficulty and serve to ward off anxiety. One of the ways they do this is by providing continuity and stability. Thus, people will naturally resist change to a new culture. (Katzenbach, 2000)

These three views suggest that managers who are interested in attempting to produce cultural changes face a difficult task. There are, however, courageous managers who believe that they can intervene and make changes in culture. One view suggests the following five intervention points for managers to consider when interested in undertaking culture change (Sathe, 1983).

1. A considerable body of knowledge suggests that one of the most effective ways of changing people's beliefs and values is to first change their behavior. However, behavior change does not necessarily produce culture change because of the process of justification. Behavioral compliance does not mean cultural commitment.
2. Managers must get employees to see the inherent worth in behaving in a new way.
3. Typically, communication is the method used by managers to motivate the new behaviors. Cultural communication can include announcements, memos, rituals, stories, dress, and other forms of communications.
4. The socialization of new members.
5. The removal of existing members who deviate from the culture.

Each of these interventions must be done after careful diagnoses are performed. Although some individuals may not perfectly fit the organization's culture, they may possess exceptional skills and talents. Weeding out cultural misfits might be necessary, but it should be done after weighing the costs and benefits of losing talented performers who deviate from the core cultural value system.

Changing an organization's culture takes time, effort, and persistence, especially in organizations with strong cultures. Older, strong culture organizations have established stories, use symbols, conduct rituals, and even use their own unique language. In a strong culture organization the core values are widely shared, respected, and protected. An organization that is steeped in history, stories, and traditions will exert significant influence on the employees. On the other hand, new organizations or ones with weak cultures do not have the tradition, real or mythical, to have a dramatic influence on their employees.

The five elements for understanding the maintenance of organizational culture identified at the end of the previous section also provide insights as to how to change an organization's culture. That is, culture may be best changed by altering what managers measure and control, changing the manner in which crises are handled, using different role models for new recruits and altering the socialization/orientation process, establishing different criteria for allocating rewards, and changing the criteria for promotion, hiring, and dismissal.

An organization's culture and values are important because they provide guidance for behavior. They are intertwined with the concept of ethics, an important dimension of individual and organizational differences that, if not properly created and maintained, can lead to a culture or climate that encourages unethical behavior—a culture or climate that the organization will undoubtedly need to change.

THE IMPORTANCE OF ETHICS IN ORGANIZATIONS

Culture is one of the most influential factors contributing to an organization's ethical posture. Organizational leaders can use organizational culture to create values that result in ethical or unethical behavior.

Ethics are the rules, principles, standards, or beliefs that commonly define right and wrong. Ethics are involved in all facets of business from decision-making to budgeting, from personnel issues to leadership. Today's managers must be able to see the ethical issues in the choices they face, make decisions within an ethical framework, and build and maintain an ethical work environment. Managers must be particularly sensitive to ethical issues because of their key role as a bridge between upper management and operating employees. For most employees, their manager is the only contact they have with middle and top management. As such, employees interpret the company's ethical standards through the actions and words of their managers. If managers take company supplies home, cheat on maintenance reports, or engage in other unethical practices, they set a tone for their work groups that is likely to undermine all the efforts by top management to create a corporate climate of high ethical standards. In a sense, therefore, managers must be even more ethical than their employees.

There are many stakeholders with interests in ethical decision making: the organization itself, corporate boards, middle and top management, managers, operating employees, customers and clients, suppliers, competitors, the industry at large, the community, and the nation. At one time or another, ethical decisions affect all of these constituencies, and ethical considerations may change based on the particular group of stakeholders affected. When an organization operates ethically, the people who manage that organization evaluate the organization's business practices in light of human values of morality. An ethical dilemma occurs when two or more values or goals (e.g., profit, growth, technological progress, desire to contribute to some basic good) conflict. The best solution to any problem almost always involves a cost of some kind.

The difficulty is that ethical behavior often collides with the bottom line at least in the short-run. But things are changing. The word is getting out: Ethical behavior is good business—it contributes to organizational success. A reputation for honesty and integrity attracts and holds customers and it will ultimately show up in the bottom line. Organizations that have strong ethical values and consistently display them in all their activities derive other benefits: improved management control, increased productivity, avoidance of litigation, and an enhanced company image that attracts talent, improves morale, and earns the public's good will. For today's managers, leading effectively therefore also means leading ethically and morally. While businesses expand over geographic and cultural boundaries, questions concerning the sense of right and wrong within an organization become more complex. It is the responsibility of managers to guide the design, implementation, and monitoring of the organization's moral environment and strategies. As organizations put increased pressure on managers and employees to cut costs and increase productivity, ethical dilemmas are almost certain to increase. By what they say and do, managers contribute toward setting their organization's ethical standards.

INDIVIDUAL ETHICS

How would you rate your own standards of ethics? Are you always ethical? Are you ethical except in situations where you can't possibly be found out? Are you ethical except when you are under pressure from your boss or your peers? Are profits or your department's success more important than your personal values? Do your career goals sometimes take precedence over principle? Is it right to bend the rules to your company's advantage whenever you can? Should you always tell the truth? Now, consider a couple of specific cases: Is it wrong to use the company telephone for personal long distance calls? Is it ethical to falsify safety reports? Is it ethical for a member of your team to offer a bribe to an Occupational Safety and Health Administration (OSHA) inspector to ignore safety violations?

Anyone can be ethical when there is no pressure to act otherwise. Pressures to be unethical come from many sources—yourself, your boss, your peers, your employees, your organization—but managers today must be able to resist. Personal ambition and self-interest are probably the most common causes of unethical decisions and behaviors. People act in self-serving or unethical ways in order to improve their personal situation or reputation, to gain advancement, to increase income, or to avoid criticism or punishment.

Your peers can also put pressure on you to behave unethically. It is always difficult to turn down a request for help, especially from a colleague; yet if you are asked to support unethical behavior, abandoning your own standards serves neither of you. Unpleasant though it may be, you should decline. Say something like, "I appreciate the difficulty of the situation you face; I would like to be able to help you, but I cannot." At some point, managers face pressure from their employees to be unethical. People might ask you to conceal absences, to overlook infractions just this time, or to help them cover up a near-accident. As a manager, you should never give in to such requests. Not only would it be unethical, but it would destroy the employees' respect for you and ruin your power as a manager and leader. The difficult but right thing to do under these conditions is to get the group together and talk to them along these lines: "I understand that you're not asking me to do this out of self-interest. But I will not tolerate dishonesty. We are going to abide by our code of conduct. We're going to do our job properly."

Pressure to be unethical can also come from your boss, usually stemming from his or her desire to look good to his or her bosses: "I don't care how you do it, but I want that safety award." Pressure from a boss is extremely difficult, particularly since it is often accompanied by a threat, either direct or implied, of some adverse action, such as a poor performance report or denial of a bonus. But the fact that the pressure comes from your boss is not an excuse to behave unethically. Don't deceive yourself into believing that you are doing something to make your department look better; recognize that your motivation is self-protection. Although it's difficult, you should refuse to compromise your values.

The culture of the organization is still another source of unethical conduct. Some organizations choose to engage in questionable practices. Other organizations are just as likely to stimulate unethical actions when they place too much emphasis on managerial aggressiveness or on organizational expansion, competitiveness, and profit.

There is little anyone can do to stop people from rationalizing about their questionable conduct, but companies can try to encourage ethical behavior. In the next section we present three different approaches that can be used to determine whether a decision is ethical.

DETERMINING WHETHER A DECISION IS ETHICAL

Managers often experience an ethical dilemma when they confront a situation that requires them to choose between two courses of action, especially if each of them is likely to serve the opposing interest of different stakeholders. To make an appropriate decision, managers might weigh the competing claims or rights of the various groups. Sometimes, making a decision is easy because some obvious standard, value, or norm of behavior applies. In other cases, managers have trouble deciding what to do.

In many large companies, managers have a code of ethics to guide them as to what constitutes acceptable and unacceptable practices. A code of ethics is a formal document that states an organization's primary values and the ethical rules it expects employees to follow. For instance, a code of ethics might instruct employees to be law-abiding in all activities, truthful and accurate in what they say and write, and to recognize that high integrity sometimes requires the company to forego business opportunities. Codes of ethics do not, however, provide enough guidance for the many difficult dilemmas managers face. Philosophers have debated for centuries about the specific criteria that should be used to determine whether decisions are ethical or unethical. The use of different criteria can result in different decisions. Three models of what determines whether a decision is ethical are the utilitarian, moral rights, and justice models. Each model offers a different and complementary way of determining whether a decision or behavior is ethical.

The Utilitarian Approach

The utilitarian approach suggests that managers should strive to provide the greatest degree of benefits for the largest number of people at the lowest cost. In other words, managers must weigh the costs against the benefits of their actions. In a manner of speaking, you do this whenever you make a decision, as you balance one alternative against another and choose the one that you believe will yield the best results for the lowest cost or least effort. The utilitarian view tends to dominate business decision making, because it's consistent with goals like efficiency, productivity, and high profits. By maximizing profits, for instance, managers can argue that they are securing the greatest good for the greatest number.

The Moral Rights Approach

The moral rights view of ethics is concerned with respecting and protecting the basic rights of individuals, such as, the rights to privacy, free speech, and due process. Even if the decision accomplishes the greatest good for the greatest number of people, it is considered unethical if it denies individual rights. This position would protect employees who report unethical or illegal practices by their organization to the press or government agencies on the grounds of their right of free speech. A manager can use this approach to assess the implications of his or her decisions on individuals and not just on groups of people. He or she should not make a decision that compromises individual rights.

The Justice Approach

The justice approach embodies democratic principles and protects the interests of those who might otherwise lack power. It requires managers to impose and enforce rules fairly and impartially so there is an equitable distribution of benefits and costs. Union members typically favor this view. It justifies paying people the same wage for a given job, regardless of performance differences, and it uses seniority as the criterion in making layoff decisions. The justice approach is based on two components: (1) the procedural justice component, which requires impartial administration of disciplinary actions, and (2) the distributive justice component, which requires people to be judged only in terms of the performance criteria and not on such characteristics as race, gender, or religious preference. For example, people who vary in job skills should be paid differently, but there should be no differences in pay based on race or gender. More will be said about these two components later in this chapter.

Combining the Approaches

It's difficult to apply a single approach consistently to all situations you encounter. All three approaches can be used as guidelines for helping individuals to sort out the ethics of a particular course of action. Each of these three models has advantages and disadvantages, however. The utilitarian view promotes efficiency and productivity, but it can ignore the rights of individuals, particularly those with minority representation in the organization. The moral rights view protects individuals from injury and is consistent with freedom and privacy, but it can create an overly legalistic work environment that hinders productivity and efficiency. The justice perspective protects the interests of the underrepresented and less powerful, but it can encourage a general sense of entitlement that reduces risk taking, innovation, and productivity.

Although individuals in business have tended to focus on utilitarianism, times are changing. New trends toward individual rights and social justice mean that managers need ethical standards based on nonutilitarian criteria, which are more difficult to evaluate. Criteria such as individual rights and social justice are far more ambiguous than utilitarian criteria such as productivity and profits. Therefore, you should ask yourself what the consequences of your actions will be in terms of each approach.

One way to identify an unethical decision is to ask whether the manager would prefer to disguise or hide it from other people because it would enable the company or a particular individual to gain at the expense of society or other stakeholders.

CONTEMPORARY CORPORATE ETHICS

The value system that makes up the organization's culture determines its ethical behavior. Managers who wish to be a part of an ethical organization have to understand the organization's ethical character or culture. Managers should be as aware of an employer's ethical character as they are of its economic health. For example, if an organization emphasizes short-term revenues over long-term results, it may be creating an unethical atmosphere. If it expects employees to leave their private ethics at home, thus encouraging unethical behavior or discouraging ethical behavior for financial reasons, it is promoting an unethical work environment. If an organization links its ethical behavior to a code of ethics but will not address the complexity of ethical dilemmas, then the code may merely be window dressing. Proactive organizations do more than adopt a document when they establish a code of ethics. They may establish board-level committees to monitor the ethical behavior of the organization, or develop ethics training courses or other programs.

The treatment of employees can also indicate the ethical nature of an organization. If employees are not treated as well as customers or if performance-appraisal standards are unfair or arbitrary, the company may be unethical. Additionally, an absence of procedures for handling ethical issues, or the lack of a whistle-blowing mechanism, or even the lack of a basic communication avenue between employees and managers can indicate an organization that is ethically at risk.

Finally, an organization may be unethical if it fails to recognize its obligations to the public as well as to its shareholders. Ethical problems are not merely public relations issues, and legal decisions may not be ethical ones.

CORPORATIONS DEMONSTRATE CORPORATE RESPONSIBILITY

What responsibility do managers have to provide benefits to their stockholders and to adopt courses of action that enhance the well-being of society at large? Social responsibility is an obligation that organizations have to society. It means going beyond legal responsibilities and profit making. Social responsibility tries to align organizational long-term goals with what is good for society. An organization should recognize the impact of its actions on others and be able to predict how those actions would threaten or further its existence. Becoming a moral actor can be a fundamental issue of survival for the organization. Social responsibility, therefore, obligates managers to make decisions that nurture, protect, and promote the welfare and well-being of stakeholders and society as a whole.

We can understand social responsibility better if we compare it with two similar concepts: social obligation and social responsiveness. Social obligation is a business's most basic duty to society. A business has fulfilled its social obligation when it meets its economic and legal responsibilities and no more. It does the minimum that the law requires. In contrast to social obligation, social responsiveness adds a moral obligation to business responsibilities. It requires business to take actions that make society better and to refrain from actions that could make it worse. Societal norms guide this process.

WHY ORGANIZATIONS SHOULD BE SOCIALLY RESPONSIBLE

Several advantages may result from socially responsible behavior. First, workers and society benefit directly when organizations bear some of the costs of helping workers that would otherwise be borne by the government. Second, if all organizations in a society were socially responsible, the quality of life as a whole would be higher. Indeed, several management experts have argued that the way organizations behave toward their employees determines many of a society's values and the ethics of its citizens. It has been suggested that if all organizations adopted a caring approach and agreed to promote the interests of their employees, a climate of caring would pervade to greater society.

Experts point to Japan, Sweden, the Netherlands, and Switzerland as countries with very socially responsible organizations and where, as a result, crime and unemployment rates are relatively low, the literacy rate is relatively high, and sociocultural values promote harmony between different groups of people. Finally, being socially responsible is the right thing to do. Evidence suggests that socially responsible managers are, in the long run, best for all organizational stakeholders. It appears that socially responsible organizations are also sought out by communities, which encourage these organizations to locate in their cities by offering them incentives such as property-tax reductions, new roads, and free utilities for their plants. Additionally, managers who promote a proactive approach to social responsibility are also sought out by organizations. There are many reasons to believe that, over time, strong support of social responsibility greatly benefits managers, their organizations, organizational stakeholders, and society at large.

HOW TO INSTITUTIONALIZE ETHICAL BEHAVIOR

How should managers and organizations decide which social issues are important and to what extent the organizations should trade profits for social gain. First, illegal behavior should not be tolerated, and managers and operating employees should be alert to its occurrence and report it promptly. The term whistle-blower is used to refer to a person who reports illegal or unethical behavior and takes a stand against unscrupulous managers and stakeholders who are pursuing their own ends. Laws now exist to protect the interest of whistle-blowers, who risk their jobs and careers to reveal unethical behavior. In part, these laws were implemented because of the experiences of two engineers at Morton Thiokol who warned that the *Challenger* space shuttle's O-ring gaskets would be adversely affected by cold weather at launch. Their warnings were ignored by everyone involved in the headlong rush to launch the shuttle. As a result, seven astronauts died when the *Challenger* exploded shortly after its launch in January 1986. Although the actions of the engineers were applauded by the committee of inquiry, their subsequent careers suffered because managers at Morton Thiokol blamed them for damaging the company's reputation and harming its interests.

Any organization must clarify that ethical considerations are valued by the organization. An organization's mission statement often details its goal of providing the highest quality product at the lowest cost and recognizes its commitment to all stakeholders. In addition, it needs to include a commitment to an ethical standard for all employee actions. An organization must communicate its commitment to ethical values to all of its employees and external stakeholders. Codes of conduct or ethics should be adopted and distributed to all employees. Communication cannot be limited to the distribution of the code of ethics, however, because actions speak louder than words. Through their actions, managers should foster employee commitment to the organization's goal of ethical behavior in the same way that they foster employee commitment to its goal.

During the promotion and recruitment process, organizations can include in their criteria an interest in ethical decision making. Several methods can be used to evaluate employees, such as honesty tests, background checks, and an employee's willingness to sign a commitment to the corporate code of ethics. Pizza Hut, Inc.'s top management looks for integrity when hiring and promoting employees in the organization. Integrity includes a personal allegiance to excellence, honesty, a sense of teamwork, and a balanced perspective on long-term goals and short-term profits. Early in a company's process, a psychological contract is formed between the employer and employee. Psychological contracts typically cover the expectations that the employer and the employee form about each other. The degree to which both parties satisfy these expectations affects the success of the relationship.

It is important for managers to understand that if the two do not or cannot agree on their fundamental needs, then the relationship will suffer. Furthermore, because ethical behavior cannot be reduced to simple "do's and don'ts," both parties' expectations will continually change and thus there must be opportunity and structure to address evolving expectations.

Training employees to make an ethical analysis as part of their decision making is critical. Training can be formal, focused on the organization's goals and objectives and on decision-making techniques. Training can also be achieved through the normal socialization that occurs during the orientation of a new employee. If the employer is operating ethically, then the role models whom the employee emulates will exhibit the proper ethical behavior. The system of rewards and punishment will confirm and reinforce ethical behavior.

MODELS FOR ETHICAL CONDUCT

This section takes a look at two models for ethical conduct. The distributive and procedural justice models each provide managers with guides for their own and others' ethical conduct.

Distributive Justice

The principle of distributive justice requires that managers not be arbitrary and use only relevant information to determine how to treat people. It demands a fair distribution of pay raises, promotions, job titles, interesting job assignments, office space, and other organizational resources among members of an organization. Fairness means that rewards should be based on the meaningful contributions that individuals have made to the organization, such as time, effort, education, skills, abilities, and performance levels, and not on irrelevant personal characteristics over which individuals have no control, such as gender, race, or age.

Managers have an obligation to ensure that their departments and organizations follow distributive justice principles. This does not mean that all members of a department or organization should be rewarded equally; rather it means that those employees who receive greater rewards than others should have made substantially higher or more significant contributions to the organization. In many countries, managers have not only an ethical obligation, but also a legal obligation to strive to achieve distributive justice in their organizations, and they risk being sued by employees who feel that they are not being fairly treated.

Procedural Justice

The principle of procedural justice requires that managers clearly state and consistently administer the rules and established procedures of the organization and not bend the rules to serve their own interests or to show favoritism. This principle applies to procedures such as appraising an employee's performance, deciding who should receive a raise or a promotion, and deciding whom to lay off when an organization is forced to downsize. Procedural justice exists, for example, when managers:

- carefully appraise the job performance of employees reporting directly to them
- take into account any environmental obstacles to high performance beyond the employees' control, such as lack of supplies, machine breakdowns, or dwindling customer demand for a product
- ignore irrelevant personal characteristics such as an employee's age or ethnicity.

Like distributive justice, procedural justice is necessary not only to ensure ethical conduct but also to avoid costly lawsuits.

MANAGING A DIVERSE WORKFORCE

As highlighted in Chapter 2, one of the most important trends to emerge in organizations over the last 30 years has been the increasing diversity of the workforce. Diversity means differences among people due to age, gender, race, ethnicity, religion, sexual orientation, socioeconomic background, and capabilities/disabilities. Diversity raises important issues of ethics and social responsibility for managers and organizations. If not handled well, diversity challenges bring an organization to its knees, especially in our increasingly global environment.

There are several reasons why diversity is valued, both in the popular press and by managers and their organizations. First, there is a strong ethical imperative that diverse people receive equal opportunities and be treated fairly and justly. In some countries, unfair treatment is also illegal. Second, when managers effectively manage diversity, they can improve organizational effectiveness. They not only improve morale by encouraging other managers to treat diverse members of an organization fairly, but also use diversity as an important resource that can give the organization a competitive advantage.

In the rest of this section we examine workplace diversity in detail. Then we look at the steps you can take to supervise diversity effectively. Effectively supervising diversity not only makes good business sense but is an ethical imperative in U.S. society.

Diversity versus Affirmative Action

Sometimes managing diversity is confused with affirmative action or other laws favoring certain types of people. Actually, the two terms are quite different. Affirmative action emphasizes achieving equality of opportunity in the work setting by changing organizational demographics—age, gender, race, ethnic mixes, and the like. It is designed to benefit specific groups that have suffered past wrongs. Affirmative action is mandated by equal employment opportunity laws, and requires written reports containing plans and statistical goals for increasing the numbers of employees that belong to specific groups. It primarily affects hiring and promotion decisions, thus opening doors for some but leading to fears of reverse discrimination against others.

The goal of effectively managing diversity is to create a setting in which everyone feels valued and accepted and differences are appreciated. It assumes that groups will retain their own characteristics and will shape the organization as well as be shaped by it, thus creating a common set of values. The proper management of diversity is designed to affect employee perceptions and attitudes, but it is resisted sometimes because of fear of change and discomfort with differences. In Canada, laws have been designed to encourage the supervision of diversity at the provincial level through employment equity legislation.

Diversity Makes Good Business Sense

A diverse workforce can be a source of creativity and competitive advantage, helping an organization provide customers with better goods and services. Diverse employees provide a variety of viewpoints and approaches to problems and opportunities that can improve managers' decision making. For example, suppose a manager is trying to find some creative ideas for responding to a broad range of business problems. Which group do you think would be more likely to come up with the most creative ideas: a group of homogeneous employees with similar backgrounds and experiences or a diverse group of employees with different backgrounds and experiences? Most people would agree that the diverse group is likely to come up with a wider range of creative ideas. Although this example is simplistic, it underscores one way in which diversity can lead to a more dynamic company with more varied approaches to its business.

Just as the workforce is becoming increasingly diverse, so too are the customers who buy an organization's product and services. Diverse members of an organization are likely to be more attuned to the goods and services desired by diverse segments of the market. Major car companies, for example, are increasingly assigning women to their design teams to ensure that the needs and desires of the growing number of female car-buyers are taken into account in new car design.

Effectively supervising a diverse workforce makes good business sense for another reason. More and more, managers and organizations concerned about diversity are insisting that their suppliers also support diversity. Managers at American Airlines, for example, recently announced that all the law firms they hire would need to submit quarterly reports indicating the extent to which diverse employees work on the airline's account. Similarly, managers at Chrysler, Aetna Life and Casualty, and General Motors all consider diversity information when they are deciding which law firms will represent them.

Managing diversity ought to be a top priority for managers in all organizations, large and small, public and private, for profit and not for profit. Organizations need to ensure that managers and all levels of employees appreciate the value that diversity brings to an organization and have the ability to interact and work effectively with men and women who are physically challenged or who differ in age, race, gender, ethnicity, nationality, or sexual orientation. An objective of today's manager is to build a team of heterogeneous employees that function at least as productively as homogeneous employees. Ideally, today's managers must be able to tap into the reservoir of a multitalented, diverse workforce that will make the organization more resourceful, more productive, more responsive to customers, and a more interesting place to work.

Developing Skills for Working with People

Today's organizations must develop and reinforce cultures committed to educating managers and their employees about why and how people differ in the ways they think, communicate, and approach work, which can help all members of the organization develop a healthy respect for diversity and at the same time facilitate mutual understanding. When American and Japanese managers interact, for example, the Americans often feel frustrated by what they view as indecisiveness in the Japanese, and the Japanese are often frustrated by what they perceive as hasty, shortsighted decision making by the Americans. If Japanese managers and American managers realize that their approaches to decision making are by-products of cultural differences and recognize the relative merits of each approach, they may be more likely to adopt a mutually satisfactory decision-making style that incorporates the advantages of each approach and minimizes the disadvantages.

Managers and their employees must learn to communicate effectively with one another if an organization is to take advantage of the skills and abilities of its diverse workforce. Different managers and employees may differ in their styles of communication, language fluency, and use of words. They may differ in the nonverbal signs they send through facial expression and body language, and in the way they perceive and interpret information. Educating them about different ways to communicate is often a good starting point. Managers and their employees must learn how to be open to different approaches and ways of doing things. This does not mean that they need to suppress their personal styles. Rather, it means that they must not feel threatened by other approaches and perspectives, and they must have the patience and flexibility needed to understand and appreciate diverse perspectives. And this all begins with the development and reinforcement of the organization's culture, a culture committed to creating an ethical climate that encourages the understanding and appreciation of diversity.

SUMMARY

Organizational cultures include the values, norms, rites, rituals, symbols, ceremonies, heroes, and scoundrels in the history of the organization. Organizational cultures define what a new employee needs to learn for acceptance as a member of the organization. Cultures are functional when they help an organization adapt to its external environment and coordinate internal activities. Organizational cultures are dysfunctional when they are the basis of resistance to change or create culture clashes when two different cultures merge.

The levels at which you see organizational culture vary from visible to almost invisible. Artifacts and other cultural symbols usually are visible to even the newest employee. Basic assumptions, a set of implicit values, are almost invisible to new employees and are learned only after a period of socialization and acceptance. Espoused values and enacted values have mid-level visibility.

Organizational culture is created by the influence of company founders, an organization's experience with the environment, and contact between groups of people. Organizational culture may be reinforced through symbols, stories, jargon, ceremonies, and statements of principle. Managers seeking to create culture change must intervene at specific points: behavior, justification for behavior, cultural communications, hiring and socialization of members, and removal of members who deviate from the culture.

Business ethics is an important topic today. Business ethics is ethical behavior in the workplace that influences how a business functions, such as individual and corporate ethics. Managers can apply ethical standards to help themselves decide on the proper way to behave toward organizational stakeholders.

Social responsibility refers to an organization's manager's duty to make decisions that nurture, protect, enhance, and promote the welfare and well-being of stakeholders and society as a whole. Promoting ethical and socially responsible behavior is a manager's major challenge. Organizations can institutionalize ethical behavior by establishing the value, communicating the value, and selecting and training employees with ethical behavior in mind. Three models available to managers to determine whether a decision is ethical are utilitarian, justice, and moral rights.

The issue of diversity (i.e., differences among people due to age, gender, race, ethnicity, religion, sexual orientation, socioeconomic background, and capabilities/disabilities) also poses ethical challenges for today's managers. Changes in the nature of the employee-employer relationship have come about in U.S. business, in part, because of the changing values of American workers.

REFERENCES

Deal, T.E., and Kennedy, A.A. 1982. *Corporate culture: The rites and rituals of corporate life*. Reading, MA: Addison-Wesley, pp. 13–15.

Katzenbach, J.R. 2000. *The path to peak performance*. Cambridge, MA: Harvard Business School Press.

Kerr, J., and Slocum, J.W., Jr. 1987. Managing corporate culture through reward systems. *Academy of Management Review* 1: 99–108.

Kilman, R.H. 1985. Corporate culture. *Psychology Today* (April): 62–68.

Martin, J. 1982. Stories and scripts in organizational settings. In A. Hastorf and A. Isen (eds.), *Cognitive social psychology*. New York: Elsevier–North Holland, pp. 255–306.

Martin, J. 1992. *Cultures in organizations: Three perspectives*. New York: Oxford University Press.

Sathe, V. 1983. Implications of corporate culture: A manager's guide to action. *Organizational Dynamics* (Autumn): 4–13.

Schein, E.H. 1985. *Organizational culture and leadership*. San Francisco: Jossey-Bass.

Schein, E.H. 1992. *Organizational culture and leaders*. San Francisco: Jossey-Bass.

Smith, C.G., and Vecchio, R.P. 1993. Organizational culture and strategic management: Issues in the management of strategic change. *Journal of Managerial Issues* 5: 53–70.

Trice, H., and Beyer, J.M. 1993. *The cultures of work organizations*. Englewood Cliffs, NJ: Prentice-Hall.

Chapter 13

The Dynamics of Organizational Change

INTRODUCTION

It is a rare organization that has the luxury to operate in a stable and predictable environment. The adjective many organizations and their employees are increasingly using to describe their world is chaotic. In today's work world, change is an everyday occurrence for organizations. The message is clear: "Change or else!"

The business landscape is not the same as it was just a few years ago. Change is everywhere. Today's organizations are not static, but continually change in response to a variety of influences coming from both outside and inside. Those companies that fail to change when required may likely find themselves out of business. For today's employee, the challenge is to anticipate and help implement change processes so that organizational performance is enhanced. In this chapter, we first discuss the challenge of and pressures for change and briefly revisit the major change challenges facing today's organizations and managers. We then take a brief look at internal and external sources of change and planned versus unplanned change. Next we examine the scope and types of change before taking a look at the process of change. The discussion then focuses on employee and manager reactions to change and how organizations can overcome resistance to change. The chapter also discusses a general model of change.

THE CHALLENGE OF CHANGE

Organization change is any substantive modification to some part of the organization. It involves movement from the present state of the organization to some future state. The future state may be a new strategy for the organization, changes in the organization's culture, introduction of new technology, and so on. Change can involve virtually any aspect of an organization including work schedules, departmentalization, span of management, machinery, organizational design, and employee selection. It is important to keep in mind that any particular change in an organization may have ripple effects. For example, when a company installed a new computerized production system at one of its plants, employees were required to learn to operate the new equipment, the compensation system was adjusted to reflect those newly acquired skills, the manager's span of management was altered, several related jobs were redesigned, the criteria for selecting new employees was changed, and a new quality control system was implemented.

Understanding and managing organizational changes presents complex challenges. Planned change may not work, or it may have consequences far different from those intended. In many sectors of the economy, organizations must have the capacity to adapt quickly and effectively in order to survive. Often the speed and complexity of change severely test the capabilities of managers and employees to adapt rapidly enough. However, when organizations fail to change, the costs of that failure may be quite high. Hence managers and employees must understand the nature of the change needed and the likely effects of alternative approaches to bring about that change.

Because organizations exist in a changing environment and are themselves constantly changing, organizations that emphasize bureaucratic or mechanistic systems are increasingly ineffective. Organizations with rigid hierarchies, high degrees of functional specialization, narrow and limited job descriptions, inflexible rules and procedures, and impersonal, autocratic management can't respond adequately to demands for change. As noted in Chapter 12, organizations need designs that are flexible and adaptable. They also need systems that both require and allow greater commitment and use of talent on the part of employees and managers alike.

Organizational change can be difficult and costly. Despite the challenges, many organizations successfully make needed changes, but at the same time, failure also is common. There is considerable evidence that adaptive, flexible organizations have a competitive advantage over rigid, static organizations. As a result, managing change has become a central focus of effective organizations, and this focus is even creating its own vocabulary (i.e., the learning organization, reengineering, core competencies, organizational architecture, time-based competition, growth strategies, mission and vision statements, and strategic alliances among others). In many respects, managing change effectively requires an understanding and use of many of the important principles and concepts or organizational behavior that we have explored in this book.

Pressures for Change

Look around your office or organization and what do you see? Computers, copiers, fax machines, robots, and close-circuit TV sets were rare, or nonexistent, only a few short years ago. Look harder and you will probably notice that your company has changed in other, subtler, ways in order to respond to a host of new conditions and constituencies, such as government regulations, political activism, and criticism of big business. Some of these changes may not affect you personally, but many do.

It is hard to adjust to change. We tend to be the willing victims of inertia—comfortable with the status quo because we are used to it. If something threatens to "rock the boat," we often view it with suspicion and distrust. The accelerating rate of change makes change even more difficult to tolerate. Those who fail to adjust to it are condemning themselves to professional obsolescence. It is important to recognize that change is a natural part of life, and that change produces progress.

Both advanced industrialized and developing countries are changing in important ways that have significant impacts on organizations. Many organizations have had to undergo a radical reorientation with regard to the way they do business. As recently reported, the following trends are expected to have profound effects on organizations in the coming years:

- Government will get out of the way.
- E-business outlays will boom.
- Biotechnology will arrive.
- Net connections will get faster.
- Gadgets will get even cooler. (Creswell, Mclean, and Koudis, 1999)

According to this analysis, companies that are well positioned to take advantage of these trends will prosper, but those that ignore them will flounder. For example, Applied Energy Services (AES) which owns power generation facilities in 16 countries, is well positioned to take advantage of the trend toward deregulation in the electrical power industry as governments around the world seek to reduce government regulation and red tape. Genentech and other large biotechnology firms should thrive in the emerging global economy.

Many organizations have also increasingly paid attention to the importance of HRM in determining their competitive advantage. And as noted in Chapter 1, some have even declared that human resources represent the only enduring source of competitive advantage available to many of today's organizations. As described in Chapter 1, a number of factors have contributed to the increased attention to effectively managing organizational behavior and the value of an organization's human resources in ongoing organizational change and success. For example, as described in Chapter 1 there are a number of changes in organizations themselves and broader trends causing these changes to occur. Perhaps most important, organizations today are under intense pressure to be better, faster, and more competitive. There are more and more efforts to squeeze productivity out of organizations while others are merging and downsizing. Why is this the case? Technological changes, deregulation, and globalization are three trends accounting for these competitive pressures. Other trends include diversity, workforce changes, and achieving societal goals through organizations.

ORGANIZATIONAL AND MANAGEMENT CHANGE CHALLENGES

It has often been said that the only thing that remains constant is change—and it's true! Today's managers will, more than ever before, need to be prepared for changing events that will have a significant effect on their lives. Some of the more recent changes and challenges have been highlighted throughout this book and this section takes a summarizing look at how some of these changes are and will continue to affect managers in organizations.

Globalization affects managers in many ways. A boundaryless world introduces new challenges for managers. These range from how managers view people from different countries to how they develop an understanding of these immigrating employees' cultures. A specific challenge for managers is recognizing differences that might exist and finding ways to make their interactions with all employees more effective.

Although downsizing, quality improvements, and changing forms of work are activities that are initiated at the top-management level of an organization, they do have an effect on managers. Managers may be heavily involved in implementing the changes. They must be prepared to deal with the organizational issues these changes bring about. For example, when an organization downsizes, an important challenge for managers is motivating a workforce that feels less secure in their jobs and less committed to their employers. Managers must also insure that their skills and those of their employees are kept up to date. Employees whose skills become obsolete are more likely to be candidates for downsizing. Those employees who keep their jobs will more than likely be expected to do the work of two or three people. This situation can create frustration, anxiety, and less motivation. For today's manager, this, too, can dramatically affect work-unit productivity.

An emphasis on quality focuses on the customer, seeks continual improvements, strives to improve the quality of work, seeks accurate measurement, and involves employees. Each manager must clearly define what quality means to the jobs in his or her unit. This needs to be communicated to every staff member. Each individual must then exert the needed effort to move toward "perfection." Managers and their employees must recognize that failing to do so could lead to unsatisfied customers taking their purchasing power to competitors. Should that happen, jobs in the unit might be in jeopardy.

Effective quality initiatives can generate a positive outcome for managers and employees. Everyone involved may now have input into how work is best done. A focus on quality provides opportunities for managers to build the participation of the people closest to the work. As such, quality can eliminate bottlenecks that have hampered work efforts in the past. Quality can help create more satisfying jobs—for both the manager and his or her employees.

Few jobs today are unaffected by advances in computer technology. How specifically is it changing the manager's job? One need only to look at how the typical office is set up to answer this question. Today's organizations have become integrated communications centers. By linking computers, telephones, fax machines, copiers, printers, and the like, managers can get more complete information more quickly than ever before. With that information, managers can better formulate plans, make faster decisions, more clearly define the jobs that employees will need to perform, and monitor work activities on an "as-they-happen" basis. In a sense, today, technology has enhanced managers' ability to more effectively and efficiently perform their jobs.

Technology is also changing where managers' work is performed since they have immediate access to information that helps them in making decisions. Technological advances assist managers who have employees in remote locations, reducing the need for face-to-face interaction with these individuals. On the other hand, effectively communicating with individuals in remote locations (for example, teleworkers), as well as ensuring that performance objectives are being met, has become a major challenge for managers.

The implications of workforce diversity for managers are widespread. However, the most significant implication for managers is the requirements of sensitivity to the differences in each individual. That means they must shift their philosophy from treating everyone alike to recognizing, valuing, and responding to these differences in ways that will ensure employee retention and greater productivity.

Today's successful managers will be those who have learned to effectively respond to and manage change. Managers will work in an environment in which change is taking place at an unprecedented rate. New competitors spring up overnight and old ones disappear through mergers, acquisitions, or failure to keep up with the changing marketplace and customer demands. Downsized organizations mean fewer workers to complete the necessary work. Constant innovations in computer and telecommunications technologies are making communications instantaneous. These factors, combined with the globalization of product and financial markets, have created an environment of never-ending change. As a result, many traditional management practices—created for a world that was far more stable and predictable—no longer apply.

New governmental and societal issues will continue to complicate the manager's job in the future. Numerous environmental concerns will remain as serious long-term problems for managers and their organizations. Energy availability and costs will continue to be of great concern internationally and domestically. These types of issues and societal pressures have to become part of the manager's and organization's planning and operations.

Federal legislation affects the managers. In addition, state and local governments have laws and regulations that impact business. The effect of such legislation can be quite costly, and managers and their organizations may be required to change their methods of operations in order to comply.

All indications are that these pressures will remain intense. In some instances, today's manager has to be more of a lawyer, cop, teacher, accountant, political scientist, and psychologist than a manager. While it may be overstating the point, this reflects a realistic aspect of every manager's contemporary role. Managers must be more flexible in their styles, smarter in how they work, quicker in making decisions, more efficient in handling scarce resources, better at satisfying the customer, and more confident in enacting massive and revolutionary changes. As management writer Tom Peters captured in one of his best-selling books: "Today's managers must be able to thrive on change and uncertainty."

As suggested throughout this book, it is important to recognize that the workplace of today and tomorrow is indeed undergoing immense and permanent changes. Organizations are being challenged to change or be "reengineered" for greater speed, efficiency, and flexibility. Teams are pushing aside the individual as the primary building block of organizations. Command-and-control management is giving way to participative management and empowerment. Authoritative leaders are being replaced by charismatic and transformational leaders. Employees increasingly are being viewed as internal customers. All this creates a mandate for a new kind of manager today.

Managers will need a broader set of skills to achieve and maintain both their own, the department's, and organization's success today. The areas in which they will need to develop expertise include strategic planning; budgeting; quality management, benchmarking, and best practices; and telecommunications and technology. Aside from honing these skills, managers can better prepare themselves for today's challenges by gaining a better understanding of the needs of their internal customers, recognizing the need for effective information systems for employees, building relationships with the best service providers, and aligning the manager's unit and organization strategies and their processes.

Today's manager, regardless of his or her level in the organization, must be a true strategic partner in the organization. Each manager must effectively respond to the constantly changing world of work and the role the manager is expected to successfully play in that world. As the pace of change quickens, managers must become a tougher and more durable, albeit more flexible, interface between their organization and the lumpy road of a changing environment.

SOURCES OF CHANGE

As evidenced by our discussion to this point, there are both internal and external sources of change. This section offers a brief discussion of both internal and external sources of change.

Internal Sources of Change

Internal sources of change exist within the organization itself, and often refer to internal pressure for change within the organization. Examples of internal pressures for change include shifts in workers' attitudes toward their supervisor or manager or their benefits package; budget adjustments; declining productivity; reorganizations; hiring new employees; changes in key organizational personnel, whose goals and values influence large populations of the organization; and changes implementation of new policies regarding overtime procedures, work schedules, or vacations. Changes in attitudes among employees (due to increased age or changes in job responsibilities) can result in changes in job satisfaction, attendance behavior, and commitment. Changes in top-level and other key individuals in an organization can alter the internal character of the organization. For example, if an incoming CEO or president emphasizes integrity, corporate ethics, and customer service to his or her staff, those concerns will come to be reflected in the creation of new programs, the restructuring of the organization, and the evolution of a different organizational culture. It is not unusual for individuals like front-line managers to have input into these decisions.

External Sources of Change

External sources of change originate in the organization's environment. Specific examples of external change include evolving government regulations (e.g., such as new tax rates or new laws), changes in economic factors (e.g., interest rates or increase in minimum wage), and social changes (e.g., changing consumer desires, shifts in population, or new political trends). Ordinarily, changes of this kind have an indirect impact on an organization's employees, and there is very little that the employees or their managers can do to influence them. It is important for today's employees to understand that any of these features of the external environment can have profound positive or negative effects on an organization. The rise and fall of competitors has clear implications for organizational performance, as does the cooperativeness and competencies of suppliers. If the preferences of customers change as a result of changes in taste, the well-being of a product line can be affected. Recessions, periods of inflation, and upturns or downturns in the economy can have both direct and indirect influences on organizations. The education, talents, and attitudes of potential employees also play an important role in an organization's well-being. Changes in these facets of the labor force can lead to a shortage of surplus of qualified employees. Lastly, legislation can produce change. Federal legislation, such as the enforcement of the policies of the Equal Employment Opportunity Commission (EEOC) and the Federal Trade Commission (FTC), can alter the procedures an organization traditionally uses in its recruiting and marketing functions.

Regardless of the type of change, today's managers are still responsible for helping to successfully implement the policies associated with that change. As a result, the manager must deal with the frustrations and anxieties that usually accompany change, and address some difficult questions: "Will the employees resist the change? When should my employees be informed of the change? Am I capable of implementing the change? What other changes will be necessary as a result of this change?"

Planned versus Unplanned Change

Organizational change is either planned well in advance or comes about as a reaction to unexpected events. Planned change is change that is designed and implemented in an orderly, systematic, and timely fashion by managers to move an organization, or a subsystem, to a new state. Planned change includes deliberately changing the organization's design, technology, tasks, people, information systems, and the like. Although managers try to follow a plan for change, it does not always move forward smoothly. The plan often hits roadblocks, causing managers to rethink their goal and plan. Unplanned change often results in piecemeal responses to events as they occur. Unplanned change occurs when pressures for change overwhelm efforts to resist the change. Such change may be unexpected by management and can result in uncontrolled, if not chaotic, effects on the organization. There is a greater potential for unplanned change to be poorly conceived and executed. Planned change is, therefore, almost always preferable to unplanned change.

Georgia-Pacific, a large forest-products business, is an excellent example of an organization that recently went through a planned and well-managed change. When CEO A.D. Correll took over the company's leadership in 1991, he quickly became alarmed at the company's high accident rate: 9 serious injuries per 100 employees each year and 26 deaths during a five-year period. Even though the forest-products business is inherently dangerous, Correll believed that the accident rate was far too high and began a major initiative to improve the situation. He and other top managers developed a multistage program intended to educate workers about safety, improve safety equipment in the plant, and eliminate a long-standing part of the company's culture that made injuries almost a badge of courage. Seven years later, Georgia-Pacific had the best safety record in the industry.

On the other hand, a few years ago, Caterpillar was caught flat-footed by a worldwide recession in the construction industry, suffered enormous losses, and took several years to recover. Had managers at Caterpillar anticipated the need for change earlier, they might have been able to respond more quickly. Similarly, Kodak recently announced plans to cut several thousand jobs, a reaction to sluggish sales and profits that had not been foreseen.

The importance of approaching change from a planned perspective is reinforced by the frequency of change in well-run organizations. Many companies implement some form of moderate change at least every year and major changes every four to five years. Organizations and managers who sit back and respond only when necessary are likely to spend time and money hastily changing and rechanging things. It is more effective to anticipate the forces urging change and plan ahead to deal with them. Responsiveness to unplanned change requires tremendous flexibility and adaptability on the part of the organization. Today's organizations and their employees must be prepared to handle both planned and unplanned forms of change.

SCOPE AND TYPES OF CHANGE

Change can be a relatively small scope, such as a modification in a work procedure. Such changes, in essence, are a fine-tuning of the organization, or the making of small improvements. Change also can be of a larger scale, such as the restructuring of an organization. In this change, the organization moves from an old state to a known new state during a controlled period of time and usually involves a series of transition steps. The most massive scope of change is when the organization moves to a radically different and sometimes unknown future state. In this change, the organization's mission, culture, goals, structure, and leadership may all change dramatically. This section briefly discusses four types of change: strategic, technological, structural, and people.

Strategic Change

Organizations often change goals and tactics. Sometimes these plans are a variation on a common theme that's specified in the organizational mission statement or elsewhere. For example, under the leadership of Jack Welch, General Electric followed a well-known strategy of retaining businesses that were first or second in their respective markets, and changing or selling those that did not measure up. Other strategic changes can turn a company 180 degrees. For instance, when IBM was losing money during 1991–1992, it adopted a turnaround strategy. After cutting costs by $6 billion in 1995, IBM changed directions. It acquired Lotus Development Corporation to become a player in the burgeoning "groupware" market.

Other organizations like these have changed their strategy (i.e., a retrenchment strategy) so they can concentrate on a few core businesses. For example, not long ago Pepsi sold its international food service division, comprised of Pizza Hut and Taco Bell restaurants, so it could concentrate on a few core businesses (soft drinks and snack foods).

It has been recommended that still other organizations like Xerox, which has struggled in recent years, needs to shift strategies. Specifically, some have recommended that Xerox abandon its efforts to catch a new technological wave on its own and instead merge with an organization that offers leading-edge technologies in a high-growth area.

Technological Change

Technological change can also range from minor to massive. Typically, when people think of technological change, they often think of computerization. Clearly, the changes brought about by the computer have been far-reaching. And the promise of even more compelling change is on the horizon. For example, the availability of inexpensive computer equipment may allow some foreign competitors to narrow the technology gap if not leapfrog some U.S. organizations.

But we also need to consider allied forms of technological change. Supermarkets, for example, are very different places than they were a few years ago. Today's cash registers are actually input terminals that are linked to servers which provide and collect information. Likewise, the operations of the U.S. Postal Service have been affected by mail-sorting and other automation technology. Regardless, technological change is one of the most common ways in which organizations are transformed.

Structural Change

There are various options for restructuring an organization. Some of these methods are more popular than others. For example, as noted in

Chapter 12, common change today involves flattening an organization to reduce bureaucratic red tape and increase employee initiative. Likewise, re-engineering (i.e., the fundamental re-thinking and radical re-design of business processes to achieve dramatic improvements in performance) and downsizing (i.e., changes aimed at reducing the size of organizations) are options for structural change. In many instances, structural changes follow technological or other changes. Consider, for example, a strategic decision to enter a new area of business by acquiring an existing company. IBM purchased Lotus primarily to enter the groupware business. The integration of Lotus into IBM followed what is probably a naturally rocky path, which affected the structural organization of the company, including reporting relationships and functional layout.

People Change

Clearly, the best laid strategic plans eventually have to be enacted by the employees themselves. Structure has a major impact on people. So it's important to think through people-related changes as fully as you would think through a change in technology or another area. As we'll note later, there is often considerable resistance to change among employees and managers alike. So plans for people-related change should be integrated into organizational strategy. This could include training opportunities for a new technology that is being implemented. It could also mean more long-term investment in employee training to expand knowledge beyond just the next new implementation. Obviously, people changes can also occur by hiring new people or by firing existing ones, either at the executive level or at the line level. These are just a few methods of people change. For some this type of change is so important that it has earned its own separate moniker: organizational development. Organizational development is a process that applies behavioral science knowledge and practices to help organizations achieve greater effectiveness, including increased financial performance and improved quality of work life.

Before moving on with our discussion it is important to emphasize several points about types of change. First, these four types of change are highly interrelated; a change in one area often necessitates changes in the others. As mentioned above, a technological change often spills over to a structural one. So a change effort might fail because its cascading effects have been overlooked. Consequently, today's managers and employees must keep in mind that changes rarely occur in isolation. Second, change in any area almost always requires some thought as to how people will be affected. Even small changes in technology can have a large impact on people. This is another reason why organizations must increase their understanding of organizational behavior and anticipating or responding to employees' reactions to change.

The Change Agent's Role

The individual or group that undertakes the task of introducing and managing a change in an organization is known as a change agent. Change agents can be internal, such as managers or employees who are appointed to oversee the change process. Change agents can also be external, such as outside consultants.

Internal change agents have certain advantages in managing the change process. They know the organization's past history, its political system, and its culture. Because they must live with the results of their change efforts, internal change agents are likely to be very careful about managing change. There are disadvantages, however, to using internal change agents. They may be associated with certain factions within the organization and may easily be accused of favoritism. Furthermore, internal change agents may be too close to the situation to have an objective view of what needs to be done.

External change agents bring an outsider's objective view to the organization. They may be preferred by employees because of their impartiality. External change agents face certain problems, including their limited knowledge of the organization's history. In addition, they may be viewed with suspicion by organization members. External change agents have more power in directing changes if employees perceive the change agents as being trustworthy, possessing important expertise, having a track record that establishes credibility, and being similar to them.

A promising approach to having the advantages of both internal and external change agents is to include them both as members of an internal-external change agent team. External change agents can combine their special expertise and objectivity with the inside knowledge and acceptance of internal change agents. The two parties can use complementary change skills while sharing the workload and possibly accomplishing more than either would by operating alone. Internal change agents, for example, can provide continuous contact with the host organization, and their external counterparts can provide specialized services periodically, such as two or three days each month. External change agents also can help train their organization partners, thus transferring change skills and knowledge to the organization.

THE PROCESS OF CHANGE IN ORGANIZATIONS

Once an organization has made the decision to change, careful planning and analysis must take place. An important way to increase the likely success of such change is for organizational leaders to attempt to anticipate the need for change and to develop creative innovations before serious problems evolve.

The Need for Anticipation

Far too frequently, managers and their organizations fail to set aside the time necessary for analyzing changing conditions and attitudes and suddenly find themselves in the middle of severe complications. Managers must learn to anticipate the need for change.

There is something of a paradox between the need for continuity and the necessity for change in organizations. For example, customers and employees usually prefer feelings of continuity in their lives because such feelings enable them to have faith that events in the future will unfold in a predictable manner. Customers hope that a continued supply of materials at comparable prices will be available. Employees want their paychecks to be secure so that they can continue to purchase the items they want and need.

However, as evidenced by our discussion on change to this point, conditions seldom remain static. Whenever possible, the need to change with the times (or even before) should be anticipated, and management should attempt to implement these changes before the crisis-state is reached. Otherwise, serious organizational behavior difficulties can result.

EMPLOYEE REACTIONS TO CHANGE

How employees perceive a change greatly affects how they react to it. While many variations are possible, there are only four basic reactions. If employees clearly see that the change is not compatible with their needs and aspirations, they will resist the change. In this situation, the employees are certain that the change will make things worse. If employees cannot foresee how the change will affect them, they will resist the change or be neutral, at best. Most people shy away from the unknown. They often assume that the change may make things worse.

If employees see that the change is going to take place regardless of their objections, they may initially resist the change and then resignedly accept it. Although their first reaction is to resist, once the change appears inevitable, they often see no other choice than to go along with it. If employees see that the change is in their best interests, they will be motivated to accept it.

Obviously, it is critical for employees to feel confident that the change will make things better. It is the manager's obligation to foster an accepting attitude. Note that three out of the four situations involve some form of resistance to change. Resistance to change is an emotional/behavioral response to real or imagined threats to an established work routine. Managers must understand resistance to change and learn techniques to overcome it.

Understanding and Managing Resistance to Change

We tend to be creatures of habit. Many people find it difficult to try new ways of doing things. It is precisely because of this basic human characteristic that most employees are not enthusiastic about change in the workplace. This resistance is well documented. As one person once put it, "Most people hate any change that doesn't jingle in their pockets." No matter how technically or administratively perfect a proposed change may be, people make or break it.

Rare is the manager who does not have several stories about carefully cultivated changes that died on the vine because of employee resistance. It is important for managers to learn to manage resistance because failed change efforts are costly. These costs may include decreased employee loyalty, a lowered probability of achieving corporate goals, a waste of money and resources, and the difficulty of fixing the failed effort.

People resist change for many reasons. Resisting change does not necessarily mean that they will never accept it. In many cases, the change may be resisted because it was introduced improperly. The manager, by implementing drastic change, could have created feelings of insecurity in the employees. Perhaps the manager did not inform the employees about the change until the last minute. Sometimes the change is introduced properly but is still resisted. The manager may use resistance to change as a means of "taking the pulse" of the department. If minor change meets with resistance, it could indicate that other problems exist, such as problems with morale, commitment, or trust.

Individual and group behavior following an organizational change can take many forms, ranging from extremes of acceptance to active resistance. Resistance can be as subtle as passive resignation or as overt as deliberate sabotage. Resistance can also be immediate or deferred. It is easiest for managers to deal with resistance when it is overt and immediate. For instance, a company proposes a change, and employees quickly respond by voicing complaints, engaging in a work slowdown, or threatening to go on strike. Although these responses may be damaging, their cause is clearly identifiable.

It is more challenging to manage resistance that is implicit or deferred. Implicit resistance is subtle—such as loss of loyalty to the organization, loss of motivation to work, increased errors or mistakes, or increased absenteeism due to "sickness"—and hence more difficult to recognize. Similarly, deferred resistance clouds the link between the source of the resistance and the reactions to it. For example, a change may produce what appears to be only a minimal reaction at the time it is initiated, but then resistance surfaces weeks, months, or even years later. In another type of deferred resistance, a single change that in and of itself might have had little impact can become the straw that breaks the camel's back. Reactions to change can build up and then explode in a response that seems totally out of proportion to the change it follows. The resistance, or course, has merely been deferred and stockpiled. What surfaces is a response to an accumulation of previous changes.

Managers need to learn to recognize the manifestations of resistance to change both in themselves and in others if they want to be more effective in creating, supporting, and managing change. So why do people resist change? A number of specific reasons are discussed in the next few paragraphs.

Predisposition against Change

Some people are predisposed to dislike change. This predisposition is highly personal and deeply ingrained. It is an outgrowth of how they learned to handle change and ambiguity as a child. Consider the hypothetical examples of Amy and Fred. Amy's parents were patient, flexible, and understanding. From the time Amy was weaned from a bottle, she was taught that there were positive compensations for the loss of immediate gratification. She learned that love and approval were associated with making changes. In contrast, Fred's parents were unreasonable and unyielding. They frequently forced him to comply with their wishes. They required him to take piano lessons even though he hated playing piano. Changes were accompanied by demands for compliance. This taught Fred to be distrustful and suspicious of change. These learned predispositions ultimately affect how Amy and Fred handle change as adults.

Habits

Habit is a wonderful thing for human beings. Can you imagine how difficult life would be without habits? Imagine if you had to think consciously about every little movement needed to drive an automobile. Would you ever make it to work in the morning? When we drive by habit our mind can think about other things, secure in the knowledge that our senses will warn us when something is wrong.

We do things by habit: routine household chores, dressing ourselves, greeting one another, sorting our mail, and so forth. Habits are easy and comfortable, freeing our minds to focus on other, more important things. Furthermore, habits are often difficult to change: Reflect on a time when you or a friend tried to alter your morning routine or to drop a bad habit. One very important reason we resist is because we do not want to change our safe, secure, habitual way of doing things.

Lack of Trust

Trust is a characteristic of high-performance teams, in which team members believe in each other's integrity, character, and ability. Managers who trust their employees make the change process an open, honest, and participative affair. Employees who trust management are more willing to expend extra effort and take chances with something different. Mutual mistrust, on the other hand, can doom an otherwise well-conceived change or project to failure.

Surprise and Fear of the Unknown

When finding yourself in the presence of an unknown insect, many of us typically choose to kill it by swatting it or stepping on it. We typically rationalize, "Better safe than sorry." It is a natural reaction to fear of the unknown. When innovative or radically different changes are introduced without warning, affected employees become fearful of the implications. Grapevine rumors fill the void created by a lack of official announcements and employees often develop negative attitudes toward the change. They may also behave dysfunctionally—complaining, purposely working more slowly, or undermining department morale—if required to go through with the change. In these situations, employees let fear paralyze them into action. Managers should therefore avoid creating situations in which employees are surprised and thus fear change. They can do this by keeping all affected employees adequately informed.

Poor Timing

The timing of change in relation to other events also may increase resistance to the change. The poor timing may be caused by events within the organization, in relation to events outside the organization, or by events occurring in someone's personal life. For example, bringing in a young manager from outside the organization at the same time that all of the equipment and procedures are being updated may increase resistance to both changes. On a personal level, changing a parent's start time just as his or her child begins school and thus preventing the parent from driving the child to kindergarten can increase resistance to the new schedule. Managers should consider other events that are occurring at the same time that a major change is proposed or implemented and avoid poor timing, if possible.

Poor Approach

The approach used in presenting a change can increase resistance to the change if people dislike the approach. A poor approach to change can be caused either by the way change is communicated or by the communications channel that is selected. Sending an e-mail message or a memo to someone, for example, may not be as effective as delivering the change message in person. An approach may also be considered poor if the person delivering the change message is already disliked. Finally, the words used to explain the change may cause the approach to be poor. Telling a workforce that there will be no raises or bonuses this year and that everyone will have to increase productivity in order to boost the stock dividend may be a poor approach because the workforce will assume the real objective is to make the stockholders wealthier. However, explaining that the change is needed so that the dividend can be increased in order to increase the stock price and avoid a hostile takeover, a liquidation of the firm, and the firing of everyone may generate more cooperation for the change.

Ignoring Change through Selective Perception

We are bombarded every moment with information pouring into our brains from our sensory organs—our eyes, ears, nose, taste buds, and various touch and balance sensors. We cannot possibly attend to all of the information, so we screen out much of it through a process called "selective perception" as discussed in Chapter 2. This means that we pay attention to those sensations, which we judge to be important, while ignoring the rest. Selective perception is a complex psychological process that occurs both intentionally and unconsciously.

How do we choose those messages to which we pay attention? When faced with messages signaling a change, we frequently attend to those that reinforce our belief in the status quo and maintain our present comfort level. In other words, too often we see only what we want to see, and hear only what we want to hear. Through selective perception, we frequently protect the status quo by filtering out troubling signals that a change is needed, or may be on its way.

Similarly, we often listen only to commentators or others with whom we agree or whose ideas resonate with our own. Dangerous messages, which somehow threaten our comfort level, are "tuned out" and ignored. The natural human tendency toward selective perception can harm our ability to deal with change. If we block out all information with which we do not agree, we often miss clear signals that change is on the horizon. Thus when change occurs we are surprised by it, unprepared for it, and afraid of it.

Too Much Dependence on Others

One way to deal with the bombardment of information at work is to specialize. We tend to gravitate to our own spheres of interest and depend on others for information and insights outside our scope of knowledge. For example, when a car needs repairs, you may take it to a trusted mechanic rather than attempt to repair it yourself. The point is that everyone depends on certain people for advice and guidance. This dependence may serve you well, but only if the people on whom you rely are well informed—not if they give you misinformation or poor advice. Although you should not immediately become suspicious of all your advisors, you should recognize that too much dependence on others could become dangerous. Managers and employees may resist change if they are advised to resist because the change may adversely affect them. Trusting in this advice, they may fail to understand for themselves the true nature of the situation, and may be "blindsided" by the change when it occurs.

Threats to Jobs and Income

Employees often fear that change may reduce their job security or income. New labor-saving equipment, for instance, may be interpreted as a signal that layoffs are imminent. When a potential change has the real possibility to cause employees harm, they are likely to resist it with all their might.

Changes in job tasks or established work routines often threaten employees. They worry that they won't be able to perform successfully, particularly where pay is closely tied to productivity. It is therefore important that managers consider any adverse effect employees might experience as a result of a proposed organizational change. If employees perceive that they will lose money, influence, clout, or status as the result of a change, managers can expect strong and active resistance. This resistance is not irrational, but is aimed at protecting employee self-interest.

Revenge

Employees may resist change out of revenge. When employees perceive that management has wronged them in the past or that a manager has not trusted or supported them, then they may feel that resisting change is a justified payback. Here also may be the time that a person seeks a return to equity when an imbalance is perceived. Herzberg (1966) has discussed a whole "revenge psychology" whereby people feel that they have been so grievously wronged that they not only resist change (in addition to taking other measures), but the story of the perceived wrong is passed on. Sometimes none of the people who were originally "wronged" are still at work, and yet people still say things like, "Remember the time management . . ." Herzberg claims that some actions by managers can create a "remembered pain" that can never be removed.

Absent Benefits

When people resist change because of absent benefits, they are really saying that there is nothing in the change for them. When a change is absent benefits, it means that the change or the change agent has provided no incentive for the people to change. In actuality, there may be benefits in the new change, but they may not be obvious, or they may not have been explained. Some people may feel this way about recycling paper or soft-drink cans at work. If no immediate benefit is seen, some may not bother. If, however, the long-term environmental benefits are explained, then these people may comply.

INEVITABLE REACTIONS TO CHANGE

In spite of attempts to minimize the resistance to change in an organization, some reactions to change are inevitable. Negative reactions may be manifested in overt behavior, or change may be resisted more passively. People show four basic identifiable reactions to change: disengagement, disidentification, disenchantment, and disorientation. Managers can use interventions to deal with these reactions (Woodward and Bucholz, 1987).

Disengagement is psychological withdrawal from change. An employee appears to lose initiative and interest in the job. Employees who disengage may fear the change but take on the approach of doing nothing and simply hoping for the best. Disengaged employees are physically present but mentally absent. They lack drive and commitment, and they simply comply without real psychological investment in their work. Disengagement can be recognized by behaviors such as being hard to find or doing only the basics to get the job done. Typical disengagement statements include "No problem" or "This won't affect me."

The basic manager strategy for dealing with disengaged individuals is to confront them with their reaction and draw them out, identifying concerns that must be addressed. Disengaged employees may not be aware of the change in their behavior, and may need to be assured of the good intentions of the manager. Helping them air their feelings can lead to productive discussions. Disengaged people seldom become cheerleaders for the change, but they can be brought closer to accepting and working with a change through open communication with an empathetic manager who is willing to listen.

Another reaction to change is *disidentification.* Individuals reacting in this way feel that their identity has been threatened by the change, and they feel very vulnerable. Many times they cling to a past procedure because they had a sense of mastery over it, and it gave them a sense of security. "My job is completely changed" and "I used to . . ." are verbal indications of disidentification. Disidentified employees often display sadness and worry. They may appear to be sulking and dwelling on the past by reminiscing about the old ways of doing things.

Disidentified employees often feel like victims in the change process because they are so vulnerable. Managers can help them through the transition by encouraging them to explore their feelings and helping them transfer their positive feelings into the new situation. One way to do this is to help them identify what it is they liked in the old situation, as well as to show them how it is possible to have the same positive experience in the new situation. Disidentified employees need to see that work itself and emotion are separable, that is, that they can let go of old ways and experience positive reactions to new ways of performing their jobs.

Disenchantment is also a common reaction to change. It is usually expressed as negativity or anger. Disenchanted employees realize that the past is gone, and they are mad about it. They may try to enlist the support of other employees by forming coalitions. Destructive behaviors like sabotage and back-stabbing may result. Typical verbal signs of disenchantment are "This will never work" and "I'm getting out of this company as soon as I can." The anger of a disenchanted performer may be directly expressed in organizational cultures where it is permissible to do so. This behavior tends to get the issues out in the open. More often, however, cultures view the expression of emotion at work as improper and unbusinesslike. In these cultures, the anger is suppressed and emerges in more passive-aggressive ways, such as badmouthing and starting rumors. One of the particular dangers of disenchantment is that it is quite contagious in the workplace.

It is often difficult to reason with disenchanted employees. Thus, the first step in managing this reaction is to bring these employees from their highly negative, emotionally charged state to a more neutral state. To neutralize the reaction does not mean to dismiss it; rather, it means to allow the individuals to let off the necessary steam so that they can come to terms with their anger. The second part of the strategy for dealing with disenchanted employees is to acknowledge that their anger is normal and that as their manager you don't hold it against them. Sometimes disenchantment is a mask for one of the other three reactions, and it must be worked through to get to the core of the employee's reaction. Employees may become cynical about change. They may lose faith in the managers and other leaders of change.

A final reaction to change is *disorientation*. Disoriented employees are lost and confused, and often are unsure of their feelings. They waste energy trying to figure out what to do instead of how to do things. Disoriented individuals ask a lot of questions and become very detail oriented. They may appear to need a good deal of guidance, and may leave their work undone until all of their questions have been answered. "Analysis paralysis" is characteristic of disoriented employees. They feel that they have lost touch with the priorities of the company, and they may want to analyze the change to death before acting on it. Disoriented employees may ask questions like "Now what do I do?" or "What do I do first?"

Disorientation is a common reaction among people who are used to clear goals and unambiguous directions. When change is introduced, it creates uncertainty and a lack of clarity. The manager's strategy for dealing with this reaction is to explain the change in a way that minimizes the ambiguity that is present. The information about the change needs to be put into a framework or an overall vision so that the disoriented individual can see where he or she fits into the grand scheme of things. Once the disoriented employee sees the broader context of the change, the manager can plan a series of steps to help this employee adjust. The employee needs a sense of priorities.

Managers need to be able to diagnose these four reactions to change. No single universal strategy can help all employees adjust because each reaction brings with it significant and different concerns. By recognizing each reaction and applying the appropriate strategy, it is possible to help even strong resisters work through a transition successfully. It is also helpful to identify some more specific ways that employees resist change as offered in the next section.

HOW EMPLOYEES SHOW THEIR RESISTANCE TO CHANGE

Besides understanding why people resist and might emotionally respond to change, it is also important to examine how people show their resistance to change. There are a number of methods by which people demonstrate resistance: absenteeism, decreased productivity, regression, resignation, transfer, and sabotage. Note that outright refusal to change is not on the list. People do not usually openly refuse to change, probably because this would be a highly visible act that carries too much risk. Instead of refusing and taking the risk of being disciplined or fired, most people choose a less obvious and less confrontational method of protesting a change.

Absenteeism

Instead of changing, people may try to escape the change by calling in sick or arriving late to work. Through their absence, they are not trying to have the change reversed as much as they are trying to avoid the change or delay its implementation. For example, given a new boss, people may be absent or late in order to escape having to deal with or work for the new manager. Absenteeism is a more complex phenomenon. First, it has causes other than just change, some of which are related to work and others that are not. Second, absenteeism not only affects the employer or the boss, it affects coworkers who must perform the extra work left by a person who is absent. By trying to escape the change rather than trying to cope with it, the resister creates stress by not facing the change. This stress can be even greater than the stress of adapting to the change.

Decreased Productivity

Decreased productivity differs from other ways people show resistance to change in that it is aimed at reversing the change and has some chance of working. This tactic involves people who deliberately slow down so that productivity declines. The thinking behind this tactic is that after the change the manager will notice that productivity is lower than it was before the change without seeing that the decline was artificial. The underlying hope is that if the manager notices the decline, he or she will blame the drop on the latest change, decide that the change is failing, and return conditions back to the way they were before the change. There are no statistics on how well this works because if it is done properly, managers will never realize that it was done—and employees certainly won't admit to it.

Regression

Regression is a relatively simple method of showing resistance to change. Here, to resist change, people regress their behavior and understanding to the level of a new, untrained worker. People who display regression are essentially saying, "If things change, you [the manager] will have to tell me how to work under this change and how to do all the rest of my job, too." The behavior is not uncommon, even though it is rather childish to pretend that one change has somehow caused people to forget how to do everything. Some people, however, use regression to make the change as painful as possible, hoping the manager will give up or return to the old ways.

Resignation

Resigning, the ultimate escape mechanism, is also a method for coping with unacceptable change. Resignation may be a poor choice for a resister because he or she may suffer more than the employer, and if the change is later rescinded, he or she will not be there. Resignation should never be used without careful consideration. A person must consider the availability of other jobs and his or her own financial needs before quitting. It can also be more difficult to go from being unemployed to employed than it is to go from being employed in one job directly to being employed in another job. On the other hand, if the change truly is unacceptable, then it may be better to leave a situation than to stay and be miserable. One might, however, be able to transfer rather than resign.

Transfer

A request for a transfer to another department in the same company may be caused by change or some other factor. Like resignation, transferring can be an escape mechanism if the person is unwilling to confront the change, or it can be a coping mechanism when the person really cannot cope with or accept the change. Transferring carries less financial worry and risk than resignation, and a transfer can help an organization retain valuable people.

Sabotage

Sabotage can be considered the severest form of resistance to change because it is tricky, damaging, and typically illegal. Sabotage is a deliberate act to harm the organization. The sabotage can be subtle—sometimes so subtle that it goes undetected. Other times, it can cause significant damage to the organization and to innocent employees. People who choose sabotage generally feel that they have been greatly wronged by the boss or the organization. They typically feel that they are justified in their actions, so sabotage may just be an example of equity theory taken to an extreme. Of course, sabotage can never be condoned; it can be costly, and it can negatively affect many innocent people, such as coworkers and customers. Still, incidences of sabotage are more frequent than one might initially suspect.

MANAGERS' ORIENTATION TO RESISTANCE TO CHANGE

Managers can react to resistance to change in two ways. They can treat resistance as a problem to overcome or view it as a signal to get more information about the reasons for the resistance. Managers who view resistance as a problem to overcome may try to forcefully reduce it. Such coercive approaches often increase the resistance.

Alternatively, managers may see resistance as a signal that those responsible for the change need more information about the intended change. Those employees who will be affected by the change may have valuable insights about its effects. An alert manager will involve the employees in diagnosing the reasons for the resistance. In this way, managers can use resistance to change as a tool to get needed information.

Should managers and others see the absence of resistance to change as a stroke of good fortune? Many reasons suggest that they should not. The absence of resistance is also a signal to managers. A change that is automatically accepted can be less effective than one that has been resisted and actively debated. The resisters play an important role by focusing the manager's attention on potentially dysfunctional aspects of the proposed change.

CHANGE MANAGEMENT

This section discusses the way in which change can be introduced effectively. We've already discussed how many individuals have a tendency to resist change. Change management, that is, the manner by which managers introduce change, regardless of how ideal their intentions may be, largely determines the success of their efforts. By understanding and applying some basic concepts, managers can improve their track records.

Change as a Three-Step Process: The Lewin Model

We've already examined how established habits tend to affect the manner in which individuals react to new things. A way to gain a better insight into what people go through when changing is to view the activity as a three-step process: (1) unfreezing, (2) changing/moving, and (3) refreezing.

Kurt Lewin, a noted organizational theorist, developed a model of the change process that has stood the test of time and continues to influence the way organizations manage planned change (Lewin, 1947). Lewin's model is based on the idea of force-field analysis. Although force-field analysis may sound like something out of a *Star Trek* movie, it is a technique that can be used to analyze a change and help overcome resistance to it.

This model contends that a person's behavior is the product of two opposing forces: one force pushes toward preserving the status quo, and another force pushes for change. When the two opposing forces are approximately equal, current behavior is maintained. For behavioral change to occur, the forces maintaining status quo must be overcome. This can be accomplished by increasing the forces for change, by weakening the forces for status quo, or by a combination of these actions.

For managers, the first step in conducting a force-field analysis is to develop a list of all the forces promoting change and all those resisting change. Then determine which of the positive and which of the negative forces are the most powerful. The forces can be ranked in order of importance or by rate of strength. To facilitate the change, managers try to remove or at least minimize some of the forces acting against the change in order to tip the balance so that the forces furthering the change outweigh those hindering the change.

Lewin's change model suggests that every change requires employees to go through the following three steps:

1. *Unfreezing*—employees recognize the need for change.
2. *Changing or Moving*—employees begin trying to behave differently.
3. *Refreezing*—the new behavior becomes a part of employees' moral behavior and procedures.

In order for change to be fully implemented, the organization must help provide a way for the new behavior to become an established practice.

Unfreezing

In the unfreezing stage, employees must see the status quo as less than ideal. The manager or other change agents—individual(s) responsible for implementing the change—must spell out clearly to affected employees why the change is necessary. Allied Signal's former CEO, Lawrence Bossidy, describes this step colorfully, as the "burning platform theory of change":

> When the roustabouts are standing on the offshore oilrig and the foreman yells, "Jump into the water," not only won't they jump but they also won't feel too kindly toward the foreman. There may be sharks in the water. They'll jump only when they themselves see the flames shooting up from the platform. . . . The leader's job is to help everyone see that the platform is burning, whether the flames are apparent or not. (Tichy and Charan, 1995)

In essence, unfreezing means overcoming fears about the change and other resistance to change. Organizations often accomplish unfreezing by eliminating the rewards for current behavior and showing that current behavior is not valued. Unfreezing on the part of individuals is an acceptance that change needs to occur. In essence, individuals surrender by allowing the boundaries of their status quo to be opened in preparation for change. The organization relies heavily on managers—as management's link to operating employees—to carry out this responsibility, for which they need good communication skills.

According to Ken Blanchard (1992), a behavioral scientist, a major reason many efforts to change fail is that management does not consider the employees' point of view. Many changes require not only performing new tasks but also adopting new attitudes, such as a willingness to assume decision-making responsibility or a strong commitment to customers. Employees may have difficulty changing their attitudes, especially if they are unsure about management's sincerity.

Changing or Moving

When employees appreciate the need for a change and have received any necessary training, they are ready to begin altering their behavior. It is practical to begin by attempting to make basic changes in employees' behavior, rather than trying to change their values. Values, by their very nature, are more resistant to change. To induce changes in behavior, managers and other change agents should offer tangible and intangible rewards. As employees' attitudes become more positive, their values may shift as well.

The key to implementing change is to build on success. Change agents should determine those aspects of the change over which they have control and then try to carry them out successfully. A change agent should point out each success the group achieves along the way. For example, a manager who has control over scheduling a change should establish reasonable deadlines. As employees meet each deadline, the manager can praise their achievements. To be more specific, imagine that an accounting department is installing a new computer system. Instead of focusing simply on whether everyone is using the system properly, a manager can establish dates for setting up various pieces of equipment and teaching employees to operate different parts of the system. Then the manager can note that the terminals arrived on time, that everyone learned how to log on and enter their passwords in a single training session, and so on. This positive reinforcement will help employees to change their behavior and their attitudes.

Refreezing

The change process is complete only when employees make the new behaviors, attitudes, and values part of their routine. In organizations that do not manage change effectively, managers may assume a change effort has succeeded simply because employees merely fulfill the basic requirements of a change without adjusting their routines or their attitudes. In such cases, backsliding is likely. Employees may revert to their old practices when the initial pressure for change eases, because new procedures are less comfortable than the old familiar ones. Changes in the reward structure may be needed to ensure that the organization is not rewarding the old behaviors and merely hoping for new behaviors.

Backsliding is a natural response to change, but it can become a problem unless the manager acts to get everyone back on track. A manager should remind employees about what they have achieved so far and what is expected of them in the future. It is important for the organization to continue to reinforce and reward employees for behavior that shows they have made the desired change.

Monsanto's approach to increasing opportunities for women within the company is an illustration of how to use the Lewin model effectively. First, Monsanto emphasized unfreezing by helping employees debunk negative stereotypes about women in business. This also helped overcome resistance to change. Second, Monsanto moved employees' attitudes and behaviors by diversity training in which differences were emphasized as positive, and supervisors learned ways of training and developing female employees. Third, Monsanto changed its reward system so managers were evaluated and paid according to how they coached and promoted women, which helped refreeze the new attitudes and behaviors.

Lewin's model proposes that for change efforts to be successful, the three-stage process must be completed. Failures in efforts to change can be traced back to one of the three stages. Successful change thus requires that old behaviors be discarded, new behaviors be introduced, and these new behaviors be institutionalized and rewarded.

MANAGING THE CHANGE PROCESS TO REDUCE RESISTANCE

Most changes are originated by an organization's middle- or senior-level managers. The changes are then passed down to the lower level or middle manager, the link between management and employees, for successful implementation. In this process, the manager is the person who must cope with employees' anxieties and fears about change. The environment created by the manager can greatly affect employees' acceptance of change. Several suggestions for creating a positive environment for change are discussed in the following paragraphs.

Build Trust

If employees trust and have confidence in the manager or organization, they are much more likely to accept change; otherwise, they are likely to resist change vigorously. Trust cannot be established overnight: It is built over a period of time. The organization's actions determine the degree of the employee's trust. Employees will trust a manager they perceive to be fair, honest, and forthright. Employees will not trust a manager who they feel is always trying to take advantage of them. Managers can go a long way toward building trust if they discuss upcoming changes with their employees, and if they actively involve the employees in the change process.

Openly Communicate and Discuss Change

Communication about impending change is essential if employees are to adjust effectively. The details of the change should be provided, but equally important is the rationale behind it. Employees want to know why change is needed. If there is no good reason for it, why should they favor it? Fear of the unknown, one of the major barriers to change, can be greatly reduced by openly discussing any upcoming or current changes with the affected employees. A manager should always begin by explaining the five *W*'s and the *H* to the employees—What the change is, Why it is needed, Whom it will affect, When it will take place, Where it will take place, and How it will take place. During this discussion, the manager should be as open and honest as possible. The more background and detail the manager can give, the more likely it is that the employees will accept the change. The manager should also outline the impact of the change on each of the affected employees. People are primarily interested in how this will affect them as individuals.

It is critical that the manager gives employees an opportunity to ask questions. This is the major advantage of an oral discussion over a written memo. Regardless of how thorough an explanation may be, employees will usually have questions that managers should answer to the fullest extent possible. When employees receive all the facts and get their questions answered, their resistance often fades. This explains why, for example, company officials at one organization allow their employees to review company profit and loss statements and answer their questions about the organization's performance. Improved communication is particularly effective in reducing problems resulting from unclear situations. For example, when the grapevine is active with rumors of cutbacks and layoffs, honest and open communication of the true facts can be a calming force. Even if the news is bad, a clear message often wins points and helps employees accept change. When communication is ambiguous and employees feel threatened, they often imagine scenarios that are considerably worse than the actual "bad news."

Involve the Employees

Changes that are "sprung" on employees with little or no warning will likely result in resistance—simply as a "knee-jerk" reaction—until employees can assess how the change affects them. In contrast, employees who are involved in the change process better understand the need for change and therefore are less likely to resist it. Additionally, people who participate in making a decision tend to be more committed to the outcome than those who are not involved. Employee involvement in change can be extremely effective. It is difficult for individuals to resist a change when they participated in the decision and helped implement it. The psychology is simple: no one wants to oppose something that he or she has helped develop. It is useful to solicit employee ideas and input as early as possible in the change process. Don't wait until the last minute to ask the employees what they think about a change. When affected employees have been involved in a change at, or near, its inception, they will usually actively support the change.

Provide Rewards and Incentives

Employers can give employees rewards and incentives to help them see that supporting a change is in their best interests. One rather obvious, and quite successful, mechanism to facilitate change is rewarding people for behaving in the desired fashion. For example, employees who are required to learn to use new equipment should be praised for their successful efforts. In order to make incentives work effectively, employers should analyze the source of the resistance, and what might overcome that resistance. For example, employees may be afraid they won't be able to do a new task. Managers could provide them with new skills—training, or a short paid leave of absence to allow them to calm down, rethink their fears, realize that their concerns are unfounded. A difficult change can also have positive aspects. Layoffs can be viewed as opportunities for those who remain, allowing jobs to be re-designed to provide new challenges and responsibilities. Other incentives that can help reduce resistance include a pay increase, a new title, flexible work hours, or increased job autonomy.

Make Sure the Changes Are Reasonable

The manager should always do whatever is possible to ensure that any proposed changes are reasonable. Managers can do this by striving to employ empathy by asking themselves, "How might my direct reports view and react to this change?" This is especially important since very often proposed changes that originate with upper management are sometimes totally unreasonable. When this is the case, it is usually because upper management is not aware of specific circumstances that make the changes unworkable. It is the manager's responsibility to intervene in such situations and communicate the problem to upper management.

Educate the Workforce

Sometimes, people are reluctant to change because they fear what the future has in store. For example, fears about economic security may be put to rest by a few reassuring words from management. As part of educating employees about what organizational change means for them, top management must show considerable emotional sensitivity. Doing so makes it possible for people affected by a change to help make it work. Some companies have found that simply answering the question "What's in it for me?" can help to allay many fears.

Avoid Threats

The manager who attempts to implement change through the use of threats is taking a negative approach likely to decrease employee trust. A natural reaction is "This must be bad news if it requires a threat." Most people also dislike being threatened into accepting something. Even though threats may get results in the short term, they may be damaging to employees' morale and attitude over a longer period of time.

Follow a Sensible Time Schedule

As mentioned previously, most changes are passed down from upper management to the middle- or lower-level managers for implementation. The manager often has control or influence over when changes should be implemented, however. Some times are better than others. For example, the week before Christmas or the height of the vacation season would ordinarily not be good times to implement a major change. Managers should rely on their valuable insights into the department and on their common sense when recommending a time schedule for implementing a change.

Implement the Changes in a Sensible Manner

The manager often has some choice about where changes will take place. When making these decisions, managers should rely on logic and common sense. For example, the manager usually decides who will get a new piece of equipment. It would be sensible to introduce the equipment through those employees who are naturally more adaptable and flexible than others. If the manager makes it a point to know his employees, he usually will have a good idea as to which are more flexible. Another consideration in introducing changes is to implement them where possible in a way that minimizes their effects on interpersonal relationships. The manager should try not to disturb smoothly working groups or teams.

Provide Empathy and Support

Another strategy for overcoming resistance is providing empathy and support to employees who have trouble dealing with the change. Active listening is an excellent tool for identifying the reasons behind resistance and for uncovering fears. An expression of concerns about the change can provide important feedback that managers can use to improve the change process. Emotional support and encouragement can help an employee deal with the anxiety that is a natural response to change. Employees who experience severe reactions to change can benefit from talking with a counselor. Some companies provide counseling through their employee assistance plans.

SUMMARY

Organizations face many pressures to change. Some forces are external, including globalization, workforce diversity, and technology advances among others. Other forces are internal, such as changing employee expectations.

Organizations face both planned and unplanned change. The individual or team who directs the change, known as a change agent, can be internal or external to the organization. Individuals resist change for many reasons, and many of these reasons are rooted in fear. Managers and other change agents should discuss the upcoming changes with employees to solicit their ideas. They should explain the five *W*'s and *H* to them: What the change is, Why it is needed, Whom it will affect, When it will take place, Where it will take place, and How it will take place.

Managers should also make sure that the implementation of the change is realistic. They should be aware that the natural reaction of many employees will be to resist the change, and they should try to overcome much of this resistance by carefully explaining what the new changes will do and how they will affect each employee. It is important that the work climate be conducive to the change being introduced, implemented, and accepted. Lewin's change model proposes three stages of a change: unfreezing, changing or moving, and refreezing.

REFERENCES

Blanchard, K. 1992. Six concerns in the change process. *Quality Design* (June): 14, 62.

Creswell, J., Mclean, B., and Koudis, S. 1999. The next big things. *Fortune* (December 20): 86–100.

Faircloth, A. 1998. Guess who's coming to Denny's. *Fortune* (August 3): 95–108.

Herzberg, F. 1966. *Work and the nature of man.* Cleveland: World Publishing.

Lewin, K. 1947. Frontiers in group dynamics: Concepts, method and reality in social science. *Human Relations* (June): 5–41.

Nelson, D.L., and Quick, J.C. 2000. *Organizational behavior: Foundations, realities, and challenges.* Cincinnati, OH: South-Western College Publishing.

Tichy, N.M., and Charan, R. 1995. The CEO as coach: An interview with Allied Signal's Lawrence Bossidy. *Harvard Business Review* (March–April): 69–78.

Woodward, H., and Bucholz, S. 1987. *Aftershock: Helping people through corporate change.* New York: John Wiley.

Chapter 14

Career Development and Management

INTRODUCTION

One of the most important changes in organizations in the past decade or two is the role of the organization in its employees' careers. It had gone from paternalism—in which the organization took nearly complete responsibility for managing its employees' careers—to supporting individuals as they take personal responsibility for their future. And careers, themselves, have gone from a series of upward moves with increasing income, authority, status, and security to one in which people adapt quickly, learn continuously, and change their work identities.

This chapter examines career development and management and its role in developing human potential. We first discuss roles in career development. The discussion then turns to implementing career development. After examining career development issues and challenges for today's diverse workforce, we conclude by discussing how organizations can evaluate career development and management activities.

UNDERSTANDING CAREER DEVELOPMENT AND MANAGEMENT

Career development and management (or what is sometimes referred to as career planning) is an integral activity in our lives. There are three reasons why it is important to understand careers. First, if we know what to look forward to over the course of our careers, we can take a proactive approach to planning and managing them. Second, as managers (or other employees), we need to understand the experiences of our employees, fellow team members, and other colleagues as they pass through various stages of careers during their tenure in the same organization or over their life spans. Third, career development and management is good business. It makes good financial sense to have highly trained employees keep up with their fields so that organizations can protect valuable investments in human resources.

A career is a pattern of work-related experiences that spans the course of a person's tenure in an organization or their life. The two elements in a career are the objective element and the subjective element. The objective element of the career is an observable, concrete environment. For example, you can manage a career by getting training to improve your skills. In contrast, the subjective element involves your perception of the situation. Rather than getting training (an objective element), you might change your aspirations (a subjective element). Thus, both objective events and the individual's perception of those elements are important in defining a career.

Effective career development is integrated with the existing HRM functions and structures in the organization. Integrating career development with other HRM programs creates synergies in which all aspects of HRM reinforce one another. For example, in planning careers, employees need organizational information on strategic planning, HRM planning. Skills inventories can provide this information. Similarly, as they obtain information about themselves and use it in career planning, employees need to know the career paths within the organization and how management views their performance.

Career management is a lifelong process of learning about self, jobs, and organizations; setting personal career goals; developing strategies for achieving the goals; and revising the goals based on work and life experiences. Whose responsibility is career development and management? It is tempting to place the responsibility on individuals, and it is appropriate. However, it is also the organization's duty to form partnerships with individuals in managing their careers. Careers are made up of exchanges between individuals and organizations. Inherent in these exchanges is the idea of reciprocity, or give and take.

The psychological contract between employees and workers has changed. Yesterday, employees "exchanged loyalty for job security." Today, employees instead exchange performance for the sort of training and learning and development that will allow them to remain marketable. This, in turn, means that the somewhat unidirectional nature of HRM activities like selection and training is starting to change; in addition to serving the organization's needs, these activities must now be designed so that the employees' long-run interests are served, and that, in particular, the employee is encouraged to grow and realize her or his potential. Table 14.1 summarizes how activities such as training and performance appraisal can be used to

Table 14.1
HRM Traditional versus Career-Development Focus

Activity	**Traditional Focus**	**Career Development Focus**
Human resource management planning	Analyzes jobs, skills, tasks—present and future. Projects needs. Uses statistical data.	Adds information about individual interests, preferences, and the like to data.
Training and development	Provides opportunities for learning skills, information, and attitudes related to the job.	Provides career path information. Adds individual growth orientation.
Performance appraisal	Rating and/or rewards.	Adds development plans and individual goal setting.
Recruitment and placement	Matching organization's needs with qualified individuals.	Matches individual and jobs based on a number of variables including employees' career interests.
Compensation and benefits	Rewards for time, productivity, talent, and so on.	Adds non-job-related activities to be rewarded, such as United Way leadership positions.

provide more of such a career planning and development focus (Otte and Hutcheson, 1992).

Like performance appraisal, training and development is an equally important element in managing organizational behavior and the enhancement of motivation and performance is the set of activities and processes that constitute career development and planning.

THE CHANGING BUSINESS LANDSCAPE

Once upon a time, people graduated from school and eagerly sought employment with a large and prosperous organization. They considered themselves most fortunate if they were hired by a major and "secure" organization. They were able to assume that they would systematically move up in the organization, eventually retiring with a gold watch and a comfortable pension.

If the phrase "once upon a time" sounds like a fairy tale, you understand why we use it. The lifetime employer with secure jobs is no longer a reality in the modern business landscape. There are exceptions, of course, but by far the more realistic picture of a typical career today involves job changes, extensive organizational restructuring (often with job cuts) to respond to increased globalization and fiercer competition, and a greatly diminished sense of loyalty. Organizations seldom feel deeply obligated to provide long-term work, and employees rarely feel loyalty to the company. Part of the reason for these dramatic shifts is the nature of the business world. The age of technology and information has created a fluid and dynamic economy where organizations must make frequent and often radical changes to compete successfully. These changes have an impact on people. Some cannot adjust. Some lack skills to deal with a company's changed mission. And some feel betrayed by "big business" when they are downsized or laid off.

Career planning used to involve assessing your personal goals and seeing how you could make these work with a current employer or a similar business. It used to involve seeing how to set goals that would help you be promoted in the organization. Even people who followed the advice of leadership gurus to develop a "vision" often did so within the context of existing organizations.

Advances in technology or what many refer as the "Information Age" has changed organizations and their people more dramatically than has any shift since the economy evolved from agricultural to industrial. At one time, the vast majority of Americans were employed in producing agricultural products. Today, less than 4 percent of the economy produces all the food we can eat. But the industrial revolution is also a thing of the past. Less than 20 percent of all workers are now employed in manufacturing. Some futurists predict that in the not-too-distant future, fewer than 10 percent of employees will produce all the manufactured goods we can use. So what will the other 85 percent of us be doing? We are, and increasingly will be, working with information.

Brain power has steadily replaced muscle power, machine power, and even electrical power. Management guru Peter Drucker (1998) says that the amount of labor needed to produce an additional unit of manufacturing output has fallen 1 percent per year since 1900 (99 percent), when machines took over what muscles once did. The years since World War II show similar drops in the amount of energy needed to increase manufacturing levels. What has taken the place of matter and energy is intelligence. Since 1900 the number of educated workers on the payroll has risen about the same rate. The major economic powers are no longer "the industrialized world," but the knowledge world. Agriculture, construction, manufacturing, and mining employ fewer than 1 in 4 Americans, and even those people work principally with their hands rather than their backs and hands. We are all knowledge workers now, working for knowledge organizations. If all this is true, then what must employees and their organizations do to develop and manage careers in the new economy? Many of the concepts covered throughout this book will improve career development and management in any type of organization, including the knowledge businesses.

MATCHING ORGANIZATION AND INDIVIDUAL NEEDS: THE GOAL OF CAREER DEVELOPMENT

Career development is an ongoing, formalized effort by an organization that focuses on developing and enriching the organization's human resources in light of both the employees' and the organization's needs. Career planning is the process by which an individual formulates career goals and develops a plan for reaching those goals. Thus, career development and career planning should reinforce each other. Career development looks at individual careers from the viewpoint of the organization, whereas career planning looks at careers through the eyes of individual employees. In the end, a career development program should be viewed as a dynamic process that matches the needs of the organization with the needs of employees.

The Organization's Role

The organization has the primary responsibility for instigating and ensuring that career development takes place. Specifically, the organization's responsibilities are to develop and communicate career options within the organization to the employee. The organization must carefully advise an employee concerning possible career paths to achieve that employee's career goals.

The organization must supply information about its mission, policies, and plans and for providing support for employee self-assessment, training, and development. Significant career growth can occur when individual initiative combines with organizational opportunity. Career development programs benefit managers by giving them increased skill in managing their own careers, greater retention of valued employees, increased understanding of the organization, and enhanced reputations as people-developers. As with other HRM programs, the inauguration of a career development program should be based on the organization's needs as well.

Assessment of needs should take a variety of approaches (surveys, informal group discussions, interviews, etc.) and should involve personnel from different groups, such as new employees, managers, plateaued employees, minority employees, and technical and professional employees. Identifying the needs and problems of these groups provides the starting point for the organization's career development efforts. Organizational needs should be linked with individual career needs in a way that joins personal effectiveness and satisfaction of employees with the achievement of the organization's strategic objectives.

HRM's Role

HRM personnel are generally responsible for ensuring that this information is kept current as new jobs are created and old ones are phased out. Working closely with both employees and their managers, HRM specialists should see that accurate information is conveyed and that interrelationships among different career paths are understood. Thus, rather than bearing the primary responsibility for preparing individual career plans, the organization should promote the conditions and create the environment that will facilitate the development of individual career plans by the employees.

Like any other HRM activity, if career development is to succeed, it must receive the complete support of top management. Ideally, senior line managers and HRM managers will work together to design and implement a career development system. The system should reflect the goals and culture of the organization, and the HRM philosophy should be woven throughout. An HRM philosophy can provide employees with a clear set of expectations and directions for their own career development. For a program to be effective, managerial personnel at all levels must be trained in the fundamentals of job design, performance appraisal, career planning, and counseling. More will be said about management's role in career development shortly.

The Employee's Role

In today's dynamic work environment, individuals are increasingly responsible for initiating and managing their own career planning. Career planning is not something one individual can do for another; it has to come from the individual. Only the individual knows what she or he really wants out of a career, and certainly those desires vary appreciably from person to person.

Career planning requires a conscious effort on the part of the employee; it is hard work, and it does not happen automatically. Each employee must identify his or her own knowledge, skills, abilities, interests, and values and seek out information about career options in order to set goals and develop career plans.

Before employees can engage in meaningful career planning, they must not only have an awareness of the organization's philosophy, but they must also have a good understanding of the organization's more immediate goals. Otherwise, they may plan for personal change and growth without knowing if or how their own goals match those of the organization. For example, if the technology of a business is changing and new skills are needed, will the organization re-train employees to meet this need or hire new talent? Is there growth, stability, or decline in the number of employees needed? How will turnover affect the need? Clearly, an organizational plan that answers these kinds of questions is essential to support individual career planning.

Although an individual may be convinced that developing a sound career plan would be in his or her best interest, finding the time to develop such a plan is often another matter. The organization can help by providing trained specialists to encourage and guide the employee. This can best be accomplished by allotting a few hours of company time each quarter to this type of planning. Individuals and organizations must constantly recognize that individuals like their organizations change over time, their needs and interests change. Thus, it would be unrealistic to expect individuals to establish their career goals with perfect understanding of where they are going or, for that matter, where the organization is going. So while goal setting is critical, building in some flexibility is a good idea.

The Manager's Role

It has been said that "the critical battleground in career development is inside the mind of the person charged with supervisory responsibility (Randolph, 1981). Although not expected to be a professional counselor, the manager can and should play a role in facilitating the development of a direct report's career. First, and foremost, the manager should serve as a catalyst and sounding board.

Managers should encourage employees to take responsibility for their own careers, offering continuing assistance in the form of feedback on individual performance and making available information about the organization, about the job, and about career opportunities that might be of interest. The manager should show an employee how to go about the process and then help the employee evaluate the conclusions.

Unfortunately, many managers do not perceive career counseling as part of their managerial duties. They are not opposed to this role; rather, they have never considered it as part of their job. To help overcome this and related problems, many organizations have designed training programs to help their managers develop the necessary skills in this area.

Successful career development results from a joint effort by the organization, HRM, the individual, and the immediate manager. The organization provides the resources and structure; the individual does the planning; and the immediate manager provides guidance and encouragement. However, none of this is possible unless efforts are made to improve the match between an employee and an organization as soon as the employee enters the organization. One way of avoiding the conflicts and mismatches is to utilize a realistic job preview.

REALISTIC JOB PREVIEWS

Conflicts between individuals and the organizations they enter can derail the career development and management process and result in unrealistic expectations on the part of the employee. People entering the world of work may expect, for example, that they will receive explicit directions from their boss, only to find that they are left with ambiguity about how to do the job. They may expect that promotions will be based on performance and find that promotions are based mainly in political considerations. Some new hires expect to be given managerial responsibilities right away; however, this is not often the case.

Giving potential employees a realistic picture of the job they are applying for is known as a realistic job preview (RJP). When job candidates are given both positive and negative information, they can make more effective job choices. Traditional recruiting practices produce unrealistically high expectations affecting the reality of the situation. RJPs tend to create expectations that are much closer to reality, and they increase the numbers of candidates who withdraw from further consideration. This occurs because candidates with unrealistic expectations tend to look for employment elsewhere.

RJPs can also be thought of as inoculation against disappointment. If new recruits know what to expect in the new job, they can prepare for the experience. Newcomers who are not given RJPs may find that their jobs don't measure up to their expectations. They may then believe that their employer was deceitful in the hiring process, become unhappy and mishandle job demands, and ultimately leave the organization.

Job candidates who receive RJPs view the organization as honest and also have a greater ability to cope with the demands of the job. RJPs perform another important function: uncertainty reduction. Knowing what to expect, both good and bad, gives a newcomer a sense of control that is important to job satisfaction and performance.

Ultimately, RJPs result in more effective matches, lower turnover, and higher organizational commitment and job satisfaction. There is much to gain, and little to risk, in providing realistic job information.

The needs and goals of individuals and organizations can clash during entry into the organization. To avoid potential mismatches, individuals should conduct a careful self-assessment and provide accurate information about themselves to potential employers. Organizations should present RJPs to show candidates both the positive and negative aspects of the job, along with what they can expect in the way of career development efforts sponsored by the organization along with the potential career paths available to the employee.

IMPLEMENTING CAREER DEVELOPMENT

Successful organizations keep a steady watch on their human resource needs and requirements through HRM planning. This ongoing process involves an analysis of the competencies or knowledge, skills and abilities (KSAs) required for jobs, the progression among related jobs, and the supply of ready (and potential) talent available to fill those jobs.

It is important for an organization to constantly study its jobs carefully in order to identify and assign weights or prioritizations to the KSAs that each one requires. This can be achieved with job analysis and evaluation systems such as those used in compensation programs.

Once the skill demands of the jobs are identified and weighted according to their importance, it is then possible to plan job progressions. A new employee with no experience is typically assigned to a "starting job." After a period of time in that job, the employee can be promoted to one that requires more KSAs. While most organizations concentrate on developing job progressions for managerial, professional, and technical jobs, progressions can be developed for all categories. These job progressions then can serve as a basis for developing career paths—the lines of advancement within an organization—for individuals. Career pathing will be discussed in more detail later in this chapter.

Although these analyses can be quite helpful to employees—and are perhaps essential for organizations—a word of caution is appropriate here for readers. Many successful careers are not this methodical, nor do they proceed in a lockstep manner. In today's working world, career progressions often occur as much through creating and capitalizing on arising opportunities as they do through rational planning.

It used to be that career development and planning systems were primarily focused on promotions and hierarchical advancement. However, in today's flatter organizations and more dynamic work environment, an individual's career advancement can occur along several different paths: transfers, demotions—even exits—as well as promotions. An organization's HRM policies have to be flexible enough to adapt as well as be helpful enough to support the career change.

A promotion is a change of assignment to a job at a higher level in the organization. The new job normally provides an increase in pay and status and demands more KSAs or carries more responsibility. Promotions enable an organization to utilize the KSAs of its personnel more effectively, and the opportunity to gain a promotion serves as an incentive for good performance.

In flatter organizations, there are fewer promotional opportunities and many individuals have found career advancement through lateral moves. A transfer is the placement of an employee in another job for which the duties, responsibilities, status, and renumeration are approximately equal to those of the previous job (although as an incentive, organizations may offer a salary adjustment). Individuals who look forward to change or want a chance to learn more may seek out transfers. In addition, transfers frequently provide a broader foundation for individuals to prepare them for an eventual promotion. A transfer may require the employee to change work group, workplace, work shift, or organizational unit; it may even necessitate moving to another geographic area. Transfers make it possible for an organization to place its employees in jobs where there is a greater need for their services and where they can acquire new KSAs.

A downward transfer, or demotion, moves an individual into a lower-level job that can provide developmental opportunities. Although such a move is ordinarily considered unfavorable, some individuals actually may request it in order to return to their "technical roots." It is not uncommon, for example, that organizations appoint temporary leaders (especially in team environments) with the proviso that they will eventually step down from this position to re-assume their former position.

Self-Assessment

Many individuals never take the time to analyze their KSAs, interests, and career goals. It isn't that these individuals don't want to analyze these factors; rather, they simply never take the time. While this is not something an organization can do for the individual, the organization can provide the impetus and structure. A variety of self-assessment materials are available commercially; and some organizations have developed tailor-made forms and training programs for the use of their employees. Another option is the use of psychological testing.

An individual's self-assessment should not necessarily be limited by current resources and abilities; career plans today increasingly require that the individual acquire additional training and KSAs. However, this assessment should be based on reality. For the individual, this involves identifying personal strengths—not only the individual's developed abilities but also the financial resources available. More will be said later about the organization's role in helping employees identify their potential and the strength of their interests.

Assessing Employee Potential

In conjunction with identifying the career opportunities and requirements for the organizations, managers and HRM personnel must also establish clear understanding of the talent base they have at their disposal. Organizations have several potential sources of information that can be used for assessing employees potential. This typically begins with the use of performance appraisal and moves into other potentially sophisticated methods (i.e., inventorying management talent and using assessment centers).

Identifying and developing talent in individuals is a role that all managers should take seriously. As they conduct formal appraisals, they should be concerned with their direct reports' potential for managerial or advanced technical jobs and encourage their growth in that direction. In addition to immediate managers, there should be others in the organization who have the power to evaluate, nominate, and sponsor employees with promise.

Skill inventories are an important tool for succession planning. These inventories provide an indication of the skills employees have as well as their interests and experiences. In this way, they help managers pay better attention to the developmental needs of employees, both in their present jobs and in managerial jobs to which they may be promoted. Organizations often turn to employee personnel records reflecting information such as education and previous work experience. An equally important part of this process is identifying high-potential employees who may be groomed as replacements for managers who are re-assigned, retire, or otherwise vacate a position.

The assessment center can also be an excellent source of information. The assessment center allows the organization to evaluate individuals as they participate in a series of situations that resemble what they might be called upon to handle on the job. It is usually a good idea for an organization not to depend on any one source of information but to use as many as are readily available. Such an approach provides a natural system of checks and balances.

As noted earlier, the organization's assessment of an individual employee should normally be conducted by HRM personnel and the individual's immediate manager, who serves as a mentor. More will be discussed about mentoring later.

Communicating Career Options

In order to set realistic career goals, employees must know the options and opportunities that are available within the organization. The organization can do several things to facilitate such awareness. Posting and advertising job vacancies is one activity that helps employees get a feel for their career options. Clearly identifying possible paths of advancement within the organization is also helpful. This can be done as part of the performance appraisal process. Another good idea is to share HRM planning forecasts with employees.

Although career management involves a good deal of analysis and planning, the reality is that it needs to provide a set of tools and techniques that help employees gauge their potential for success in the organization. Informal counseling by HRM personnel and managers is used widely.

Many organizations give their employees information on educational assistance, Equal Employment Opportunity/Affirmative Action (EEO/AA) programs and policies, salary administration, and job requirements. Career pathing and career planning workbooks and workshops are also popular means of helping employees identify their potential and the strength of their interests.

Career Pathing

Career pathing is a technique that addresses the specifics of progressing from one job to another in the organization. It can be defined as a sequence of developmental activities involving informal and formal education, training, and job experiences that help make an individual capable of holding more advanced jobs. Career paths exist on an informal basis in almost all organizations. However, career paths are much more useful when formally defined and documented. Such formalization results in specific descriptions of sequential work experiences, as well as how the different sequences relate to one another. This information could be generated by computer.

Traditional career paths have emphasized upward mobility in a single occupation. An alternative to traditional career pathing is to base career paths on real-world experiences and individualized preferences. Paths of this kind would have several characteristics:

1. They would include lateral and downward possibilities, as well as upward possibilities, and they would not be tied to "normal" rates of progress.
2. They would be tentative and responsive to changes in organizational needs.
3. They would be flexible enough to take into account the qualities of individuals.
4. Each job along the paths would be specified in terms of acquirable skills, knowledge, and other specific attributes, not merely in terms of educational credentials, age, or work experience. (Jackson, 1999)

Realistic career paths, rather than traditional ones, are necessary for effective employee counseling. In the absence of such information, the employee can only guess at what is available.

Career Planning Workbooks and Workshops

Several organizations have prepared workbooks to guide their employees individually through systematic self-assessment of values, interests, abilities, goals, and personal development plans. General Electric has developed an extensive set of manuals for its career development program, including two workbooks to help employees explore life issues that affect career decisions. Other companies prefer to use workbooks written for the general public, for example, Richard N. Bolles' *What Color Is Your Parachute 1999: A Practical Manual for Job-Hunters & Career-Changers* and Julie Griffin Levitt's *Your Career—How to Make It Happen.*

Workshops offer experiences similar to those provided by workbooks. However, they have the advantage of providing a chance to compare and discuss attitudes, concerns, and plans with others in similar situations. Some workshops focus on current job performance and development plans. Others deal with broader life and career plans and values.

A career workshop can help employees assume responsibilities for their careers. It can also help them learn how to make career decisions, set career goals, create career options, seek career planning information, and at the same time build confidence and self-esteem.

Career Counseling

Career counseling is the activity that integrates the different steps in the career-planning process. Career counseling may be performed by an employee's immediate manager, an HRM specialist (or a combination of the two), or outside consultants. In most cases, it is preferable to have the counseling conducted by the immediate manager with appropriate input from HRM personnel. The immediate manager generally has the advantage of practical experience, knows the company, and is in a position to make a realistic appraisal of organizational opportunities.

Some managers are reluctant to attempt counseling because they haven't been trained in the area. However, it is not necessary to be a trained psychologist to be a successful counselor. Generally, managers who are skilled in basic human relations are successful as career counselors. Developing a caring attitude toward employees and their careers is of prime importance. Being receptive to employee concerns and problems is another requirement.

One interesting development in recent years has been the establishment of the Workforce Investment Act of 1998. With the signing of this act, Congress established a new law that consolidates a wide variety of federally sponsored career-development and job-training programs. Under the new arrangement, one-stop service centers will be set up in cooperation among businesses and local governments to provide jobseekers with a variety of services, including career counseling, skill assessments, training, job-search assistance, and referrals to related program and services (Pantazis, 1999).

Career Self-Management and Training

Career self-management is closely related to the concept of career pathing. Career self-management is the ability to keep pace with the speed at which change occurs within the organization and the industry and to prepare for the future (Meister, 1998). A relatively new concept, career self-management emphasizes the need of individual employees to keep learning because jobs that are held today may evolve into something different tomorrow, or may simply disappear entirely. Career self-management also involves identifying and obtaining new KSAs and competencies that allow the employee to move to a new position. The payoff of career self-management is more highly skilled and flexible employees and the retention of these employees. Career self-management requires commitment to the idea of employee self-development on the part of the organization and the providing of self-development programs and experiences for employees.

In response to the growing view that employees should assume greater responsibility for their own career management, many organizations are establishing training programs for employees on how they can engage in career self-management. The training focuses on two major objectives: (1) helping employees learn to continuously gather feedback and information about their careers and (2) encouraging them to prepare for mobility.

The training is not geared to KSAs and behaviors associated with a specific job, but rather toward their long-term personal effectiveness. Employees often undertake self-assessments to increase awareness of their own career attitudes and values along with a wider viewpoint beyond the next company promotion to broader opportunities in the workplace.

Mentoring

The success of many individuals in their careers can often be tied back to others who influenced them. These individuals frequently mention immediate managers who were especially helpful as career developers. Many of these individuals also mention others at higher levels in the organization who provided guidance and support to them in the development of their careers. These executives and managers who coach, advise, and encourage employees of lesser rank are called mentors.

Generally, the mentor initiates the relationship, but sometimes an employee will approach a potential mentor for advice. Most mentoring relationships develop over time on an informal basis. However, in proactive organizations there is an emphasis on formal mentoring plans that call for the assignment of a mentor to those employees considered for upward movement in the organization. Under a good mentor, learning focuses on goals, opportunities, expectations, standards, and assistance in fulfilling one's potential (Starcevich and Friend, 1999).

Mentoring functions can be divided into two broad categories: career functions and psychosocial functions:

- *Career functions.* Career functions are those aspects of the relationship that enhance career advancement. They include sponsorship, exposure and visibility, coaching, protection, and challenging assignments.

- *Psychosocial functions.* Psychosocial functions are those aspects that enhance the protégé's sense of competence, identity, and effectiveness in a professional role.

They include role modeling, acceptance and confirmation, counseling, and friendship. Both functions are viewed as critical to management development.

Many organizations have developed formal mentoring programs. Alternatively, given the importance of the issue, a number of mentoring organizations have begun to spring up. Often the main purpose of these organizations is to help create and monitor mentoring partnerships so that the right people are matched with one another. When done well, the mentoring process is beneficial for both the pupil and the mentor.

Not surprisingly, mentoring is also being done over the Internet. Known as *e-mentoring*, the process is mediated via web sites that bring experienced business professionals together with individuals needing counseling. Even though participants in e-mentoring typically never meet in person, many form long-lasting e-mail connections that tend to be very beneficial. Still, most participants see these connections as supplements to—rather than substitutes for—in-company mentors.

Career Plateaus

A career plateau is defined as "the point in a career where the likelihood of additional hierarchical promotion is very low" (Ferrence, Stoner, and Warren, 1977). Career plateauing takes place when an employee reaches a position from which he or she is not likely to be promoted further. Virtually all people reach a plateau in their careers; however, some individuals reach their promotional ceiling long before they retire.

Organizations can help employees cope with plateaus by providing opportunities for lateral growth where opportunities for advancement do not exist. Other actions that can aid in managing the plateau process are: (1) prevent plateauees from becoming ineffective (prevent a problem from occurring); (2) integrate relevant career-related information systems (improve monitoring so that emerging problems can be detected and treated early); and (3) manage ineffective plateauees and frustrated employees more effectively (cure the problem once it has arisen). The first action basically involves helping plateauees adjust to the solid-citizen category and realize they have not necessarily failed. Available avenues for personal development and growth should be pointed out. The second suggestion can largely be implemented through a thorough performance appraisal system. Such a system should encourage open communication between the managers and the person being appraised.

Because plateaued employees often include a significant number of employees who are worth rehabilitating it would pay for most organizations to address this issue seriously. At least five possibilities exist:

1. Provide alternative means of recognition. Some possibilities include assigning the employee to a task force or giving other special assignments, participation in brainstorming sessions, representation of the organization to others, and training of new employees.
2. Develop new ways to make their current jobs more satisfying. Some possibilities here include relating employees' performance to total organizational goals and creating competition in the job.
3. Effect revitalization through reassignment. The idea here is to implement systematic job switching to positions at the same level that require many similar, though not exactly the same, skills and experiences as the present job.
4. Utilize reality-based self-development programs. Instead of assigning plateauees to developmental programs designed to help them move into future jobs (which a majority of development programs do), assign them to development programs that can help them perform better in their present jobs.
5. Change managerial attitudes toward plateaued employees. It is not unusual for managers (and supervisors) to give up on and neglect plateaued employees. Such actions are quickly picked up by the affected employees and only compound the problem. (Payne, 1984)

DUAL-CAREER COUPLES

Economic necessity and social forces have encouraged the trend of the employment of both members of a couple. In these dual-career partnerships, both members follow their own careers and actively support each other's career development.

As with most lifestyles, the dual-career arrangement has its positive and negative side. A significant number of organizations are concerned with the problems facing dual-career couples and offer assistance to them. Flexible working schedules are the most frequent organizational accommodation to these couples. Other arrangements include leave policies where either parent may stay home with a newborn, policies that allow work to be performed at home, day care on organization premises, and job sharing.

The difficulties that dual-career couples face include the need for quality childcare, the time demands, and the emotional stress. Time demands or pressures, for example, is a key stressor in the lives of dual-career couples. When both partners work outside the home, there may be a time crunch in fitting in work, family, and leisure time. However, the main problem these couples face is the threat of relocation and the accompanying problem of jealousy. When one partner's career blooms before the other's, that partner may feel threatened. Another issue that must be worked out is whose career takes precedence. For example, what happens if one partner is transferred to another city? Must the other partner make a move that might threaten his or her own career in order to be with the individual who was transferred? Who, if anyone, will stay home and take care of a new baby?

Many large organizations now offer job-finding assistance for spouses of employees who are relocated, including payment of fees charged by employment agencies, job counseling firms, and executive search firms. Organizations are also developing networking relationships with other employers to find jobs for the spouses of their relocating employees. These networks can provide a way to "share the wealth and talent" in a community while simultaneously assisting in the recruitment efforts of the participating organizations (Fraze, 1999).

Working out a dual-career partnership takes careful planning and consistent communication between the partners. Each partner must serve as a source of social support for the other. Couples can also turn to other family members, friends, and professionals for support if the need arises.

PERSONAL CAREER DEVELOPMENT

As noted at several points throughout this chapter, regardless of whether or not an employer routinely offers development programs, it is essential that employees take responsibility for working out their own development plan. Today managers and employees who neglect to do this risk stagnation and obsolescence. Even if their KSAs are not outdated, a downsizing or merger may put employees at risk of being terminated. It has happened to many employees already and there is every indication that this trend will continue in the years to come.

Becoming your own career coach. The best way to stay employed is to see yourself as being in business for yourself, even if you work for someone else. You must know what skills are state of the art. Organizations need employees who have acquired multiple skills and are adept at more than one job. Employers want employees who demonstrate competence in dealing with change. To be successful, think of organizational change not as a disruption to your work, but instead as the central focus of your work. You will also need to develop self-reliance to deal effectively with the stress of change. Self-reliant individuals take an interdependent approach to relationships and are comfortable both giving and receiving support from others.

The people who will be most successful in tomorrow's organizations are individuals who are flexible, team oriented (rather than hierarchical), energized by change, and tolerant of ambiguity. Those who will become frustrated in the new career are individuals who are rigid in their thinking and learning styles, and who have high needs for control. A commitment to continuous, lifelong learning will prevent you from becoming a professional dinosaur. An intentional and purposeful commitment to taking charge of your professional life will be necessary in managing your career in today's world of work.

Conducting regular self-assessments. Planning for one's career should include an ongoing assessment and consideration of how an individual can demonstrate that they make a difference to the organization. The following suggestions can help an individual make this case if they find that their job and career are vulnerable to the fallout from business decisions such as mergers and downsizings:

1. *Assess yourself.* How are your job skills? How do your skills compare with your peers in your organization and in other organizations? How important is your role? Would profits or customer satisfaction be negatively affected if your job or department were eliminated? What do you contribute? Have you become quicker or more productive? Can you show an increase in customer satisfaction associated with your efforts? If you're in a management position, do employees like you and tend to stick with you?
2. *Cultivate a positive relationship with your boss and your boss's boss.* Can your boss count on you? Is your boss aware of your contributions?
3. *Get plugged into the networks.* What kind of reputation do you have with others both inside and outside of the organization? Are others in the organization aware of your skills and contributions? Do you get calls from headhunters suggesting other employment opportunities? (Kennedy, 1999)

Clearly, in planning a career one should attend to more than simply acquiring specific job knowledge and skills. Job know-how is clearly essential, but as the list above highlights there are other skills one must develop to be successful as an employee. To succeed as a manager, one must achieve a still-higher level of proficiency in such major areas as communications, time management, self-motivation, interpersonal relationships, and the broad area of leadership.

Below is a list of a set of suggestions to help employees enhance their own development and increase their opportunities for advancement. The *development suggestions* focus on personal growth and direction, while the *advancement suggestions* focus on the steps employees can take to improve their promotability in the organization.

Development

1. Create your own personal mission statement that indicates the business you would like to be in and the role you would like to play.
2. Take responsibility for your own direction and growth and avoid placing all of your hopes in an organization-provided development program.
3. Make enhancement, rather than advancement, your priority by constantly searching for opportunities to broaden your skills in the short run.

4. Talk to people in positions to which you aspire and get suggestions on how to proceed to make it to that level.
5. Set reasonable career goals by breaking them into smaller, more manageable goals along the way to your ultimate goal.
6. Make investment in yourself a priority by not neglecting self-development activities.

Advancement

1. Remember that performance in your function is important, but interpersonal performance is critical.
2. Set the right values and priorities by aligning your behavior with the organization's values.
3. Provide solutions, not problems, by taking the time to think issues through and offer potential solutions.
4. Be a team player by working to shine the spotlight on the group's efforts.
5. Be customer-oriented by always keeping in mind that anyone with whom you have an exchange is your "customer."
6. Act as if what you're doing makes a difference by approaching each activity with a positive attitude.

It is important for organizations to understand that a systematic program of career development is a valuable tool in attracting, retaining, and motivating employees. The benefits of such a program are many, including:

1. Developing an employee's capabilities is consistent with an HRM policy of promotion from within.
2. Training enables an employee to acquire the KSAs needed for promotion to higher-level positions. It eases the transition from an employee's present job to one involving greater responsibilities.
3. Training assists in retention. Those organizations that fail to provide training often lose their most promising employees. Frustrated by the lack of opportunity, achievement-oriented employees often seek employment with other organizations that provide training for career advancement.
4. Training can increase an employee's level of commitment to the organization and improve perceptions that the organization is a good place to work. By developing and promoting trained employees, organizations create a competent, motivated, and satisfied workforce.

In general, most organizations have implemented the use of individual development plans (IDPs) for all categories of employees. Special interest programs related to upward mobility for minorities, women, and handicapped workers have also become quite prevalent in the organizations resulting from changes in workforce demographics. As suggested throughout this chapter a number of career development tools, techniques, and programs have evolved, including training workshops, individual counseling, career information centers, career ladders, assessment and testing centers, skills inventories, job rotation, and mentoring.

Today's successful organizations should ensure that they have a viable career development system in place that addresses the demands of a changing workforce. It can be an investment with very high returns.

CAREER DEVELOPMENT FOR TODAY'S DIVERSE WORKFORCE

To meet the career development needs of today's diverse workforce, organizations need to break down the barriers some employees face in achieving advancement. The first major study of the glass ceiling in 1991 revealed that women and minorities are held back not only from top executive positions but also from lower-level management positions and directorships. The Department of Labor defines the glass ceiling as "Those artificial barriers based on attitudinal or organizational bias that prevent qualified individuals from advancing upward in their organizations into management level positions" ("Glass Ceiling report," 2001). The study revealed that women and minorities are frequently excluded from informal career development activities such as networking, mentoring, and participation in policy-making committees. In addition to outright discrimination, some of the practices that contribute to their exclusion are informal word-of-mouth recruitment, companies' failure to sensitize and instruct managers about EEO requirements, lack of mentoring, and the too-swift identification of high-potential employees (Kalish, 1992).

Barriers to the advancement of women and minorities continue to exist 10 years after the initial government study of the glass ceiling. The Office of Federal Contract Compliance Programs (OFCCP) enforces antidiscrimination laws covering federal contractors. The OFCCP began monitoring the pay and promotion practices of companies doing business with the government in 1991. It has found problems in about half of the companies it has audited. However, some of these difficulties have to do with gender- or race-based pay differences, rather than with mobility and promotion opportunities (Swoboda, 1998).

The imbalance in the proportion of women in top management positions and minorities in middle- and top-management positions indicates the ongoing need for special career development programs for both these groups. Systematic on-the-job approaches such as coaching, job rotations and transfers, underway assignments, and mentoring, can be particularly helpful. Challenging, successfully completed projects like troubleshooting, start-ups, and international assignments are especially important to the career progression of executives, yet women and minorities are less likely to be assigned to those projects. Therefore, careful attention must be paid to HRM planning and decisions about assignments to ensure that women and minorities have equal opportunities.

Many employers now offer special training to women and minorities who are on a management career path. They may use their own staff or outside firms to conduct the training. Opportunities are also available for women and minorities to participate in seminars and workshops that provide instruction and experiences in a wide variety of management topics. Often these training programs stress the special problems often faced by women and minorities in managerial positions. These problems include potential lack of acceptance by their white male counterparts and by direct reports and lack of support from family for women with career aspirations.

Amendments to the Age Discrimination in Employment Act removing ceilings on retirement make it even more important that organizations pay attention to the long-term career development of all employees, including the older worker. There are at least four myths about older workers that tend to make them vulnerable to discrimination in training and advancement opportunities.

One myth is that older workers are less motivated, less efficient, and less productive than younger workers. A second myth is that older workers are resistant to change and less flexible than younger workers. A third myth is that older workers tend to have poor attendance records. A fourth myth is that older workers have more accidents. Despite the fact that research has dispelled all of these myths (Mitchell, 1988), subtle discrimination stemming from such myths can, of course, affect the self-confidence and risk taking of older workers, and might discourage them from pursuing training opportunities. With people living longer and thus staying in the workforce longer, organizations must recognize the importance of ensuring that their career management system addresses the challenges presented by the older worker.

Regardless of whether the organization is confronted with a more diverse workforce that is dominated by more women, minorities, older workers or the disabled, successful organizations would do well to follow the Glass Ceiling Commission's suggestions for toppling job-advancement barriers:

- Demonstrate commitment. Top management should communicate its dedication to diversity and enact policies that promote it.
- Hold line managers accountable for progress by including diversity in all strategic business plans. Performance appraisals, compensation incentives, and other evaluation measures should reflect this priority.
- Use affirmative action as a tool to ensure that all qualified individuals compete based on ability and merit.
- Expand your pool of candidates. Look for prospects from noncustomary sources who may have nontraditional backgrounds and experiences.

- Educate all employees about the strengths and challenges of gender, racial, ethnic, and cultural differences.
- Initiate family-friendly programs that help women and men balance their work and family responsibilities. ("The glass ceiling," 1991)

If followed, the suggestions from the Glass Ceiling Commission should go a long way toward creating a culture that evaluates, hires, and promotes on the basis of merit.

CAREER DEVELOPMENT ONLINE

Many of today's organizations are developing comprehensive, online career development centers. These online career development centers provide access to a wide variety of services to help employees manage their careers and, in some instances, even find jobs outside their present organization. Online capabilities can provide many types of career-related information on demand. For example, employees can look up the competencies and KSA's required for jobs they aspire to have. Some of the online career planning resources being offered include:

- Information about employment trends and job opportunities.
- Self-assessment tools, such as personality tests and interest indicators, that employees can use to determine which types of jobs they might best pursue.
- Links to online employment resources such as job listings and career development information.
- Individual online job counseling, including advice on preparing for interviews. ("Dismantling the glass ceiling," 1996)

As noted earlier, in addition to company-sponsored online services, many resources are available on the Internet to help individuals with career development. These resources include job-search guides, resume-preparation aids, job listings, career-related articles, and other similar services. There is little doubt that career-development resources online will continue to expand in the future.

NEW ORGANIZATIONAL STRUCTURES AND CHANGING CAREER PATTERNS

The changing economic environment, increased global competition, and the glut of middle-aged baby boom workers have sparked a further set of changes in organizational structures and employee career paths. Restructuring, downsizing, or rightsizing has been the norm for many organizations for the past decade and a half. In an effort to reduce labor costs organizations have reduced the size of their permanent full-time staff. These cuts have affected middle managers as well as lower-level employees. Entire levels of management have been abolished to become "flatter," quicker to respond, and closer to the customer. To meet varying labor needs, the new rightsized organizations hire temporary workers or outsource work to smaller organizations and consultants. There also has been a substantial rise in part-time employment both because part-timers are less expensive and receive fewer fringe benefits and because they provide greater flexibility in scheduling employees for peak demand periods. In general, it is safe to say that for many employees, the "psychological contract" they have with their employer has changed from one of "If you do your job well, we'll employ you until you retire" to "We'll employ you as long as we need your contribution to help us succeed in business." In today's world of work, employability has replaced the idea of employment security.

Consequently, career patterns for individual employees are changing. Research suggests that the traditional linear career path in which one enters an organization near the bottom, works in the same organization for many years, and gradually and predictably moves up, retiring from a fairly high-level position in the same organization may become the exception rather than the rule over the next few decades. The bulge of baby boomers has made climbing the hierarchy much more competitive, the flattening of organizational structures has reduced the number of management positions just as the number of candidates has increased, and massive layoffs have destroyed faith in the employer as a long-term source of security. These changes have caused a great deal of frustration as middle-aged employees fail to advance as they had expected.

In efforts to maintain the motivation and creativity of career-plateaued employees, organizations are developing alternatives to the traditional linear-career success model. To some extent, the meaning of career success is changing. Some feel that career success now has more to do with self-actualization, skill growth, and self-satisfaction than climbing a fixed ladder of jobs. Balancing family and life commitments with work also seems to be taking on more importance for many employees. Four possible career paths that an employee could follow are expert, spiral, transitory, and linear (Brousseau, Driver, Eneroth and Larson, 1996).

An expert, or professional, career ladder rewards growing expertise in a single technical specialty without the need to move into management. Professional ladders allow for career advancement within a single employer, even a "flat" one. For example, scientists and engineers can follow such ladders of increasing technical competence and status (junior engineer, engineer, senior engineer, etc.) without managerial responsibilities.

Another possibility is the spiral career path that involves a number of lateral moves between functional areas within the same organization. This combines broadening experience and the continuous challenge of new tasks with slower hierarchical progress. As an example, one might begin a career in sales, move to operations after several years, move to a different operations job, and then move into the finance area by midcareer. To make these complex spiral career paths work, organizations need to design sophisticated career planning and career information systems to generate and disseminate information about lateral career opportunities throughout the organization (Vaughn and Wilson, 1994).

The transitory career path is another common path. In this approach, the career occurs virtually independent of any single organization. The individual may move into and out of organizations and even occupations on a regular basis, either in search of better jobs and more satisfying challenges or because there is little choice when secure permanent jobs are rare. Some or even most of a transitory career may be spent as a consultant or independent contractor, short-term contract employee, part-timer, or entrepreneur. Individuals on this career path think of themselves as possessing and maintaining a portfolio of competencies that give them security and employability rather than assuming that security and employment are provided by a single organization. Career and development planning is critical for individuals on a transitory career path, but they are more likely to become their own career strategists than rely on input from formal employer-provided career-planning systems (Brousseau et al., 1996).

Spiral or transitory career paths may offer another attraction to today's employees: the possibility of staying in one location much longer. With the increasing number of dual-career couples, individuals may prefer to remain in the same community for a longer period, moving between different types of jobs within the same establishment or moving within the same specialty across local employers.

Today's and tomorrow's organizations need to continue to find ways to wrestle with the prevailing "up-or-out" culture of most organizations, which defines lack of upward progress as failure. Traditional linear career planning is less feasible than before, and employer-initiated creative career planning is even more important to effectively utilize talent and provide satisfying careers for today's employees. It has been suggested that the most successful organizations of the future will provide all four types of career paths (linear, expert, spiral, and transitory) in varying proportions to meet the needs of their workforce and provide the combination of stable and flexible staffing necessary to carry out their business plans (Brousseau et al., 1996).

EVALUATING CAREER DEVELOPMENT AND MANAGEMENT ACTIVITIES

Career development programs are much more difficult to evaluate than other HRM programs. One of the primary difficulties involves establishing specific objectives. General objectives, such as to create better employees provide little guidance for evaluation purposes. Even when good objectives are established, it is difficult to design a career development program that can fulfill all of them. Career development tends to be an ongoing process, which compounds the difficulties of evaluation.

One systematic approach to evaluating programs consists of five steps:

1. Determine the history and rationale of the program.
2. Determine the degree to which the program places primary emphasis on its most important goals.
3. Analyze change occurring in employees and the organization, that is, program effectiveness, comparing the outcomes of the program with its stated objectives.
4. Examine the general adaptability of the program.
5. Introduce modifications as required.

Feedback from employees and their managers about the usefulness of specific elements of a career development program is one of the most critical elements of the evaluation process.

While the systematic evaluation process presented above is a start it is important to understand that the ultimate goal of career management is to have employees that have reached their full potential at work, enjoy productive and satisfying work careers, and then successfully move into retirement. As such, full appreciation of career management activities may not come until after retirement. But as employees are increasingly unlikely to spend their entire careers in a single organization, success in retirement is much more likely to be a function of the individual's own career management efforts, as well as the good fortune to remain healthy through retirement years. Furthermore, for many employees (especially those in higher status jobs or those for whom work is an important part of self-image) leaving one's career does not mean the end of work. For these employees managing the transition to what has been called "bridge" jobs (and eventually on to full retirement) is most important for their continued satisfaction (Doeringer, 1990).

Therefore, the success of career management activities can be judged only at one point in time. If an employee is satisfied with her or his career at this point, then career management must be judged successful up to that point. While there is a lot that organizations can do to manage this process, clearly, a great deal depends on the individual's efforts at career management. Employees who go into careers for which they are not well suited (either in terms of abilities or temperament) will obviously be more likely to suffer dissatisfaction with their careers than will those who have made more appropriate career choices. Therefore, although organizational career management efforts are important, the successful management of one's career in today's dynamic world of work depends heavily on each individual's efforts to accurately assess his or her own KSAs and interests and to formulate a plan for what a successful career should look like.

In bringing this chapter to an end, Andy Grove, CEO of Intel Corporation, suggests that as a general rule, you must accept that no matter where you work, you are not an employee. Instead, your are in a business with one employee: yourself. You face tremendous competition with millions of other businesses. You own your career as a sole proprietor. Grove (1995) poses three key questions that are central to managing your career.

1. Continually ask: Am I adding real value? You add real value by continually looking for ways to make things truly better in your organization. In principle, every hour of your day should be spent increasing the value of the output of the people for whom you're responsible.
2. Continually ask: Am I plugged into what's happening around me? Inside the company? The industry? Are you a node in a network of plugged-in people, or are you floating around by yourself?
3. Are you trying new ideas, new techniques and new technologies? Try them personally—don't just read about them. (pp. 229–230)

SUMMARY

Today, organizations and individuals need to take a more active, systematic approach to career development and management. A career development program is a dynamic process that should integrate individual employee needs with those of the organization. The individual employee, the manager, the employer (especially HRM personnel) all have roles in the individual's career development.

It is the responsibility of the employee to identify her or his own KSAs as well as interests and values and to seek out information about career options. The organization should provide information about its mission, policies, and plans and what it will provide in the way of training and development for the employee.

Organizations must keep a steady watch on their human resource needs and requirements. This ongoing analysis involves an analysis of the competences or KSAs required for jobs, the progression among related jobs, and the supply of ready (and potential) talent available to fill those jobs. Employees must take responsibility for analyzing their KSAs, interests, and career goals. Organizations must also identify the career opportunities and requirements for the organization and establish a clear understanding of the talent base they have at their disposal. Organizations often rely on various mechanisms to communicate career options to include posting and advertising job vacancies and sharing HRM planning forecasts with employees. Successful career development efforts really begins before a new employee enters the organization and starts with a realistic picture or job preview of what the employee can expect upon entering the organization.

Career-counseling programs are very important to an organization interested in career development for its employees. Such programs usually address a wide variety of career-related issues and are readily accessible to people in the organization. Helping dual-career couples and meeting the challenges for today's workforce require that organizations work to break down the barriers such employees face in achieving advancement.

An environment of increasing competition, continuous change, increased globalization, and new organizational structures have resulted in changes in career patterns for individual employees. Organizations have recognized that the traditional career paths are no longer feasible and are increasingly relying on creative career planning to meet the demands of the new world of work.

Unlike other HRM activities career development, planning, and management are much harder to evaluate. Thus, career management activities can be judged only by individuals at that point in their lives where they feel they have or have not realized their potential.

REFERENCES

Bolles, R. 1999. *What color is your parachute 1999: A practical manual for job-hunters & career-changers*. Berkeley, CA: Ten Speed Press.

Brousseau, K.R., Driver, M.J., Eneroth, K., and Larson, R. 1996. Career pandemonium: Realigning organizations and individuals. *Academy of Management Executive* (November): 52–66.

Dismantling the glass ceiling. 1996. *HRFocus* (May): 12.

Doeringer, P.B. 1990. Economic security, labor market flexibility, and bridges to retirement. In P.B. Doeringer (ed.), *Bridges to retirement*. Ithaca, NY: Cornell University, ILR Press, pp. 3–22.

Drucker, P. 1998. Management's new paradigm. *Forbes* (October 6): 152–157.

Ferrence, T.P., Stoner, J.A.E., and Warren, E.K. 1977. Managing the career plateau. *Management Review* (October): 602.

Fraze, V. 1999. Expert help for dual-career spouses. *Workforce* (March): 18–20.

The glass ceiling. 1991. *HRMagazine* (October): 91–92.

Glass ceiling report. 2001. U.S. Department of Labor. www.dol.gov.

Grove, A.S. 1995. A high-tech CEO updates his views on managing and careers. *Fortune* (September 18): 229–230.

Jackson, C. 1999. Career path. *Hospital & Health Networks* (August): 20.

Kalish, B.B. 1992. Dismantling the glass ceiling. *Management Review* (March): 64.

Kennedy, M.M. 1999. How do you prove you make a difference? *Across the Board* 36: 44–48.

Levitt, J.G. 1995. *Your career—how to make it happen*. 3rd ed. Cincinnati, OH: South-Western Publishing.

Meister, J.C. 1998. The quest for lifetime employability. *Journal of Business Strategy* (May/June): 25–28.

Mitchell, O.S. 1988. The relation of age to workplace injuries. *Monthly Labor Review* (July): 8–13.

Otte, F.L., and Hutcheson, P.G. 1992. *Helping employees manage careers.* Englewood Cliffs, NJ: Prentice-Hall, p. 10.

Pantazis, C. 1999. The new workforce investment act. *Training and Development* (August): 48–50.

Payne, R.C. 1984. Mid-career block. *Personnel Journal* (April): 42.

Peiperl, M., and Baruch, Y. 1997. The post-corporate career. *Organizational Dynamics* (Spring): 7–22.

Randolph, A.B. 1981. Managerial career counseling. *Training and Development Journal* (July): 54–55.

Starcevich, M., and Friend, F. 1999. Effective mentoring relationships from the mentee's perspective. *Workforce*, supplement (July): 2–3.

Swoboda, F. 1998. US Airways settles "glass ceiling" case. *The Washington Post* (December 3): E2.

Vaughn, R.H., and Wilson, M.C. 1994. Career management using job trees: Charting a path through the changing organization. *Human Resource Planning* 17(4): 43–55.

Index

About the Author

RONALD R. SIMS is the Floyd Dewey Gottwald Senior Professor of Business Administration in the Graduate School of Business at the College of William & Mary, Williamsburg, Virginia. He holds a doctorate in organizational behavior and consults widely with organizations in the private, public, and not-for-profit sectors. Dr. Sims is author or coauthor of more than 75 scholarly and professional articles and more than 20 books. Among his more recent ones are *Organizational Success Through Effective Human Resources Management* (2002), *Teaching Business Ethics for Effective Learning* (2002), and *The Challenge of Front-Line Management* (2000).

LaVergne, TN USA
03 November 2009

162885LV00002B/2/P